The Essentials of Teaching Health Education

Curriculum, Instruction, and Assessment

Sarah Benes, EdD

Holly Alperin, EdM

SHAPE America
SOCIETY OF HEALTH AND PHYSICAL EDUCATORS®

health. moves. minds.

Human Kinetics

Library of Congress Cataloging-in-Publication Data

Names: Benes, Sarah, 1982- author. | Alperin, Holly, 1977- author.
Title: The essentials of teaching health education: curriculum, instruction, and assessment / Sarah Benes, Holly Alperin.
Description: Champaign, IL : Human Kinetics, 2016. | Includes bibliographical references and index.
Identifiers: LCCN 2015025904
Subjects: LCSH: Health education--United States. | Health education--Curricula--United States. | Health education--Standards--United States. | Health education teachers--Training of--United States.
Classification: LCC LB1587.A3 B46 2016 | DDC 613.071--dc23 LC record available at http://lccn.loc.gov/2015025904

ISBN: 978-1-4925-0763-5 (print)

The web addresses cited in this text were current as of October 2015, unless otherwise noted.

Acquisitions Editor: Ray Vallese; **SHAPE America Editors:** Joe Halowich and Joe McGavin; **Developmental Editor:** Bethany J. Bentley; **Managing Editor:** Anne E. Mrozek; **Copyeditors:** Alisha Jeddeloh and Jan Feeney; **Indexer:** Dan Connolly; **Permissions Manager:** Dalene Reeder; **Graphic Designer:** Joe Buck; **Cover Designer:** Keith Blomberg; **Photograph (cover):** © Ragnar Schmuck/age fotostock; **Photographs (interior):** © Human Kinetics, unless otherwise noted; **Photo Asset Manager:** Laura Fitch; **Photo Production Manager:** Jason Allen; **Art Manager:** Kelly Hendren; **Associate Art Manager:** Alan L. Wilborn; **Illustrations:** © Human Kinetics; **Printer:** Walsworth

SHAPE America – Society of Health and Physical Educators
1900 Association Drive
Reston, VA 20191
800-213-7193
www.shapeamerica.org

Printed in the United States of America   10 9 8 7 6

The paper in this book was manufactured using responsible forestry methods.

Human Kinetics
1607 N. Market Street
Champaign, IL 61820
USA

United States and International
Website: **US.HumanKinetics.com**
Email: info@hkusa.com
Phone: 1-800-747-4457

Canada
Website: **Canada.HumanKinetics.com**
Email: info@hkcanada.com

Tell us what you think!
Human Kinetics would love to hear what we can do to improve the customer experience. Use this QR code to take our brief survey.

To the educators "in the trenches" working to support
the health and wellness of students.

Contents

Part V   Beyond the Classroom   257

Preface

Many of us are familiar with the phrase "Knowledge is power." Many of us have also experienced at least one health education course that embodied this philosophy—a traditional health education course in which the emphasis was on learning facts and figures, disease names and symptoms, or the vitamins and minerals that help a body grow. But did any of that information change the way you behaved? Did you select foods with more vitamin C in them or remember the chemicals that caused the blackened lung? The answer is, probably not. But, what if you attended a health education class that asked you to think critically about a goal you have for the future and then determine the best strategies to achieve that goal? Or, what if your teacher had you consider what factors might influence whether or not you drink alcohol at a party, engage in sexual activity, or wear a helmet while riding your bike? Hopefully that would be a health class that you would remember, a class that helped you develop some key skills that would influence your health-related behaviors long after the class ended.

This textbook focuses on the latter health education class. It provides a new perspective on health education that shifts the emphasis from primarily knowledge acquisition (learning a lot of new information) to skill acquisition (learning how to do something that will affect your health in a positive way). We believe that after you read this book, the new phrase you will be using is "Skills are power."

We call the approach presented in this text a *skills-based approach* to health education. As you learn more about the skills-based approach, you will understand how its strategies can lead to empowered students who are able to maintain and enhance their health and wellness by developing the skills, attitudes, and knowledge necessary for being health literate.

The authors of this book want students to experience a health education class that is meaningful, makes the most out of the limited amount of time health educators have, and provides students an opportunity to explore how their behaviors influence their health and well-being. We want health teachers to contribute to the development of students who are critical thinkers and ready to tackle the 21st century because they have learned how to lead healthy lifestyles. Learning new information is interesting, but knowledge acquisition alone will not lead to meaningful behavior change because students haven't learned the skills necessary to *apply* their knowledge. This book is a how-to guide for designing your health education program to support the application of knowledge and skills in order to maintain or improve students' health.

With the National Health Education Standards (accessing information, analyzing influences, decision making, interpersonal communication, goal setting, self-management, and advocacy) as the foundation, this text supports the development and implementation of a skills-based health education program. We discuss the importance of including key topics and information in your curriculum, and we encourage you to select topics that are relevant to your students, determined by student needs, and *functional*—that is, topics with the primary purpose of providing students with the information they *need* to know in order to *develop* and *apply* the skills. Information can be powerful, but it is most powerful when used to apply a health skill in a meaningful way. We believe that, in a skills-based curriculum, information provides the context for discussing health behaviors and the skills necessary to improve or maintain one's health. An approach that emphasizes skills also aligns with efforts to ensure that today's high school graduates have the 21st-century skills (skills that are necessary for college and career readiness in the 21st century) to lead lives that are not only healthy but successful and productive as well.

We designed this text to assist anyone who wants to implement a skills-based approach. Whether you are a current health teacher, physical education teacher, school nurse, elementary teacher, student in a HETE (health education teacher education) or PETE (physical education teacher education) preservice program, physical and health education curriculum coordinator, principal, higher education faculty, or other stakeholder interested in improving the health literacy of students, you will be able to find information and strategies throughout that will help in your quest to improve your health education program. This text will fill the gap that educators often find once they begin to plan a curriculum that focuses on skill development rooted in the National Health Education Standards. Many educators transitioning from a curriculum that focuses on knowledge acquisition find themselves asking, "What now?" They may understand that shifting to a skills-based approach is valuable but don't know how to begin the transition. Or, they may have begun to integrate skills but need support to truly make their curriculum and instruction skills based. We regularly work with educators and school districts to improve their health education programs. We find that once people understand a skills-based approach, they are on board and excited about trying it, but then ask, "OK, but *how* do I *do* this?" This text provides you with the tools and guidance to answer these questions and to implement a skills-based approach in a cohesive, systematic, and accessible format.

We recognize that embracing a skills-based approach takes time, can require a significant paradigm shift in your view of health education, and requires support. Our goal is to the make your transition efforts as smooth as possible. We do this by addressing the critical aspects of a skills-based approach, including how to teach and develop health-related skills (with a focus on the National Health Education Standards), how to emphasize skill development in the curriculum, and how to implement the approach in the classroom.

The sequence of the book will orient you to a skills-based approach and provide concrete strategies for developing and implementing this approach. The first three chapters (part I—Building the Foundation of a Skills-Based Approach) set the stage, outline the role of health literacy in a health education course, and explain what we mean when we use the term *skills-based health education*. Chapter 1, Developing Health-Literate Individuals, defines health literacy and explains how health and health literacy are connected to academic outcomes. Chapter 2, Understanding a Skills-Based Approach, outlines the components of a skills-based approach to health education,

shows examples of what it might look like in the classroom, and provides theoretical support for it. Chapter 3, Examining Student Motivation, discusses theories of motivation, how development affects motivation, and considerations for meeting the needs of your students.

The middle of the text (part II—Teaching to the National Health Education Standards) takes an in-depth look at each skill of the National Health Education Standards. Each chapter focuses on one skill and provides steps for skill development (procedural knowledge), a definition of the skill, suggested skill cues for each skill, strategies for teaching and modeling the skill, developmentally appropriate skill-based learning activities, strategies and activities for skill practice and application in the real world, and health topics that could also be taught in conjunction with that skill. A significant amount of the text is dedicated to the skills because they are the foundation of the approach and teachers need a thorough understanding of the skills in order to plan an effective curriculum for their students.

The final chapters (parts III-V) pull everything together and describe the process of developing and implementing this approach in schools as well as strategies for professional learning and engagement. Part III, Developing Curricula and Assessments, begins with chapter 11, Using Data to Inform Curriculum Planning, which describes how to use data to determine the needs of students and determine topics to include in the curriculum. It also offers guidance for using data to make decisions about curriculum and support your health education program. Chapter 12, Eight Steps for Curriculum Development, discusses how to use a backward design to create a skills-based curriculum for preK-12 health education programs. We included the curriculum development chapters after the skill chapters because it is important for readers to have a strong understanding of the skills before beginning the curriculum development process. Chapter 13, Designing Meaningful Assessments, provides guidance on how to develop assessments to evaluate skill development and proficiency in ways that are relevant and meaningful for students.

Part IV, Strategies for Effective Instruction, focuses on the implementation of a skills-based approach. Chapter 14, Creating a Positive

Learning Environment, focuses on establishing and maintaining a positive learning environment, which is critical to the success of a skills-based approach. We examine multiple aspects of the learning environment and strategies that can be applied at any level. Chapter 15, Implementing a Skills-Based Approach, examines teaching strategies and classroom practices that support a skills-based approach. Importantly, this chapter also looks at the role of the teacher in a skills-based classroom, which is that of guide or facilitator. Chapter 16, Meeting the Unique Challenges of Elementary Health Education, looks at the challenges and special considerations of teaching health education at the elementary level. This chapter addresses challenges and their possible solutions, skills-based strategies specific to elementary students, and ways to use literature to support health education.

Finally, part V, Beyond the Classroom, includes two chapters. Chapter 17, Professional Development and Advocacy, describes core principles of professional development, suggestions of ways for teachers to support their growth as professionals, and strategies for advocating for skills-based health education in schools. Chapter 18, Making Cross-Curricular Connections, explains the critical role of health education in schools, especially as it relates to other components of a whole-school approach in supporting the health and academic achievement of students. This chapter also describes ways to connect health education with other subjects to extend health education beyond health class and into the larger school context.

In addition to the content just outlined, this book includes several special features to enhance the text:

- **Practical examples for educators.** We believe in the importance of offering practical strategies that readers can use immediately. The examples help bring the text to life for those implementing health education.

- **Advice from educators in the field.** Receiving advice from people in the field who have implemented a skills-based approach can have a profound impact on those working to adopt this approach. There are many challenges but also many rewards to this approach. By soliciting input from educators who have worked to make the switch, we hope to provide you with personal experiences and reflections as well as advice on the struggles and successes of moving toward a skills-based approach.

- **Online resources with further information.** In addition to this text, you have access to ancillary materials online. These materials include additional practical examples, ideas for learning activities, sample scope and sequences, lesson plans, and other supporting materials. Visit **www.HumanKinetics.com/TheEssentialsOfTeachingHealthEducation**.

To summarize, this book provides practical, relevant, and applicable information to assist you in improving the effectiveness of your health education program. You will find this book easy to read and easy to use to meet your program development and improvement needs. We hope this book will become a frequently used and highly valued resource throughout your teaching career.

eBook
available at
HumanKinetics.com

About SHAPE America

SHAPE America—Society of Health and Physical Educators—is committed to ensuring that all children have the opportunity to lead healthy, physically active lives. As the nation's largest membership organization of health and physical education professionals, SHAPE America works with its 50 state affiliates and is a founding partner of national initiatives including the Presidential Youth Fitness Program, *Let's Move!* Active Schools and the Jump Rope for Heart and Hoops for Heart programs.

Since its founding in 1885, the organization has defined excellence in physical education, most recently creating *National Standards & Grade-Level Outcomes for K-12 Physical Education* (2014), *National Standards & Guidelines for Physical Education Teacher Education* (2009), and *National Standards for Sport Coaches* (2006), and participating as a member of the Joint Committee on National Health Education Standards, which published *National Health Education Standards, Second Edition: Achieving Excellence* (2007). Our programs, products and services provide the leadership, professional development and advocacy that support health and physical educators at every level, from preschool through university graduate programs.

Every spring, SHAPE America hosts its National Convention and Expo, the premier national professional-development event for health and physical educators.

Advocacy is an essential element in the fulfillment of our mission. By speaking out for the school health and physical education professions, SHAPE America strives to make an impact on the national policy landscape.

Our Vision: Healthy People—Physically Educated and Physically Active!

Our Mission: To advance professional practice and promote research related to health and physical education, physical activity, dance and sport.

Our Commitment: 50 Million Strong by 2029

Approximately 50 million students are currently enrolled in America's elementary and secondary schools (grades pre-K to 12). SHAPE America is leading the effort to ensure that by the time today's preschoolers graduate from high school in 2029, all of America's students will have developed the skills, knowledge and confidence to enjoy healthy, meaningful physical activity.

Acknowledgments

We are grateful for the support and encouragement of many people who have helped make our dream of writing a book to support skills-based health education a reality. First and foremost we would like to express our love and gratitude for our families who have been there for us through all the ups and downs of this process. Sarah would like to thank Rick, Lillian, and Brynn for putting up with long nights, sometimes crabby mornings, and for helping mom share her passion with you – the reader! She would also like to thank her parents for their unwavering belief that she could make her dreams come true and her sister for her support and encouragement along the way – the best little sister a person could ask for.

Holly would like to thank Todd, Taylor, and Jenna for all of their patience and support throughout this process of writing, re-writing, and filling in "just one more thing" all in an effort to share our passion. She would also like to thank her parents, in-laws, and siblings for being constant supporters of her work. Without her family as her biggest cheerleaders, Holly knows it would not be possible to keep doing what she does.

Even with the support of all of our families, we could not have made this book what it is without our colleagues in the field who provide their advice to support future and current teachers, our students who provide insight and new ideas and who challenge us to clarify and articulate our vision for health education, and educators and staff who are tirelessly working to support the health of students and for whom we hope this text can be a source of support!

We owe a debt of gratitude to the all of the staff members at SHAPE America and Human Kinetics who assisted with the development, writing, designing, editing, and publishing of this book. We would especially like to thank Joe McGavin, Joe Halowich, Scott Wikgren, Ray Vallese, and Bethany Bentley for being invaluable resources on this journey. From their consistent encouragement to their thoughtful feedback, they made two first time authors feel confident, calm, and capable. We are grateful for their support of our vision and their assistance in bringing this book to you! We truly could not have done it without them.

Our two names are on the cover of this book but this book would not be possible without the many people who played a role in helping us realize this dream! Lastly, thank you to you the reader. We realize that there are many experienced and respected educators in the field of health education. We appreciate your taking the time to improve the health of your students through this approach to health education.

How to Access the Web Resource

You will notice references throughout *The Essentials of Teaching Health Education* to a web resource. This online content is available to you for free upon purchase of a new print book or an e-book. All you need to do is register with the Human Kinetics website to access the online content. The steps below will explain how to register. The web resource offers supplemental learning activities.

Follow these steps to access the web resource:

1. Visit www.HumanKinetics.com/TheEssentialsOfTeachingHealthEducation.
2. Click the first edition link next to the corresponding first edition book cover.
3. Click the Sign In link on the left or top of the page. If you do not have an account with Human Kinetics, you will be prompted to create one.
4. After you register, if the online product does not appear in the Ancillary Items box on the left of the page, click the Enter Pass Code option in that box. Enter the following pass code exactly as it is printed here, including capitalization and all hyphens: **BENES-9NTQ-WR**
5. Click the Submit button to unlock your online product.
6. After you have entered your pass code the first time, you will never have to enter it again to access this online product. Once unlocked, a link to your product will permanently appear in the menu on the left. All you need to do to access your online content on subsequent visits is sign in to **www.HumanKinetics.com/TheEssentialsOfTeachingHealthEducation** and follow the link!

Click the Need Help? button on the book's website if you need assistance along the way.

Connections to 21st-Century Skills

What do we need to be successful in the world? Money, time, luck, intelligence, perseverance, food, health care, a career—any of these could be considered necessary for success, and there are many more items that we could add to the list. In reality, this question is entirely dependent on who you ask. However, schools are tasked with preparing students to be future ready—that is, ready to tackle college, a career, or whatever life has in store for them once they graduate from high school. You may wonder, how can schools that are already responsible for preparing students for their future also make health a priority? The answer is skills-based health education. Skills developed through a skills-based health education program include decision making, goal setting, self-management, interpersonal communication, accessing information, analyzing influences, and advocacy. All of these skills are necessary for being future ready and successful in life regardless of the path chosen.

The skills developed through skills-based health education are tools that students need to succeed in the "real world." However, that is not the only advantage to this approach. When the skills are combined with functional health information, students have the knowledge and

skills they need to be healthy. In short, we provide the environment and learning opportunities so students can demonstrate both the skill application and acquired knowledge through strategies presented in the chapters of this text.

The beginning of this text makes two important points: Skills are critical to maintaining and adopting health behaviors, and a skills-based approach supports both health outcomes and 21st-century skills and learning outcomes. Teaching in the 21st century comes with many challenges but also many opportunities and rewards. This text provides you with strategies for developing and implementing a skills-based approach to health education that will also help students to be successful in tomorrow's world.

This generation of students presents unique challenges for health educators. Not only does information change at a rapid pace, but information delivery and technology are constantly evolving and saturate all areas of life. Students are also exposed to many more health-related challenges, including media influences, misinformation, cyberbullying, access to products and services, and a decrease in face-to-face communication as we become ever more reliant on texting, e-mailing, and other media. These barriers to keeping students healthy are significant, but the good news is that there is a way to help students navigate life in the 21st century—teaching them skills that they can use throughout their lives.

Throughout this text you will find the information you need to create a meaningful, engaging, and relevant health curriculum that is structured around the skills of the National Health Education Standards. If you help students develop the skills of decision making, interpersonal communication, analyzing influences, accessing valid and reliable information, goal setting, self-management, and advocacy, you will be giving them the tools they need to build and maintain a healthy lifestyle. Perhaps even more importantly, these skills are constant—no matter the technology, the situation, or the location, these are the skills necessary to maintain and enhance health. You don't need to worry about the skills becoming outdated or irrelevant—we will always need these skills if we want to maintain or adopt healthy behaviors. Effective implementation of a skills-based approach can lead to improved health outcomes in students because they have developed the knowledge and skills to engage in health-enhancing behaviors outside the classroom.

Twenty-first-century skills are similar to health-related skills in that they are the skills that will help prepare students for college and career in the 21st century—one set of skills prepares students to be successful in their careers, the other prepares them to be healthy. These skills, as discussed in the following table, do not stand alone but rather are supported with the implementation of a skills-based approach in the health education classroom. When you teach health-related skills, you are teaching the acquisition of 21st-century skills as well—one supports the other, and this integration can lead to more effective outcomes for students in both academics and health.

The idea of teaching 21st-century skills is widespread, and the foundation of these skills has been discussed in both the education and business sectors. Both sectors have a stake in ensuring that students about to enter the workforce have the knowledge and skills necessary to be productive, effective, and efficient. For the purposes of this book, we use the Framework for 21st Century Learning created by the Partnership for 21st Century Learning (www.p21.org) as a foundation for our discussion. The Partnership for 21st Century Learning is a coalition of education, business, community, and government leaders interested in bridging the gap between schooling and the workforce. A mission of the coalition is to serve as a catalyst for 21st-century readiness, and it has defined 21st-century skills in three main categories: life and career skills, learning and innovation skills, and information, media, and technology skills. The following table describes each set of skills in detail.

As you may notice in the Twenty-First-Century Skills table, there are many opportunities for a direct connection to 21st-century skills in a skills-based health education classroom. In fact, several chapters in this book focus on topics and skills similar to the ones listed in this chart. Some examples include analyzing influences (analyze media), accessing valid and reliable information (access and evaluate information), decision making (make judgments and decisions and solve problems), and goal setting (manage goals and time and work independently).

Although some of the skills listed in the table are not as explicit within the National Health Education Standards, you can include them in your classroom in other ways. For example, interacting effectively with others is critical for many of the listed strategies. Interacting effectively with others also becomes part of the discussion to develop class norms and expectations. Students practice collaborating with others when they work in diverse teams with the expectation that team members are respectful of each other's opinions and create a rich dialogue and exchange of ideas that support the participatory nature of a skills-based health education classroom.

A second component of the Partnership for 21st Century Learning that directly supports the implementation of a skills-based approach is the emphasis on 21st-century support systems. Within the Framework for 21st Century Learning, the support systems are as follows.

Twenty-First-Century Standards

■ Skills, content, and expertise

■ Deeper understanding

TWENTY-FIRST-CENTURY SKILLS

LIFE AND CAREER SKILLS	LEARNING AND INNOVATION SKILLS	INFORMATION, MEDIA, AND TECHNOLOGY SKILLS
Flexibility and Adaptability • Adapt to change • Be flexible **Initiative and Self-Direction** • Manage goals and time • Work independently • Be a self-directed learner **Social and Cross-Cultural Skills** • Interact effectively with others • Work effectively in diverse teams **Productivity and Accountability** • Manage projects • Produce results **Leadership and Responsibility** • Guide and lead others • Be responsible to others	**Creativity and Innovation** • Think creatively • Work creatively with others • Implement innovations **Critical Thinking and Problem Solving** • Reason effectively • Use systems thinking • Make judgments and decisions • Solve problems **Communication and Collaboration** • Communicate clearly • Collaborate with others	**Information Literacy** • Access and evaluate information • Use and manage information **Media Literacy** • Analyze media • Create media products **Information, Communication, and Technology Literacy** • Apply technology effectively

- Emphasizing real-world data, tools, and experts; best ways to solve meaningful problems
- Multiple measures of mastery

Assessment of 21st-Century Skills

- Using effective formative and summative assessments
- Emphasizing useful and productive feedback
- Balancing technology-based formative and summative assessments
- Developing portfolios that students can use to demonstrate learning
- Developing a balanced portfolio to measure how well the educational system is helping students to become proficient in the 21st-century skills

Twenty-First-Century Curriculum and Instruction

- Teaching 21st-century skills discretely within subjects
- Applying 21st-century skills across content areas
- Using innovative learning methods that use supportive technology, inquiry, and problem-based learning approaches and higher-order thinking
- Encouraging integration of community resources

Twenty-First-Century Professional Development

- Helping teachers integrate 21st-century skills by providing support and training
- Balancing direct instruction with project-based methods
- Helping teachers identify and meet individual learning styles, intelligences, and weaknesses
- Encouraging knowledge sharing and building a community of practice among educators

Twenty-First-Century Learning Environments

- Creating the learning environments, human supports, and physical space that support teaching and learning
- Enabling students to learn in a real-world context
- Allowing equitable access to learning tools, technologies, and resources

Adapted from P21 Framework Definitions, 2009.

As these lists indicate, and as reinforced in the chapters in this text, a skills-based health education program includes more than just good instruction on meaningful and relevant topics. It also includes assessments and learning environments that help students feel supported and provide opportunities to experience success. Each of these components of a skills-based approach becomes the precursor to students leaving your program prepared for college, careers, and meaningful citizenship.

Our work in health education is about more than providing students with the information to know what is healthy and what isn't. It is our responsibility through effective implementation of a skills-based approach to require students to think critically about health topics and why they choose the behaviors that they do. If we are unable to help students to see the connection between their behaviors and health outcomes, we have failed to provide them with a pathway for success. Specifically, employers need employees who show up ready to work and who are reliable, competent, and critical thinkers. If employees are sick, under the influence of a substance, or having difficulty managing a breakup with a partner, their productivity will suffer. If we are able to provide these same employees with health education that teaches them how to stay healthier, analyze the influences around them to avoid substance abuse, and manage stressful situations and get help if they are feeling depressed, we increase their productivity while they are on the job.

We want to develop the dispositions (mindset or habits) of workers to be good problem solvers and communicators, adaptable to new ways of working, innovative, or even leaders among their peers, and this takes consistent practice and reinforcement in an environment that challenges students to find answers to their problems and allows for the creativity to try something new. Many of these dispositions can be developed within the methods suggested throughout this text. For example, you can monitor and evaluate communication through group work and group discussions. Using questioning techniques and problem-solving activities, you can foster creativity and allow students to explore solutions to challenges and complex issues.

We have a prime opportunity as health educators to challenge and support our students as they develop the skills that support their dispositions. We do this by providing meaningful lessons that require students to be active participants and problem solvers in their health and the health of those around them. We talk less and students do more.

The five main goals of a skills-based approach are

1. to facilitate learning experiences through which students engage with the content;

2. to use a lesson format that supports knowledge and skill acquisition;

3. to provide engaging, relevant experiences for students;

4. to foster participation and active learning; and

5. to provide opportunities for self-reflection, internalization, and personalization of the content (information and skills).

We hope that you will keep these goals in mind as you continue through this text. Skills-based health education not only helps students develop the knowledge and skills necessary for leading a healthy lifestyle but also supports the development of 21st-century skills, thereby helping students to become healthy and productive citizens.

Our goal is to support your work as a health educator by providing you with a strong foundation in a skills-based approach so that you can improve your existing program or make the change to a skills-based approach. All of this is so that you can improve outcomes for the people who matter most—your students!

PART I

Building the Foundation of a Skills-Based Approach

Implementing a skills-based approach in your health education classroom requires thoughtful planning. In part I, we set the stage for planning and implementing a skills-based approach by providing the background context and research base. The goal is to provide you with the foundation necessary to support your efforts to make skills-based health education a reality in your school.

By the end of this part, you will be able to describe health literacy, its relevance in schools, and how a well-designed health education program can support health literacy. You will also be able to describe key components of a skills-based approach. Finally, you will better understand ways to increase student motivation at any developmental level. Reading part I will provide the context necessary to move on to part II, in which we examine each skill of the National Health Education Standards in detail.

Fotolia

CHAPTER 1

Developing Health-Literate Individuals

Learning Objectives

After reading this chapter, you will be able to do the following:

- Define *health literacy.*
- Discuss dimensions of health literacy.
- Discuss characteristics of health-literate people.
- Explain how schools can support the development of health literacy.

Key Terms

competency

e-health literacy

health literacy

knowledge

literacy

motivation

protective factors

risk factors

socioecological model

The goal of health education is to provide students with the knowledge and skills needed to adopt and maintain healthy lifestyles. One indication of students' ability to do this is their level of health literacy. Health-literate people are able to address their own health needs along with the needs of others. They are able to obtain and apply knowledge and skills to enhance their own health and the health of others—both now and in the future as their needs change throughout their lives. Therefore, health literacy is an important measure of the effectiveness of health education and is critical to ensuring that students have the ability to be healthy throughout their lives.

This chapter provides a working definition of *health literacy*, describes the levels of health literacy, and discusses how to develop health literacy through comprehensive health education in schools. Not only can high-quality health education support the development of health literacy, but skills-based health education in particular can support the educational mission of schools and have a positive effect on students' ability to think critically in other educational domains.

COMPONENTS OF HEALTH LITERACY

Health literacy is not a new concept; it has been around since the 1970s. However, multiple definitions of and approaches to health literacy have appeared in the literature. In this book, we use the definition established by Sorenson et al. (2012) because it is based on an extensive review of literature that considered the leading constructs of health literacy:

> *Health literacy is linked to literacy and entails people's knowledge, motivation, and competencies to access, understand, appraise, and apply health information in order to make judgments and make decisions in everyday life concerning healthcare, disease prevention, and health promotion to maintain or improve quality of life during the life course. (p. 3)*

This all-encompassing definition builds on the original concept of health literacy that was developed in the medical field. Similar to many traditional definitions of health literacy, this definition includes the ability to navigate the medical or clinical side of health and wellness. However, more recent definitions have emerged that view health literacy as an asset, a valuable quality that can help people improve their health outcomes. This suggests that when students recognize that their choices directly influence their ability to stay healthy, and when they feel empowered with the knowledge and skills to live a healthy life (i.e., they are health literate), they are likely to experience improved health outcomes, make health-enhancing choices, and have an increase in positive opportunities in a range of "personal, social, and environmental determinants of health" (Nutbeam, 2008, p. 2074).

When educators view health literacy as an asset that students can develop in the classroom, they recognize that they have the opportunity to help students develop this critical ability and thus contribute to positive health outcomes. For example, if middle school students learn how to effectively refuse drugs and feel empowered to make a healthier choice, they are more likely to abstain from drug use and avoid negative health outcomes. Additionally, if students learn to view health literacy as an asset, they may be more invested in developing it and more motivated to engage with their health (see figure 1.1).

To better understand health literacy and its connection to health education, we will examine key aspects of Sorenson et al.'s (2012) definition in more detail. Let's begin with a discussion of the term *literacy*.

Literacy

Many hear the term *literacy* and make a connection to reading and writing. In our case, **literacy** is included in part because people must be able to read and write in order to be healthy. However, literacy means more than reading and writing. It has a broader definition that refers to having knowledge related to a specific subject. Literacy as a construct (an idea or theory) is driven by context (subject or setting), and to be literate in a specific topic, a person must learn about that topic. We cannot assume that because people are literate in biology that they are also literate in anatomy.

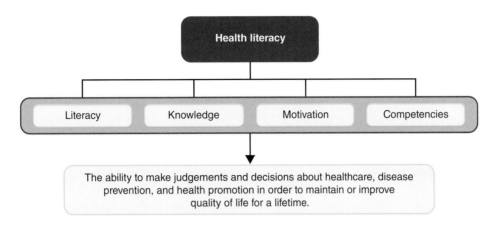

FIGURE 1.1 Each component of health literacy is necessary for it to become an asset that has a positive impact on a student's health outcomes.

Health literacy specifically focuses on understanding and interpreting a wide array of health-related information. It requires visual literacy (understanding visual information, such as in a graph or chart), computer literacy (using computers), information literacy (obtaining, understanding, and applying information), and numerical literacy (understanding and applying numbers and computations) (National Network of Libraries of Medicine, 2013). Clearly health literacy involves a varied set of skills that are needed in order to maintain or enhance health.

One additional literacy context worth mentioning is **e-health literacy**, or the ability to find, understand, and appraise health information from electronic sources and use that information to address a health problem (Norman & Skinner, 2006). In other words, e-health literacy is the ability to apply the competencies of health literacy in an online environment (Paek & Hove, 2012). This is important because students today are growing up in a more global and electronic world. A 2015 report found that 84 percent of teens have received health information from online sources (Wartella, Rideout, Zupancic, Beaudoin-Ryan, & Lauricella 2015). Adolescents use the Internet regularly as a way to gather information. Fifty-three percent report using the Internet for a school project, and 45 percent report using the Internet to gather health-related information about how to take better care of themselves (Wartella et al., 2015). Given this, it is important for adolescents to develop the skills to think critically and use the Internet safely, responsibly, and effectively so they are accessing and interpreting credible information from reliable sources.

Health literacy and the other types of literacy just described are relevant to health education because the competencies within each type of literacy should all be learned in health education even if they are also included in other subjects. For example, students may be considered literate and able to read and interpret nonfiction texts, but unless they have also learned how to read and interpret informational text about a specific disease, how to read and interpret the dosage requirements of a medication, or how to decipher accurate versus inaccurate information related to nutrition, their ability to engage in health-enhancing behaviors will be limited. A skills-based health education course can emphasize the application of literacy competencies and critical thinking specifically in the context of health behaviors and outcomes.

Finally, literacy and health literacy connect with a critical goal of the greater education community: producing people who are ready for college and careers. To do this, each state has identified core competencies that students are responsible for achieving in subjects such as English language arts, math, and science. Within these standards, emphasis may be given to areas such as reading, writing, speaking, and listening in English language arts (National Governors Association Center for Best Practices, 2010); counting, mathematical operations, measurements and data, and statistics within math (National Governors Association Center for Best Practices, 2010); and patterns, cause and effect, structure and function, and stability and change (NGSS Lead States, 2013). The intent is for students to learn these concepts across multiple content areas in preparation for college and careers. The development of these standards within the health classroom helps students develop their health literacy while also applying skills from other courses, which may enhance academic outcomes and support their preparation for college and careers.

Knowledge

Knowledge refers to the compilation of information that forms the foundation of what a person understands and believes. Knowledge is the result of learning—not just formal learning in school but also general learning through personal experiences. The more information you gather, process, and retain, the greater your knowledge base is. In other words, knowledge is what stays with you when you have internalized learning and can access and apply the information learned.

The Institute of Medicine (IOM, 2004) supports the acquisition of knowledge through their definition of *health literacy* as an individual's capacity to obtain, process, and understand basic health information and services. Within a health education course, this definition supports the need for students to use the skill of accessing valid information when identifying which information can be believed and internalized (leading to knowledge) and which information is based on conjecture, built on weak evidence, or completely untrue.

Motivation

People must play an active role in keeping themselves healthy; good health is not something that happens on its own. **Motivation** is the driving force behind individual actions, whether derived from an internal conviction or exerted from an external source such as a friend, parent, or teacher. Ultimately, motivation guides your level of participation in health-related choices and behaviors. Without motivation, the ability to maintain your health and the health of those around you is limited. In other words, motivation can start with one person, but it soon can become a driving force behind a community initiative that increases positive health outcomes at a community level.

Although a health education course cannot teach motivation in and of itself, students can become empowered to take ownership of their health. An example is when students see the connection between their behaviors and immediate health outcomes. Adolescents pay little attention to the connection between their current behaviors and health outcomes later in life. For example, adolescents are unlikely to be motivated to change their eating habits even if you explain how a poor diet can lead to weight gain, high blood pressure, or high cholesterol and can increase the risk of chronic diseases such as type 2 diabetes, heart disease, and stroke later in life. The adolescent brain makes it difficult for students to prioritize future consequences, and thus those consequences are not as motivating. It would be more effective to explain to students how poor diet can affect their energy levels, their ability to perform on the field or in the orchestra, and their weight. You can still discuss the long-term effects of health behaviors, but the emphasis is on the more immediate effects.

Educators are even more effective when they make connections that are meaningful for their students. For example, student athletes might be most concerned with how health behaviors will affect their performance in a game, students who are musicians might be most interested in how health behaviors can affect their ability to perform, and students concerned with grades might be most interested in how health behaviors can affect their ability to be successful in school and get into a good college. Your job is to discover the best motivators and leverage them to help students actively engage in their health and well-being. We will discuss motivation in more detail in chapter 3.

Competencies

Being competent means having requisite abilities or qualities. In terms of health literacy, it is not enough to have the *capacity* to obtain, process, and understand health information and services. One must also have the *competence* to apply these understandings in a health-enhancing manner. Sorenson and colleagues' (2012) definition of **competency** specifically mentions *access*, *appraise*, and *apply health information* as competencies needed for health literacy. Within a health education course,

Health education can help students develop skills that will lead to positive health outcomes such as fostering positive relationships, engaging in physical activity and other behaviors that can help them stay healthy for a lifetime.

students achieve these competencies and more by learning both the skills they can use to be healthy and the functional information (that they will hopefully internalize as knowledge) that allows them to make meaningful connections to their world. For example, if the outcome for an elementary student is to demonstrate effective handwashing in order to reduce the spread of germs, you must spend more time teaching the steps of handwashing and allowing students to practice than you spend teaching which germs lead to which illnesses and associated symptoms. This is meaningful to elementary students because they can understand that germs are all around them and the simple task of handwashing is a proven way to minimize the likelihood of getting sick.

The ultimate goal is that, through the development of specific competencies, students are able to engage in health-enhancing behaviors, avoid risky behaviors, and be healthy, productive people. In this text, we discuss the following skills, all based on the National Health Education Standards (Joint Committee, 2007), as the main competencies to develop in the health education classroom:

- Accessing valid and reliable information, products, and services
- Analyzing influences
- Interpersonal communication
- Decision making
- Goal setting
- Self-management
- Advocacy

Parameters

The Sorenson et al. (2012) definition of health literacy mentions "health care, disease prevention, and health promotion to maintain or improve quality of life during the life course" (p. 3) as the parameters for health literacy. Of the three parameters, health promotion lends itself best to health education in schools. Although it is always a goal of health education to prevent disease, and helping students become proficient in health-related skills and knowledge will certainly support this effort, disease prevention is complex and health education alone is not enough to solve the problem. Health promotion, on the other hand, is strongly influenced by health education. When students learn how to set a goal related to improving their physical fitness or how to analyze community influences and norms related to underage drinking, they are taking ownership of their health. When students can advocate for a healthy cause, they are able to promote the health of those around them. Teaching students how to have an impact on health promotion is a responsibility of health educators. In addition, even though the strongest connection is to health promotion, all the skills developed in skills-based health education can also apply to the contexts of health care and disease prevention, leading to improved health outcomes and quality of life in all areas.

CONTINUUM OF HEALTH LITERACY

As we just discussed, health literacy is complex. Understanding the intent of health literacy by dissecting the definition lays the groundwork for a conversation about how the dimensions (or levels) of health literacy intersect with health education. As a process, health literacy takes time to understand and develop on a continuum from simple to complex.

The levels described in this section—functional health literacy, interactive health literacy, and critical health literacy—were originally introduced by Nutbeam (2000). Recently, a fourth level, holistic health literacy (Rask, Uusiautti, & Maatta, 2013-2014), has been suggested (see figure 1.2). This section examines each level and provides examples of how a health education course might address it.

Functional Health Literacy

The first, most basic level of health literacy is functional health literacy. This level of health

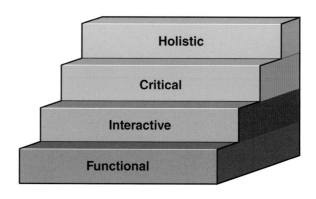

FIGURE 1.2 Levels of health literacy.

literacy relates to acquiring factual information of health risks and health services (Nutbeam, 2000). This level reflects a more traditional approach to health education—disseminating information to students without a focus on interactive communication, skill development, or autonomy. This level addresses fundamentals such as drugs, relationships, hygiene, and safety, leading to outcomes such as increased knowledge of factors that could enhance or decrease health (St. Leger, 2001). Functional health literacy is represented in approaches to health education that are topic based and include teacher-led direct instruction. This foundational level is important because information provides the context for developing health-related skills. For example, people cannot make a health-enhancing, informed choice about the level of physical activity to engage in if they have not received any information about how much activity is optimal for a healthy body. However, as we discuss in chapter 2, there is a place for information in the skills-based classroom because it provides the context you need in order to develop and apply skills.

Many health behavior theories, including the health belief model and social cognitive theory, suggest that knowledge, especially of risks and

KEY POINTS

■ Literacy develops within a specific context. Literacy in one area does not guarantee literacy in another; it must be specifically developed in a given area. Therefore, it is necessary to help students develop health literacy, as well as other forms of literacy.

■ Health education provides an opportunity to teach students how to take ownership of their own health and that of others. It directly contributes to a student's level of health literacy.

■ A person's health literacy is complex and is influenced by multiple factors.

Health Belief Model and Social Cognitive Theory

HEALTH BELIEF MODEL

The health belief model (HBM) was developed in the 1950s as a framework for understanding how to promote preventative health behaviors (Murray-Johnson et al., 2005-2006). The model suggests that behavior is determined by the following six factors: perceived susceptibility, perceived severity, perceived benefits, perceived barriers, health motivation, and cues to action (Armitage & Conner, 2000). This theory suggests that perceived susceptibility to and perceived severity of a behavior strongly influence health motivation, highlighting the importance of relevant, factual information about health behaviors (Murray-Johnson et al., 2005).

SOCIAL COGNITIVE THEORY

With respect to health education, social cognitive theory (SCT) proposes that health behavior is determined by knowledge, perceived self-efficacy over one's health habits, outcome expectations, health goals, and perceived facilitators and impediments to action (Bandura, 2004). This theory is discussed in greater detail in chapter 2.

benefits, is one piece of making behavior change (see sidebar). However, knowledge alone will not lead to changes in behavior. Social cognitive theory suggests that knowledge is the precondition for change but is not typically enough to complete a behavior change (Bandura, 2004). Think about how many people engage in behaviors that they know are unhealthy, such as tobacco use. There is a wealth of knowledge about the risks of tobacco use and yet many people still use tobacco. People have (and can find) information but may not have the skills or confidence to use the information to meet their health needs. Because of this, we need to move beyond the functional level of health literacy in health education courses.

Interactive Health Literacy

The second level, interactive health literacy, focuses on "the development of personal skills in a supportive environment. This approach to education is directed towards improving personal capacity to act independently on knowledge, specifically to improve motivation and self-confidence to act on advice received" (Nutbeam, 2000, p. 265). At this level, the functional information in a health education course would include opportunities to develop specific skills such as problem solving, food preparation, and communication. This level emphasizes

the ability to independently engage in positive health behaviors and access information and services (St. Leger, 2001).

Interactive health literacy begins to address aspects of health behavior beyond knowledge, including skills, motivation, and self-confidence. The goal for this level is for students to be able to act on knowledge and actually adopt or change behavior. To do this, current best practice in health education suggests a focus on skill development and opportunities for practice within the curriculum. This level also begins to consider the impact of moving beyond the individual and toward greater understanding of how relationships and the community can affect behavior. The benefits of health literacy extend beyond the individual and contribute to domains such as work, society, and culture (Sorenson et al., 2012). Many effective health education programs address the first two levels of health literacy.

Critical Health Literacy

The third level proposed by Nutbeam (2000) is critical health literacy. This level is oriented toward individual, social, and political action. Critical health literacy focuses on broader perspectives of community, national, and global capacity to address health issues. Curriculum content at this level addresses social inequities, policy development, and affecting change. Outcomes include the capacity to participate in community and societal initiatives that bring about positive change for disadvantaged populations (St. Leger, 2001).

When people reach this level of health literacy, they are empowered to take action for themselves and others. This level requires them to actively work for change to benefit the broader population. In a health education class, teaching the National Health Education Standard of advocacy with a focus on making an impact on the broader community helps students to reach critical health literacy.

Holistic Health Literacy

Whereas the previous levels of health literacy are widely accepted, holistic health literacy continues to be part of the wider discussion about health literacy both in the education and medical fields. Holistic health literacy, as defined by Rask et al. (2013-2014), includes "tolerance; understanding the culture as a wide and multidimensional phenomenon; environmental consciousness; and analyzing the state of the world from various points of view" (p. 58). This level looks beyond what is for the greater good of the broader population and requires people to embody a fundamental acceptance that each individual has a rich history and many multidimensional facets. Holistic health literacy is achieved when one perceives that health is not just about disease prevention and the impact of cultural beliefs on health but also about opportunity, environment, norms, and traditions.

In an increasingly globalized world, students need to look beyond themselves and their communities to the big picture. Although holistic health literacy is an important consideration, the concept has been discussed for many years and is important to consider when discussing the connection between health education and health literacy. Holistic health literacy recognizes that we live in an ever-changing world where globalization is the norm and communities no longer exist in a single dimension. Students can travel to another country and see familiar restaurants and stores or just as easily walk down their block and encounter other youth who speak a different native language or celebrate other religious traditions. This affects learning because, as students begin to understand that differences exist, they are able to recognize what their personal beliefs are and how those beliefs and the beliefs of the people around them influence their health behaviors.

As a health educator, you must teach your students how to navigate the world as global citizens with a small footprint, recognizing the role each person plays within the larger society and that all of our actions have an impact on available resources. This includes assisting students in understanding those around them, assessing the impact of policies and practices on the environment, and knowing how food availability and production affects global health. By preparing students to better understand the world around them and those who live in this world with them, you prepare them to be contributing members of society.

DEVELOPING HEALTH LITERACY AS AN ASSET

As mentioned, conceptualizing health literacy as an asset to develop in youth is a recent but important development. This approach, which has foundations in public health, suggests that health literacy is a quality a person can develop that is both useful and valuable because it can

KEY POINTS

- ■ Health literacy is ever evolving, and a person can be anywhere on the continuum.
- ■ Many health education programs only help students achieve lower levels of health literacy and fail to help students reach more complex levels of health literacy.
- ■ Each dimension of health literacy builds upon the previous level in order to develop students who are able to function across many levels.
- ■ A health education course that helps develop health literacy at higher levels is beneficial to students and society.

lead to improved health outcomes, choices, and opportunities (Nutbeam, 2008). This approach takes into account the broader potential of health literacy as well as the socioecological model of health behaviors.

The **socioecological model** suggests that health behaviors are influenced at three levels: intrapersonal (individual), interpersonal, and community. Intrapersonal or individual traits such as age, cultural background, motivation, attitudes, race, gender, cognitive and physical abilities, and knowledge affect health literacy and health outcomes (Manganello, 2008). Other individual factors include general literacy, experience with illness and the health care system, media use, socioeconomic status, and social support, as well as more general competencies such as vision, hearing, memory, and social skills (Sorenson, 2012).

At the interpersonal level, people are influenced by their relationships with peers, family, teachers, coworkers, coaches, significant others, and so on. When working with youth, especially adolescents, peer and parent influences are particularly important at this level. Both parents and peers have been shown to directly influence health literacy and health outcomes, and both should be a focus of health literacy efforts with adolescents (Manganello, 2008).

The third level, community, encompasses a variety of organizations and systems, including media, school, health care, public policy, religious communities, and neighborhoods. Systems at the community level are thought to contribute to the development of health literacy, especially during adolescence. Because adolescents are still engaged with these organizations (such as schools), the organizations should be considered when developing health literacy interventions. Manganello (2008) states that there is a "need for schools to play an important role in improving health literacy for adolescents, as schools have a direct influence on the education and development of adolescents" (p. 842). Figure 1.3 is a framework for studying adolescent health literacy.

ESTABLISHING HEALTH LITERACY FOR LIFE

As discussed earlier, when individual health literacy rises, so does the ability to be in control of one's health. Young people who can take care of themselves will more easily engage in health-enhancing behaviors and avoid risky behaviors. For example, a study examining adolescent levels of health literacy and self-efficacy found

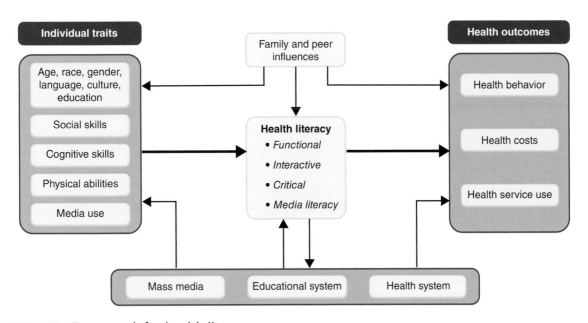

FIGURE 1.3 Framework for health literacy.

Adapted, by permission, from J.A. Manganello, 2008, "Health literacy and adolescents: A framework and agenda for future research," *Health Education Research* 23(5): 840-847.

KEY POINTS

■ Assets support the health of individuals. Health literacy as an asset supports improved outcomes, choices, and opportunities.

■ Each level of the socioecological model (intrapersonal, interpersonal, and community) has an important impact on health outcomes.

■ Schools have a direct influence on youth and must be actively involved in developing the asset of health literacy in their students.

that the ability to read and understand food labels increased health literacy and dietary quality (Cha et al., 2014). Because poor dietary patterns are a leading **risk factor** for overweight and obesity, having the ability to read, understand, and use the information on food labels could help someone make healthier food choices. This is just one example of how health literacy can directly affect health behaviors.

Health literacy plays a role in many aspects of life and is a significant contributor to the health behaviors of individuals and those around them (Cha, 2014; U.S. Department of Health and Human Services [HHS], n.d.; Sorenson, 2012). Given this, we can argue that when adolescents have learned how to take control of their health and how to choose health-enhancing behaviors, they are better

positioned to learn during the school day because some of the other confounding factors have been addressed. Bradley and Greene's 2013 meta-analysis supports this argument. It reviewed 122 research studies examining the relationship between the six leading health risk behaviors and their relationship to academic outcomes. Table 1.1 highlights some key findings from this research.

Moreover, many studies support the idea that good health can help students achieve higher academic outcomes in school because healthy children are more likely to attend school, to be able to concentrate, and to perform well—they are more ready and able to learn (Centers for Disease Control and Prevention [CDC], 2015; Lewallan, 2004; World Health Organization [WHO], 2003). Health and academic outcomes

TABLE 1.1 Relationship Between Leading Health Risk Behaviors and Academic Outcomes

Violence-related behaviors	• Students with higher academic achievement are less likely to engage in or be victims of violence. • Being forced to engage in or forcing another to have nonconsensual sexual activity is associated with lower academic outcomes.
Tobacco use	• Tobacco use has a direct relationship with poorer academic outcomes. • Those using tobacco don't perform as well on academic measures compared with non-tobacco-using peers.
Alcohol and other drug use	• Students who engage in binge drinking, marijuana use, illicit drug use, or misuse of prescription medications are more likely to do worse in school. • High school seniors who report binge drinking (more than five drinks) are 7 to 9 percent less likely to enter college.
Sexual behaviors	• The earlier students engage in sexual activity, the more likely the behavior is to have a negative effect on academic outcomes. • Those who engage in other risky behaviors are more likely to engage in risky sexual behaviors.
Physical inactivity	• Physical activity is positively associated with academic achievement. • Moderate to vigorous physical activity has a positive impact on GPA.
Nutrition	• Participation in school breakfast or lunch has a positive association with academic outcomes. • Inadequate dietary intake has a negative effect on academic measures.

Advice From the Field

BENEFITS OF TEACHING HEALTH EDUCATION

Amy Lauren Smith
Shanghai American School, Shanghai, China

In your experience, what are the benefits of teaching health education in schools?

I often tell my students that it doesn't matter what you want to be when you grow up, but I am pretty sure you'll want to be healthy. The skills taught in health are ones that all students will absolutely, without a doubt, need when they get older. While some argue that these are skills that could be taught at home, we have to understand that many parents aren't comfortable with the subject matter or might not have been educated on it correctly themselves.

Health education needs to take more of a priority in our schools. We offer limited contact hours of health education K-12 and then wonder why our college students are having such issues with alcohol abuse, sexual assault, and mental health. We scramble to solve our health care issues after they arise, often taking a reactionary approach. More comprehensive, skills-based health education is a critical aspect of prevention that our country desperately needs.

How does health education contribute to health literacy?

The skills-based National Health Education Standards aim to equip students with the tools they will need for health literacy. We have no idea what concerns will pop up in their lives or in our society in the future. Students need to know where to go for information, how to make healthy decisions, how to set goals, and how to advocate for themselves, their families, and their communities (just to list a few). Health education teaches them to be ready for challenges as they arise.

What advice do you have for other health educators in the field?

For me, it comes down to three main goals. For a curriculum to be effective, it needs to be current, relevant, and adaptable.

The health concerns and issues for our students are vastly different than they were 20, 10, even 5 years ago, and new research is coming out all the time. By staying on top of the latest research and trends, we are modeling that health literacy is an ongoing skill that they're going to need for the rest of their lives.

In order to get buy-in from the students, we need to make sure that the topics covered are relevant to them and their unique needs. Use formative assessments to gauge what's going on in their lives. Build your curriculum around that.

Design your units around the skills, not the content. This gives you the freedom to address issues as they arise and adapt your curriculum accordingly.

Lastly, I believe in collaboration. Health educators often work in isolation and might be the only one at their school, or they might also be teaching another subject such as physical education, giving them very little time for prep. By broadening the net and reaching out to health teachers through professional development and social networking sites such as Twitter, we can share lessons, ideas, and resources that work for us—and ask for help when we need it.

are linked such that improving one is likely to improve the other. Schools, then, provide a unique opportunity to support the development of health literacy in youth.

Not only is it possible that a well-constructed health education program may have a positive effect on individual academic performance, but it may also help schools attain objectives within the following four areas (Kolbe, 2002):

1. Improving health knowledge, attitudes, and skills

2. Improving health behaviors and health outcomes

3. Improving educational outcomes

4. Improving social outcomes

Acknowledging the significant role that health education can play in helping schools to reach these goals outlines the potential impact of health education in supporting other school initiatives. Let's take a look at each of the four goals to further understand their importance.

Improving Health Knowledge, Skills, and Attitudes

This goal can be achieved through the inclusion of a comprehensive, skills-based health education program that is built upon the National Health Education Standards and includes a variety of health topics as well as skills needed to live a healthy life. The National Health Education Standards suggest that health education programs should be designed to promote seven skills: analyzing influences, accessing valid information, interpersonal communication, decision making, goal setting, self-management (ability to practice health-enhancing behaviors and avoid or reduce health risks), and advocacy (Joint Committee, 2007). In addition, the first National Standard, which is dedicated to "comprehending the concepts of health promotion and disease prevention to improve health" (Joint Committee, 2007, p. 8), identifies the importance of meaningful, relevant content as an accompaniment to the skills being taught. A skills-based approach is discussed in greater detail in chapter 2.

Improving Health Behaviors and Outcomes

This goal is important for schools and society as a whole. Healthy People 2020—a U.S. initiative to improve health and prevent disease nationwide—has adopted a number of objectives that involve educational programming in schools and address the health of adolescents (www.healthypeople.gov). There is also an Adolescent and Young Adult Health Program that has the following aims (Health Resources and Services Administration [HRSA], n.d.):

■ Elevate the national, state, and community focus on and commitment to the health, safety, positive development, and well-being of adolescents, young adults, and their families.

■ Increase access to quality health and safety education and health care, including comprehensive general health, oral health, mental health, and substance abuse prevention and treatment services.

■ Address the influence of social determinants on health, safety, and well-being.

■ Improve health and safety outcomes in such areas as mortality, unintentional injury, violence, oral and mental health, tobacco and substance use, reproductive health, nutrition and physical activity, and the prevention of adult chronic diseases.

■ Eliminate disparities in health, safety, and well-being among adolescents and young adults.

Schools are in a unique position to help meet the second goal of improving health behavior and outcomes through health education because they assume a primary role in adolescent education and reach many students on a regular basis (Association for Supervision and Curriculum Development [ASCD], 2011; CDC, 2015; Fisher et al., 2003; St. Leger, 2001). By educating students before they adopt unhealthy habits, schools can lessen the likelihood of students engaging in risky behaviors. Effective health education programs in schools can provide students with the knowledge and skills to make health-enhancing decisions and can influence their health-related behaviors (Hale, Fitzgerald-Yau, & Vine, 2014; Kirby et al., 1994; Rosemond, Blake, Jenkins, Buff, & Moore, 2015). Quality health education programs in schools can result in healthier students and thus a healthier nation.

Improving Educational Outcomes

Enhancing the health of students through comprehensive health education can improve educational outcomes. The key message is that healthy students are better learners (CDC, 2015). As discussed, good health can have a positive impact on academic performance, and health education can improve health through the development of health literacy and other outcomes (Michael, Merlo, Basch, Wentzel & Wechsler, 2015). This has a direct impact on student outcomes and can play a significant role in closing the achievement gap. Another key opportunity to address the achievement gap is by addressing health disparities among young people.

As Basch (2011) writes, "No matter how well teachers are prepared to teach, no matter what accountability measures are put in place . . . education professionals will be profoundly limited if students are not motivated and able to learn" (p. 593). Health problems linked to health disparity can lead to a lack of motivation and a decreased ability to learn. This is especially true for urban minority youth who are at greater risk of health disparities and therefore are at greater risk for health problems and negative academic outcomes (Basch, 2011).

Additional research examining urban youth suggests that students with health assets such as maintaining a healthy weight, consuming less soda, having a stable food source, having less screen time, and being emotionally healthy are more likely to achieve the goal for standardized test scores in reading, writing, and mathematics (Ickovics et al., 2014). These findings suggest that "health-promoting behaviors should be considered nontraditional school achievement strategies with the potential to enhance both student health and academic achievement" (Ickovics et al., 2014, p. 44). This research supports the link between health and academics, but rather than focusing on the absence of risky behaviors, it focuses on positive health behaviors, or **protective factors**, as supporters of academic outcomes. Quality health education should not only focus on reducing risky behaviors but also on enhancing protective factors. According to recent data, this could have a positive impact on both health and academics.

Another research-supported connection between health and education outcomes is the negative relationship between risky behaviors and achievement. Students who engage in risky behaviors such as smoking cigarettes, using drugs, drinking alcohol, and being sexually active are more likely to have lower grades (Michael, Merlo, Basch, Wentzel & Wechsler, 2015). For example, in 2009 (the most recent data available), 62 percent of students who were currently using alcohol reported receiving Ds and Fs (CDC, 2012).

This research clearly shows that students engaging in risky behaviors are more likely to perform poorly in school. A report from the Washington State Board of Health (Diley, 2009) also found that the more health risks students had, the more likely the students were to be at academic risk. Interestingly, the report also found that each health risk similarly increased academic risk and that all of the factors that they examined contributed to academic risk, whether it was using marijuana or watching three or more hours of TV per day. In short, these data reveal that risky health behaviors affect academic performance. The good news is that health education "allows students to learn and practice communication and social skills" which can reduce the likelihood of students engaging in these negative behaviors (Michael, Merlo, Basch, Wentzel & Wechsler, 2015, p. 751).

Improving Social Outcomes

One way schools can address risky behaviors is by designing a health education curriculum that helps students build character—that is, a character education or social competency curriculum (Kolbe, 2002). *Character education* is the "explicit teaching of positive values by teachers supported by the school" (Beachum, McCray, Yawn, & Obiakor, 2013, p. 471). Within skills-based health education, teaching positive values, especially as they relate to health, is a core part of this approach (see chapter 2).

Another connection is in the teaching method. Character education is most effective when it is interactive and cooperative and when it uses real-life examples—just like in a skills-based approach to health education (Lewis, Robinson, & Hays, 2011).

Finally, the skills themselves can support the teaching and development of positive values. For example, teaching the skill of interpersonal communication could include strategies for conflict resolution, empathy building, and

KEY POINTS

■ Comprehensive health education programs can be an effective way for schools to achieve multiple educational goals while improving students' health.

■ Many health behavior, educational, and social outcomes overlap and do not function independently of one another.

■ Teaching students skills and information can play a key role in breaking the cycle of risky behaviors.

listening. In addition, you could use real-life scenarios in the classroom to help students practice these skills, and you could use teachable moments that naturally occur in class to create a learning environment that fosters mutual respect, honesty, and caring for other students. For instance, when conflict arises in the hallway or on the playground, you have the opportunity to reinforce what students learned in the classroom. The similarities between effective character education and effective health education suggest that integrating character education into the health education curriculum would require minimal effort but result in positive outcomes, including helping students build character and encouraging them to be a positive part of the school community (Kolbe, 2002).

A second way that a health education program can address social outcomes is by teaching skills and information that can break cycles of risky behaviors. It is widely noted that the earlier young people engage in risk behaviors (e.g., smoking, sexual activity, substance use), the poorer the health outcomes they will encounter throughout their lives. Additionally, because the risk factors for many health indicators overlap and do not occur independently, Hale et al. (2014) argue for the integration of strategies that influence multiple health risk factors: "For example, sexual intercourse accompanied by alcohol or illicit drug use is linked to a lower likelihood of condom use, so targeting substance misuse may be a feasible approach to reducing unsafe sex" (p. e19). Social outcomes improve when risk behavior decreases. This is because risk behaviors affect not only students' own health but also the health of those around them, including their peers, family, and community.

SUMMARY

Health literacy affects a person's ability to achieve positive health outcomes. It is a multifaceted concept that involves developing competencies within a series of levels that relate to students' ability to look beyond themselves and have broader perspectives of health. School-based health education is critical in the development of health literacy and has relevance to positive health outcomes across the population.

The goal of health education is to develop students who are able to access, understand, appraise, and apply health information in order to maintain or enhance health for themselves and others. Health-literate people are more likely to experience positive health outcomes throughout their lives. In addition, if health literacy develops during adolescence, it increases the likelihood that healthy behaviors will continue into adulthood. Although schools have the primary goal of producing students who are academically prepared for college and careers, the data and literature suggest that schools should also address the health of students. This will not only have a positive impact on academic performance but can also address a significant issue in the larger community: the importance of improving the health of our society and world.

Review Questions

1. What is health literacy, and why is it important in relation to health education?

2. What are the dimensions of health literacy? Provide an example of what skills or abilities a person should have at each level of literacy.

3. How does a socioecological approach relate to health literacy?

4. How can improving health literacy in adolescents affect overall academic achievement?

To find supplementary materials for this chapter, such as worksheets and extended learning activities, visit the web resource at
www.HumanKinetics.com/TheEssentialsOfTeachingHealthEducation

CHAPTER 2

Understanding a Skills-Based Approach

Learning Objectives

After reading this chapter, you will be able to do the following:

- Define a skills-based approach to health education.
- Describe key aspects of a skills-based approach.
- List and describe the steps in a skill development model.
- Discuss the theory and research behind a skills-based approach to health education and how it differs from a content-based approach.

Key Terms

functional information

functional knowledge

outcome expectations

participatory methods

self-efficacy

skill proficiency

skills-based health education

social cognitive theory (SCT)

transfer

The first edition of the National Health Education Standards, released in 1995, emphasized skill development over learning information. The second edition, released in 2007, built on the first edition by fine-tuning the skills that are important components of a health education course (Joint Committee, 2007). However, even with two editions of the National Standards focusing on skills and skill development, most health education programs in the United States have placed more emphasis on ensuring that students learn information rather than developing the skills necessary to apply that information.

This text seeks to change this practice by encouraging you to use **skills-based health education** to make skill development, specifically the development of skills to proficiency (discussed in part II of this book), the emphasis of your health education program. For many, this change in emphasis from presenting information (perhaps with some inclusion of skills) to helping students develop skills to proficiency (with the inclusion of functional information to support the skill development) is a paradigm shift in the way they view health education. We provide evidence in this chapter to support the transition to a skills-based approach. We discuss why this approach is more likely to lead to behavior change, **transfer** outside the health classroom, and improve ability to apply learning throughout life. Specifically, this chapter defines a skills-based approach, discusses its core components, and provides support for its efficacy.

COMPONENTS OF SKILLS-BASED HEALTH EDUCATION

The approach presented in this text is called *skills-based health education* or a *skills-based approach*. A skills-based health education program is a planned, sequential, comprehensive, and relevant curriculum that is implemented through participatory methods in order to help students develop the skills, attitudes, and functional knowledge needed to lead health-enhancing lives. As asserted in chapter 1, health literacy is an important outcome of effective health education, but the goal of health education should go beyond health literacy.

The definition of skills-based health education presented here allows for the development of higher levels of health literacy while also leaving room for broader outcomes for students. Health literacy is one asset that can help people lead health-enhancing lives, but there are many other necessary skills, behaviors, and competencies (all of which can be considered assets) that can be developed through a skills-based approach to health education.

It is important to make one clarification before continuing the discussion of skills-based health education. Often the term *standards-based health education* is used interchangeably with *skills-based health education*. Although both terms refer to programs aligned with the National Health Education Standards, standards-based health education and skills-based health education are not the same (Tappe, Wilbur, Telljohann, & Jensen, 2009). A standards-based health education curriculum is designed using the National Health Education Standards, but it does not directly refer to other health education components such as instructional style. Though skills-based health education should also be standards based, in this text *skills-based health education* refers to the written curriculum, instructional style, and implementation of the curriculum in the classroom. Even educators who are implementing a standards-based approach must consider the importance of a skills-based approach for focusing on skill development and proficiency. Now, let's take a deeper look at the core aspects of skills-based health education.

Uses Planned and Sequential Curriculum

Ideally, health education curriculum is planned and sequenced from preK-12 with a written scope and sequence (what is taught and when; see chapter 12). Even if the curriculum is not planned in coordination with other health educators in a school or district, any educators implementing a skills-based approach, even if just in their courses, can have a planned and sequential curriculum within their classroom. *Planned* means that you have thought about, made decisions about, and drafted written versions of intended outcomes, units, and lesson plans (more on this in chapter 12). A sequential

A skills-based approach can lead to skill proficiency which is more likely to support behavior change and enhance health.

curriculum is one that has a logical order, builds on prior learning, and helps students develop the skills and functional knowledge necessary for the course of instruction and beyond. This is important because without a planned set of outcomes, the likelihood of students being able to demonstrate growth and **skill proficiency** is low—how can you get to where you are going if you don't have a specific destination? When a course is not sequential, it is likely that holes will exist in student learning, valuable time will be wasted on duplicated efforts, and important parts of the curriculum will not be conveyed.

Comprehensively Addresses Dimensions of Health

Comprehensive means the curriculum addresses a variety of topics within multiple dimensions of health (i.e., physical, social, environmental, emotional, mental, spiritual). The specific topics and depth of coverage will depend on

state and district regulations, frameworks and standards, local health behaviors, data, and time dedicated to health education. The key here is that the course should include multiple dimensions of health and should not be limited to a single topic. The National Health Education Standards identify the following topics for inclusion in health education: substance use and abuse, injury prevention and safety, environmental health, community health, disease prevention and control, nutrition, personal health, mental and emotional health, consumer health, and family life (Joint Committee, 2007). These can be a starting place when determining what topics to include (see the National Health Education Standards Sidebar and chapter 12 for more details).

Relevant to Students

Relevant means having significant and demonstrable bearing on the matter at hand, in this instance the health and wellness of

National Health Education Standards

1. Students will comprehend concepts related to health promotion and disease prevention to enhance health.
2. Students will analyze the influence of family, peers, culture, media, technology, and other factors on health behaviors.
3. Students will demonstrate the ability to access valid information, products, and services to enhance health.
4. Students will demonstrate the ability to use interpersonal communication skills to enhance health and avoid or reduce health risks.
5. Students will demonstrate the ability to use decision-making skills to enhance health.
6. Students will demonstrate the ability to use goal-setting skills to enhance health.
7. Students will demonstrate the ability to practice health-enhancing behaviors and avoid or reduce health risks.
8. Students will demonstrate the ability to advocate for personal, family, and community health.

your students. The curriculum must take into consideration all students in the classroom and must not be designed with a one-size-fits-all approach. This is about more than just being up to date and using factual information or trends. It means that you consider skills, topics, instructional methods, terminology, and activities that are engaging and meaningful for *your* students prior to and during instruction. It also means that the curriculum and instructional methods are developmentally appropriate, age appropriate, and culturally inclusive.

Uses Participatory Methods

Participatory methods are discussed in greater detail later in the chapter, but in brief, they are methods through which people naturally learn behaviors, including observation, modeling, and interaction (WHO, 2003). An important component of participatory teaching, especially relating to skills-based health education, is that teachers give students time to practice the skills they have learned.

Develops Skill Proficiency

In a skills-based approach, the primary skills developed are those included in the National Standards: accessing valid and reliable information, analyzing influences, interpersonal communication, decision making, goal setting, self-management, and advocacy. However, the standards cover overarching topics, and within each of those standards additional skills are necessary in order to achieve proficiency. Examples include analyzing advertising techniques (part of analyzing influences), reading food labels (part of accessing valid and reliable information), and appropriately using condoms (part of decision making and self-management). Each primary skill will be covered in more detail in part II.

Fosters Health-Enhancing Attitudes

An important part of skills-based health education is addressing student attitudes toward health, healthy behaviors, and healthy decision making. Attitudes are not easily changed and are typically rooted in values and beliefs that students have developed over their lifetimes. Therefore, the goal is not to force students to change or to impose values, beliefs, or attitudes. Rather, curriculum and instruction are designed to encourage critical thinking and

- ■ Skills-based health education focuses on students attaining knowledge and skills through participatory classroom methods.
- ■ A skills-based curriculum should be planned, sequential, relevant, and comprehensive.
- ■ A skills-based approach is similar to but not the same as a standards-based approach.

allow students to develop health-enhancing priorities and attitudes that support their ability to make healthy decisions and engage in health-enhancing behaviors outside the classroom.

Builds Functional Knowledge

The inclusion of functional information in a curriculum allows students to process and internalize that information into **functional knowledge** (remember from chapter 1 that knowledge is the result of learning and internalizing information). You cannot simply use facts and figures in the hope that this information will prompt students to make a healthy choice. Rather, you must only include information that is important for students to learn based on the intended outcome, the skill with which it will be taught and connected to student need. In other words, the information must be functional and useful. A good question to ask is, "What information about this topic do my students need in order to effectively apply the skill being covered?" Or, "If my students do not learn this information, will they be able to apply this skill to achieve the desired outcome?" Though simple in theory, these two questions require you to analyze why you are including the information you identify as functional, which builds a stronger justification for your course. Determining functional information is further discussed in chapter 11.

SKILLS-BASED HEALTH EDUCATION IN PRACTICE

It is important to have a clear understanding of what skills-based health education looks like in practice (see figure 2.1). In this chapter we examine the ways skills-based health education differs from content-based health education, key aspects of skills-based health education, and practical, classroom-based examples of this approach.

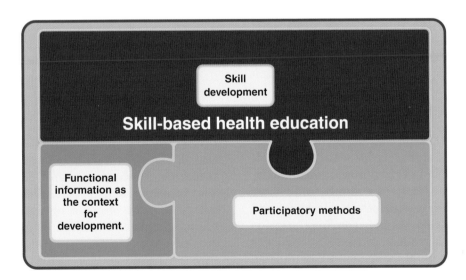

FIGURE 2.1 Key aspects of skills-based health education.

Before we continue the discussion about implementing a skills-based approach to health education, we first must explain how skills-based health education differs from traditional or content-based health education. Comparing the two helps highlight some key components of the skills-based approach.

Traditional or content-based health education typically emphasizes knowledge acquisition, includes the typical content areas described earlier, and relies on direct instruction and changes in knowledge and attitudes to change behaviors (Allensworth, 1994). Traditional health education is like any other lesson. It teaches issues that are not always relevant to the students and focuses on future outcomes rather than present outcomes, which is not as effective with adolescents (Arborelius & Bremberg, 1991). These characteristics highlight the major differences between traditional and skills-based health education, so we will describe each in more detail.

The first major difference between traditional health education and skills-based health education is that skills-based health education does not rely on knowledge and attitude change alone to drive behavior change. To achieve behavior change, a curriculum must include knowledge, attitudes, and skills. As discussed previously, the National Health Education Standards reflect the shift from traditional health education to skills-based health education in their primary outcome goal of students engaging in healthy behaviors (Tappe et al., 2009). This means that a curriculum must address not only knowledge and skills but also beliefs, values, and norms that are health enhancing (Tappe et al., 2009). It is clear that the focus of the standards is not merely on knowing but also on applying learned information in a meaningful, health-enhancing way.

The National Health Education Standards further demonstrate this paradigm shift through the use of performance indicators for each standard. The performance indicators communicate what students should know and be able to do for each standard during the grade spans of preK to grade 2, grades 3 to 5, grades 6 to 8, and grades 9 to 12 (Joint Committee, 2007). For example, it is not enough to know that smoking is detrimental to one's health.

Students must be able to analyze the pressures they are feeling to smoke, they must be able to make health-enhancing decisions regarding whether or not to smoke, and they must be able to say no to smoking in a variety of situations. Skills-based health education means teaching more than just health-related concepts; it means providing students with the necessary skills to navigate a life filled with tough decisions about staying healthy.

A second way in which skills-based health education differs from traditional health education is in the area of instruction. Effective skills-based health education uses participatory teaching methods, including skill development techniques, interactive teaching, and a social context for learning (WHO, 2003). This results in instruction that allows students to see change in the present as opposed to teaching knowledge that might be useful in the future. Students become directly involved in their learning experiences, and much of the instruction focuses on giving students the knowledge and skills they need both now and in the future versus focusing on didactic learning for fact acquisition. Teaching students how to use these skills and having an opportunity to shape their attitudes through participatory methods will assist them in creating and maintaining a healthy lifestyle.

To further your understanding of the components of a skills-based approach, we will now explore skill development, participatory methods, and functional information as the context for skill development.

Skill Development

In order to change behavior, a health education curriculum must help students apply what they have learned. In a skills-based approach, the emphasis is on students acquiring both the skills and knowledge that can lead them to make health-enhancing choices in a variety of situations. However, before students can learn how to use a skill in a real-life setting, they must learn the steps of performing the skill, see examples of the skill being used in real life, have opportunities to practice in real-life situations, and receive appropriate feedback. These aspects of skill development fit easily into participatory instruction (WHO, 2003).

There are two main models for skill development related to health and health education: one from the National Health Education Standards and one from the World Health Organization (WHO). Here we present a model that combines the two.

- ■ Step 1: Discuss the importance of the skill, its relevance, and its relationship to other learned skills.
  - Define the skill.
  - Determine educational objectives (what should students be able to do if they learn the skill correctly?).
- ■ Step 2: Present steps for development of the skill.
- ■ Step 3: Model the skill.
  - Generate positive and negative examples of how the skill might be applied.
  - Provide students the opportunity to observe the skill being applied effectively.
  - Correct misconceptions about what the skill is and how to perform it.
- ■ Step 4: Practice the skill using real-life scenarios.
  - Encourage verbal rehearsal and action.
  - Provide opportunities for practice with coaching and feedback.
- ■ Step 5: Provide feedback and reinforcement.
  - Evaluate student performance.
  - Provide opportunities for personal practice (students practice the skill in real life outside the classroom).
  - Foster self-evaluation and skill adjustment.

In a skills-based classroom, this model provides a framework for the curriculum. Every step is covered for every skill in the curriculum. The length and depth of coverage for each step depends on a variety of factors, but all steps should be included. The steps are listed in the order in which they should be presented, but you can return to previous steps at any time if necessary. Let's use an example to illustrate what this might look like in a classroom.

The skill being taught in a ninth-grade classroom is decision making. On the first day of the decision-making unit, the class begins with a do-now activity (an activity for reflecting on the topic of the day that students begin as soon as they come into the classroom): How can decisions affect a teen's health? The question provides an opportunity for students to develop their own ideas about the relevance of the skill. Next, the teacher facilitates a few activities that reinforce the relevance of decision making, especially as it relates to health. The teacher then provides students with the educational objectives—what students should know and be able to do when they become proficient in decision making. This tells students the outcomes of the unit for developing the skill proficiency and the topics that they will cover while discussing decision making. The teacher can now move to step 2.

In step 2, the teacher presents the steps, or skill cues, of the skill and highlights the critical elements. *Skill cues* are the components of the skill that are necessary to perform the skill correctly.

Step 3 is where the teacher provides opportunities for students to observe examples of the skill being performed effectively and ineffectively. These should be examples that directly relate to the educational objectives and skill cues presented in step 2. The examples do not have to be teacher directed. The goal is to model the skill to help students see what the skill should look like when performed at the level described in steps 1 and 2. For example, the teacher might use an activity in which students write a story or a script about a teenager who engaged in the decision-making process. After students learn the skill cues, they create a story that highlights all of the cues. Students then share their stories, and the whole class reviews the skill cues and the teacher addresses any confusion or misconceptions. If students have not yet done a decision-making unit, the teacher should create this story and then walk through the story with the group, highlighting the skill cues. However the teacher addresses this step, the outcome should be that students have opportunities to see the skill in action and see the skill cues modeled effectively.

Step 4 is critical to a skills-based approach because it allows students practice the skill in meaningful and relevant ways. The teacher provides class time for students to practice individually or in groups, working through each of the decision-making steps in multiple ways. The teacher needs to provide opportunities for practice that will reasonably lead to the educational objectives in step 1 and skill proficiency. Time spent on this step includes providing students with meaningful feedback and will depend on students' ability to understand and apply what you have presented. Monitor the opportunities and adapt them as necessary to meet student need and ability.

Feedback can be teacher to student, student to student, or self-directed (individual). The practice opportunities might also lead to the final product that the students are asked to demonstrate. Examples of activities for step 4 are included in part II of this text; the main takeaway in this chapter is that students need ample time for practice, and the practice needs to include feedback to improve the students' ability to become proficient in the skill.

The final step, step 5, is when students demonstrate decision making for final evaluation. Through their own work, students must be able to demonstrate their ability to apply the skill properly. The demonstration could be done outside the classroom as homework, the teacher might have the students practice outside the classroom before the final product is presented in class, or there could be an in- or out-of-class extension activity at the end of the unit. Regardless of how students take their learning out of the classroom, this step needs to be explicitly included in the curriculum and instruction.

One way to think of skill development in the classroom is to think of the health educator as a coach. When you coach a team, you teach the athletes specific skills they need in order to be successful during a game. Let's take basketball as an example. The coach teaches dribbling, passing, and shooting, as well as offensive and defensive strategies. Each of the skills needs to be learned on its own and then combined in a gamelike setting. The coach shows the athletes how to dribble correctly and explains the critical elements or skill cues of dribbling. The coach demonstrates what the skill looks like in a real-life setting, showing athletes the application of the skill. The coach then runs drills where the athletes practice dribbling to ensure that they can perform the skill correctly. As the athletes advance, the coach provides practice

opportunities that mimic gameplay, including creating real-life conditions so that athletes practice in a context as similar to a game as possible. During all of this practice, the coach is providing feedback to help the athletes successfully perform the skill. Finally, it is game day. The coach hopes that working with the athletes has resulted in effective application of skills and ideally in a win.

In health education, the game is real life and the coach is the teacher. Of course, you can't be there in the student's life outside school, but that means it is even more important to do as much as you can during class to ensure that students have authentic practice opportunities that mimic real-life situations and are ready to apply these skills in their lives.

Although the coaching analogy focuses on athletes, this approach holds true in many other contexts as well. Consider skill development in terms of a violin teacher helping a student prepare for a concert, a literacy coach helping a student improve reading skills, or a dance teacher helping students with choreography for a performance. These situations all require implementation of the skill development model in order to assist students with their goal of being able to perform a set of skills in a specific context.

Participatory Methods

Instructional methods in skills-based health education should be "student-centered, interactive and experiential" (CDC, 2015). This includes the following instructional strategies: role-play, large- and small-group discussions, debates, cooperative learning, problem solving, brainstorming, and games and simulations (CDC, 2015; WHO, 2003). Lecture or direct instruction, usually associated with disseminating factual information or concepts, is not included in this list. The implication is that skills-based health education focuses not on acquiring facts alone but also on the larger aim of teaching skills, changing attitudes, and influencing behaviors through interactive teaching methods.

The instructional methods in skills-based health education are based on the premise that learning occurs in a social context and that the learning environment is student centered and

Fotolia/gajatz

Participatory methods engage students in their learning experience and provide opportunities for social interactions.

allows for social interactions (Borders, 2009). Students learn from the people around them, including their teachers, peers, parents, and other role models in their lives. We further discuss how to create, implement, and support a positive classroom environment in detail in chapter 14.

Peer pressure and the perception of peer behaviors have been found to influence behavior during adolescence (Bongardt, Reitz, Sandfort, & Dekovic, 2014; Monahan, Rhew, Hawkins, & Brown, 2013). It would follow that it is important to address norms of health-related behaviors to help influence students' attitudes toward certain behaviors, to acknowledge and listen to what behaviors students believe their peers are engaging in, to allow time for practice and feedback so that students can see each other applying skills successfully, and to address the influences in students' lives that will guide their decisions. Direct instruction may not have the same impact on the students

because it eliminates much of the social context of learning. Student-centered learning environments and social interaction can be facilitated best through participatory learning via discussion, brainstorming, role-play, and other techniques discussed earlier (Borders, 2009; WHO, 2003).

One of the main characteristics of participatory methods in a skills-based approach is that the teacher becomes a guide who plans and facilitates learning activities and experiences that allow students to engage in the material and take ownership over their learning. In essence, the teacher is a participant in the journey as well. Students are the leaders and teachers work to get to know their students and to be active observers in the class who adjust instruction as needed. This does not mean that you can't make a plan or that students take over the class; rather, it means you can adjust the course to meet students' needs year to year, semester to semester, and within the duration of the course. Here are some examples of how the teacher can act as a guide:

- Ask students what topics they are interested in learning about (this would also increase the relevance for students).
- Include a pretest or preassessment to determine students' areas of strength (this can be skill, topic, or information based).
- Provide differentiated options in the classroom and in projects and assignments (this can increase relevance).
- Give students ownership of their learning—have them research, design, and present projects.
- Have students design learning activities to use in the classroom.
- Ask for regular feedback from students on activities, information, and projects, and use the feedback as appropriate.

Functional Information

Functional information will be discussed in greater detail in chapter 11, but here we provide a brief introduction to the term. **Functional information** is information that is useable, applicable, and relevant. It is not arbitrary, traditional, or extensive. It is the *context* in which the skills are taught and the base for developing functional knowledge. Remember from chapter 1 that information that is learned becomes knowledge, so functional information that is learned and internalized will result in functional knowledge.

As we have discussed, the focus of a skills-based classroom is skill development; however, health skills must be developed using health-related information. For example, it would be difficult for students to develop interpersonal communication to improve or maintain their health if they are not given information to communicate about. It is also difficult to focus on developing skills if students are overwhelmed with information that is not easily applied or transferred or that is not clearly connected to skills, their lives, or previous learning in the course. The solution, then, is to determine the functional information about a topic that you can use to teach, practice, and apply a skill.

Let's think about the following outcome: Students will be able to refuse alcohol offered

by a peer. What do the students need to know in order to do this? They might need to know how to make an effective refusal, the negative effects of alcohol, and their own values about underage drinking. Is this enough? Let's play it out.

Tristan: Come on, Fatima, just have a drink. No one will find out, and everyone's drinking. You can't be at this party and not drink—don't be a loser.

Fatima: No thanks, Tristan. I don't want to drink.

Tristan: Fatima, come on! You're being a loser. Just do it!

Fatima: No. I don't want to drink. If my coach finds out, I'll be suspended.

Tristan: Whatever.

This is a simplistic example, but it highlights the fact that students can deliver an effective refusal with limited information. The information the student did use was relevant to her—the possibility of getting in trouble because she's on a sport team. In this instance, she didn't need to explain what alcohol is, what the long- and short-term effects of alcohol are, or what alcoholism is. She simply needed a limited amount of functional information that she could use to support her refusal. This is in essence what would happen in the classroom, and it is core to a skills-based approach. You present limited, functional information to students, and they use it to develop the skill of making refusals.

SUPPORT FOR SKILLS-BASED HEALTH EDUCATION

Now that we have discussed the key aspects of skills-based health education, it is useful to understand the theoretical support for this approach. Multiple health behavior theories, including the health belief model and the theory of reasoned action, support a skills-based approach. However, social cognitive theory, discussed below, provides the best support and relates to many ideas discussed throughout the text. We also discuss how a skills-based approach meets the CDC's characteristics of effective health education curricula, and we go over research support for the effectiveness of skills-based health education.

Social Cognitive Theory

Social cognitive theory (SCT) addresses the multidimensional aspect of the skills-based approach and provides a strong theoretical basis for using this approach in the classroom. According to SCT (Bandura, 2004), health behavior is influenced by knowledge, perceived self-efficacy (i.e., the perception that you have control over your health habits), outcome expectations, health goals, and perceived facilitators and impediments to action (see figure 2.2).

Knowledge

Knowledge about health-related concepts and behaviors is the impetus for change, the first step toward behavior modification. Knowledge forms when you acquire information and apply it in a particular situation. Based on the definition of skills-based health education presented earlier, knowledge would include the physical, mental, emotional, and social dimensions of health as well as a variety of health-related concepts, such as nutrition, physical inactivity, alcohol and drug prevention, violence prevention, injury prevention, and sexuality education. It would also include knowledge of health-promoting skills. In a skills-based approach, students must learn the skills (as identified in the National Standards) before they are able to use them in other traditional content areas. The knowledge in skills-based health education needs to be presented in the form of health-

FIGURE 2.2 Components of SCT.

related concepts *and* skills because concepts alone are not enough to stimulate behavior change (Greenberg et al., 2003; Tappe et al., 2009). SCT supports this view through the fact that there are many other determinants (such as self-efficacy) that influence health practices. The knowledge component lays the foundation, but without the other influences, health behavior will not change.

Self-Efficacy

Once a student has the knowledge necessary for health behavior change, the next step is developing self-efficacy. SCT suggests that

self-efficacy is the "foundation of human motivation and action. Unless people believe they can produce desired effects by their actions, they have little incentive to act or to persevere in the face of difficulties" (Bandura, 2004, p. 144). The implication for skills-based health education is that we must use methods in the classroom to build students' self-efficacy around the skills and behaviors that will help them lead healthy lives.

Bandura (2004) suggests that self-efficacy can be developed by providing students with opportunities to experience success, which can increase their ability to control situations and produce desired results. If students are given opportunities to experience success by applying skills in the classroom, they are more likely to develop high self-efficacy regarding those skills because they have had positive results from their performance. A study conducted by Brown, Teufel, and Birch (2007) found that adolescents (aged 9-13) who perceived that they had "at least some control over future health outcomes" were three to four times as likely to be interested in health, and subjects who felt they had "a lot" of control were more likely to report interest and attempts to follow what they were taught (Brown et al., 2007, p. 12). These findings suggest that developing students' self-efficacy about controlling their health can be an effective tool in health education. It is clear that helping students develop self-efficacy in a variety of health-related skills learned in the classroom will have a significant impact on other health behavior determinants, including goals and outcomes.

Outcome Expectations

Outcome expectations are the expectations people have about the outcomes of their health-related actions (Bandura, 2004). To facilitate positive outcome expectations, the skills-based approach includes education about attitudes and beliefs surrounding health behaviors and actions. This is particularly relevant because most health education occurs in the adolescent years, when peer pressure and peer acceptance are extremely important. For example, you might teach students refusal skills that they can use to say no to drugs. You model, observe, and provide feedback to students in realistic scenarios in the classroom. The students have

high levels of self-efficacy in refusing drugs, but at a social function outside the classroom they may encounter intense peer pressure to use drugs. This may lead to feelings of guilt, shame, or being uncool. Despite the self-efficacy they developed in the classroom, they might *expect* a negative outcome as a result of these pressures that weren't present in the classroom. To best prepare students for the real world, you need to address outcome expectations by discussing these outside factors while also trying to influence more positive attitudes toward health-enhancing behaviors.

Goals

According to SCT, another key determinant in health behavior is having goals and plans for accomplishing those goals (Bandura, 2004). The National Health Education Standards include goal setting as one of the eight standards for health education, highlighting its importance within the curriculum. Students must be able to set appropriate, realistic goals and formulate plans to accomplish those goals. This can help keep students motivated in the face of setbacks and negative experiences. Additionally, Bandura (2004) suggests that long-term goals "set the course for personal change" (p. 144), signifying the importance of goals in making long-term lifestyle changes, which is the aim of most health education programs. Skills-based health education not only teaches students goal-setting skills but allows them opportunities to apply these skills and develop goals to live healthier lives.

Perceived Facilitators and Impediments

The last major determinants in health behavior change are perceived facilitators and impediments (Bandura, 2004). The National Health Education Standards include analyzing influences, accessing valid and reliable information, and advocating for self and others, which all address potential facilitators and impediments to behavior change. Skills-based health education provides students with the knowledge necessary to identify and hopefully overcome obstacles and to take advantage of facilitating factors in their lives, encouraging positive health behavior change.

IMPLEMENTING A SKILLS-BASED APPROACH

Claudia T. Brown, MEd
North Reading Public Schools, North Reading, Massachusetts

What are the benefits of implementing a skills-based approach to health education?

Implementing a skills-based approach to health education has afforded many benefits to me as a teacher. I have been able to facilitate student practice of real-world skills, many of which can change previously learned behaviors. For instance, in our communication unit, students repeatedly practice refusal skills needed in peer-pressure situations. As I coach them, I remind them that effective communication in healthy relationships is a learned behavior and practice makes permanent. Would a coach send a player onto a field if that player had not practiced her skills? Probably not! Similarly, we should not send students into the adult world without practicing the essential skills of communication, decision making, goal setting, advocacy, accessing valid and reliable health information, and analyzing those things that influence our health.

What is the biggest challenge of a skills-based approach and how have you dealt with the challenge?

Initially, I was overwhelmed not only by the transformation process but also by the responsibility I felt to my students to make this a success. I felt that I had to make this transition immediately and effectively and I wanted my department members to buy in completely. When I realized that this was unrealistic, I found that by adding one skills-based unit in year 1 of the transition, I could become more comfortable with this method and feel more confident in leading my teachers.

What advice do you have for other health educators in the field?

Time will not wait for us to change; it is up to us to move forward in education, offering the most reliable tools to ensure our students' ability to live healthy lives. Don't be afraid to take a chance on this method of teaching health! Aside from being engaging and fun, it is, in fact, the best way for us to reach our students and prepare them to take responsibility for their health now and in the future.

Characteristics of Effective Health Education

Following is a list from the Centers for Disease Control and Prevention (CDC) of characteristics of effective health education. The skills-based approach presented in this text can help you address these characteristics in your classroom. The characteristics are organized according to key points of the definition of skills-based health education provided earlier in the chapter (CDC, 2015).

■ Planned and sequential
  ● Provides age-appropriate and developmentally appropriate information, learning strategies, teaching methods, and materials.
  ● Provides adequate time for instruction and learning.
  ● Focuses on specific behavioral outcomes.
  ● Is research based and theory driven.
■ Comprehensive
  ● Increases the personal perception of risk and harmfulness of engaging in specific health risk behaviors.
  ● Reinforces protective factors.
■ Relevant and participatory methods
  ● Provides basic functional health knowledge that is accurate and that directly contributes to health-promoting decisions and behaviors.
  ● Uses strategies to personalize information and engage students.

- Incorporates learning strategies, teaching methods, and materials that are culturally inclusive.
- Provides opportunities to reinforce skills and positive health behaviors.
- Provides opportunities to make positive connections with influential others.
■ Focus on skills, attitudes, and knowledge
  - Addresses individual values and group norms that support health-enhancing behaviors.
  - Addresses social pressures and influences.
  - Builds personal competence, social competence, and self-efficacy by addressing skills.

There is one other characteristic of effective health education curriculum: It includes teacher information and plans for professional development and training that enhances instruction and student learning. It is not included in this list because it is more of an administrative concern. Professional development is important, however, and is discussed in chapter 17. A skills-based approach as defined in this text can meet all the characteristics of an effective health education curriculum. We will discuss aspects of the approach in more detail throughout the text. However, first we need to demonstrate how the approach is based on current knowledge and literature about effective health education.

Research Support

The research studies presented in this section support the effectiveness of skills-based health education. Research has shown that health education that includes skills can decrease risky behaviors and increase health-enhancing behaviors. Additionally, it has shown that characteristics of effective health programming align with core principles of a skills-based approach (Botvin et al., 2005; Kirby et al, 1994; Nation, 2003; Greenberg, 2003; CDC, 2015). The evaluation of effective programs also supports the importance and effectiveness of interactive, participatory methods of instruction. In sum, evidence supports the efficacy of a skills-based approach.

In an article discussing effective prevention programs, Nation et al. (2003) discussed five key principles related to prevention: varied teaching methods, comprehensive programs, theory-driven programs, opportunities for positive relationships, and sufficient dosage. Most relevant to health education are varied teaching methods, comprehensive programs, and opportunities for positive relationships. The authors found that the most successful teaching methods are active, skills-based approaches that include interactive, hands-on experiences to increase participants' skills. Further, Greenberg et al. (2003) found that modeling behaviors with opportunity for rehearsal and feedback, having students set behavioral goals, and including cues to prompt behavior in a variety of settings are effective techniques in prevention programs. These are all methods of the participatory learning style associated with skills-based health education.

Nation et al. (2003) identified comprehensive programs as ones that have multiple interventions and multiple settings. *Multiple interventions* refers to addressing issues from multiple perspectives, such as increasing awareness and teaching skills (Nation et al., 2003). Skills-based health education uses a variety of learning experiences and interventions, such as skills teaching and practice, providing relevant information about health-related concepts, addressing norms about behaviors, and using group processes for learning. Research about prevention programs has revealed that teaching across multiple settings (e.g., school, community, peers) improves outcomes. In skills-based health education, health-related concepts and skills should be taught and applied in a variety of settings, particularly the peer setting because of the significant influence peers have on health behaviors during adolescence.

Finally, the interactive nature of participatory teaching methods in skills-based health education provides an opportunity to work with other students in a safe environment through role-play, small- and large-group discussions, and other group processes that foster positive relationships among students. Additionally, one characteristic of effective health education is providing opportunities for students to build relationships with influential people who can affirm positive health behaviors (CDC, 2015). All of these examples demonstrate that skills-based health education can teach concepts and skills in a variety of settings.

Similar to prevention, long-term behavior change is a major goal of any health education program. A study in the field of substance use examined a middle school program for drug abuse prevention and found significant reductions in drug and polydrug (tobacco, alcohol, and marijuana) use that lasted until the end of high school (Botvin et al., 1995). The prevention program ran for 15 class periods in seventh grade, 10 booster sessions in eighth grade, and another 5 booster sessions in ninth grade. The focus was on teaching information and skills (including resistance skills and personal and social skills) for resisting social influences to use drugs. Skills were taught using a participatory teaching method, including rehearsal, feedback and reinforcement, and demonstration (Botvin et al., 1995). Instead of focusing on long-term health consequences, the program offered information about immediate consequences, decreasing social acceptability, and actual prevalence rates (norming or perceptions). This program, still used in many schools today, has many parallels with skills-based health education, including participatory methods, skills teaching, focus on social aspects of health behaviors, and information that is not only relevant to adolescents but is also based in the present. Because the prevention program and skills-based health education are so similar, the efficacy of the program in preventing substance use both immediately and in the future strongly supports the use of skills-based health education in school.

Research also supports the use of active instruction methods where students are involved in experiential activities such as role-playing, group discussions, locating contraceptives in stores, and games or simulations. Kirby et al. (1994) give the examples of how "role-playing activities that ended successfully in the avoidance of unprotected intercourse reinforced the norms against unprotected sex; small group discussions . . . reinforced peer norms against risk-taking behaviors" (p. 354). These findings support the claim that participatory learning with a variety of learning experiences and activities that include skills

in the National Health Education Standards (e.g., accessing valid and reliable information, analyzing influences)—that is, skills-based health education—is effective in sexual behavior interventions.

This research is not new; it has provided the foundation on which many programs are built and is still relevant today. However, the lack of new research about health education is reflective of trends in the field. There have been few recent studies that would add to the research presented here. For example, in a recent article about the connections between health and academics the authors state that "Studies have not yet examined how health education curricula and instruction alone are directly associated with academic achievement. However, nine programs that included a health education component increased academic grades and test scores, decreased school absences, improved student behavior, and reduced school dropout." (Michael, Merlo, Basch, Wentzel & Wechsler, 2015, p. 751). There is still much work to be done to build the research support for the benefits of school-based health education. However, much of the research presented here can be found as support in other studies, including the research discussed next. The dates of the research do not detract from the support for the skills-based approach or the value of the findings.

In 2014, we reviewed school-based interventions that are included in the Substance Abuse and Mental Health Services Administration (SAMHSA) National Registry of Evidence-based Programs and Practices (www.nrepp.samhsa.gov/search.aspx). Interventions in this registry must meet certain criteria, and the most recent period for consideration of inclusion in the registry ended in February 2014. We reviewed programs that were school based for children aged 5 to 18 that related to the skills-based approach presented here or that had the most recent research.

The programs reviewed varied by length, instructional methods, training for people implementing the programs, evaluation, and so on. However, many of the programs included self-reporting as the main method of assessment, many successfully increased knowledge, and some, especially those that specifically mentioned a focus on skills, showed improvements among students in skills such as goal

KEY POINTS

- Social cognitive theory supports the skills-based approach presented in this text.
- According to SCT, health behavior is influenced by knowledge, self-efficacy, outcome expectations, goals, and perceived facilitators and impediments.
- A skills-based approach aligns with the characteristics of effective health education curricula.
- Research to date focuses mainly on specific topic areas but does support key aspects of the skills-based approach.
- The registry of evidence-based programs includes interventions that focus on skills.
- School-based health interventions can result in positive student outcomes.

setting, decision making, and refusal. These assessments were mainly questionnaires, not performance-based assessments; nonetheless, the evidence from these interventions does suggest that skills can be developed in the classroom, adding further support for the approach.

Finally, this review also revealed that school-based programs can decrease substance use, decrease intentions to use, increase risk perceptions, and influence attitudes. It is not within the scope of this text to discuss the various programs in detail. However, we wanted to review the most recent evidence for health-related programs to provide further support for not only health interventions in school but also programs that specifically include a focus on skills. The take-home message is that effective curricula that emphasize skill development can lead to positive student outcomes.

SUMMARY

A skills-based approach is supported by theory and research. It highlights skill development, uses participatory methods that emphasize a student-centered approach with the teacher as a guide, and includes functional information in order to build a functional knowledge base. It includes multiple topics and addresses multiple dimensions of health. It is relevant and engaging for students, and it addresses the skills, attitudes, and knowledge that students need in order to be healthy throughout their lives.

Review Questions

1. What is the definition of skills-based health education? List the critical pieces of the definition and briefly explain each.

2. What are the three core aspects of a skills-based approach?

3. What are the five steps of the skill development model? Provide a practical, classroom-based example for each.

4. What are some examples of participatory teaching methods?

5. What is functional information? How is it used in a skills-based approach?

6. What support exists for a skills-based approach to health education?

To find supplementary materials for this chapter, such as worksheets and extended learning activities, visit the web resource at
www.HumanKinetics.com/TheEssentialsOfTeachingHealthEducation

CHAPTER 3

Examining Student Motivation

Learning Objectives

After reading this chapter, you will be able to do the following:

- Discuss motivation theories as they relate to behavior choices.
- Define how student motivation influences behavior across a variety of developmental levels.
- Explain teaching strategies across developmental levels and how they motivate students to be proactive in their own health and wellness.

Key Terms

extrinsic motivation

intrinsic motivation

Maslow's hierarchy of needs

need

self-actualization

self-determination theory

self-esteem

From birth, we all have an innate motivation to meet our basic needs. As we grow and develop, our needs become more complex and our ability to meet those needs, which is influenced in part by the motivation to do so, becomes more sophisticated. Each person is motivated by different things and for different reasons. Some people are motivated by an internal drive while others are motivated by an external force such as the approval of others. Motivation can also be influenced by the person's age and developmental level, social setting (e.g., community norms and values, parental views, peer-group attitudes), or specific needs the person is trying to address.

For our purposes, a **need** is something that is innate—it is part of who we are and is not learned or placed upon us by others. We each must determine what we need. Others can suggest areas of concern, but ultimately we are responsible for accepting (or not accepting) those suggestions and recognizing and addressing our own needs. When we discuss student motivation across various developmental levels later in the chapter, remember that students can develop the ability to meet their needs if they have the proper tools and resources.

THEORIES OF MOTIVATION

Many theories exist to explain what motivates people. Some focus on internal motivators, some on external motivators, some on the role that one's social circle plays, and even some on how a person plans and executes specific behaviors. To help students increase their motivation to maintain and enhance their health, we need to understand how students are motivated and what strategies we can use to support their motivation. Two theories form the basis of our discussion in this text: the theory of human motivation and the self-determination theory. These two theories recognize that individuals are motivated by factors that are unique to them. Each theory specifically considers how people's needs affect both their level of motivation and their ability to use that motivation productively. These theories form a framework to discuss what educators can do in order to support students' efforts to be healthy.

Theory of Human Motivation

The theory of human motivation (Maslow, 1943), better known as **Maslow's hierarchy of needs**, is considered a cornerstone of understanding human motivation. Even today it continues to be used as a foundation for other theories of motivation and behavior. The theory of human motivation asserts that we each have a set of basic needs that must be met, including biological and psychological, safety, belongingness and love, self-esteem, and self-actualization. Once our basic needs are met, such as having shelter or feeling loved, we are able to focus on our higher-order needs such as self-esteem and self-actualization.

Further research has expanded upon the original needs identified by Maslow to include three additional levels—cognitive, aesthetic, and transcendence. For the purposes of preK-12 health education, the original basic needs are more relevant for two main reasons. First, within the context of a health education classroom, educators must understand that whether or not a student's basic needs are being met will directly impact their ability to learn. Second, research on adolescent brain development notes the role that the prefrontal cortex plays in impulse control and decision making. It is unrealistic to expect adolescents to be developmentally able to move past these basic needs to a higher level of transcendence.

Maslow's hierarchy of needs is organized in a pyramid (see figure 3.1). The basic needs are at the base of the pyramid. As people meet their needs at each level, they are able to meet more complex needs, and they work their way closer to self-fulfillment and achieving their full potential. However, this is not a one-way process. People may find themselves revisiting levels based on life circumstances at a given time. This model provides a framework for understanding why people may be motivated toward certain behaviors at a given time; it does not provide specific steps that must be taken in order. The following sections look at each level in the hierarchy.

Biological and Physiological Needs

The first level includes needs such as food, shelter, sleep, and homeostasis (the body's ability to

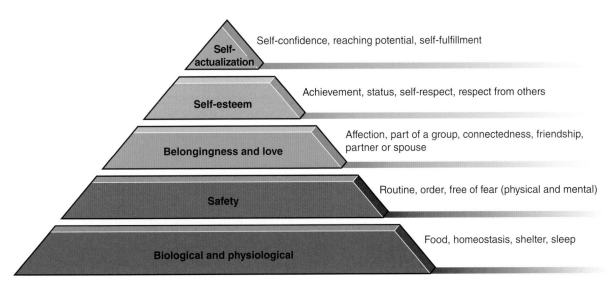

FIGURE 3.1   Maslow's hierarchy of needs.

maintain its natural state). These are the needs that are critical for survival. If they aren't being met, it is difficult to focus on anything else. For example, a student sitting in your classroom who has not eaten breakfast or is worried about where she's going to sleep tonight will have a hard time concentrating on learning.

Safety

In Maslow's hierarchy, safety expands beyond the physical to include emotional safety, order and predictability, routines, and stability. This includes being in familiar surroundings and not having to worry about a lot of unexpected change. In the classroom, a student may not be willing to participate in an activity or lesson, and as the educator you must consider whether or not resistance to participation is due to safety concerns (physical, emotional, or social) about participating. Will the student be teased for his response, is he afraid to try something new or unexpected, could he be physically hurt by the activity, or does the activity challenge his beliefs? Is there something going on at home that is preventing him from feeling safe and secure? If so, the student's reluctance may be rooted in a deeper issue and will likely only change if his safety concerns are addressed.

Belongingness and Love

Once a person is physically content and feels safe, the need to belong and be loved by others becomes important. The need for belongingness and love recognizes that each person needs more than just food and shelter. We need to belong to something greater than ourselves, to be part of a partnership or group that values us as an individual yet provides us with a sense of purpose greater than ourselves. This need may be met through nurturing friendships, having a trusted person to talk to, being in a romantic relationship, or feeling connected to a cause, such as a club or team. Belongingness and love are not necessarily taught to students. However, in health education we can teach students empathy, how to be a good friend, the difference between helpful and hurtful relationships, and assertive communication skills. We can also make the classroom a positive, supportive environment in which students feel a sense of safety and belonging. All of these feed into our need to belong and feel loved.

Self-Esteem

This level is best described as people having "a need or desire for a stable, firmly based, (usually) high evaluation of themselves, for self-respect, or self-esteem, and for the esteem of others" (Maslow, 1943, p. 381). We need to develop a respect of self that is fostered by an understanding of our own self-worth and abilities. If a student does not believe that she is worthy of being treated well, she is less likely to treat her body or mind well. **Self-esteem** also considers the need to be respected by others. It is connected to the self-efficacy (one's belief that one has the ability to reach a goal) aspect of SCT discussed in chapter 2. People with higher levels of self-esteem will likely also have higher levels of self-efficacy, which influences their ability to change or engage in certain behaviors. Teaching students the importance of respecting themselves and others is the foundation for developing skills to maintain or improve health. For example, we cannot expect students to set a goal for the future if they do not believe that they are able to control the outcome.

Self-Actualization

After all of the other needs are met, the need for **self-actualization** can be addressed. This need is based on the personal desire to do something substantial that helps us to reach our fullest potential. Specifically, self-actualization is about finding a sense of purpose in our work or actions. For students, this may be developing a plan and advocating for a cause that is important to them or choosing a behavior they wish to change and then establishing a plan to improve in that area. You must listen to what students are saying during discussions, watch how they are behaving in class, and look deeper at the meaning behind it all. Your students bring with them a variety of issues, concerns, and needs that, if not addressed, will hinder their motivation to succeed and ultimately their performance both in and out of class.

Self-Determination Theory

Self-determination theory is similar to the theory of human motivation in that it relates to needs. However, it focuses on three specific needs:

1. Competence, or the desire to effectively handle our environment (Deci & Vansteenkiste, 2004; White, 1959)
2. Relatedness, or the need to interact with and be connected to others (Baumeister & Leary, 1995; Deci & Vansteenkiste, 2004)
3. Autonomy, or acting in accordance with one's beliefs and values whether out of a personal choice or a duty to others (Chirkov, Ryan, Kim, & Kaplan, 2003; Deci & Vansteenkiste, 2004)

Additionally, self-determination theory is driven by three assumptions (Deci & Vansteenkiste, 2004):

1. Human beings have the ability to act on and master inner drives and emotions and external forces that are presented to them.
2. Human beings are always growing and learning, specifically through learning that engages our inner thoughts (feelings and beliefs) and outer environments (peers, surroundings, and social contexts) in ways that promote positive outcomes.
3. Although human beings are always striving to grow and develop, this does not happen automatically. Growth happens when we are nurtured by our social surroundings.

Adolescence in particular can be a confusing and unsettling time as students try to understand what is going on inside their head and body while also trying to navigate the world of friends, family, and society. Health educators typically work with students in this important phase of their lives—the time of life when they are figuring out who they are and when they are adopting behaviors that will likely remain into adulthood. One way of supporting students during this time and helping them to develop motivation to engage in health-enhancing behaviors is to help them understand what is important to them and how that shapes behavior. This can be achieved by addressing the two types of motivation: intrinsic and extrinsic.

Intrinsic motivation is a person's internal drive to engage in behaviors that are interesting and provide an opportunity to feel competent and self-determined (Deci & Ryan, 2000). Intrinsically motivated behaviors are different for each person and are based on individual needs, beliefs, and desires. These behaviors are not done to meet the needs or requirements of others. Often they make us feel good and provide an opportunity to learn something new or participate in something important to us.

On the other hand, **extrinsic motivation** is driven by factors outside of oneself, such as fame, money, and consequence. Extrinsic motivators may get someone to act in a particular way, but the results are often derived because there is a reward or punishment at stake. For example, students may study harder if they know they will receive money for each high grade they earn. However, the results of extrinsically motivated actions do not often lead to long-term change. So, once students stop getting paid for good grades, they may let their grades slip. Once the reward or punishment is removed, people are likely to revert to previous behaviors that they are intrinsically motivated to do. This means that students would be better served by engaging in learning that helps them see the value of what they are learning and how it relates to their world.

Motivation Theories in the Classroom

Intrinsic and extrinsic motivation are directly applicable to a skills-based health education classroom because one role of health educators is to provide a learning environment that stimulates students' thoughts and creativity and allows for personal exploration. Creating an environment that fosters student discovery, questioning, and understanding of what is intrinsically important will allow them to navigate their lives outside the classroom. If students leave a health education course with a strong sense of self and an awareness of what is important to them, they will be more likely to choose behaviors that are in alignment with their personal growth.

Let's look at an example that demonstrates motivation theory in action in a middle school classroom that is discussing goal setting. After presenting the steps of goal setting and giving students a chance to consider why setting goals is important for health and well-being, the teacher asks the students to each select a health goal that is important to them and write a goal statement that will take them one month to accomplish. In addition, the students must identify the steps they are going to take in order to accomplish this goal. Students leave

Christopher Futcher/iStock.com

Using motivation theory as a lens for planning and implementing a skills-based approach can lead to higher levels of student engagement.

KEY POINTS

- Each person has biological and physiological, safety, belongingness and love, self-esteem, and self-actualization needs. At any given time people may find themselves on a different level of having their needs met.

- Failing to address our basic needs results in an inability to focus on higher-order needs or tasks such as learning and school engagement.

- Each person is striving to develop competence, relatedness, and autonomy in order to meet individual needs. Any efforts to meet a personal need must address these areas.

- Intrinsic motivation to change a behavior is more likely to lead to lasting change compared with motivation from an extrinsic source. Students must learn the necessary skills to support their intrinsic ability to solve problems and meet their needs.

the class with the assignment to work on their goals. The teacher checks in periodically with students about their progress and at the end of the month provides a handout that asks students to assess their progress and whether or not they have been able to accomplish their goals. Through the reflection students discuss why their goals were important to them and how they will continue (or discontinue) work toward their goals.

In this example, the educator implements motivation theory by allowing students to choose goals that are meaningful to them and acknowledging that students have unique personal context for their goal—what is happening in their lives—rather than preselecting a health goal for the entire class. Based on the theories presented thus far, this approach is more likely to lead to increased motivation because it allows students to work on something related to their circumstances, wants, and needs; it helps build their competence; and it provides an opportunity to explore their values and beliefs.

This activity also makes no assumptions for where each student is on Maslow's hierarchy of needs. For example, one student may set a goal to make a better routine for managing his time (addressing a safety need) because he's feeling disorganized and is not able to complete all of his school work, extracurricular activities, and household chores. Another student may set a goal to turn off her electronics and get more sleep at night because she now understands that lack of sleep is affecting her ability to do well in class (addressing the need for self-actualization). Both of these students will leave

class with the ability to set a goal and see it through to completion while at the same time having a sense of ownership and motivation over the choices they make.

DEVELOPMENTAL LEVELS AND MOTIVATION

As students move from kindergarten through grade 12, many changes occur physically, mentally, socially, and cognitively. During this time of growth, needs and motivations change in large part due to the changes associated with each developmental stage. The changes that occur during childhood and adolescence are both natural and necessary for students to become productive adults. Although changes are to be expected, not all students develop at the same rate and the effect that development has on needs and motivation is not the same for all students. However, understanding the developmental level of your students will allow you to teach lessons in a way that is relevant to the situations and needs of the students in the room (see sidebar). You must also keep in mind that age and developmental level are not always aligned; for example, students might be physically mature or emotionally mature for their age. Understanding key characteristics of developmental levels can be helpful, but it does not replace the need to get to know your students and adjust instruction as necessary.

In the health education classroom, it is important to know not only what is developmentally appropriate in the social, mental, emotional, and physical domains but also

Example of Tailoring Lessons, Assignments, Assessments, and Expectations to Students

During a class discussion at the high school level, students may discuss how they can avoid peer pressure to smoke while out with their friends and to instead avoid those situations or make an alternative plan that includes refusal language. At the elementary level, a similar discussion on peer pressure related to tobacco use may include practicing simple refusal messages, identifying allies, and knowing when to consult a trusted adult for help. This could also play out in the classroom during discussions about group and community norms of appropriate behaviors and choices. At the high school level, students may be asked to brainstorm community norms that promote or allow risky behaviors (such as returning to play after a concussion) and then strategies to change those unhealthy norms. At the elementary level, the brainstorm may be about how to be a good friend and to encourage students to create a school culture of respect and empathy. Age differences will also be apparent when developing requirements for student assignments, scenarios for learning activities, and expectations about the type and depth of information students should share with the class about their lives.

what is to be expected in terms of behavior. For instance, typical behavior varies from age to age. In high school it is likely acceptable for students to meet up with their friends without an adult present, whereas in elementary school students are likely to need permission and are taken to meet friends by an adult who stays in the vicinity. Knowing this will allow you to tailor lessons, assignments, assessments, and expectations to make them reasonable and appropriate—in other words, relevant and authentic—for students.

The National Health Education Standards are presented by developmental stages (preK-grade 2 and grades 3-5, 6-8, and 9-12). They provide a basis for teaching skills at an appropriate level for each developmental stage. The performance indicators include behavioral outcomes that are characteristic of the developmental stage. When examining the standards, it becomes clear that, as students get older, developmental changes such as moving from concrete to abstract thinking, moving from reliance on adults to independence and autonomy, and the strengthening of reasoning skills are reflected in the behavioral outcomes for the skills (e.g., emphasis moves from identifying in younger grades to analyzing and evaluating in older grades). However, the standards do not provide a background for understanding

key characteristics and considerations for each stage. In this section we examine the characteristics of each developmental level, including how to teach students based on their developmental stage and examples of what activities to teach based on the performance indicator of the National Standards.

First we provide an overview of developmental characteristics within each of the following stages: early childhood, late elementary, middle school, and high school. For each level, there is a discussion of characteristics and teaching considerations as well as tables that provide examples of National Health Education Standards within each developmental stage. This section is organized by the verb or action language (e.g., identify, analyze, evaluate) in the performance indicators of the standards across a sampling of skills within each level. We also provide examples of developmentally appropriate activities that could be used to address the verb of the performance indicator (i.e., ideas that would require the students to perform the verb). Note that not all performance indicators are listed in these tables for each skill, and the activities are not intended to be a direct match with the performance indicators listed. The goal of this section is to demonstrate how the performance indicators relate to developmental characteristics and ideas for the classroom.

Early Elementary (PreK-2)

Table 3.1 provides characteristics of children in early childhood, from prekindergarten to grade 2, along with teaching considerations for each characteristic. Children at this age are egocentric, have short attention spans, need simple and concise instruction, are curious, and seek approval and feedback from adults.

TABLE 3.1 Developmental Characteristics and Teaching Considerations for Children in Early Childhood (PreK-2)

CHARACTERISTICS	TEACHING CONSIDERATIONS
PHYSICAL DOMAIN	
Enjoy being physically active and moving	Use learning activities that encourage movement, include physical activity bursts in your classroom, and include learning activities that explore types of movement.
Better control over gross motor activities than fine motor activities	Hands-on activities and crafts are great ways to engage students at this age, but be sure that beginners can complete the activities successfully. Limit (or progress) the amount of fine motor skills necessary for completion (e.g., cutting out bones for a skeleton; some students may have trouble using scissors).
Slow and steady physical growth	This is a good time to provide opportunities for students to explore what their bodies can do. Assign homework and projects that provide opportunities to do so (can connect with self-management, goal setting, and so on).
SOCIAL	
Learning how to be friends	Use small groups during class time to help students develop their social skills while providing the opportunity to meet individual needs.
Egocentric but beginning to develop empathy	Role-play, acting, and stories can help students develop empathy and think beyond themselves. Encourage dialogue to acknowledge how others are feeling.
Prefer same-gender groups by the end of this developmental stage	Encourage mixed-gender activities and positive social interactions in the classroom.
INTELLECTUAL	
Motivated by things that are new and exciting	Use a variety of teaching methods and plan multiple activities during lessons.
Short attention span	Keep directions short and simple, mix up activities so that students don't have to focus for too long, and include physical activity in the classroom.
More interested in doing things rather than finishing things	Engage students in the process of learning; help them find success and validation in the process as well as the product.
Concrete thinkers	Use demonstration often in the classroom, engage all the senses when possible, and be clear in your directions and examples.
Curious	Encourage curiosity through questioning, create a positive learning environment that encourages students to ask questions to find out more information, and provide students an opportunity to voice areas of interest and then address them in the class.
EMOTIONAL	
Sensitive to criticism	Use positive feedback and encouragement but be specific (e.g., avoid "Good job everyone" but rather "I like that the class was able to freeze and listen to me when I clapped my hands" or "Ruby, I like how you raised your hand before asking the question"), plan activities in which students can experience success, and provide guidelines for receiving constructive feedback.
Still seeking adult approval, attention, and affection	Help students begin to develop independence through group and individual work and develop intrinsic motivation rather than relying on the extrinsic feedback of an adult (e.g., "I'm glad that you enjoyed that activity. Can you tell me how you feel now that you have completed it?", "What made that activity enjoyable for you?").

Based on Tomek and Williams, *Ages and stages of 4-H youth development.*

At this stage, the performance indicators focus on simple verbs such as *identification* and *demonstration* as students are beginning to build the foundations for higher-level actions and thinking (see table 3.2).

TABLE 3.2 Performance Indicators and Developmentally Appropriate Activities for Prekindergarten to Grade 2

IDENTIFICATION PERFORMANCE INDICATORS	SAMPLE LEARNING ACTIVITIES
Analyzing Influences 2.2.1 Identify how the family influences personal health practices and behaviors. 2.2.2 Identify what the school can do to support personal health practices. **Goal Setting** 6.2.1 Identify a short-term personal health goal and take action toward achieving the goal. 6.2.2 Identify who can help when assistance is needed to achieve a personal health goal.	• Students draw a picture (either written or spoken) about a particular health behavior and describe it, such as drawing a picture of a community helper and then explaining why that helper is a good person to ask for help. • Students cut out pictures from a magazine or book or use stickers to create a collage that demonstrates a healthy choice, such as using pictures to create a healthy snack or lunch. • Students look at pictures and interpret what they mean, such as pictures of people's faces or body language as a means of understanding emotional and social cues. • Students work in small groups to match a person who can help with a goal. • The teacher reads a story or a series of situations and the students demonstrate through nonverbal behaviors how that person might be feeling (e.g., "This made Owen feel sad. Can you show me what Owen might do when he is sad? What can we do to help Owen?").
DEMONSTRATION PERFORMANCE INDICATORS	SAMPLE LEARNING ACTIVITIES
Interpersonal Communication 4.2.1 Demonstrate healthy ways to express needs, wants, and feelings. 4.2.3 Demonstrate ways to respond in an unwanted, threatening, or dangerous situation. **Self-Management** 7.2.1 Demonstrate healthy practices and behaviors to maintain or improve personal health. 7.2.2 Demonstrate behaviors that avoid or reduce health risks. **Advocacy** 8.2.1 Make requests to promote personal health.* 8.2.2 Encourage peers to make positive health choices.*	• Students practice the steps of a healthy behavior, such as demonstrating how to wash hands properly. • Students role-play talking with a friend and encouraging the friend to make a healthy choice. • Students role-play healthy ways to express anger. • Students role-play appropriate ways to express a need.

*Even though the verbs here are *make* and *encourage*, both of these verbs are a demonstration of the behavior.

Based on Tomek and Williams, *Ages and stages of 4-H youth development.*

Late Elementary (Grades 3-5)

Table 3.3 presents key developmental characteristics and teaching considerations for the late elementary classroom. In general, girls and boys are beginning to go through puberty (especially girls), students are looking up to older kids around them, and while they still want adult approval they are becoming more independent and reliant on peers. They also have longer attention spans and are able to handle more complex activities and directions.

TABLE 3.3 Developmental Characteristics and Teaching Considerations for Late Elementary (Grades 3-5)

CHARACTERISTICS	TEACHING CONSIDERATIONS
PHYSICAL	
Energetic	Incorporate physical activity regularly; plan activities that involve movement (stations, incorporate movement with each skill cue).
Girls maturing faster than boys	Avoid competition between girls and boys, make sure students are aware of changes during puberty, and discuss strategies for managing changing bodies.
SOCIAL	
Enjoy group activities and cooperation; like to belong	Plan small- and large-group activities, discuss and develop interpersonal skills within groups, and provide opportunities for collaboration.
Prefer to be with members of the same gender	Provide opportunities for same-gender and mixed-gender group work; establish and enforce proper interpersonal communication. Do not assume where students will feel most comfortable and assign students to a particular gender group. Not all students will feel comfortable in those preselected groups.
Admire and imitate older students	Bring in students from upper grades to support lessons or activities, set up a pen-pal system with older students, and have your students do presentations for older students.
Need guidance from adults to put in their best effort	Provide ample opportunities for feedback during skill practice sessions, develop clear expectations for assignments and activities, and closely monitor and supervise activities to ensure students are on task.
INTELLECTUAL	
Interests change rapidly (longer attention spans than early elementary but still limited)	Use a variety of examples during modeling to keep students interested, vary activities and situations to engage students, and allow students to offer input about topics or ideas they are interested in.
Individual students vary greatly in academic skills, abilities, and interests	Get to know your students so you can tailor activities to their abilities, differentiate activities with options for students at varying levels, and develop activities where all students can experience success with options for added challenges.
Easily motivated and eager to try new things	Encourage students to explore their interests and motivations as a part of a skill unit, use current events or examples to pique interest, and try to use new activities in every unit.
EMOTIONAL	
Comparisons with others challenge self-esteem	Limit competition (even activities where two students are on a team but may have to face off can be a negative experience) and focus on cooperation, help students see the strength in themselves and others, be sure to give positive feedback to all students in the class, and focus on recognizing and praising individual students' successes and strengths.

Adapted from Tomek and Williams, *Ages and stages of 4-H youth development.*

During this grade span, the National Standards ask students to take a more active role in their health by better understanding the world around them and then using that information to maintain or improve their health. The performance indicators of the National Standards focus on students describing and explaining. Both are a progression of outcomes from identifying, but students are still asked to demonstrate particular skills. Some of the indicators still ask students to identify information, but this is a precursor to demonstrating a particular strategy or behavior within the skill. Table 3.4 gives examples of performance indicators from the National Health Education Standards (Joint Committee, 2007).

TABLE 3.4 Performance Indicators and Developmentally Appropriate Activities for Grades 3 to 5

DESCRIBING OR EXPLAINING PERFORMANCE INDICATORS	SAMPLE LEARNING ACTIVITIES
Analyzing Influences 2.5.4 Describe how the school and community can support personal health practices and behaviors. 2.5.5 Explain how media influences thoughts, feelings, and healthy behaviors. 2.5.6 Describe ways that technology can influence personal health.	• Students make lists of positive and negative influences on health within the school and community. For each influence, describe why that factor has a positive or negative influence on health. • Students make a list of media influences and then describe how their current time spent on the Internet or watching TV could influence their health choices.
DEMONSTRATING PERFORMANCE INDICATORS	**SAMPLE LEARNING ACTIVITIES**
Interpersonal Communication 4.5.1 Demonstrate effective verbal and nonverbal communication skills to enhance health. 4.5.3 Demonstrate nonviolent strategies to manage or resolve conflict. 4.5.4 Demonstrate how to ask for assistance to enhance personal health. **Goal Setting** 6.5.1 Set a personal health goal and track progress toward its achievement.* **Advocacy** 8.5.1 Express opinions and give accurate information about health issues.* 8.5.2: Encourage others to make positive health choices.*	• Model the steps of goal setting and then have students write out the steps they would take to set a goal. Be sure to have students list potential options for the problem identified and then predict the outcome of various options. • With a partner, students practice refusal skills. Be sure to include practice of how to ask for help if they are not being well received by the person they are refusing. • Students create a poster campaign that advocates for a health issue, such as a no-smoking campaign. Create an ad that is persuasive and includes relevant information about smoking that will encourage others not to smoke.

*Even though the verbs here are *set, express,* and *encourage,* these verbs are all forms of demonstrating a behavior.

Middle School (Grades 6-8)

Table 3.5 presents characteristics of the early teen years with corresponding teaching implications. At this stage, students are experiencing rapid changes and growth spurts, and they tend to be emotional and self-conscious. Students are becoming more independent both in and out of the classroom and are beginning to be influenced by peers more than parents and other family.

At this age, students are able to go beyond

TABLE 3.5 Developmental Characteristics and Teaching Considerations for the Early Teen Years (Grades 6-8)

CHARACTERISTICS	TEACHING CONSIDERATIONS
PHYSICAL	
Rapid growth and changes in physical appearance	Discuss physical changes, and include activities in which students explore physical changes and learn more about why and what occurs in the body. This is also a good time to include activities to develop positive body image.
Intense physical feelings and an interest in their bodies	Provide opportunities for students to ask questions, validate their curiosity, and help them develop skills to access appropriate information about sexual activity and development.
SOCIAL	
Concerned about appearance and peer acceptance	Facilitate learning experiences in which students develop self-awareness, help students develop self-confidence not connected to the validation of peers, encourage mixed-gender activities, and work on interpersonal communication skills.
Parental influence is decreasing while peer influence is increasing	Provide opportunities for students to explore how their parents have helped shape who they are, provide activities for students to explore their values and beliefs, and discuss positive and negative peer pressure.
INTELLECTUAL	
Independent thinkers	Provide opportunities for students to formulate questions and answers, engage students in planning and creating course materials, and encourage expression of ideas and opinions.
Developing abstract thinking and metacognition	Provide opportunities to reflect on their work, include time for reflection on their health and health behaviors, and include open-ended questions and problems that require students to think outside the box.
Developing academic skills such as planning, evaluating, and taking responsibly for their work	Support students in developing time management and study skills, and provide opportunities for students to choose methods for completing assignments.
EMOTIONAL	
Can be self-conscious and critical; may experience low self-esteem	Include activities that allow students to experience success, provide opportunities to self-reflect on strengths, encourage students to express strength, and provide strategies to handle feedback.
Experience mood swings	Include activities that help students develop strategies for recognizing and managing emotions.
Want to be independent but still need support	Include opportunities for students to choose activities or subjects to explore in class, and extend offers to help but allow students to be successful on their own.

Based on Tomek and Williams, *Ages and stages of 4-H youth development.*

identifying and describing into analyzing and the critical thinking of predicting when to use specific products or services. Although students in this age group focus more on the present, they are beginning to see future consequences of their actions, even if this awareness doesn't always guide their decision making. Table 3.6 gives sample performance indicators from the National Health Education Standards (Joint Committee, 2007) for analyzing, critical thinking, and describing in the middle school grades.

TABLE 3.6 Performance Indicators and Developmentally Appropriate Activities for Grades 6 to 8

ANALYZING PERFORMANCE INDICATORS	SAMPLE LEARNING ACTIVITIES
Accessing Information 3.8.1 Analyze the validity of health information, products, and services. **Decision Making** 5.8.4 Distinguish between healthy and unhealthy alternatives to health-related issues or problems. 5.8.7 Analyze the outcomes of health-related decisions.	• Students review the claims for three similar products and discuss why the product claims are valid or invalid. • While working through a decision-making model, students write a list of pros and cons for two choices they are considering.
DETERMINING PERFORMANCE INDICATORS	SAMPLE LEARNING ACTIVITIES
Accessing Information 3.8.2 Determine the accessibility of products to enhance health. 3.8.4 Determine situations that may require professional health services. **Decision Making** 5.8.2 Determine when health-related situations require the application of a thoughtful decision-making process.	• Students take a health-related scenario and create a mind map determining whether the person should seek professional medical advice to address the problem. • Students identify a health behavior they wish to change and then work through a decision-making process related to this change. Make sure students describe why the decision is important, what skills they have to support this change, and what they will need help with.
DEMONSTRATING PERFORMANCE INDICATORS	SAMPLE LEARNING ACTIVITIES
Self-Management 7.8.2 Demonstrate healthy practices and behaviors that will maintain or improve the health of self and others. 7.8.3 Demonstrate behaviors that avoid or reduce health risks to self and others.	• Practice communication and refusal skills using authentic scenarios that students can relate to. Students could write a scenario that results in a positive health behavior or outcome and work with a partner to present the situation to the class. • Students create a role-play or comic strip that has the main character choosing a health-related behavior that ultimately keeps the character or a friend of the character safe.

High School (Grades 9-12)

Table 3.7 presents developmental characteristics and teaching suggestions for students in late adolescence. During this stage students continue to gain independence, develop community consciousness, and begin seeing beyond themselves. Students often strive for status and acceptance among their peer groups and seek out leadership opportunities to demonstrate their independence.

High school students are capable of complex

TABLE 3.7 Developmental Characteristics and Teaching Considerations for Late Adolescence (Grades 9-12)

CHARACTERISTICS	TEACHING CONSIDERATIONS
PHYSICAL	
Concerned with body image, overcoming the awkwardness experienced during puberty	Continue to include opportunities for self-reflection and confidence building, discuss influences on body image and self-esteem, provide strategies for increased self-confidence, and give a realistic view of the variety within a healthy range of body types.
SOCIAL	
Desire status in their peer groups	Focus on cooperation, avoid hierarchical structures within the class, and assist in the development of interpersonal skills.
Seeking leadership opportunities	Include projects that provide opportunities for students to assume leadership roles, and structure courses such that students can be leaders in a variety of ways.
Desire a sense of belonging but also want to be recognized as individuals	Have students tap into their creativity during projects. Allow students to select the way they present their work to the class (e.g., visual drawing, performance, writing).
INTELLECTUAL	
Increase levels of abstract thinking and problem solving	Provide problems and scenarios of health issues for students to create solutions. Include social issues of importance to students or have them create solutions for a health-related problem of students in their community.
Developing community consciousness and concern for others	Introduce students to a variety of ways to become involved in health-related causes.
Increasing their self-knowledge and awareness	Provide opportunities for self-reflection and feedback (self, peer, or teacher). Encourage students to be realistic in their feedback to promote self-growth.
Need support to plan for the future	Structure assignments and practical application of classroom material to encourage future goals and dreams. Allow students to consider many options as they think about their future plans.
EMOTIONAL	
Can experience low self-esteem and feelings of inadequacy	Provide opportunities for students to define and achieve success. Include discussion and activities that value different views, beliefs, social values, and so on to help students understand that different people have different views on issues.
Gaining independence	Encourage self-directed thinking and study. Allow students to take a proactive role in topic selection and problem solving.

Based on Tomek and Williams, *Ages and stages of 4-H youth development.*

Understanding the general characteristics of development can help health teachers meet student needs.

thinking and are expected to use reasoning and deduction to address issues. The National Standards at this level require students to take ownership of their learning and to critically analyze how each skill is important to their world. It is necessary for students to consider both immediate and long-term consequences for themselves and others. As mentioned earlier, even though impulse control is still limited, having a perspective of the potential outcomes is important because students will often process that information at a later time.

High school students are able to see others' perspectives, but they are still self-centered in how they think. Imagine a teen who is trying to get ready to leave the house in the morning. While this is occurring, other family members are also trying to use the bathroom, eat breakfast, and get out the door. The teen may be so completely focused on getting himself out the door that he is unable to recognize how his extended use of the bathroom has put everyone else in the house behind. He truly believes that his needs and decisions are the most important

priority at that moment. This is not just the teen being egocentric but also his brain working to understand the world around him. He likely understands that his actions could have contributed to the stressful situation, but he is unlikely to change his routine without a further plan to avoid this problem in the future. As the health educator, your job is to help teens critically assess what their behavior means for their world and how it may affect other things that are important to them. For instance, a class assignment on time management might ask students to consider their own schedule and the schedules of others in their household during the same time period.

Performance indicators for this age group are more complex, requiring students to collaborate with others and also apply the skill in a larger setting. The indicators no longer singularly focus on the student but instead bring into account how one's actions affect others. Table 3.8 gives sample performance indicators from the National Health Education Standards (Joint Committee, 2007) that require critical thinking in the high school grades.

TABLE 3.8 Performance Indicators and Developmentally Appropriate Activities for Grades 9 to 12

DEMONSTRATING PERFORMANCE INDICATORS	SAMPLE LEARNING ACTIVITIES
Interpersonal Communication 4.12.2 Use skills for communicating effectively with family, peers, and others to enhance health. 4.12.3 Demonstrate strategies to prevent, manage, or resolve interpersonal conflict without harming self or others. 4.12.4 Demonstrate how to ask for and offer assistance to enhance the health of self and others. 8.12.4 Adapt health messages and communication techniques to specific target audience.	• Students write and perform a role-play that demonstrates strategies to resolve interpersonal conflict in a constructive way. • Students write a comic strip that has two characters discussing a health issue with the end result being that the main character convinces the secondary character to seek medical advice on a health-related matter. • Students interview a family member or other trusted adult about how culture or environment may have influenced their current health. They write about how their own culture and environment affect their health and what strategies they will use to ensure they maintain or improve their health. • Students research a health risk factor among students in the school and create a public service announcement (PSA) that promotes a healthy alternative to that behavior.
CRITICAL-THINKING PERFORMANCE INDICATORS	SAMPLE LEARNING ACTIVITIES
Decision Making 5.12.3 Justify when individual or collaborative decision making is appropriate. 5.12.5 Predict the potential short-term and long-term impact of each alternative on self and others.	• Students predict potential short-term and long-terms consequences of a risky health behavior along with strategies to mitigate those consequences. • Students research a local community agency that provides services to adolescents and present information that informs other students of what the organization does, why it is health enhancing, and how others can locate the organization.

GENERAL CONSIDERATIONS ACROSS AGE LEVELS

As described earlier, student motivation is directly connected to developmental level, and knowing key characteristics of students at each level can help you develop and implement a health education program that motivates students. Though some aspects of development are relevant to specific age and grade groupings, there are two general areas that can affect motivation at any age: the impact of friendship and peer groups on motivation and the importance of identifying and discussing community norms and values. In this section, we discuss these two areas and explore considerations for addressing them in the classroom.

Friendship and Peer Groups

Young children form bonds, develop friendships, and watch their peers for behavior cues about what is acceptable, but it is not until later in childhood that friendship begins to influence behavior. For example, a protective factor for children in early elementary is that adults provide them with opportunities to be around other children who are a positive influence. In middle school and high school, the same protective factor changes to adolescents having their closest friends modeling positive and responsible behaviors (Search Institute, 2006). The onus shifts from adults being responsible for choosing friends for children to adolescents selecting friends on their own.

This applies to student motivation because helping students to understand the influence that friends and peers may have both inside and outside of school allows them to recognize why they choose certain behaviors. For instance, research on peer influence noted that students whose friends participated in risk-taking behaviors were more likely to participate in similar behaviors (van de Bongardt, Reitz, Sandfort, & Dekovic, 2014;

MOTIVATION

Erica Gambrell

White Knoll High School, Lexington, South Carolina

What is the biggest barrier to student motivation?

The biggest barrier to student motivation is the lack of self-motivation. Some of my students are not goal oriented and have no vision of success in their life. In order to know where you are going, you've got to know how to get there. It is so important to incorporate self-confidence and self-motivation into your curriculum. Regardless of what you teach, these skills will always benefit students in every aspect of life.

What is your best strategy for motivating students?

My biggest strategy for motivating students is building a relationship with them. I do an activity the first week of school where my students finish the sentence "I want my teacher to know. . ." I have a wide range of answers, but I explain to them that I want to be able to teach them more effectively and this is their way of letting me know how to do that. When my students know that I care about them and their success, it is easier for them to be relaxed and comfortable. When they walk through my classroom doors, it should be a welcoming and calming experience. Being in a relaxed and stress free environment compliments motivation.

What piece of advice do you have for other health educators in the field?

Be honest with your students. My students are always saying how they appreciate my stories and how I bring the subject to life. So many students have the disbelief that teachers are not "real" and we cannot make mistakes. They need to know that although you make mistakes, as we all do, you can bounce back from them. I teach them there is no such thing as a mistake as long as you learn from it and do not continue to make the same one.

Buckley et al., 2010; Hawkins et al., 1992; Monahan, Rhew, Hawkins, & Brown, 2013). Given this, it is important to discuss the impact that peers and friends can have on our decisions.

Another study noted that many children have multiple groups of friends, such as through school, through extracurricular activities, and through their parents' friends (Li, Iannotti, Haynie, Perlus, & Simons-Morton, 2014). This particular study found that each group had an impact on the amount of physical activity a child was performing. Groups that had a norm of doing physical activity were more likely to be active. Groups where the relationship was built around sedentary activities or where physical activity was not a priority showed students participating in less physical activity. Peer support for physical activity was found to increase internal motivation to participate (Li et al., 2014).

Normalizing Behaviors and Community Norms

Every family, school, and community has its own norms and rules for acceptable behavior. For example, in the United States alcohol use is illegal for anyone under the age of 21, yet in some communities it has become acceptable practice to allow teens to drink under certain circumstances. This establishes alcohol consumption by teens as a community norm, which makes efforts to curb underage drinking difficult because the community is sending messages to teens and creating a norm that this behavior is acceptable.

Research indicates that the more normal or common a behavior, the more likely it is that people will engage in that behavior even if they do not have the traditional risk factors and would not normally participate in the behavior.

KEY POINTS

- Elementary students are focused on learning skills and information and then demonstrating it in meaningful ways with concrete applications.

- Middle school students are going through many developmental changes that can be both exciting and challenging. Providing these students with a safe environment to explore and grow is vital to supporting their success.

- High school students are on the verge of adulthood but have brains that are not fully developed. These students must be challenged to incorporate what they learn with how it affects the world around them.

For example, the more socially acceptable it is for teens to have parties with alcohol, the more likely it is that the number of teens who are drinking at those parties will increase, even among the kids who may not normally be likely to drink. Normalization of a risky behavior tends to occur once 40 percent of the population (or sample) engages in a particular behavior (Sznitman et al., 2013). This means that not only are a high number of young people (more than 40 percent) participating in that risky behavior, but also more young people who may not have otherwise engaged in that behavior are doing it. As another example, students who are firmly connected to school and have strong parental relationships are less likely to use marijuana. If fewer peers are using marijuana and marijuana use is seen as deviant and socially unacceptable, these students are less likely to use marijuana. However, once approximately 40 percent of their peers are using marijuana, even the students who would not normally be at risk for marijuana use are more likely to participate because it is has become more socially acceptable (Sznitman et al., 2013).

For health education classrooms, this highlights the importance of understanding community norms around risky behaviors and reviewing the data about rates of risky behavior. Then lessons can be tailored to address the information and skills necessary to reduce those behaviors.

One last piece related to this subject is the power of promoting positive social norms and emphasizing how many students are *not* engaging in risky behavior. Using accurate behavioral norms in the classroom can be an effective way of developing health-enhancing attitudes and behaviors. Not everyone is engaging in risky behaviors, and showing students the actual data rather than what they think their peers are doing can help students understand that many peers are choosing health-enhancing behaviors. In addition, a positive approach to youth development encourages us to focus on what students are doing well and to capitalize on those behaviors. For example, students may wish to create an advocacy campaign that highlights the number of students who do not smoke or who have not ridden in a car with a driver who has been drinking. At the younger grades, a social norms campaign could include a "caught you doing good" prize or a friendly competition to see who chooses milk or water at lunch versus another beverage. Students thus hear positive messages about their choices and are encouraged to choose healthy behaviors over unhealthy ones.

SUMMARY

The development of children into adolescence and adulthood is complex. As health educators, it is our responsibility to guide students down a path that helps them grow into responsible and healthy human beings. In order to do this, however, we must consider both the age and developmental level of the individual student along with the factors that may be working for or against the student. For example, does the student have her basic needs met, or is she struggling because she does not have a trusted adult to confide in or she believes she may be in danger from another student? It is not until we take the time to learn these things about our students that we can teach them how best to attain health outcomes.

KEY POINTS

- An adolescent may have multiple friendship or peer groups that influence behaviors in a given situation. Students need to understand how each group could play a role in what healthy or risky behavior choices they make. Then they can learn strategies to mitigate the negative influences within a particular group.

- If we want students to participate in health-enhancing behaviors, these behaviors must become the default choice that is also seen as the normal or mainstream choice.

- Community norms and acceptance rates of risk behaviors play a critical role in how children and adolescents view healthy behaviors.

Students are motivated to learn and participate when they feel that doing so will assist them in meeting their needs. This includes their needs for competence, relatedness, and autonomy. Meeting these needs allows students to take action and be intrinsically motivated to succeed. Health educators in a skills-based classroom are well poised to provide the space to make this happen.

Review Questions

1. Describe the theory of human motivation and why it is important in health education.

2. Describe the self-determination theory and why it is important in health education.

3. How does the developmental level of students affect what is taught in health education?

4. Describe two teaching strategies for each developmental level (preK-2, 3-5, 6-8, and 9-12) that build on student readiness and ability to perform a skill.

To find supplementary materials for this chapter, such as worksheets and extended learning activities, visit the web resource at
www.HumanKinetics.com/TheEssentialsOfTeachingHealthEducation

Teaching to the National Health Education Standards

The second part of this book focuses on the seven skills of the National Health Education Standards: analyzing influences, accessing valid and reliable information, decision making, interpersonal communication, goal setting, self-management, and advocacy. Each skill is covered in a chapter dedicated to helping you understand what students need to learn in order to develop the ability to apply the skill. The chapters in this part also provide tips and strategies for teaching the skills in your classroom. Deepening your understanding of each skill using the skill development model (introduced in chapter 2) is critical to your ability to successfully implement a skills-based approach. The skill development model includes the following steps:

- Step 1: Discuss the importance of the skill, its relevance, and its relationship to other learned skills.
- Step 2: Present steps for development of the skill.
- Step 3: Model the skill.
- Step 4: Practice the skill using real-life scenarios.
- Step 5: Provide feedback and reinforcement.

By the end of this part, you should be able to define each skill of the National Health Education Standards and discuss its impact on health. You should also be able to list skill cues (the critical elements of the skills) and design activities to present the skill cues to your students. You will be able to create and implement modeling activities to demonstrate the skills, practice activities to support students' development of the skills, and practice activities to reinforce the skills both in and out of the classroom. Essentially, after reading this part, you will have the tools you need to help students develop the skills of the National Health Education Standards in a meaningful and relevant way.

Monkey Business-Fotolia

CHAPTER 4

Accessing Valid and Reliable Information, Products, and Services

Learning Objectives

After reading this chapter, you will be able to do the following:

- Implement all steps of the skill development model for accessing valid and reliable information.
- Describe appropriate student outcomes for accessing valid and reliable information at each developmental level.
- Create high-quality classroom activities for developing the skill of accessing valid and reliable information, products, and services.

Key Terms

anchor chart

authentic situation

feedback

information

procedural knowledge

product

service

On any given day, we encounter vast amounts of health-related information coming at us from many sources (e.g., other people, television, Internet, radio, social media). In addition, we have access to a variety of health-related products and services claiming to maintain or improve our health. This includes products such as energy drinks, supplements/vitamins, exercise equipment, and cold medicine, as well as services such as acupuncturists, reproductive health clinics, chiropractors, yoga, liposuction, and personal injury lawyers. Because of this, the skill of accessing valid and reliable information, products and services—the ability to determine what will enhance or promote our health and to discard what is not valid or reliable—is critical to improving or maintaining one's health. Note that the National Health Education Standards include only the "valid" qualifier. We believe that an important component of this skill is to be able to access information, products, and services that also are *reliable*, i.e., resources that someone could reasonably expect to be satisfied with and to reuse with confidence. Teaching students how to access valid and reliable information, products, and services prepares them to become actively engaged consumers of information and health-related resources. They develop the procedural knowledge necessary to perform the skill successfully, which is the ability to locate, understand, interpret, and make judgments about information, products, and services in order to enhance health (see figure 4.1).

This may sound familiar because the definition of accessing valid and reliable information, products, and services is similar to the definition of health literacy presented in chapter 1. The ability to access valid and reliable information, products, and services directly addresses four aspects of health literacy: literacy, knowledge, competencies (access, appraise, and

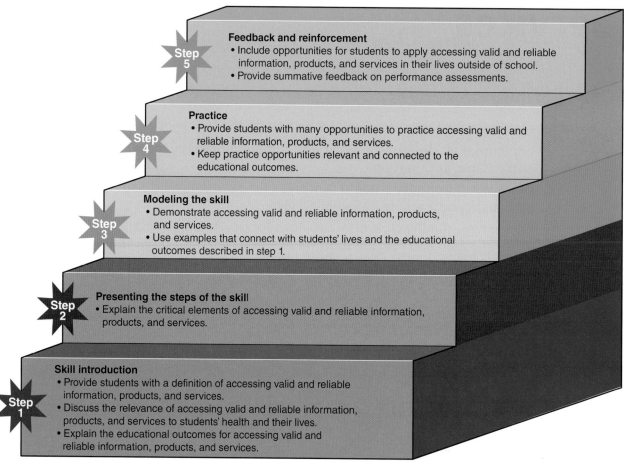

Step 5

Feedback and reinforcement
- Include opportunities for students to apply accessing valid and reliable information, products, and services in their lives outside of school.
- Provide summative feedback on performance assessments.

Step 4

Practice
- Provide students with many opportunities to practice accessing valid and reliable information, products, and services.
- Keep practice opportunities relevant and connected to the educational outcomes.

Step 3

Modeling the skill
- Demonstrate accessing valid and reliable information, products, and services.
- Use examples that connect with students' lives and the educational outcomes described in step 1.

Step 2

Presenting the steps of the skill
- Explain the critical elements of accessing valid and reliable information, products, and services.

Step 1

Skill introduction
- Provide students with a definition of accessing valid and reliable information, products, and services.
- Discuss the relevance of accessing valid and reliable information, products, and services to students' health and their lives.
- Explain the educational outcomes for accessing valid and reliable information, products, and services.

FIGURE 4.1 Steps for developing the skills of accessing products and services and processing information.

apply), and parameters (the context in which health literacy is applied). The fifth aspect of health literacy, motivation, also might be supported by this skill because if students feel confident and competent in their ability to access valid and reliable information, products, and services when they need them, they may become more motivated to take care of their health needs and work toward health goals. (This relates to the self-determination theory discussed in chapter 3.) Accessing valid and reliable information, products, and services is a multifaceted skill that helps students develop health literacy by helping them become healthy skeptics when it comes to finding and using information, products, and services to make more informed and healthier choices.

Accessing valid and reliable information, products, and services is the first skill presented in part II because if health educators include this skill early it allows students to be more thoughtful in how they locate products and services and use and apply information to their world. If you lay the foundation early, you will spend less time explaining why valid and reliable information, products, and services are important and more time developing other skills. This is because most of the other skills in the National Standards require students to use information in some way. For example, a student needs to choose a snack. After participating in a unit on accessing valid and reliable information, products, and services that focused on developing the ability to locate, access, interpret, and make judgments about nutrition-related information through activities such as reading and interpreting food labels, the student can make a more informed decision about which snack is the healthiest option. Another student wants to advocate for a cause he believes in. In order to effectively advocate, the student needs to be able to cite evidence to support his position—he needs to access information from reliable sources and use that information effectively. Finally, a student who wants to set a goal might be more successful if she can access valid and reliable information about products or services to help her achieve her goal.

This chapter explores each step of the skill development model presented in chapter 2 for the skill of accessing valid and reliable information, products, and services.

STEP 1: SKILL INTRODUCTION

Accessing valid and reliable information, products, and services is a complex but essential skill. It is particularly relevant today because a vast amount of information is easily available (think back to the discussion of e-health literacy in chapter 1), information is constantly changing, and products are being developed and distributed at a rapid pace. Students need to learn to sort through information, products, and services to determine not only what is accurate, reliable, and valid but also what will be the most helpful to meet their needs. If you cover this skill early, students can use it during the remainder of the course, in their other courses, and throughout their lives, leading to more opportunities for application and reinforcement of the skill.

Understanding the **procedural knowledge** of each component of accessing valid and reliable information is critical in being able to develop the skill in the health education classroom. We will explore each component of the definition in order to highlight the broad scope of what the skill includes.

Information, Products, and Services

The first major component of accessing valid and reliable information, products, and services pertains to *what* is being accessed. Table 4.1 lists just a few examples of what **information**, **products**, and **services** can be accessed. It is intended to provide you with some ideas, but it is important to think about each component as it relates to your students—what is available in the community, what types of products might students be using, and what kind of information do students want or need to inform their choices?

Locate

Once students have an understanding of what the terms *information*, *products*, and *services* mean and relevant examples of each, the next

TABLE 4.1 Sample Products, Services, and Information

PRODUCTS	SERVICES	INFORMATION
Vitamins	Physicians	Health topics
Supplements	Mental health providers	Health questions
Medications	Ob-gyn	Food labels
Hygiene-related	Specialists	Prescription labels
Contraceptive methods	Health clinics	Health articles

aspect of the skill pertains to *where* and *how* to find valid and reliable information, services, and products. For example, a student might know that he can use the Internet to find an answer to a question, but then he needs to know which websites (where) to go to in order to get current information and how to evaluate the validity and reliability (how). Another example is that students might know where the community health clinic is located (where), but they might not know the best way to get there or what they should have prepared, such as questions to ask the doctor, things to bring with them, and their rights as patients (how).

Understand

Once students are able to locate information, they need to be able to understand it. This aspect of the skill relates directly to health literacy. Written information requires students to be able to read and process the information. If the written information is difficult to understand, such as if it is written at a level beyond the student's abilities, the student may need to find additional resources to help with understanding the information. Verbal information or instruction (as from a doctor or other health professional) requires a student to listen carefully, interpret what has been said, and remember the information in order to apply what she has heard. Students need to be able to understand the information to move to the next aspect of the skill, which is interpreting the information and making judgments about it.

Interpret and Make Judgments

So far, we have covered what types of information, products, and services students need in order to be healthy, where and how to locate this information, and understanding it. The final step is to develop the ability to interpret and make judgments about the information, product,

or service as it relates to one's health. Note that health literacy and accessing valid and reliable information have a reciprocal relationship. As health literacy increases, so too does the ability to access valid and reliable information, products, and services and as students develop the ability to access valid and reliable information, products, and services they directly contribute to their level of health literacy.

This component of the skill requires students to understand the context in which the information, products, and services exist, translate and apply this information to their situation, determine whether this information, products, and services are useful (or to what extent they are useful), and decide whether they should act on the information or use a particular product or service based on what they have learned. For example, many supplements are available in stores and online, with some being safer and more effective than others. Students need to be able to articulate why a supplement is necessary and the most appropriate way to introduce it into the body, read and understand the active and inactive ingredients in the product, evaluate the validity of product claims, determine the safety and efficacy of the product, and then decide if the product is right for them. A second example is when a student goes to the doctor and is given a series of options. The student has to choose which option is right for her based on the available information. This aspect of accessing valid and reliable information, products, and services taps into higher-order thinking skills such as critical thinking and problem solving, and it connects to other health skills such as decision making, self-management, and advocacy.

Educational Outcomes

When teaching students the procedural knowledge for the skill of accessing valid and reliable information, products, and services it is important to define the skill, discuss its relevance in age-appropriate terms, and define its educational outcomes for students. In this section we outline a four-step process that will lead you to determine the educational outcomes for the skill of accessing valid and reliable information, products, and services. To start this process, you need the performance indicators for the skill. Table 4.2 provides the performance indicators from the National Health Education Standards for standard 3, which is accessing valid information, products, and services.

Step 1: Choosing Indicators

It is not always as simple as providing students with the performance indicators. Accessing valid and reliable information, products, and services is a skill with multiple aspects. Even though there are only 14 indicators for standard 3 from preK to grade 12, many of them are complex with multiple parts (information, products, and services). In addition, some outcomes (such as evaluate) involve multiple steps and require significant amounts of practice. Therefore, it is critical to be thoughtful about which indicators you will cover in the unit on accessing valid and reliable information, products, and services.

Accessing valid and reliable information, products, and services is part of the sixth-grade health education curriculum but students also have health in eighth grade. As you work with your program and school administration, you decide that in your sixth-grade course, you will focus on indicators 3.8.1 and 3.8.2 because the outcomes of analyzing and accessing are complex and will be enough for the eight-lesson unit on accessing information. The eighth-grade teacher will cover 3.8.3 through 3.8.5.

Step 2: Coverage of Indicators

Once you have chosen indicators, you must decide which parts (or all) of the indicators will be covered within the unit and perhaps across the year. At this point, you need to consider what the assessment for the unit will be in order to ensure clear expectations for the unit. For example, performance indicator 3.8.1 includes analyzing information, products, and services. Although the analysis might be similar for each, it might not be feasible (or appropriate) to completely cover information, products, *and* services in the unit. Therefore, you might decide to focus on analyzing information. This means that the assessment for the unit must also focus on analyzing information (and not products and services). There is no right way to cover the

TABLE 4.2 Performance Indicators for Standard 3 of the National Health Education Standards

PREK-GRADE 2	GRADES 3-5	GRADES 6-8	GRADES 9-12
3.2.1 Identify trusted adults and professionals who can help promote health.	3.5.1 Identify characteristics of valid health information, products, and services.	3.8.1 Analyze the validity of health information, products, and services.	3.12.1 Evaluate the validity of health information, products, and services.
3.2.2 Identify ways to locate school and community health helpers.	3.5.2 Locate resources from home, school, and community that provide valid health information.	3.8.2 Access valid health information from home, school, and community.	3.12.2 Use resources from home, school, and community that provide valid health information.
		3.8.3 Determine the accessibility of products that enhance health.	3.12.3 Determine the accessibility of products and services that enhance health.
		3.8.4 Describe situations that may require professional health services.	3.12.4 Determine when professional health services may be required.
		3.8.5 Locate valid and reliable health products and services.	3.12.5 Access valid and reliable health products and services.

indicators. What is important is that you make thoughtful, collaborative (when possible) decisions to ensure the most complete coverage of the indicators within the developmental grade span.

You are planning to address accessing valid and reliable information, products, and services at the beginning of the year. You don't want it to take too long, but you want to make sure you set the stage for students to be able to use the skill throughout the rest of the course. You decide that for this unit you will focus on analyzing valid and reliable information from indicator 3.8.1 (analyze the validity). This ties in nicely with 3.8.2 (access information), which also focuses on information. Other aspects of 3.8.1 (products and services) are taught during a unit later in the year.

Step 3: Student-Appropriate Terms

Now that you have identified and modified the indicators for the unit, the next step is to review the indicators in order to determine which concepts may need to be explained in more detail for students or need to be modified. When you present the indicators to the class, it is important to review the actual performance indicator as written in the National Standards so students become familiar with the vocabulary and concepts of the standards. However, *your* indicators for your curriculum must meet your students' needs and offer the appropriate level of support or scaffolding to ensure students can understand and then achieve the tasks set in the indicators. Remember that modifications should be based on the needs of your students but should still accurately reflect the indicators.

Instead of using 3.8.1, "Analyze the validity of health information," as the educational outcome in your course, you decide to modify it to "Examine critically the truthfulness and accuracy of health information" because these are terms that your students are familiar with and that your school is using across courses. When you present the educational objectives to the class, you read the entire indicators as written in the standards (i.e., "3.8.1 Analyze the validity of health information, products, and services") and then explain how you arrived at your modified version.

Step 4: Educational Outcomes

The final version of the performance indicators derived from the previous three steps are the educational outcomes for the skill. To finish our example, the educational outcome for the skill of accessing valid and reliable information, products, and services in the sixth-grade class is that students will be able to examine critically the truthfulness and accuracy of health information.

The following scenario demonstrates how step 1 of the skill development model in its entirety may look in the classroom for accessing valid and reliable information, products, and services.

Step 1 in the Classroom: Skill Introduction

The two examples presented here show how educators at all levels can implement participatory methods (discussed in chapter 2) to address step 1 of the skill development model. Step 1 may occur during one lesson, but students might need more time to work on this step or to complete an activity for a hook. In any case, this example provides a framework for planning step 1.

Scenario A: Grades 3 to 5

In preparation to teach a third-grade class, you decide to cover objectives 3.5.1 and 3.5.2 in the unit on accessing valid and reliable information, products, and services. You plan to focus on the information portion of the performance indicators. On the first day of the unit, it is important to hook the students and get them interested in the skill and the unit. Knowing that the students enjoy stories (also a nice connection to English language arts), you create a short story about a third grader who has a question about her health and goes to a series of invalid resources, leading to a comical adventure trying to find the answer to her question. You then lead the class in a large-group discussion about why the various resources were not appropriate and also why it is important to know where to find appropriate answers to our questions. The activity ends by providing students with a definition of the skill of accessing valid and reliable information (being able to access information when you need it from home, school, and community). You then tell students that they will be learning how they can access information and that by the end of the unit they will be able to determine which people, places, and things in their lives are good resources when they have questions about their health. They will also be able to tell when the information is truthful and appropriate.

Scenario B: Grades 9 to 12

You have selected performance indicators 3.12.1, 3.12.2, and 3.12.5 for the unit on accessing valid and reliable information for a ninth-grade health education course. The focus is on students' ability to independently access information, evaluate resources, and apply them to a health-related question. You have decided that this will be a project-based unit in which class time will be spent on the development of their project. Therefore, on the first day of the unit, you review the definition of accessing valid and reliable information in a large-group discussion. Then time is spent reviewing the educational outcomes for the skill. Because these are ninth graders, it is appropriate to use the indicators as they are written in the National Health Education Standards. You then explain the unit project: In small groups, students will come up with what they believe is a common question that teens have about their health (it could be a question the group would like answered, making the project topic relevant to their needs). The students must find three valid and reliable websites that provide information, identify one valid and reliable community resource that addresses the question, evaluate the validity of the identified websites and the community resource, and go to the community resource for information or interview a staff member for the project. (Note that this project allows students to address all three objectives by applying material in a relevant and personalized way). The students form small groups and work on the project for the remainder of class.

STEP 2: PRESENTING THE STEPS OF THE SKILL

This step of the model articulates the parts (referred to in the remainder of the text as *skill cues*) of the skill that students need to perform in order to meet the educational objectives (which are the modified performance indicators from step 1). You need to deconstruct the indicators for students so that they know exactly what they need to do to perform the skill and meet the educational objectives. Table 4.3 provides examples of ways to present the skill cues of accessing valid and reliable information, products, and services to students at each developmental level.

As with step 1, there are many ways to introduce step 2 that are not teacher directed. The following scenarios provide some examples.

Step 2 in the Classroom: Presenting the Steps of the Skill

PreK to Grade 2

Read a story about community helpers and have an **anchor chart** with the skill cues that students fill in based on the story. Ask guiding questions about the story and post student answers to use as a visual aid in the classroom. Prepare cards ahead of time with various people and places in the community. In class, ask students questions with built-in scenarios, such as "Whom would you go to if you felt sick at school?" You could then place a visual for nurse under the Who category on an anchor chart. Talk to students about where the school nurse is located and put a map to the office in the Where column of the anchor chart. Finally, lead students on a school and community tour, so to speak, where you point out the trusted adults and safe places on the visual aids. At the end of the activity, review the skill cues before moving on.

Grades 3 to 5

After you have introduced or reviewed the skill cues, have students work in groups and complete a scavenger hunt in the school where they have to determine who and where they can go to for help in a given situation (e.g., "You would go here if . . . "). Debrief the activity using the RACE model (see table 4.3) as a way to present and reinforce the skill cues. For example, you would ask students to report how the people and places they found fit the model (e.g., why is the school nurse reliable? Will he give you accurate and current information? Is he easy to find? Easy to talk to? Around during the whole school day?) Consider having students in small groups match the steps of the model to their definitions as a preassessment or opening activity. Then review as a class.

KEY POINTS

- The skill of accessing valid and reliable information, products, and services includes locating, understanding, interpreting, and making judgments about information, products, and services.
- Accessing valid and reliable information, products, and services is a complex but critical skill for not only increasing health literacy but also other skills.
- Presenting the performance indicators to students using the actual terminology is important, but they should always be explained to students in language they can understand.

TABLE 4.3 Skill Cues for Accessing Valid and Reliable Information, Products, and Services

PREK-GRADE 2	
Focus: Identifying people and places that can help with health needs	**People** *What*—What do I need help with? *Who*—Who are people I trust and can help me? *How*—How do I find the person? How do I ask for the help I need? **Places** *What*—What do I need help with? *Where*—Where should I go to get help? *How*—How can I get to the place I need?
GRADES 3-5	
Focus: Understanding what it means for a source to be valid and reliable	**RACE** • Is it **R**eliable? • Is it **A**ccurate? • Is it **C**urrent? • Is it **E**asy to use and access? (Here students are beginning to evaluate resources so the steps are focused on evaluating sources. Each step is further broken down later in the chapter.)
GRADES 6-8	
Focus: Analyzing sources to determine validity	**ACCESS** • Is it **A**ccurate? • Is it **C**redible? • Is it **C**urrent? • Is it **E**asy to use and access? • What **S**ituations is it best used in? • Are claims or information **S**upported? (These steps reflect the shift from discussing what valid and reliable information, services, and products look like to being able to evaluate the sources. The *ACCESS* acronym encompasses all of the performance indicators and can be applied to information, products, and services. Each piece is explained in more detail later.)
GRADES 9-12	
Focus: Using resources to maintain or enhance their health or the health of others	ACCESS can be used again here with an emphasis on students applying the skill in their own lives.

Grades 6 to 8

Emphasize the application of the skill in students' lives. Consider having students write about a time when they had to access information, products, or services relating to their health. Then introduce the ACCESS model (see table 4.3) and have students analyze the situation they wrote about. Students should describe how their situation meets or doesn't meet the criteria for each part of the ACCESS model. Have students match the steps of the model to their definitions as a preassessment or opening activity. Review as a class.

Grades 9 to 12

Emphasize application of the skill and also make connections between this and other skills. Similar activities from grades 6 to 8 can be adjusted for grades 9 through 12. You could also use scenarios or even videos or current news stories that show teens in situations where they had to access (or should have accessed) information, products, or services. Use the newspaper or video clips as a framework for discussing the ACCESS model.

- Skill cues for accessing valid and reliable information, products, and services should include all aspects of the skill necessary for effective performance in simple, helpful terms.
- Skill cues are intended to assist students as they locate, understand, interpret, and judge information, products, and services.
- Step 2 should be implemented through participatory examples, activities, and methods.

STEP 3: MODELING THE SKILL

In this step, the focus is on modeling the skill in real-life situations that are relevant to students. At least some of the modeling should demonstrate a proficient performance of the skill in the context in which the students will be evaluated. For example, if the final assessment is to find and evaluate a website, one of the modeling examples should be the proficient performance of what the students are expected to do. For this step to be most effective, modeling should be representative of how students will be using the skill in their lives.

This part of the lesson will be shaped by the educational objectives determined in step 1 of the skill development model. For example, a unit could focus only on accessing information and not products and services based on the educational outcomes determined in step 1. If this is the case, the modeling should not include the skill as it relates to products and services; the examples should all relate to accessing information. Examples of modeling activities include the following:

PreK to Grade 2

- Students observe a role-play in which you explain, using the skill cues presented, where or to whom you went for help when you had a problem.
- Students complete a matching worksheet that matches community helpers with their locations.
- Students are put into groups and given a visual of a community helper. You read a situation (relevant for the age group) and ask the class, "Which group has the trusted adult I should ask to help me?"

- Students read (or listen to) an age-appropriate letter that is written to a friend telling the friend where to go if she needs help in a situation.

Grades 3 to 5

- Students read or create a comic strip that shows someone correctly implementing the RACE model.
- Students watch a video (recorded previously with students in another class or in another year) implementing the RACE model.
- Students read a story about another student who tries to implement the RACE model but makes some errors along the way. Students have to read and identify where the character made mistakes and what he can do to fix it.

Grades 6 to 8

- Using a current event (celebrities, local heroes, or sport stars are often engaging for students), small groups of students discuss how the ACCESS model could apply (e.g., for an example of drug use, students have to think about where they could have gone to prevent the drug use or where they could go once they had a problem).
- Students observe or act out a scenario where a student is at a doctor's appointment.
- Students evaluate common sources of information (e.g., food labels, prescription labels, news stories). Review the evaluation as a class and discuss implications.

Grades 9 to 12

- Set up papers or posters in the room that have one part of the ACCESS model written

Monkey Business/fotolia.com

Helping students to develop the skill of accessing valid and reliable information, products, and services can help connect them with resources they need in order to maintain or enhance health.

on them. Provide students with examples from each part of the model and have students move to the part of the ACCESS model their example fits (e.g., "The author is a registered dietitian posting about nutrition tips for teens—this would go in the *Credible* category.").

■ Students create a list of valid and reliable resources in the school and community. Write each one on a piece of paper (or poster). Post the papers around the room. Read the situations (e.g., "Your friend tells you that he has been feeling really sad lately.") and ask students to move to the resource that they would go to in that situation. During the debriefing, refer to the model to reinforce those connections.

■ Given examples of unreliable information, products, or services, students use the ACCESS model to identify why the examples are unreliable. Then students present reliable alternatives.

STEP 4: PRACTICE

In step 4, students are provided with multiple and varied practice opportunities where they apply the skill. Sample activities for practicing each component of accessing information are provided later. These are general ideas that can be modified for any grade level with scaffolding and increased challenge or progression. Each section includes considerations and tips. **Feedback** is a crucial part of this step and must be meaningful and effective. The feedback could be based on self-evaluation, peer feedback, informal teacher feedback, or formal teacher feedback. See chapter 13 for more information on providing effective feedback.

Information

There are many forms of information, but in this discussion the focus is on written information from online resources. From a young age,

KEY POINTS

■ You can use a variety of activities to model the skill of accessing information, products, and services. As with all steps, remember to use examples that are engaging and relevant to your students.

■ Modeling the skill of accessing valid and reliable information, products, and services focuses on effective application of the skill components that the unit is addressing (as determined by the educational objectives).

■ Skill cues can be taught in student-directed ways. Determine the strategies that work best with your students and employ participatory methods when possible.

students are inundated with information. They have access to a variety of information from a variety of sources, and they use the Internet as a primary source. One of the biggest challenges is to help students gain the knowledge, skills, and self-efficacy to find accurate, reliable information when they search for it. This is true no matter what type of information they are searching for, but it is especially important for health information because the consequences of misinformation can be significant.

Before students begin practicing the evaluation of online resources, it would be appropriate, especially with younger students, to review Internet safety. Students need a solid foundation for using the Internet safely and appropriately before they even begin to search for information. It is also important to consider that many school districts have Internet policies that must be followed during school. Once it has been established that students know how to be safe online, they are ready to move on to finding and evaluating Internet resources. One concept that might arise here that we suggest addressing within the unit on analyzing influences is *media literacy*. Although it certainly connects to accessing valid and reliable information, the core of media literacy relates to developing critical-thinking skills about the purpose of media and the messages we receive. Media literacy is important in order to maintain and enhance health, as we discuss in chapter 5, but for now the focus is on helping students find valid and reliable information.

Due to the complexity of accessing valid and reliable information, we suggest that you scaffold the practice activities into stages. Because the focus in this example is online information, it would be best to have students practice on a computer. If this is not possible, you can use

screenshots as long as they include all the critical items that students need to examine in order to determine validity and reliability. Keep in mind that while we are focusing on online information, everything described in this section could be applied to other forms of written information such as an article or non-fiction text.

■ Stage 1: Along with the teacher, students evaluate a website that the teacher provides (the website should be an example of a valid and reliable resource).

■ Stage 2: Students compare two similar websites to determine which one is more valid and reliable using a compare-and-contrast model.

■ Stage 3: Students find resources on their own. This could be for a question or topic that you provide, or they could develop a research question to answer (this would be best in terms of relevance, personalization, and autonomy). The students must evaluate the website in order to justify why it is valid and reliable.

■ Stage 4: Students research, evaluate, and then use a variety of websites in order to become more knowledgeable about a certain health-related topic. Students might then share this information with their classmates, other grades, or the community.

Students constantly practice the skill cues throughout these stages, but the activities are modified based on student performance and needs.

The Tools for Evaluating Information sidebar includes tools that can be used in the classroom to evaluate information. It expands the skill cues to be relevant for the component

Tools for Evaluating Information

RACE

Reliable

- Is the domain a .gov, .org, or .edu?
- Can you find the author or authors of the website? Are they credible sources of information? Why or why not?
- Are there lots of advertisements on the page?

Accurate

- Is the information supported by research?
- Is the information listed with an author (not just for the website but for actual content)?
- Is the information confirmed by another source (provided on the website or via student research)?

Current

- When was the website developed?
- When was it last reviewed? Last updated?
- Do specific articles or content within the website include dates?
- Do the links on the website work?

Ease of use and access

- Is the website easy to use?
- Can you easily find the information you are looking for?
- Is the information easy to read and understand?

ACCESS

Accuracy

- Is the information listed with an author (not just for the website but for actual content)?
- Is the information confirmed by another source (provided on the website or via student research)?
- Does the website have an agenda or a specific target audience?

Credibility

- Is the domain a .gov, .org, or .edu?
- Can you find the author or authors of the website? Are they credible sources of information?
- Are there lots of advertisements on the page?

Current

- When was the website developed?
- When was it last reviewed? Last updated?
- Do specific articles or content within the website include dates?
- Do the links on the website work?

Ease of use and access

- Is the website easy to use?
- Can you easily find the information you are looking for?
- Is the information easy to read and understand?

Situations

- What types of information is this website best used for?
- Who should use this website?
- What types of questions can be answered at this website?

Support

- Is the content on the website supported by appropriate research?
- Is the content on the website supported by other reputable resources?
- Is the website supported or funded by reputable and reliable sources?

of information (but could be easily modified for information from other sources or for products or services; see tables 4.4 and 4.5) and can be used by students in their evaluation. Keep in mind that these models are designed so teachers can differentiate for student ability as needed. The ACCESS model is a more in-depth evaluation that is generally appropriate for older students but could be used with younger students who need more of a challenge. In addition, the RACE model, while designed for younger students, could be used if older students need more support or accommodations.

Products

As with information, a variety of health-related products are available, including toothpaste, deodorant, vitamins, sanitary napkins, condoms, and food, to name a few. Depending on how broadly the term *product* is defined, the list can be almost endless. A key aspect of accessing valid and reliable products relates to understanding the influence of media on our choices, as we will discuss in greater detail in chapter 5. Let's now focus on how the models (which were created based on the skill cues) provided in step 2 can be applied to products. One benefit of broad models is that they can easily apply in many contexts (information versus products). You can implement a similar model of progression (stages) used with accessing information in

the context of a product. Modified models are presented side by side in table 4.4 (questions might need to be modified for the developmental level and needs of students).

Services

The final context for accessing information, products, and services is services. This can be defined in many ways, but the main idea is that students can find and use services such as doctors, clinics, hospitals, and community services. Accessing services differs from accessing information and products in that it often requires face-to-face interaction and might not be as easy to access, especially for students. In this case, much of the practice should involve locating resources—how can students find services in their area for a variety of health-related topics? You may need to provide students with lists or guide them in the creation of a list of community resources and identify which are the most appropriate for students. However, it is helpful to show students how to find services regardless of their location. The RACE and ACCESS models can also apply to services (see table 4.5; questions might need to be modified for the developmental level and needs of students).

Once you have established a resource list and students know the questions to ask when evaluating a service, practice should focus on

TABLE 4.4   Skill Cues for Products

	RACE FOR PRODUCTS	
	INFORMATION	**PRODUCTS**
Reliable	• Is the domain a .gov, .org, or .edu? • Can you find the author or authors of the website? Are they credible sources of information? • Are there lots of advertisements on the page?	• Who makes or manufactures the product? • What are the company's background and reputation? • What are the ingredients? Are they even listed? Are they safe?
Accurate	• Is the information supported by research? • Is the information listed with an author (not just for the website but for actual content)? • Is the information confirmed by another source (provided on the website or via student research)?	• Are product claims supported by research? • Is information about the product (not advertisements) easily accessible?
Current	• When was the website developed? • When was it last reviewed? Last updated? • Do specific articles or content within the website include dates? • Do the links on the website work?	• What is the product expiration date? • Is the product new? Has it been tested?
Ease of use and access	• Is the website easy to use? • Can you easily find the information you are looking for? • Is the information easy to read and understand?	• Is the product easy to use? • Is the product easy to buy?
	ACCESS FOR PRODUCTS	
	INFORMATION	**PRODUCTS**
Accuracy	• Is the information listed with an author (not just for the website but for actual content)? • Is the information confirmed by another source (provided on the website or via student research)? • Does the website have an agenda or a specific target audience?	• Is information about the product (not advertisements) easily accessible? • Are product claims appropriate? • Are product claims correct?
Credibility	• Is the domain a .gov, .org, or .edu? • Can you find the author or authors of the website? Are they credible sources of information? • Are there lots of advertisements on the page?	• Who makes or manufactures the product? • What are the company's background and reputation? • What are the ingredients? Are they even listed? Are they safe?
Current	• When was the website developed? • When was it last reviewed? Last updated? • Do specific articles or content within the website include dates? • Do the links on the website work?	• What is the product expiration date? • Is the product new? Has it been tested?
Ease of use and access	• Is the website easy to use? • Can you easily find the information you are looking for? • Is the information easy to read and understand?	• Is the product easy to use? • Is the product easy to buy?
Situations	• What types of information is this website best used for? • Who should use this website? • What types of questions can be answered at this website?	• Who should use this product? • What are the indications for use? • Is the product safe for anyone?
Support	• Is the content on the website supported by research? • Is the content on the website supported by other reputable resources? • Is the website supported or funded by reputable and reliable sources?	• Does the product have research to support use and claims? • Does the product have reviews? • Is the product recommended by doctors or other medical professionals?

TABLE 4.5 Skill Cues for Services

RACE FOR SERVICES	
INFORMATION	
Reliable	• Does the service have an affiliation with a particular cause? • What is the reputation of the service or service provider?
Accurate	• Does the provider have an appropriate background related to the topic? • Does the provider or service provide accurate information?
Current	• Are facilities up to date? • Are best practices being implemented?
Ease of use and access	• Is the service easy to access? • Is the service provider easy to speak to?
ACCESS FOR SERVICES	
INFORMATION	
Accuracy	• Does the service provider have an appropriate background related to the topic? • Does the provider or service provide accurate information?
Credibility	• What are the qualifications of service providers? • What training have service providers received? • What other companies and/or organizations are the service providers connected to? Funded by?
Current	• Are facilities up to date? • Are best practices being followed?
Ease of use and access	• Is the service easy to access? • Is the service provider easy to speak to?
Situations	• When should this service be accessed (what situations require this service)? • Who should access this service?
Support	• Are there reviews for the service or provider? • Was the service or provider referred to you by a reliable source?

preparing students to use the service. Students can face many barriers from parents, social stigma around youth, and even peer pressure. Your job in the health education classroom is to prepare students and help them develop the self-confidence and self-efficacy to use these resources and services when needed. Practice should focus on the following:

■ Determining which services are needed in a given situation

■ Determining whether a minor needs parental consent

■ Determining if a health care provider is right for you

■ Determining what you need to bring and what you should be prepared for when visiting a health care provider

■ Role-playing scenarios between the service provider and the student

■ Discussing possible options in situations

Students should have many opportunities to practice in **authentic situations** in order to feel more comfortable engaging with providers, asking questions, speaking to their parents, and so on.

STEP 5: FEEDBACK AND REINFORCEMENT

This step occurs mostly outside the classroom, but reinforcing activities should be included within the unit on accessing valid and reliable information, products, and services and throughout the health education course.

ACCESSING INFORMATION

Melanie Lynch, MEd

State College Area High School, State College, Pennsylvania

What is your best strategy for teaching the skill of accessing valid and reliable information, products, and services?

When teaching any skills-based lesson, you must first take extra time in the semester to teach the skills themselves. You can't just assign a project and expect the students to know how to master the skill without your guidance. The first time in the semester that I teach accessing information, I have students find a website that they feel that they want to use with their project. They then have to answer questions about the website. Sample questions include the following:

- Who runs the website?
- Who pays for the website?
- What is the purpose of the website?
- How is the information on the website documented?
- How is information reviewed before it is posted on the website?

If the answers are not favorable for the site, they must start over with a new site. They quickly learn how to be more selective in consulting valid websites for their projects. It is important to note that learning to be proficient with the National Health Education Standards is a process. The more I teach to the skills, the more proficient my students become in these skills, improving their health literacy. Rome was not built in a day.

What is one pitfall to avoid when teaching the skill of accessing valid and reliable information?

Students today love to go straight to Wikipedia for the one-stop shop. They want to get all of the information there because it is easy and sometimes there is accurate information on it. The problem is knowing what information is accurate and what isn't. I found that if you say that Wikipedia has no valuable or accurate information on the site, some students will be all too eager to prove you wrong. Instead of saying that Wikipedia has no value, I simply state that it is too difficult to know whether or not it is accurate. Therefore, it is not a reliable website.

What advice do you have for other health educators in the field?

My best piece of advice for health educators is to make your health class as fun as possible. Be an edu-tainer. Try new things and always be open to ideas. Never be afraid to fail. To the outside observer, my classroom could best be described some days as controlled chaos. This provides my students a lot of room to try new things and possibly even fail at those new things, but they feel the safety net and I feel that I can push my students past their comfort zone because of that safety net. I am always assessing but not always grading. They reach further when they know it is not graded. Once they are confident with their skills, I give them some type of assessment that I turn into a grade.

I am not always the leader of my classroom. Once you give up the need for ultimate control, the students are more relaxed, they self-regulate more, and they are generally happier. Even though I am not always the leader, a lot of planning goes into making sure that I am able to facilitate an increase in my students' health literacy. When students find the class to be relaxed, useful, and fun, they really buy into the lessons and really try to look at their wellness behaviors and try to improve those behaviors.

KEY POINTS

■ Students need to practice all aspects of the skill of accessing valid and reliable information in all contexts throughout their health education courses. Practice opportunities within a given course should be directly aligned with educational outcomes determined in Step 1 of the skill development model.

■ All practice opportunities should be conducted in authentic situations that students are likely to experience.

■ Each of the three contexts (information, products, and services) has different points of emphasis. It is not necessary to cover all three at one time, but all should be covered by the time students complete grade 12.

Although this is step 5, you can incorporate these strategies during step 4 and even in other units after this one is complete. Reinforcement is critical, and the more connections you point out for students, the more likely the skill is to remain with the students.

Strategies for this step involve facilitating student engagement in real-life scenarios. In general, this will occur through homework and projects. Students can be assigned tasks where they have to take what they learned in class and try it at home. For example, once they have learned how to evaluate a product in class, students could have a homework assignment where they have to evaluate a product from their home. If the unit focused on accessing resources, they might have an assignment where they need to go to a community resource and gather information. Students might have to complete a brief evaluation of web resources used in this or other units. Or, a community resource (e.g., police officer, service provider) could be invited to class to demonstrate or speak about a topic related to the unit, or you could have a panel or health fair of services. There are many ways to reinforce the skill of accessing information in students' lives. The key is to ensure that the methods are embedded in the curriculum and that students understand the relevance of extending the learning beyond the classroom.

SUMMARY

Accessing valid and reliable information, products, and services is a multifaceted skill involving multiple components in multiple contexts (i.e., information, products, and services). If covered first in a health education course, it can lay the foundation for application during the rest of the course and can be used in the development of other skills.

Units need to focus on specific aspects of accessing valid and reliable information, products, and services to result in the most effective development of such a complex skill. In step 1, you define the skill and help students understand its relevance, and you present the educational objectives. During step 2, you present the skill cues for the educational objectives. In step 3, you model the skill of accessing valid and reliable information, emphasizing effective application of the skill. Step 4, practice, needs to be specific to the context in which the skill is being applied (information, products, and services) and should be designed to engage students in authentic situations. Finally, in step 5 students apply the skill in their own lives in order to continue to develop the skill and to see the relevance of accessing information in their lives.

Review Questions

1. How is accessing valid information related to health literacy?

2. Why is this such a complex skill?

3. How are educational objectives determined?

4. How is practice different for each context of accessing valid information: information, products, and services?

To find supplementary materials for this chapter, such as worksheets and extended learning activities, visit the web resource at
www.HumanKinetics.com/TheEssentialsOfTeachingHealthEducation

Monkey Business/fotolia.com

CHAPTER 5

Analyzing Influences

Learning Objectives

After reading this chapter, you will be able to do the following:

- Implement all steps of the skill development model for analyzing influences.
- Describe appropriate student outcomes for analyzing influences at each developmental level.
- Create high-quality classroom activities for developing the skill of analyzing influences.

Key Terms

culture

external influence

influence

internal influence

Our health is influenced, both directly and indirectly, by what we encounter around us. Perhaps it's the people in our life (e.g., family, friends and peers, teachers, clergy, neighbors, even those we pass by on our way to school or work), the culture(s) we are raised in, or even the advertisement that was playing as the alarm radio sounded, reminding us that a hot cup of coffee and a donut are the best way to perk up any day. Regardless of whether or not we realize that our behaviors are being influenced, it is safe to say that once we start to evaluate the choices we make every day, it becomes easier to see exactly which influences have a strong pull on our choices and which are more easily dismissed.

The skill of analyzing influences (standard 2 of the National Health Education Standards) helps students identify what is influencing their behavior, analyze whether the influence is positive or negative, evaluate why a particular influence has such a strong pull on their decision making, and mitigate influences that are supporting unhealthy behaviors. In chapter 4, we discussed the importance of developing students who are healthy skeptics about the information, products, and services they are using. Here in chapter 5, the emphasis is on creating healthy skeptics who think critically about influences on their health.

For example, Veronica, a sexually active high school student, finds valid and reliable information online about the importance of getting tested for sexually transmitted infections by a medical professional because undiagnosed STIs can lead to long-term reproductive health problems and even infertility. The information emphasizes that it is a myth that STIs always have symptoms and that a person would know when she has one. When Veronica shares this information with her friends, Megan tells her that the website where she found the information is wrong. Megan tells Veronica that there is no way an STI can have long-lasting effects on future health and that the site is just saying that to scare her into spending money to get tested at the doctor's office. In fact, Megan doesn't know of anyone who can't have kids because they had an STI when they were younger. Veronica doesn't think Megan is right, but she is confused. Veronica doesn't want to insult Megan by disagreeing with her

in front of their friends, and she fears that if she keeps trying to educate her friends, Megan will make her look like a fool. Because of this, she chooses to forget about what she read and hope that Megan knows what she is talking about.

Veronica's situation highlights both the importance of finding information from valid and reliable sources and the power of influences in our lives to affect whether or not we apply the information we have accessed in order to enhance our health. When we analyze what is influencing us, we are better able to recognize which factors can help and which can hinder us in making healthy choices. In this case, Veronica could critically analyze how her friends' influence (both Megan's inaccurate response and Veronica's social standing in the group) might potentially affect her long-term health.

A key element of this skill is that students not only take into consideration external influences but that they also critically analyze internal influences such as beliefs, attitudes, motivation, values, and needs. This internal reflection allows students to further develop their sense of self while providing the opportunity to align their beliefs, values, needs, and other internal influences with behaviors that support healthy lifestyles. For example, during a classroom activity, students compare advertisements for three brands of toothpaste and then explain the key selling points in each advertisement. Students then explain which advertisement is most appealing to them and why it is more likely to persuade them to brush their teeth than the others. A skilled health educator will use this conversation as a starting point to help students tap into the larger idea that strategies have different meanings for different people because individuals have their own beliefs, values, and needs. This sets the stage for understanding how external influences (e.g., advertisements) either complement or compete with our internal values, beliefs, or needs. Self-reflection is beneficial not just for understanding the dynamic between internal and external influences but also for increasing self-awareness of who we are, which directly enhances our ability to take control of our health.

There are so many potential influences that it can seem daunting to analyze them. However, the good news is that regardless of the influence (e.g., media, family, peers, culture, personal beliefs), the strategies are the same for analyzing its impact. This means that you don't have to ensure that students analyze all possible influences during class—you can develop the skill to proficiency by highlighting a few influences and then pointing out that the strategies the students learned will easily transfer to any influence they might encounter in the future. Your role is to ensure that students learn how to identify both internal and external influences on their health and provide the space necessary to critically evaluate multiple influences across a variety of domains. Figure 5.1 presents the steps of the skill development model for this chapter.

STEP 1: SKILL INTRODUCTION

Analyzing influences, like accessing valid and reliable information, is a foundational skill. The ability to recognize what influences our choices and actions directly affects our ability to apply the other skills (interpersonal communication,

decision making, goal setting, self-management, and advocacy). This is especially true because human beings do not operate in isolation. We operate amid a constant stream of messages and information, and we must be able to filter what is worth holding onto and what we should ignore.

Each message or bit of information has the potential to be an **influence**, which is anything that has an effect on an outcome. In this case, we explore those things that can influence feelings, actions and behaviors, or beliefs. As described in the National Health Education Standards, the skill of analyzing influences is the ability to "analyze the influence of family, peers, culture, media, technology, and other factors on health behaviors" (Joint Committee, 2007). This complex skill teaches students how to look critically at influences from a variety of angles (e.g., positive versus negative, external versus internal) and contexts (e.g., nutrition, sexual health, mental health). Students become able to understand what influences their health behaviors and also how their own actions could

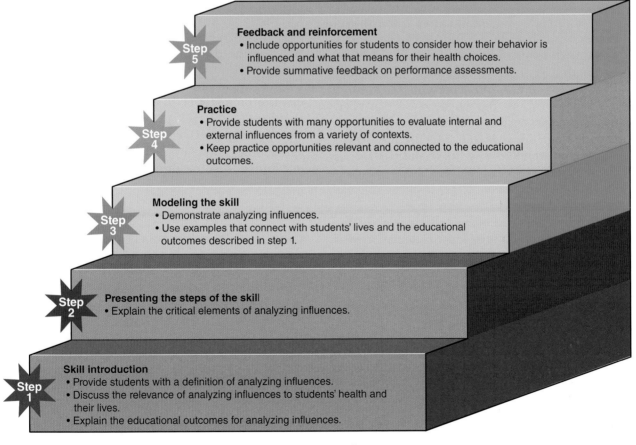

FIGURE 5.1 Steps for developing the skill of analyzing influences.

influence the health behaviors of others. They also become able to see that some influences have a positive effect on their choices and others have a negative impact (and some might be both positive and negative depending on the situation). The challenges are determining how to decipher their influences and figuring out what to do (if anything) about those influences.

Positive Versus Negative Influences

A positive influence is one that encourages decisions and actions that help a person maintain or enhance health and well-being. Conversely, a negative influence is anything (or anyone) that encourages unhealthy behavior or reduces the ability to achieve a healthy outcome. However, the reality is that determining whether an influence is positive or negative is not that simple. Influences are not absolute and they do not have the same effect on all people. For example, Jax and Peyton are friends. Jax is a good student who is actively involved in many extracurricular activities and community service projects. Peyton has had a hard time academically but understands that good grades are important. Jax likes to help his friend, often by helping him with his homework. To help Peyton, Jax offers him some pills to improve his concentration. Peyton becomes confused by Jax's behavior and what it means for their friendship. He knows that pills are not a good choice and wonders why his friend is offering them, but he has appreciated Jax's tutoring and his encouragement to get involved in community service.

This example resembles the types of dilemmas your students may face. It demonstrates how one influence (a friend) can be both a negative and a positive influence, the complexity of how influences affect us, and the importance of taking these factors into consideration when you are planning and teaching the unit on analyzing information.

However, influences change (e.g., people come and go, we move to a new city) as we grow and mature over time. For example, maybe Jax and Peyton remain in touch for the next five years but they choose different paths after high school. Peyton is able to find his passion and become successful in his career. Although he still appreciates the support Jax gave him years ago, Jax is no longer such a strong influence on him. He now has a new group of friends and a significant other on whom he relies for support. In addition, Peyton has gained self-confidence and feels that he has more control over his actions than he did five years ago. Peyton himself is different and so are his influences. However, even with these changes, the process that Peyton uses to determine whether his current influences are positive or negative is the same one he learned five years ago. Once you teach students how to analyze influences, they will have the ability to apply the skill throughout their lives.

External Influences

An **external influence** is anything that affects our feelings, actions and behaviors, or beliefs and is introduced from an outside source. Let's take a moment to explore some of the external influences most relevant to health education.

People

Humans are social creatures. We are born with the need to be loved and to belong (see Maslow's hierarchy of needs in chapter 3). Due to this innate need, we sometimes search out the opinions of those who are important to us, and we sometimes hear and internalize their opinions even when we are not asking for them. This category includes any person we encounter, such as family, peers, classmates, coworkers, and clergy.

Culture

Culture refers to the beliefs, customs, ways of thinking, or behaviors among a group of people. Any group that assembles for a shared purpose will develop an identity of its own. For example, in the case of a nationality or an ethnic group, there are often customs and traditions that are carried over time and location. Religious groups also have a strong cultural identity that has been carried across time and location. Among a group of students, there can be a culture at a grade level (elementary, middle, or high school), among organizations (e.g., drama, sports, academic clubs), or among any other configuration that students (or adults) create. The interesting thing about culture is that there are no specific parameters or rules about what defines a group to allow it to form a culture. Rather, group culture is an organic process that occurs as members of a group define their own identity.

In the classroom, encourage students to explore the idea of culture and how it affects their choices. Help students recognize that they belong to many cultures, each with its own rules and norms for behavior. Sometimes various group cultures will conflict, leaving students to determine which group they feel a stronger connection with and which norms they will allow to influence their behavior. One choice is not necessarily right while the other is wrong, but one choice will prevail.

For example, a student may belong to a culture that values privacy and believes that discussing health problems openly is inappropriate. However, the same student may be assigned a class project that requires him to interview his relatives about health conditions that run in the family in order to become more informed about potential risk factors he may encounter. The student must now decide how to handle this situation because he risks acting in a way that conflicts with his family values (by completing the assignment), and he risks acting in a way that might jeopardize his academic success (by not completing the assignment). There is likely a positive resolution to this dilemma if the student speaks with the teacher, but he must first be able to recognize the influences that are causing the problem. A second example, a female student who is a part of a peer group that dislikes exercise because it is sweaty, messy, and leaves you looking unattractive, but she enjoys the camaraderie of her lacrosse team, feels good after she plays, and is a strong player. She must find a way to balance these competing forces because she doesn't want to lose her friends or the sport she enjoys. Again, there is likely a positive solution to this dilemma, but before she can resolve the problem, she needs to understand the competing influences that are causing it.

It is the job of health educators to recognize that students live among multiple cultures at any given time. We must encourage student growth and honest exploration of cultural norms of groups in which they are members. Additionally, we must recognize that a student's

culture may sometimes be at odds with course content. Perhaps it is a religious view or a family value, or perhaps the student learned about this topic in another setting and the information is contradictory or challenges personal beliefs. It may even be a personal feeling of uneasiness or insecurity that is a result of discussing a sensitive topic related to personal habits. In this situation, you must go beyond sensitivity and support how cultural differences make us unique and can affect our health and wellness. This does not mean that students have to agree with a conflicting belief or idea. Rather, it is about having an open mind and using the classroom as a safe space to explore the rationale behind the belief, reflect on the students' own beliefs, thoughtfully consider the new belief or information presented, and decide what makes sense for them. You have to be careful to help students recognize health-enhancing beliefs and actions while not imposing ideas or values on your students. Health is unique and personal—there is no one right way to be healthy, but there are healthier beliefs, values, ideas, and actions. Your job is to guide students so that they construct their own understandings about health that are aligned with their personal values but that also encourage growth and exploration in hopes that students will move the needle toward health-enhancing beliefs, values, attitudes, and ideas.

To gain a better understanding of cultural roles and norms in your students' lives, take the time to get to know your students. Once you have established a positive, safe learning environment, consider doing an activity that encourages students to share the influence of culture in their lives. When appropriate, and with rules for acceptable group sharing that allow students to opt out of sharing without penalty, encourage open dialogue about cultural norms around a particular topic and allow students to share why their beliefs are important to them and how those beliefs influence their health. For example, ask students to think about the way they are taken care of when they get sick. Who takes care of them? What are the house rules? How sick do they have to be before they can stay home from school? What foods do they eat? How do they decide when to go to a doctor? Is there someone else they may visit first instead of a medical doctor? Overall, how do these actions and predictable behaviors make them feel about what to expect when they get sick?

This kind of conversation can illustrate for the class that even something as simple as staying home sick from school can be greatly influenced by family values and cultural beliefs. This opens the door for students to listen as classmates share stories and to become less judgmental about why behaviors differ from person to person. They can become more in tune to the fact that a variety of approaches to solving a problem can provide insight into particular behaviors and in turn create an opportunity to support healthy behaviors in meaningful and appropriate ways.

Media and Technology

As discussed in chapter 1, we live in a media-saturated society, so much so that a newer dimension of health literacy, e-health literacy, has become a necessary part of improving the health outcomes of youth. In fact, 32 percent of teens who accessed health information online reported changing their behavior because of that information (Wartella, Rideout, Zupancic, Beaudoin-Ryan, & Lauricella, 2015). From magazines to television, the Internet to social media, messages about the norms of various behaviors are all around us. Even so, most teens still report that their parents (57 percent) are their primary source of health information, followed by a doctor or nurse (54 percent) and health class at school (38 percent) (Wartella et al., 2015). However, media literacy and analysis are important, and we need to teach students how to analyze the influences of various forms of media.

Media are a vital context for analyzing influences on choices and behavior. When the skill of analyzing influences is appropriately taught, media become another influence that students must consider, not an influence that requires special consideration or a separate curriculum. This does not mean that you can't spend additional time examining media as it is an extremely complex influence with multiple facets. To delve deeply into this takes time, and it is fine to take the time if it works in your curriculum. However, the process of analyzing the influence of media is the same as for other influences, so do not feel obligated to teach media as a separate influence. When examining media, have students explore websites, social media, or print media (among others) and provide a critical analysis of how the media could influence a person's behavior. Additionally, have students provide strategies for mitigating the negative influence from the sites, develop conversation points to support their view, and find alternative forms of media that provide a positive influence. It may also be worth coordinating with your school's media specialist to support media literacy across topic areas.

Students today are participating in online environments without a full understanding of how their behaviors online could have lasting consequences. Although this behavior is completely aligned with adolescent brain development, it is vital that students receive the education and tools to mitigate future negative effects.

Law, Policy, and Regulation

The conversation about external influences must include the laws, policies, and regulations that students are subject to. These could include student handbook policies, such as for tardiness, harassment, and hazing, as well as state and federal legislation. For example, students who are looking to impress their friends by doing something daring might consider shoplifting because they've heard friends talk about the thrill of getting away with it. Because shoplifting is illegal and can result in getting arrested, it may be important to discuss how shoplifting is associated with other risk-taking behaviors and can lead to negative outcomes (e.g., how an arrest record may affect the ability to participate in school or school activities such as sports). Other students who must drive to work to earn extra money might consider how texting and driving not only puts their life at risk but could cost them their job if they are caught and end up losing their license (again affecting multiple dimensions of wellness).

Policies and regulations are important to both student safety and classroom management. While discussing laws and regulations, always remember your role as a mandated reporter. It is important that all students feel safe in the classroom, but you must be aware of conversations where you might receive information that you must report. As with all conversations, setting appropriate guidelines helps to discourage inappropriate self-disclosure within a classroom while still providing an opportunity for students to seek help privately. You will want to be up front with students regarding your role as a mandated reporter. It is inappropriate to tell students that you can be a confidant and that you will not divulge any information they tell you. This is misleading and can cause students to misunderstand your role. There are many ways to become a trusted resource for students, but you must set appropriate expectations and boundaries.

Life Circumstances

Not all influences fit into one of the previously mentioned categories. Many events and circumstances beyond our control can have a big impact on the choices we make. Examples include personal or family illness, financial status, personal crisis, marriage or separation of parents or caregivers, loss of a pet, and being cut from a team or activity. Life events can have an impact on behavior even though students may not readily acknowledge the event. Encourage students to consider these types of factors when they are looking at the big picture of external influences.

Internal Influences

Internal influences are an innate part of who we are. Our main internal influences are our values, beliefs, attitudes, motivation, and needs. They can often be managed and even modified, but they cannot be removed. For example, internal influences such as temperament, personality, cognitive ability, sense of humor, fears, drive to succeed, and other personal needs are part of who we are. Although they are independent of each other, external forces can also affect internal influences and vice versa. For example, a person with an outgoing personality may find it difficult to resist the temptation of a thrill-seeking experience, such as getting high for the first time, and her likelihood of engaging in this behavior is compounded if she is also surrounded by external influences that encourage the behavior. Another example is a shy student who has a hard time expressing his needs or opinions openly. When placed in a situation where he is a bystander to another student being bullied, he may not take a stand against

the bullying unless he has built the confidence and skill for that situation and anticipates a positive outcome.

In the classroom, it is important for students to spend time considering what parts of themselves influence their choices and behaviors. Unless they consciously spend time trying to understand what internally drives them, they are likely to overlook these influences.

Educational Outcomes

When teaching students the procedural knowledge for the skill of analyzing influences, it is important to consider what influences are occurring at each developmental level and how students define a given term. For example, the idea of family may be narrower in lower grades and more encompassing in later grades. It is also important to consider that although the types of influences don't change across grade spans, the expectations in the performance indicators become more sophisticated as the grade levels increase. For example, family is an influence that shows up in each developmental grade span. However, the outcome for the grade spans is different. In preK to grade 2, students *identify*, in grades 3 to 5 they *describe*, in grades 6 to 8 they *examine*, and finally in grades 9 to 12 they *analyze*. These actions all relate to family but illustrate the increasing sophistication of expectations as students develop their critical-thinking and analytical skills.

Step 1: Choosing Indicators

The skill of analyzing influences contains the most performance indicators of any of the National Standards (see table 5.1). Each area of influence identified in the standard (family, peers, culture, media, technology, and other factors) has a separate performance indicator at each grade level. It is probably unrealistic to spend multiple class periods discussing each indicator, but it is realistic to determine a few influences that will receive the majority of the focus. Another approach is to highlight types of influences and allow students to complete an assignment where they choose to focus on multiple influences and their impact on personal health behaviors and practices. This may lead to students selecting several influences but will highlight the connections between influences.

TABLE 5.1   Performance Indicators for Standard 2 of the National Health Education Standards

PREK-GRADE 2	GRADES 3-5	GRADES 6-8	GRADES 9-12
2.2.1 Identify how the family influences personal health practices and behaviors.	2.5.1 Describe how family influences personal health practices and behaviors.	2.8.1 Examine how the family influences the health of adolescents.	2.12.1 Analyze how the family influences the health of individuals.
2.2.2 Identify what the school can do to support personal health practices and behaviors.	2.5.2 Identify the influence of culture on health practices and behaviors.	2.8.2 Describe the influence of culture on health beliefs, practices, and behaviors.	2.12.2 Analyze how the culture supports and challenges health beliefs, practices, and behaviors.
2.2.3 Describe how the media can influence health behaviors.	2.5.3 Identify how peers can influence healthy and unhealthy behaviors.	2.8.3 Describe how peers influence healthy and unhealthy behaviors.	2.12.3 Analyze how peers influence healthy and unhealthy behaviors.
	2.5.4 Describe how the school and community can support personal health practices and behaviors.	2.8.4 Analyze how the school and community can affect personal health practices and behaviors.	2.12.4 Evaluate how the school and community can affect personal health practice and behaviors.
	2.5.5 Explain how media influence thoughts, feelings, and health behaviors.	2.8.5 Analyze how messages from media influence health behaviors.	2.12.5 Evaluate the effect of media on personal and family health.
	2.5.6 Describe ways that technology can influence personal health.	2.8.6 Analyze the influence of technology on personal and family health.	2.12.6 Evaluate the impact of technology on personal, family, and community health.
		2.8.7 Explain how the perceptions of norms influence healthy and unhealthy behaviors.	2.12.7 Analyze how the perceptions of norms influence healthy and unhealthy behaviors.
		2.8.8 Explain the influence of personal values and beliefs on individual health practices and behaviors.	2.12.8 Analyze the influence of personal values and beliefs on individual health practices and behaviors.
		2.8.9 Describe how some health risk behaviors can influence the likelihood of engaging in unhealthy behaviors.	2.12.9 Analyze how some health risk behaviors can influence the likelihood of engaging in unhealthy behaviors.
		2.8.10 Explain how school and public health policies can influence health promotion and disease prevention.	2.12.10 Analyze how public health policies and government regulations can influence health promotion and disease prevention.

This approach also allows for personalization and for students to explore the influences that they believe have the greatest impact on them, which might be more relevant and meaningful to them.

When selecting performance indicators for the class, question to ask include the following:

■ Am I avoiding duplication of influences students have discussed in a previous course?

■ Do my students have specific needs?

■ Do I have data that highlight the need to focus on a particular area? For example, recent acts of cyberbullying may lead to an emphasis on the use of technology and social media.

The following scenario provides an example of choosing performance indicators.

You are teaching the skill of analyzing influences in your ninth-grade health class. The students have previously been exposed to this skill in their seventh-grade health education course, which focused on the influence of family and media on health behaviors. In this course, you decide that focusing on just a few factors does not give students the full scope of this skill. Instead, you decide to highlight each potential area of influence (performance indicators 2.12.1-2.12.6). You then create an assessment that asks students to identify an unhealthy behavior they currently engage in and to describe how two of the previously discussed influences along with the influence of personal values (2.12.8) and the perception of norms (2.12.7) have contributed to their unhealthy behavior. The final step is for students to identify strategies to turn the unhealthy behavior into a healthier one and describe how they will mitigate negative influences and seek out positive influences. The students might not be demonstrating the performance indicators as written, but all are being covered through the unit. In this example, it would be important that you rewrite or modify the performance indicators into clear objectives that make sense for the unit.

Step 2: Coverage of Indicators

Once you have selected the indicators, and as you begin to determine how students will demonstrate learning for these indicators, it is necessary to plan activities and assignments to help students develop the knowledge and skills to meet the objectives. When considering coverage of indicators, remember that it is critical for students to learn how to analyze multiple influences in a variety of settings.

You have chosen performance indicators 2.12.1 through 2.12.8 for this unit. Your students must learn what each indicator means and how it may influence behavior and health practices. For example, students must, at a minimum, have a conversation, brainstorm in a group, or complete a worksheet that explores the definition of each influence (e.g., personal values, peers, family, community, religious groups, social media) and how it can affect health behaviors positively or negatively. This builds a foundation and alleviates confusion as to the exact meaning of the influence in the context of the class.

Then, once students understand the types of influences, they need to explore the influences across a variety of settings. This occurs when students participate in activities where they apply the concepts discussed for each influence across multiple contexts (e.g., media, technology, school and community environment). For example, using the school and community setting, have students create a mind map with school and community in the center. Each spoke of the map leads to an influence. Have students explore each influence by identifying how the influence and the setting intersect with one another.

Step 3: Student-Appropriate Terms

For the skill of analyzing influences, most terms are ones that students are familiar with and are easy to understand. However, at the start of the unit and before requiring students to complete an assignment for any given performance indicator, you should review and ask students if they have any questions or need clarification.

Step 4: Educational Outcomes

The final version of the performance indicators derived from the previous three steps are the educational outcomes for the skill.

The following scenarios demonstrate how step 1 of the skill development model may look in the classroom for analyzing influences. The two examples show how educators at all levels can implement participatory methods to address step 1 of the skill development model in one lesson. Although presented here as a single lesson, actual implementation time for step 1 may vary based on the length of your class, student learning needs, and types of activities.

Step 1 in the Classroom: Skill Introduction

Scenario A: PreK to Grade 2

Before teaching a first-grade class, you review the performance indicators and select 2.2.1 (family influences) and 2.2.3 (media influences) for the unit on analyzing influences. On the first day of the unit, you ask the students to tell you one rule their family has to keep them safe. After students have answered, you ask some follow-up questions, such as "Have you ever watched a TV show where one of the characters broke a rule that you have in your house? How did that make you feel to see someone breaking a rule that you have in your house?"

You then continue a discussion with the class that emphasizes the importance of rules for keeping people healthy and safe. In addition, you highlight that different families have different rules, and that is OK. Sometimes we see things on TV or in a magazine that are not the same as the rules in our house, and it is important to understand that the media doesn't always follow the safety rules, but we shouldn't let someone breaking the rules influence us to break the rules, too. You end the discussion by ensuring students have made a clear connection between the influence of family on the making and enforcing of rules, how that affects behavior, and how media influences relate to the situation. You then share the educational outcomes of the skill with students so they know what they will be able to do by the end of the unit.

Scenario B: Grades 6 to 8

After speaking with the school nutrition director, you learn that new requirements for students mean that they are being served more fruits and vegetables at lunch, but unfortunately many are not eating the food they are taking and it appears to be going to waste. You decide to use the unit on analyzing influences to better understand why this is happening. You select performance indicators 2.8.3 (peer influence), 2.8.4 (how school and community can affect behaviors), and 2.8.7 (how perceived norms influence behavior). As students enter the class, you ask them to complete an instant activity and write down the first thing that comes to mind when they hear the words fruits and vegetables and then the words school lunch. Once this task is complete, you share with the students that the premise of this unit is to think critically about what influences their health choices and behaviors. Then you inform the class about your conversation with the nutrition director and how fruits and vegetables are going to waste.

Next, you review the performance indicators and educational objectives to inform the students about the unit. The students are placed in small groups to create a Venn diagram that includes a circle for peers and a circle for the school and community. Within each circle they list how each group currently influences fruit and vegetable consumption, and they make another set of circles that show how each could influence a person to eat more fruits and vegetables. Once this is complete, a larger class discussion occurs about the perceived norms related to fruit and vegetable consumption and how to shift those perceived norms to a positive influence on consuming more fruits and vegetables. You also include questions about why it is important to examine influences on food choices both in and out of school.

STEP 2: PRESENTING THE STEPS OF THE SKILL

Skill cues are used in step 2 as a way of breaking the skill into manageable parts and providing students with the concrete steps they need to achieve before they can demonstrate proficiency in the skill (i.e., what students need to be able to do in order to meet the educational objectives). Remember, you can modify skill cues at each grade level as long as they provide a way to perform and measure the skill. Here are the key points to remember for analyzing influences.

Students will be able to do the following:

- List influences on health behavior from multiple sources.
- Examine a variety of influences (both internal and external), explain how they receive messages from these influences (and what the messages are), and explain how the influences affect health behaviors (positively or negatively).
- Critically analyze how influences interact with each other to have an effect on health behaviors, beliefs, values, and needs.
- Develop strategies to mitigate negative influences and foster positive influences.

Sample skill cues for analyzing influences are presented in table 5.2.

KEY POINTS

- Analyzing influences includes examining family, peers, culture, media, technology, and other social factors that can have an impact on health practices and behaviors.
- Analyzing influences is a multifaceted skill, but learning and understanding how to interpret and mitigate influences is a similar process regardless of the factors being considered.
- A person's beliefs and values are critical in successfully implementing this skill. Without an understanding of our internal views, it is hard to evaluate influences on our choices and behaviors.

As with step 1, there are many ways to introduce step 2 that are not teacher directed. Following are some examples.

Step 2 in the Classroom: Presenting the Steps of the Skill

PreK to Grade 2

In class, you read a story where the character is trying to make a healthy choice but is having a hard time because obstacles keep getting in the way. For example, the character is trying to eat a healthy lunch, but her friends keep saying that vegetables are gross, her parent packs her something she doesn't like, and all of her friends' snacks have cartoons on them and look more fun to eat. Then the character starts to run out of time because lunch is ending and most of her food goes to waste.

After reading the story, ask the class to talk about a time when they wanted to make a healthy choice but it was hard because there were so many other reasons not to make the healthy choice. Explain that this happens a lot and for many reasons, and then identify this as being influenced by things around us. At the end of the conversation, ask students to draw a picture of something or someone that influences (who from the skill cues) what they choose to eat and then explain why it is influential (how from the skill cues).

TABLE 5.2 Skill Cues for Analyzing Influences

PREK-GRADE 2	
Focus: Developing an understanding of what influences are and how they can affect choices	**Who and How** *or* **What and How** **Things That Influence Me** *Who* influences me . . . I know they influence me because . . . *What* influences me . . . I know it influences me because . . .
GRADES 3-5	
Focus: Beginning to identify a variety of influences across multiple contexts and providing explanations for how certain things can be influential	**People** *Who*—Who are the people (e.g., family, peers) who influence my behaviors and actions? *How*—How do these people influence my behaviors and actions? *So what*—Explain what I may do differently as a result of this influence. **Other Factors (e.g., Culture, Media, Technology)** *What*—What are the factors that influence my behaviors and actions? *How*—How do these factors influence my behaviors and actions? *So what*—Explain what I may do differently as a result of this influence.
GRADES 6-8	
Focus: Taking a deeper look at influences across multiple contexts and factors and then analyzing how those influences have an impact on actions and behaviors	*Identify* the influence. *Analyze* the influence: • How do I know it is influencing me? • What messages am I receiving from this influence? • Is this a positive or negative influence? • How much is this influencing my thoughts, values, beliefs, or actions? *Examine* how other factors may be interacting with this influence and how that may be affecting my thoughts, values, beliefs, and behavior choices. *Consider* whether I need to do anything about this influence. What is the best plan of action to handle this influence in my life?
GRADES 9-12	
Focus: Critically analyzing and evaluating how influences support or hinder healthy behaviors, practices, and beliefs	Same skill cues used in grades 6-8 can be used here.

Grades 3 to 5

After choosing media influences to start the conversation, invite students to think about their favorite television show, app, online game, or social media and the kinds of advertisements they see when they are using that media. As a class, make a list of products being sold in the advertisements. Either individually or in small groups, students complete a worksheet that answers the questions of the skill cues—what, how, so what—for one of the commercial products. Ensure that each group is working on a different product. Review as a class and have students report what they wrote down for each skill cue about their product. Be sure to provide feedback so that students understand the skill cues and how to use the skill cues to analyze influences.

Grades 6 to 8

Put up sheets of poster paper that each list an influence, such as personal values, peers, family, community, religious group, and social media. Have students form small groups and stand at a poster. While at the poster, students take five to eight minutes to write down (analyze) how that topic could influence the health behaviors of middle schoolers (both positively and negatively) and why this topic is important to discuss in a unit on analyzing influences. After students have had time to brainstorm, present the rest of the skill cues (examine, consider) and have the group write a response for the remaining skill cues. At the end of the time, each group shares key points with the class using the skill cues as a framework (i.e., the students explain their responses to each skill cue). This is a critical time for feedback to ensure that students have correctly applied the skill cues and have successfully implemented the skill.

Grades 9 to 12

Provide high school students with data on youth risk behaviors in your community and assign the students into pairs or small groups. Have students look through the data and highlight the areas they feel are alarming, consistent with their thinking, or inconsistent with what they see going on around them. Engage in a group discussion about each topic and briefly brainstorm ideas for why students engage in the risky behaviors. Following this activity, highlight for students that behaviors do not happen in a vacuum and that they are influenced at multiple levels all around them. Assign each pair or group one influence (e.g., personal values, peers, family, community,

religious group, social media) and one risk behavior. Have each pair or group work through the skill cues to identify, analyze, examine, and consider a plan to address the significant influence (or influences) on their assigned risk factor. Use this conversation as a starting point for further exploration of specific topics and contexts.

STEP 3: MODELING THE SKILL

To model the skill of analyzing influences, you must take into account what proficiency looks like and how it is defined. Modeling should reflect how students interact with the skill during the unit and in their lives.

This part of the lesson will be shaped by the educational objectives from step 1. For example, a unit on analyzing influences can focus on multiple influences, or it can be limited to one or two influences. Either way, the key is to provide examples that show students how, by the end of the unit, they will be able to apply the strategies they've learned to any influence. Following are examples of modeling activities.

PreK to Grade 2

- Students brainstorm a list of things that could influence a specific behavior that students regularly engage in, such as being on time or doing physical activity. Facilitate the brainstorming by asking questions that pertain to the skill cues (e.g., Who might influence you? How do you know?).

- Students create a list of influences in their school that support them in making positive health choices.

- Students analyze media advertisements using the skill cues. This could be done as a large-group activity with the teacher facilitating and scaffolding the discussion to clearly highlight the connections to the skill cues.

- Students participate in a discussion about how family can influence what they do (actions and behaviors).

Grades 3 to 5

- Students watch a video clip of a positive family or peer interaction and then dis-

KEY POINTS

- Skill cues for analyzing influences must be written in such a way that supports the analysis of influences across a variety of contexts.

- Students at all levels can articulate what is happening in the world around them in a developmentally appropriate way. Your role is to assist students in understanding how the world around them can influence the choices they make.

- Not only is it important to understand what influences behavior, but students must also be able to articulate how they will mitigate the influence and strive to make healthier choices (if the influence is negative) or embrace the influence to support their current behaviors (if it's positive).

cuss why the interaction was positive and how it influenced the situation (e.g., did it influence another character's behaviors, thoughts, or beliefs?).

- Students discuss the qualities of a good friend and how to tell if people are not your friend because they are trying to get you to do things that could get you hurt or in trouble (among other things).

- In small groups, students discuss the influence of video games and handheld devices on health behaviors.

- Students listen to a story where the lead character is a strong role model for healthy behavior. They discuss what the character does to choose healthy habits and what might be influencing the character's beliefs, values, and actions.

Grades 6 to 8

- Students examine pictures of the kinds and amount of food people eat around the world and then discuss how family and community culture influence food choices in the United States.

- Students reflect on the choices they made the day before. Then they identify what external and internal factors affected those choices.

- Students discuss what activities are available in the community for staying active. How might these activities influence youth behaviors?

- Students examine magazine advertisements for health and beauty products and then discuss the image they portray of both boys and girls and how this might influence thoughts, beliefs, values, and behaviors.

Grades 9 to 12

- Individually, in small groups, or as a large group, students create a Wheel of Influence that has a topic in the center (e.g., drinking and driving, positive body image, STIs) and spokes to various influences. Then they list messages that they might receive from these influences and how the influences might affect behavior.

- Students listen while you explain how your personal beliefs and values have influenced a behavior. For example, you might discuss stress management and explain what influences your stress levels, how you manage them, and what the outcomes are. Be sure to use the skill cues when sharing the story.

- Students watch a video clip that compares a healthy relationship interaction with an unhealthy one and discuss influences on the interaction.

- Students examine data on youth risk behavior that show the connection between better grades and reduced levels of risky behaviors. Students then brainstorm why this might be the case—how does avoiding risky behaviors affect academic success?

© ClarkandCompany/iStock.com

Supporting students in the analysis of influences in their lives can help them increase their self-awareness and empower them to make changes when necessary.

STEP 4: PRACTICE

Step 4 gives students the opportunity to articulate their thoughts in a concrete manner, whether it is on paper or in a presentation, and to practice applying the skill cues in ways that are relevant to their lives. For example, a fourth-grade class is given the topic of technology and is asked to work through the skill cues of *what*, *how*, *why*, and *so what* related to their own technology use and how their behavior is influenced by technology or how their technology use is influenced by other external or internal influences. This provides an opportunity for students to practice the skill cues while also encouraging thoughtful reflection about a specific health behavior at the individual level. Step 4 is also the time when students could be given an assignment that allows them to demonstrate the skill cues in action and their understanding of the skill. For instance, in an 11th-grade personal wellness course perhaps students are asked to identify one personal unhealthy behavior they would like to understand the influences on. Each student would then complete a worksheet with each skill cue listed (identify, analyze, examine, consider) to further examine this health behavior and the influences that affect the behavior. As a large group, solicit volunteers to share their process and receive feedback. Remember, a key element of skill practice is effective feedback.

KEY POINTS

- The key to engaging students in the skill of analyzing influences is to start with topic areas that all students in the class can relate to and that are low risk to talk about openly. As the unit progresses, more intense and personal topics may emerge, but the modeling portion is intended to provide a safe place to discuss the skill cues and intention of the skill, as evident through the educational objectives, in a way that hooks students and encourages further self-exploration.

- Students engage best when the topics are relevant to their world. Consider topics that have an immediate impact.

- Use student-level data to determine topics and guide activities.

Skill Cues for Practicing Analyzing Influences

GRADES 3 TO 5

People

Who: Who are the people (e.g., family, peers) who influence my behaviors and actions?
- Are these people close to me? Do I trust their opinion?
- Are there other people who are not close to me that have an influence on my behavior?

How: How do these people influence my behaviors and actions?
- What actions, words, or behaviors expressed by the identified people influence my behavior?
- Are there specific places where the influences happen?
- Does this person want me to do something different?

So what: Explain what I may do differently as a result of this influence.
- Tell your teacher some ways this influence causes you to do certain things.
- Discuss what you can do if the person is influencing you in ways that are not healthy.

Other Factors (e.g., Culture, Media, Technology)

What: What are the factors that influence my behaviors and actions?
- List the factors that have an influence.
- Where are these factors coming from (e.g., TV, magazines, video games)?

How: How do these factors influence my behaviors and actions?
- What do I like about these things?
- Do these factors use fun images (such as characters, bright colors, or hip language) to persuade me?

So what: Explain what I may do differently as a result of this influence.
- If I never saw this product or factor, would I believe what it is trying to get me to believe?
- How can I avoid this influence or make sure I don't do the unhealthy things it encourages?

Grades 6 to 8 and 9 to 12 (Same Skill Cues for Both)

Identify the influence.
- List who and what can influence behavior—could be people or other factors.
- List both internal influences and external influences.

Analyze how the influence has an impact on behaviors, thoughts, values, and beliefs.
- How do I know it is influencing me?
- What messages am I receiving from this influence?
- Is this a positive or negative influence?
- How much is this influencing my thoughts, values, beliefs, or actions?

(continued)

Skill Cues... *(continued)*

Examine how other factors interact with this influence and have an effect on behavior choices.

- Are there other influences that work together with this one (e.g., media messages and peer values or family and religious beliefs)?
- Do my internal influences support or contradict this influence?
- Do some external influences send me different messages about a behavior?

Consider whether I need to do anything about this influence. What is the best plan of action to handle this influence in my life?

- Does it change my behavior for better or for worse?
- If this influence were not in my life, would I be better off? Would I be worse off?
- Do I need to do anything about this influence? Is it strong enough that I should make a change?
- Should I be more aware of this influence in the future?
- Do I need to remove myself from this influence?

It may be useful to employ collective group feedback at some points and teacher-directed feedback at others.

The Skill Cues for Practicing Analyzing Influences sidebar takes an in-depth look at each skill cue for grades 3 to 5 and grades 6 to 8 and 9 to 12 presented in step 2, and it provides more information on what to expect from students in order to see their proficiency. The skill cues presented in the sidebar are intended to support teaching and learning, and they can be differentiated for students as needed.

STEP 5: FEEDBACK AND REINFORCEMENT

Step 5 focuses on the evaluation and reinforcement of the skill. When students are given a performance task that requires them to identify and then assess how a behavior is influenced,

they inevitably will be tackling tough information. They may have to acknowledge that some things that they previously felt had no impact on their behavior actually might have a big impact on them. This realization could be unsettling for some students as they grapple with how to control the influence. For example, if a student hadn't previously considered how her friends who smoke marijuana occasionally could be a negative influence on her choice to smoke marijuana (considering that she only smokes marijuana when around those friends), she may have a difficult time acknowledging this influence on an assessment. Once the student takes a look at this situation, she may choose not to acknowledge the influence of these friends on her behaviors, or she may become upset because she realizes that she does need to make a change. You must be prepared for these issues to arise, and be ready to support students.

KEY POINTS

- Analyzing influences requires students to look critically at influences that may be difficult to acknowledge.
- Providing practice and support while students explore this skill is vital.
- Defining and further breaking down the skill cues may be necessary for students to be able to apply the cues.

ANALYZING INFLUENCES

Lindsay R. Armbruster
O'Rourke Middle School, Burnt Hills-Ballston Lake Central School District, Burnt Hills, New York

What is your best strategy for teaching the skill of analyzing influences?

The best thing we can do when teaching this skill (and any skill, really!) is to make sure that each individual student personalizes the content. I have students create a web with their name and a health issue (e.g., underage drinking, sex, going to a party, participating in a particular trend) in the center and 8 to 10 spokes coming off that center point. Each of these spokes signifies an influence in the individual's life: family, culture, peers, friends, teammates, coaches and other important adults, school, community, religion, laws and rules, television, social media, and so on. The categories can be adjusted based on the population. The students identify the message that they receive from each influence about that particular topic. Then students draw a line connecting the source to themselves—the thicker and bolder the line, the more powerful they feel that influence is on their decisions and behaviors about this particular topic. Sharing the messages that students receive and the thickness of the lines provides for great discussion among students. Finally, students identify what their personal feelings and beliefs are about this topic and identify with which sources of influence their personal beliefs are in line with. If this activity is completed several times over the course of a semester on varying topics, by the end of the semester students have a portfolio of influence webs and are able to see and analyze trends about what influences their personal health decisions and behaviors.

What is one pitfall to avoid when teaching the skill of analyzing influences?

Assuming you know the messages that students receive from various sources. Kids are extremely resilient and often have background stories we couldn't even imagine that influence their decisions and relationships.

What advice do you have for other health educators in the field?

Often school health educators are a team of one or two in a school or district. It is important to build a network of colleagues outside of your school or district to work on learning experiences, share ideas, and discuss challenges. There are so many great health educators around us and so many are willing to share and collaborate. The best way to start that networking is through a professional organization such as SHAPE America.

Remember that it's OK to be innovative and try something new. It may bomb the first time around (and maybe even the second and third), but chalk it up to a learning experience. By continually being creative and trying new things, you stay fresh and the kids appreciate that!

In health education, we address personal and sometimes sensitive topics and we have a lot of curriculum to cover in a short time. However, students need a chance to get to know their teacher and the dynamics of their class and classmates. Take the time to build a sense of community and a positive, enriching culture within each class. When students are connected to the class (including the teacher), they learn better. Once the kids are connected with you and each other, let them talk, discuss, and debate. Some of the best and most powerful a-ha moments come for students when they're just chatting about a health topic.

Read professional journals, valid websites, and news sources. Our content area is always changing—there is always new information and studies that our kids may hear about. We need to be well informed. Students (and families) often look to health educators to know it all—there is no way to do that, but we do need to stay informed as much as possible.

KEY POINTS

- Transfer of information is vital and will only happen if it is part of the lesson and students are directed to consider an influence in a variety of contexts.
- The skill of analyzing influences touches both on real-life situations with those around a student as well as what is going on in a student's head.
- Internal influences can be powerful and should be addressed in a thoughtful manner.

It is vital to be supportive of students but also realistic. Telling this student she has bad friends isn't likely to change her behavior. Having the student talk through some of her goals and how smoking marijuana hinders achieving those goals may have a greater impact.

The second piece of this step is to be deliberate in the transfer of the skill across contexts. Remember, the adolescent brain is not built to transfer information, and it needs a lot of support and redirection to solidify a new concept in another context. For example, when talking about how media influence our sleep habits, also point out that media could affect how much physical activity we get, how we talk to our friends and family, or even how we view the school principal.

SUMMARY

The skill of analyzing influences is complex with many moving parts. We are all bombarded by internal, external, positive, and negative influences. This skill has the potential to affect most other skills as classes progress through the National Health Education Standards. Decisions are based on influences, goals are based on feasibility and desire (internally built off the interpretation of influences), and advocacy requires an individual to persuade others and to become an influential voice. The more students can work through this skill in a thoughtful and proactive manner, the more beneficial it will be as they consider the other skills.

Review Questions

1. Why is it important to understand the impact of influences on behavior, values, and norms?

2. What are some strategies to ensure students are able to transfer the skill of analyzing influences across multiple contexts?

3. Discuss which influences seem most important to include in a health education class. Why do you believe this?

To find supplementary materials for this chapter, such as worksheets and extended learning activities, visit the web resource at
www.HumanKinetics.com/TheEssentialsOfTeachingHealthEducation

Photodisc

CHAPTER 6

Interpersonal Communication

Learning Objectives

After reading this chapter, you will be able to do the following:

- Implement all steps of the skill development model for interpersonal communication.
- Describe appropriate student outcomes for interpersonal communication at each developmental level.
- Create high-quality classroom activities for developing interpersonal communication.

Key Terms

conflict resolution

interpersonal communication

listening

negotiation

refusal

self-expression

We interact with people in almost every aspect of our lives: at school, at home, at work, and in the community. Even in a world becoming more and more connected by technology, there will always be times when we must communicate with another person verbally, whether face to face or via another medium, in order to maintain or enhance health. The skill of interpersonal communication focuses on developing effective communicators who can express wants, feelings, and needs; make refusals when appropriate; and listen to others. Effective communication is the foundation of healthy personal relationships and is essential for resolving conflict. Learning to communicate can empower students to find their voice and take control of situations in many areas of their lives. This chapter focuses on helping students develop interpersonal communication skills in face-to-face situations, but much of what it discusses can apply to communication in e-mail, texts, or other non-face-to-face situations. Following are the aspects of interpersonal communication that we address in this chapter:

■ listening (being an active, engaged listener)

■ self-expression (appropriately expressing feelings, wants, and needs)

■ refusal (saying no in a variety of situations)

■ conflict resolution (resolving or avoiding conflict)

■ negotiation (working together to come to an agreement)

As with many of the National Health Education Standards, interpersonal communication connects with other skills. In particular, it relates to decision making, analyzing influences, and advocacy. Although the skills do not have to be taught in any specific order, it is better to teach interpersonal communication before decision making and advocacy but after analyzing influences. This is so students can

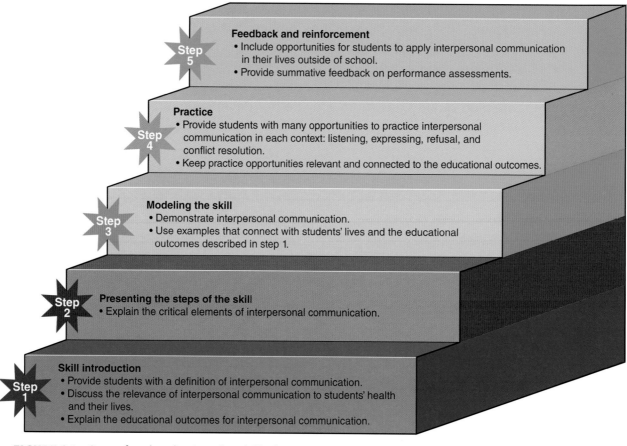

Feedback and reinforcement
• Include opportunities for students to apply interpersonal communication in their lives outside of school.
• Provide summative feedback on performance assessments.

Step 5

Practice
• Provide students with many opportunities to practice interpersonal communication in each context: listening, expressing, refusal, and conflict resolution.
• Keep practice opportunities relevant and connected to the educational outcomes.

Step 4

Modeling the skill
• Demonstrate interpersonal communication.
• Use examples that connect with students' lives and the educational outcomes described in step 1.

Step 3

Presenting the steps of the skill
• Explain the critical elements of interpersonal communication.

Step 2

Skill introduction
• Provide students with a definition of interpersonal communication.
• Discuss the relevance of interpersonal communication to students' health and their lives.
• Explain the educational outcomes for interpersonal communication.

Step 1

FIGURE 6.1 Steps for developing the skill of interpersonal communication.

continue to practice and apply the skill of interpersonal communication in real-life situations in decision-making and advocacy units while also being able to apply the skill of analyzing the influences that might be impacting their interpersonal communication.

For example, during the decision-making unit, students might be asked to make a decision about referring a friend for help because they are worried that their friend has been having a hard time coping with a breakup. This resonates with one student, Taylor, whose friend Maya has seemed sad lately. Taylor is glad for this assignment because she has made the decision to help her friend but is unsure of how to approach her or what to say. During the assignment she learns that writing out what she wants to say and practicing with a trusted adult is a good strategy for preparing to talk to Maya. Because Taylor has participated in the unit on analyzing influences, she realizes that many of her peers feel that the friend in the scenario should just suck it up, but she also knows that because her family values supporting others, she feels compelled to help Maya. Taylor recognizes that the influence of her peers isn't enough to change her mind and she is able to act on behalf of her friend.

This is just one example of how students could apply interpersonal communication within a decision-making unit. There is also a strong connection between interpersonal communication and advocacy—you will be more successful as an advocate if you can communicate your ideas in a way that will persuade others. There are many other examples of how this skill connects with other skills in real-life situations.

Figure 6.1 displays the steps of the skill development model as they apply to communication. Let's take some time to consider how the skill of interpersonal communication is implemented in health education.

STEP 1: SKILL INTRODUCTION

Interpersonal communication is the exchange of information between two or more people. A message is developed and sent by the sender. It is transmitted to, received by, and interpreted by the receiver. This seems relatively simple; however, the process is complex with many opportunities for miscommunication. It is important to clearly define and discuss each part of the exchange early in the unit. Figure 6.2 depicts the communication process.

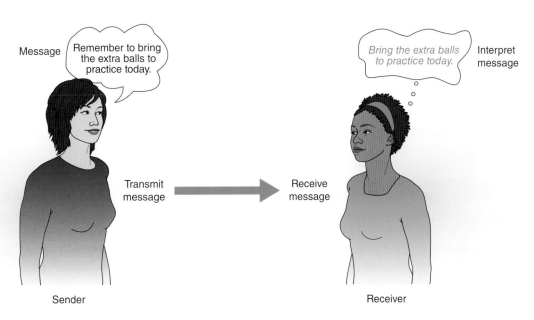

FIGURE 6.2 The process of communication.

Aspects of Communication

As described earlier, this chapter focuses on five main aspects of communication:

- **Listening:** Listening is an interpretive action in which the listener (receiver) attempts to understand and make meaning of the message.
- **Self-expression:** This is the transmission of your thoughts, feelings, needs, wants, or ideas through verbal or nonverbal communication.
- **Refusal:** This is the act of saying or showing that you will not take, do, or give something.
- **Conflict resolution:** This refers to the methods and process of managing a disagreement or conflict in a healthy way.
- **Negotiation:** This is when two or more parties are working to come to agreement on something.

We all have to communicate in some way in order to obtain our wants, address our needs, and share our ideas, feelings, or thoughts. Likewise, we must listen in order to receive messages from a variety of sources. Effective listening, through which we are able to clearly and accurately interpret messages, can help us in many situations and contexts, from absorbing information and advice to understanding someone else's point of view or information about a medical diagnosis.

Self-expression, being able to transmit messages about or from yourself, is critical to navigating life and maintaining and enhancing health. For example, emotional and social health are two dimensions that contribute to overall health and wellness. Being able to express yourself in positive ways can lead to happiness, positive relationships, and less conflict.

Being able to refuse something is important because there are many times when we need to say no to something, whether it's the pressure to drink and drive, to smoke a cigarette, to take drugs, or to be in a sexual relationship. We need to be able to stand up for ourselves in order to stay healthy.

Conflict is inevitable. This is especially relevant when working with adolescents because they are likely to be experiencing conflict with their parents, family, and peers. Students need to be able to implement strategies to avoid conflict as well as to resolve conflict in a healthy manner. This allows them to avoid the negative consequences that can arise from poor conflict resolution or unresolved conflict, such as violence, ending of a friendship or relationship, mental health problems, or consequences with school administration or law enforcement. These are only a few examples of how each aspect of interpersonal communication can affect multiple areas of health and wellness.

Finally, we engage in negotiation throughout the day and with many different people. Whether the negotiation is on the time we have to leave for school, whether or not it is necessary to wear a jacket outside, or the amount of screen time allowed, negotiations are taking place. Negotiation is a method for getting our needs met while recognizing that our needs may conflict with another person's needs or values. Teaching students to proactively negotiate in order to meet their needs allows them to better communicate in a way that will enhance or maintain their health. Because of this, students will need to be reminded as the other aspects (self-expression, refusal, and conflict resolution) are discussed that negotiation does not often stand alone but is an important component in applying each of the other aspects.

Before we move on to other aspects of interpersonal communication, we need to address two premises that set the stage for the rest of the chapter. First is the premise that health is multidimensional. Many resources use the term *dimensions of wellness* to describe this concept. Although various dimensions are used in the literature, commonly accepted ones include social, emotional, intellectual, physical, spiritual, occupational, and environmental. Figure 6.3 presents a brief overview of the dimensions. The dimensions of wellness are covered in more detail in Chapter 9.

Effective communication in particular highlights the nontraditional aspects of health and wellness. For example, communication plays a large part in relationships, which can fall under the social, emotional, and even spiritual dimensions but may not be something that people typically think of when they think about being healthy. In addition, communication plays a role in all dimensions, but its impact on health

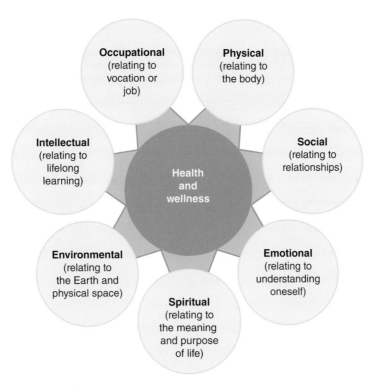

FIGURE 6.3 Dimensions of wellness.

might not be as clear as the impact of healthy eating or exercise. If someone is unhappy at work (occupational health) and he does not feel able to communicate with anyone about the issue, it can lead to unhappiness, stress, anxiety, and other negative consequences. These issues may also physically affect a person's performance or concentration and lead to an accident or injury. These are only two examples that illustrate the importance of viewing health holistically, especially the skill of interpersonal communication.

The second premise is that interpersonal communication will be effective in face-to-face as well as other forms of communication, such as texting, posting to social media, and almost any other form of communication that students might use. However, because students are inundated with technology and often use technology as their primary form of communication, it is critical to help students develop the skills to communicate face to face. Many health decisions, such as engaging in sexual activity, communicating a need for a partner to use protection, visiting a doctor, refusing drugs or alcohol, or telling someone about feelings of

depression, require face-to-face interactions. You will likely find yourself encouraging face-to-face communication as a better way of working through problems and as a way to avoid issues such as misunderstandings based on texts or online posts.

This is not to say that you should avoid addressing current issues such as cyberbullying or digital communication, but rather you should reinforce the importance of effective communication, whether it is in person or through another media, and you should highlight the transferability of skill cues for many forms of communication. It is critical to have open discussions with your students about online media and encourage them to limit or avoid online that make them uncomfortable.

Educational Outcomes

The first step in determining educational outcomes is to examine the performance indicators of standard 4 of the National Health Education Standards (see table 6.1).

Determining educational outcomes for interpersonal communication requires you

TABLE 6.1 Performance Indicators for Standard 4 of the National Health Education Standards

PREK-GRADE 2	GRADES 3-5	GRADES 6-8	GRADES 9-12
4.2.1 Demonstrate healthy ways to express needs, wants, and feelings.	4.5.1 Demonstrate effective verbal and nonverbal communication skills to enhance health.	4.8.1 Apply effective verbal and nonverbal communication skills to enhance health.	4.12.1 Use skills for communicating effectively with family, peers, and others to enhance health.
4.2.2 Demonstrate listening skills to enhance health.	4.5.2 Demonstrate refusal skills that avoid or reduce health risks.	4.8.2 Demonstrate refusal and negotiation skills that avoid or reduce health risks.	4.12.2 Demonstrate refusal, negotiation, and collaboration skills to enhance health and avoid or reduce health risks.
4.2.3 Demonstrate ways to respond in an unwanted, threatening, or dangerous situation.	4.5.3 Demonstrate nonviolent strategies to manage or resolve conflict.	4.8.3 Demonstrate effective conflict management or resolution strategies.	4.12.3 Demonstrate strategies to prevent, manage, or resolve interpersonal conflicts without harming self or others.
4.2.4 Demonstrate ways to tell a trusted adult if threatened or harmed.	4.5.4 Demonstrate how to ask for assistance to enhance personal health.	4.8.4 Demonstrate how to ask for assistance to enhance the health of self and others.	4.12.4 Demonstrate how to ask for and offer assistance to enhance the health of self and others.

to examine the performance indicators along with the aspects of communication and determine what the focus of the interpersonal communication unit will be. The following section highlights some considerations when determining educational outcomes.

Step 1: Choosing Indicators

Many of the indicators are complex and involve multiple aspects of interpersonal communication. For example, 4.8.2 involves both refusal and negotiation skills, each of which is a significant skill on its own and could be addressed in multiple contexts. Additionally, in the upper grades, listening is not listed as an indicator, and self-expression, though seemingly addressed in 4.12.1 (effectively using communication skills) and 4.12.4 (offering and asking for assistance), would need to be more explicit. For instance, communicating a need to your family may be different than communicating an idea to a friend.

You are planning your fifth-grade interpersonal communication unit. You start by looking at the performance indicators. Your school has been dealing with an increase in fights on campus. Therefore, you

feel that the most relevant performance indicators are 4.5.1, because it will help more students avoid conflict, and 4.5.3, because it will help them resolve any conflicts that do arise.

Step 2: Coverage of Indicators

Once you have chosen indicators, the next decision is the extent to which you will cover the indicators. Questions to ask include the following: How much time can I dedicate to the unit? Have aspects of the performance indicator been covered in previous years? Do students have specific needs that should be addressed? Remember, these decisions are unique to the situation. Coverage can look different in every school and every district. As long as efforts are made to cover all indicators within the grade spans, make thoughtful and deliberate decisions, and progress skills appropriately, the final decision is up to the teachers and administration about how best to address the performance indicators.

You choose 4.5.1 and 4.5.3 as indicators for the unit. You decide that because of the issues in your school you will dedicate more time for this unit, extending it an additional four lessons so that you can adequately cover both indicators completely. You feel it is worth spending the most time in your curriculum on this unit because it is relevant and directly addresses a need in your community.

Step 3: Student-Appropriate Terms

Although we recommend posting the National Standards in your classroom, it is also important that students understand the terms used to describe the skill and educational outcomes. You must decide whether or not to modify the language in order to meet the needs of your students.

You decide that it is important that students know all the terms in the performance indicators even though some may be unfamiliar at first. Additional time is spent at the beginning of the unit ensuring that students are familiar with the terms before moving on to other steps of the skill.

Step 4: Educational Outcomes

The final versions of the performance indicators, resulting from the work in the previous steps, are the educational outcomes for the unit. The following scenario demonstrates how step 1 of the skill development model might look in the classroom for interpersonal communication.

Step 1 in the Classroom: Skill Introduction

Scenario A: PreK to Grade 2

You have decided to focus on objectives 4.2.1 (self-expression) and 4.2.2 (listening) in the interpersonal communication unit for grade 2. On the first day of the unit, you know that you need to get your students interested in the skill. In addition, your school is focusing on literacy initiatives and your students enjoy listening and discussing books, so you decide to read a story that involves characters who are trying to communicate effectively with one another. After reading the book, you lead your students in a discussion relating to the educational outcomes of listening and self-expression. Then students make costumes, dress up as the characters, and act out positive ways to communicate based on the stories. Finally, you wrap up by telling the students that, like the characters in the story, they will be learning how to communicate with other people and how to listen to other people. You present the specific educational outcomes and lead a review of what the students learned from the book and activities.

Scenario B: Grades 9 to 12

You have decided to focus on 4.12.1 (effective communication) in your ninth-grade unit on interpersonal communication. You know that there will be more emphasis on refusal skills, conflict resolution, and negotiation in grade 10, and you believe that if students can communicate effectively, they can avoid or reduce conflict. Your students are very connected to technology and social media, and they are constantly discussing celebrities and popular culture. You think that the best way to engage the students is to show them examples of interpersonal communication from Instagram, Vine, Twitter, and Pheed. You will focus on face-to-face communication in the unit but engage students during the first lesson by hooking them with both positive and negative examples from social media and other forms of online communication used by students. You show several examples, leading students in a discussion about effective and ineffective communication. Then you ask students to think about a time when they effectively or ineffectively communicated with someone in their lives. The discussion centers on consequences of both effective and ineffective communication and why it is important for ninth graders to be able to communicate well. The lesson concludes with an explanation of the educational outcomes for the upcoming unit.

KEY POINTS

■ Interpersonal communication is an exchange of information between two or more people. It includes a sender, a message, and a receiver.

■ Interpersonal communication includes listening, self-expression, refusal, conflict resolution, and negotiation.

■ Interpersonal communication occurs in many areas of life, including home, school, work, and community, and it relates to many dimensions of wellness.

STEP 2: PRESENTING THE STEPS OF THE SKILL

After introducing the skill, the next step is to present the parts of the skill, the critical pieces that students need to be able to do in order to meet the educational outcomes. Table 6.2 provides sample skill cues for interpersonal communication at varying developmental levels.

The focus of step 2 is to present the steps of the skill so that students know exactly what

TABLE 6.2 Skill Cues for Interpersonal Communication

PREK-GRADE 2	

Focus: Listening and expressing feelings	• Effective communication
	  I TELL
	  Identify feelings (thoughts, ideas)
	  Tell feelings (thoughts, ideas)
	  Express using I-statements
	  Look at the person you are talking to
	  Listen to the response
	• Active listening
	  HEAR
	  Heads up, voices off
	  Eyes on speaker, **E**ars open
	  Ask questions if you don't understand
	  Relax bodies (hands and feet still)

GRADES 3-5	

Focus: Increasing the complexity of self-expression; introducing nonverbal communication, refusal, negotiation, and conflict resolution	• Effective verbal communication
	  I TELL YA
	  Identify feelings (thoughts, ideas)
	  Tell feelings (thoughts, ideas)
	  Express using I-statements
	  Look at the person you are talking to
	  Listen to the response
	  Your body language is appropriate
	  Assertive communication style
	• Effective nonverbal communication
	  FACE
	  Facial expressions and body language
	  Attentive
	  Comfortable and confident
	  Eyes on speaker
	• Refusal*
	  I SAY NO
	  I-statement
	  State a reason
	  Assertive
	  You are in control
	  No statement that is clear
	  Options (e.g., you can leave, get help)
	• Conflict resolution*
	  I'M MAD
	  I-statements
	  Manage stress
	  Mutual conversation
	  Focus on **A**ction, not person ("I'm not mad at *you*, I'm mad at what you *did*.")
	  Discuss feelings and negotiate a solution together

GRADES 6-8

Focus: Continuing to advance and expand self-expression and conflict resolution
(Note: FACE and I SAY NO are appropriate for this age group as well.)
	• Effective verbal communication
	    I TELL YOU
	    Identify feelings (thoughts, ideas)
	    Tell feelings (thoughts, ideas)
	    Express using I-statements
	    Look at the person (people) you are speaking to
	    Listen to the response
	    Your body language is appropriate
	    Open mind
	    Use assertive communication style
	• Conflict resolution
	    CONFLICT*
	    Calm attitude, manage stress
	    Open to opposing views
	    Never make assumptions about what the other person (party) is thinking or feeling
	    Focus on action, not person ("I'm not mad at *you*, I'm mad at what you *did*.")
	    Look for other options
	    I-statements
	    Compromise (Negotiate a solution.)
	    Teamwork (Make the decision together.)
	• Negotiation
	    SLIDE
	    State what you want/need
	    Listen and clarify
	    Identify with other perspectives
	    Determine common ground
	    Elicit agreement

GRADES 9-12

Focus: Advancing conflict resolution and practicing other skills	• Conflict resolution
	    CONFLICTTS*
	    Calm attitude, manage stress
	    Open to opposing views
	    Never make assumptions about what the other person (party) is thinking or feeling
	    Focus on action, not person ("I'm not mad at *you*, I'm mad at what you *did*.")
	    Look for other options
	    I-statements
	    Compromise (Negotiate a solution.)
	    Teamwork (Make the decision together.)
	    Timing (Conflict resolution needs the correct timing and environment to be discussed well; using technology might not be appropriate.)
	    Setting (What is the appropriate setting to work through the conflict? At home? With parents? With school support? Online forums are not appropriate.)
	• Negotiation
	    SLIDE
	    State what you want/need
	    Listen and clarify
	    Identify with other perspectives
	    Determine common ground
	    Elicit agreement

*All skill cues can be applied in technology contexts.

KEY POINTS

- Skill cues should be generated for any aspects of interpersonal communication that you are going to address in the unit.
- Skill cues should be applied in varying contexts, such as home, school, work, and community.
- Emphasize participatory methods during step 2.

they need to do in order to perform the skill. Emphasize the skill cues by using examples that are relatable and relevant to the students. The following scenario provides some examples of ways to address step 2 in the classroom.

Step 2 in the Classroom: Presenting the Steps of the Skill

PreK to Grade 2

Begin this step by asking students, "What do we need to do when we listen?" Students at this age have likely discussed how to listen, and it will be helpful to use this activity as a preassessment to determine what the students already know and also how to relate what they already know to support the skill cues. After soliciting student ideas, use visual aids to explain the skill cues for listening (HEAR). Explain each cue while referencing how the visual connects with the cue. After explaining, ask students to demonstrate what listening looks like. You can use a similar approach to teach I TELL, but you can begin practicing the skill of listening by reminding students about the HEAR expectations and having them practice during the discussion of expressing feelings. During the discussion use examples related to how listening connects to health.

Grades 3 to 5

In these grades, students are beginning to develop problem-solving skills and work more independently. An engaging way to introduce students to the skill cues is to create an activity in which students are given just the acronym for the skill (e.g., just I'm MAD on a piece of paper). You've already placed the skill cues around the classroom, and you've prepared a color scheme where each group has its own color of paper so that groups can work simultaneously. The students find all their cues for the skill and then put them in order. Once they're done, they check with you. When you confirm that the skill cues are correct, the students attach the cues they collected on a large poster that they decorate and then hang in the classroom or around the school. After the activity is complete, you debrief the activity by discussing the skills and skill cues and answering any questions.

Grades 6 to 8

To teach the skill cues in grades 6 through 8, it can be helpful to use students' experiences and access their knowledge. You can provide the students with just the acronym and ask students to create the skill cues that fit with each letter. Once groups have completed the work on their own, bring them together to share ideas and come to a consensus. If students are able to identify key aspects of the skill, even if the language is different than what you intended, it would be empowering to use the students' language in the final version, which you can then post and use for the remainder of the course.

Grades 9 to 12

By grades 9 to 12, students should be familiar with the skill cues because they have seen them many times over the years. Therefore, it is appropriate to use this step as a review or preassessment by asking students to list the skill cues for the various aspects of interpersonal communication. This could be done as a large group or within small groups depending on the students and the amount of scaffolding needed. (If more scaffolding is needed, use a large group so that you can lead the discussion.) Once you've reviewed the previous skill cues, you introduce the next skill cue, which represents a more sophisticated skill application.

STEP 3: MODELING THE SKILL

Step 3 is where you facilitate opportunities for students to observe the skill of interpersonal communication being applied effectively. This should include modeling the skill, which fulfills the educational objectives determined in step 1. It is important to model the skills using examples that students can connect with—relevant examples are critical to students' skill development. Following are some examples of modeling activities.

KEY POINT

Modeling is an important part of the skill development process. This is the time to ensure that students have observed the skill being performed correctly in health-related situations that are relevant and meaningful to the students. You can incorporate other strategies that are not all demonstration, but at least one activity must involve students observing people effectively communicating.

PreK to Grade 2

- Students watch examples of TV characters using effective communication skills in a health-related situation relevant to students (e.g., asking a parent to buy a fruit or vegetable, telling a parent about something that is upsetting, telling a friend they are mad).

- Students observe a role-play that demonstrates effective communication in relevant health-related situations.

- Students listen to communication scenarios and identify which ones are effective and which are ineffective. All examples should relate to health situations with a focus on expressing feelings, wants, and needs or handling an unwanted situation (e.g., inappropriate touching is an important topic for young students and would be good for examples relating to communication).

- Students listen to a story in which the characters use effective communication. (Many stories are available related to friendship, going to a doctor, and so on.)

Grades 3 to 5

- Students volunteer to present role-plays, with the teacher modeling effective communication in health-related situations that students choose independently or from a list of options.

- Students from upper grades come to class to model effective communication. (This could also be an opportunity for students in upper grades to apply the skill.)

- Students watch appropriate clips from popular TV that show effective communication in situations dealing with peer pressure, drugs and alcohol, relationships, or other health issues.

Grades 6 to 8

- After collaborating with the English teacher, the students read a play or novel that involves interpersonal communication in a friendship, parent–child relationship, or romantic relationship. The communication examples can be examined or acted out in class.

- Students fill out a worksheet or script (created by the teacher) with examples of effective communication. They then share their work with the large group, reviewing effective skill application.

Grades 9 to 12

- Students use the Internet (if school policy allows) to find examples of effective communication related to a variety of health contexts. Students justify to the class how the examples demonstrate effective communication.

- Students are given examples of effective and ineffective communication within multiple domains of health. The students need to evaluate the examples to determine which are effective or ineffective and prepare to justify their evaluations.

STEP 4: PRACTICE

During step 4, students must practice the skill, ideally for as much time as needed in order to develop proficiency, in varied contexts. Educational theory suggests that multiple practice opportunities across varying contexts will improve transfer (Bransford, Brown, & Cocking, 2000). This section provides considerations and examples for practicing each aspect of interpersonal communication within multiple domains of health. As with modeling, remember that it is vital to make practice opportunities relevant to students.

TEACHING INTERPERSONAL COMMUNICATION

Jeff Bartlett

Holten Richmond Middle School, Danvers Public Schools, Danvers, Massachusetts

What is your best strategy for teaching interpersonal communication?

I use an activity where students can receive feedback multiple times before presenting an interpersonal communication role-play to the class. After spending class time going through the process of teaching interpersonal communication skills, students develop a script in groups, using a skills-based rubric as their guide. Students then practice their role-play and engage in a self-assessment based on their rubric. Next, I have groups rotate to other groups so they are presenting their role-play to the other groups in the class one on one, and they evaluate the presenters using the rubric, too. Every group then goes back and reworks their script, adding and clarifying as needed. I'll cycle through all the groups during these activities and provide feedback as needed. By allowing students to evaluate their peers, students become experts at identifying the interpersonal communication skill being taught. It also helps them further develop and strengthen their own role-plays.

What is one pitfall to avoid when teaching interpersonal communication?

With interpersonal communication skills, it's important to account for cultural differences among students. A pitfall to avoid would be to remain ignorant about different cultural norms regarding communication. By working with students, a teacher can find ways to still accomplish the interpersonal communication skill objectives by infusing aspects of other cultures.

What advice do you have for other health educators in the field?

It's vital to stay involved professionally, either through state organizations, national organizations such as SHAPE America, or by collaborating with other health educators online through social media. With technology today, professional development and ongoing professional dialogue can occur 24/7. By reaching out to other health educators, everyone works together to bring the field of health education to the highest level possible for teachers and students.

Listening

Listening is a critical part of the communication process. If we don't listen well, we might miss the message, misinterpret the message, or not communicate at all. Being an active, engaged listener takes practice. There are two main components to focus on when providing students with practice opportunities. The first is the ability to perform the skill cues. The second is the listener's ability to receive and correctly interpret meaning and to identify key aspects of the message. Increasing students' ability to listen will benefit them in many aspects of their lives. The following scenario illustrates a practice activity that could be modified for any grade level.

The teacher reviews the skill cues for listening before beginning the activity. Students are put into groups of three. One person in the group is the speaker, one is the listener, and one is the observer. The speaker speaks about a topic for two minutes. The listener's job is to listen by applying the skill cues. The observer has an observation form that includes the skill cues for listening. The observer is watching the interaction, trying to determine which skill cues are demonstrated by the listener and other notes about the interaction. After the two minutes, the listener tells the speaker what the main messages were. Then the speaker and listener discuss the interaction. Did the listener correctly interpret the speaker's message? Did the speaker feel that the listener was listening? Finally, the observer should discuss the observations. The group then rotates roles. Each person should have an opportunity to be in each role. You debrief the activity and discuss how listening relates to health.

Self-Expression

Self-expression is a broad term that relates to many areas of life. We often need to be able to express ourselves to maintain or enhance our health. Examples include telling people you love them, discussing sexual activity and relationship boundaries, discussing time management strategies, sharing your fitness goals with others, telling a doctor you are uncomfortable with a certain treatment option, telling a trusted adult you feel afraid for your safety while on the bus, or explaining to a waiter at a restaurant that you have a food allergy. Therefore, self-expression is an aspect of interpersonal communication that might require more practice time in many situations. For example, Logan wants to seek help for the feelings of depression he has been experiencing. Telling his parents might be different than telling his friend and different still from telling the school counselor or a licensed medical professional. Theoretically, these are four practice situations for one example of self-expression.

It isn't practical to try to cover every possible situation, but it is important to provide varied practice opportunities across multiple dimen-

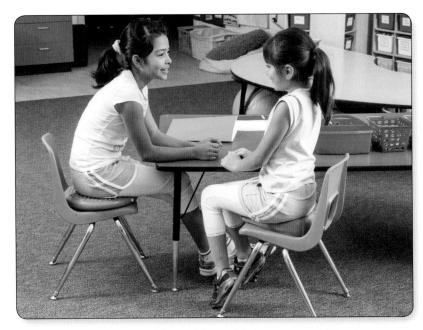

Students who are provided with multiple opportunities to practice effective communication will be better prepared to apply this skill in their lives.

sions. It may be helpful to ask students which types of communication they need the most support with or to focus on areas that you notice need to be addressed based on your knowledge of your students. The more opportunities you can create that directly meet the needs of students, the more likely the information will be lasting, relevant, and personalized and will be applied outside the classroom. The following scenario illustrates an activity that could be used at any level with appropriate modifications.

You create a version of the following worksheet:

SELECT *ONE* OPTION FROM THIS COLUMN.	WRITE A HEALTH-RELATED WANT, NEED, FEELING, OR THOUGHT.	WRITE THE PERSON YOU WILL TELL THIS INFORMATION TO.	WHERE WILL YOU TELL THE PERSON THE INFORMATION?
I . . .	What?	Whom will I tell?	Where?
Want Need Feel Think			
Write a brief role-play about the conversation. Try to be as realistic as possible.			

Allow students time to complete the worksheet individually, in partners, or in small groups. Once they have completed the worksheet, students have the opportunity to act out their role-play and receive feedback. This could be peer feedback (using a rubric), teacher feedback, or self-reflection. It is also important to help students understand how various audiences might receive their message. Provide opportunity for self-reflection as well as group discussion about how to communicate messages in ways that minimize the chance for miscommunication or misinterpretation.

Refusal

As with self-expression, there are many situations in which we might have to refuse something. The focus of refusal should be on helping students build self-efficacy (chapter 2) around saying no and discussing outcome expectations (chapter 2). This gives students the opportunity to prepare for the consequences (positive or negative) when they need to make a refusal and build the confidence to say *no*. Students need to practice and to receive feedback on saying no in an effective way (using the skill cues). Effective refusals might not always feel natural and might not use realistic language that students would use among their peers. However, it is important that, in the context of skill development in the classroom, students practice making a clear, concise refusal. You should discuss outcome expectations (what they want to happen because of their refusal versus what might actually happen) and encourage open dialogue about the challenges of implementing effective refusals in real-life situations.

Keep in mind that, as the prefrontal cortex (responsible for judgment and impulse control) develops, especially during adolescence, students are less likely to make well-reasoned decisions. Add the fact that adolescents are heavily influenced by their peers, and you have an equation for risky behaviors. Given this, it is critical that students practice and develop their self-efficacy in making an effective, concise refusal that uses the skill cues. It is better to have students say an awkward but effective refusal than to allow them to modify and possibly weaken their refusal because it is more realistic.

Your job is to ensure that students can apply the skill of refusal effectively. If you offer real-life, relevant situations, your students should gain the confidence to make effective refusals

without having to modify them. Once they have confidence saying an effective refusal, they can then modify their refusals as needed in their own lives.

The following scenario illustrates an activity for practicing refusals in the classroom. The activity can be modified as appropriate.

Students develop a real-life example of a situation in which a refusal is the healthiest choice. Another group of students is given the scenario and creates a role-play that includes the key components of an effective refusal and continues to play out past the refusal (don't have students stop at the refusal; ask them to think about what would happen in the scene once the effective refusal is delivered). The group then acts out the role-play. The most important piece is having students practice the refusals and receive feedback. In this instance, it would be important for students to receive structured feedback from you or a peer.

Conflict Resolution

Though this aspect of interpersonal communication is conflict *resolution*, it is also important to emphasize how to communicate to avoid conflict. The focus of conflict resolution is managing a situation once it is occurring using effective communication. Conflict usually involves heightened emotions, so conflict resolution requires analysis of emotions and how they might affect the situation (as well as how to manage those emotions during the conflict). Developing empathy can also help during conflicts because being able to put yourself into someone's shoes may help diffuse your emotions when conflicts arise. Empathy should be addressed during any conflict resolution unit. It is also important to help students see the bigger picture by analyzing the situation to determine why the conflict arose in the first place as well as steps to take after the immediate problem is resolved. The following scenario provides an activity that can be used in the classroom (modify as necessary).

A group of students develops a realistic, relevant example of a common conflict that people their age might face. Another group receives the scenario. The groups must accomplish two tasks: Identify ways that this conflict might have been avoided in the first place, and create a role-play in which the students apply the skill cues to resolve the conflict. The role-play can then be performed by the groups or the written script could be evaluated by another group for demonstration of the skill cues. The group receives revisions and feedback, and finally the role-play is performed. It is important that the students perform the role-play because writing a script is not the same as demonstrating the skill cues for communication.

Negotiation

This aspect of interpersonal communication is focused on helping students to better understand how to ask for what they need. While negotiation is often a necessary part of conflict resolution, because we must be flexible in understanding the other person's point of view, it is also a key part of refusal since there are times that a negotiation either fails or isn't appropriate and either a direct refusal or self-expression is necessary. When we express ourselves we must do so in a way that aligns with our values and beliefs while also understanding that another's values and beliefs may be different than our own.

As with self-expression, it is unreasonable to identify every possible scenario where negotiation may need to take place. This is why there are no specific skill cues noted for negotiation. Rather, we suggest integrating into discussions the concept of negotiation and the value of effective communication. Students must understand that while negotiation strategies are an important (and often effective) tool for helping to ensure that our needs are met, we should never negotiate in an instance related to our personal safety or well-being. For example, it would be inappropriate to negotiate in a situation where a student is being bullied, a partner or friend is being physically or verbally abusive,

or the negotiation would result in further harm. Negotiation is appropriate in situations of disagreement or when both parties maintain equal standing or power in the negotiation and are looking for an alternative to the issue at hand. Examples include negotiating alternatives to avoid texting while driving, setting boundaries on how social media is used between friends, or discussing with a trusted adult strategies to get more sleep while balancing current obligations. The following scenario illustrates an activity for practicing negotiation in the classroom. The activity can be modified as appropriate.

Students watch a video where two students are negotiating the boundaries in their relationship. After watching the video, ask students to partner up and write down strategies used by the characters that were effective and those that seemed less effective to achieve a healthy outcome. Ask the pairs to report to the class and use the responses to highlight effective strategies versus less effective or harmful strategies. Use this as a time to also discuss how negotiation fits with other components of interpersonal communication and when negotiation may be appropriate.

STEP 5: FEEDBACK AND REINFORCEMENT

In the final step, students should receive feedback on an assessment that requires demonstration of the educational objectives that were established in step 1. It is vital to evaluate students *demonstrating* the skill of interpersonal communication. Keep in mind that if one educational objective relates to making an appropriate refusal and you ask students to perform a role-play, only the person who actually makes the refusal can be evaluated for the educational objective. The other students have only watched the refusal occur; they have not demonstrated their own ability to make a refusal. This may bring up logistical concerns related to ensuring all students have an opportunity to demonstrate the skill, but with planning, technology, and creativity, you can create assessments that allow all students to demonstrate their ability to meet the educational objectives.

There are many ways to reinforce this skill both in and out of the classroom. For example, once you have covered effective communication and created a scoring rubric to assess proficiency, you could then use the same rubric any time students are doing a presentation regardless of the topic. Collaboration with other teachers would allow a single rubric to be used across classes and provide consistency for students. Outside the classroom, you can assign homework in which interactions with others need to be recorded, evaluated by family members, or reflected on by students. You need to help students see the connection between what they are doing in the classroom and the communication occurring in their lives through both relevant classroom activities and hands-on practical application outside the classroom.

SUMMARY

Interpersonal communication is a dynamic skill that is critical for maintaining and enhancing health. It involves the exchange of information between two or more people. During communication there is a sender, a message, and a receiver. No matter what the form (e.g., face to face, via phone, via computer), these three elements are involved. Within this broad definition of interpersonal communication, there are five aspects: listening, self-expression, refusal, conflict resolution, and negotiation.

When developing interpersonal communication in the classroom, you must present skill cues clearly and model effective application of the skill. Practice opportunities should involve all aspects of the skill (listening, self-expression, refusal, and conflict resolution), should be examined from the point of view of the sender and the receiver, should be performed in a variety of health-related contexts (home, school, work, community), and should be reinforced in other classes and outside school. Finally, you should provide immediate, specific, and appropriate feedback during development of the skill and in a final evaluation.

Review Questions

1. What is the definition of *interpersonal communication*?

2. List and define the five aspects of interpersonal communication.

3. How do the skill cues for interpersonal communication advance through the grade levels?

4. How does interpersonal communication affect health?

To find supplementary materials for this chapter, such as worksheets and extended learning activities, visit the web resource at
www.HumanKinetics.com/TheEssentialsOfTeachingHealthEducation

Three Rocksimages/fotolia.com

CHAPTER 7

Decision Making

Learning Objectives

After reading this chapter, you will be able to do the following:

- Implement all steps of the skill development model for decision making.
- Describe appropriate student outcomes for decision making at each developmental level.
- Create high-quality classroom activities for developing the skill of decision making.

Key Terms

data-driven approach

decision making

values

From the moment we wake up, whether consciously or unconsciously, we are making decisions. Should we floss our teeth? What should we eat for breakfast? (Is there time to eat breakfast?) What should we wear? Even the way we choose to talk to the people around us is a decision. Although we are continually making decisions (some thoughtful, some less so), the process to get from "What should I do?" (contemplation) to "How did that work out for me?" (evaluation and reflection) is rarely considered. Even when facing a big decision that requires thoughtful consideration, most people instinctively jump straight to the final choice without considering the pros and cons or how the outcome of the decision may affect other aspects of their life.

This scenario is precisely why the National Health Education Standards include **decision making** as one of the key skills students must learn in order to be healthy and advance their health literacy. The skill is fairly straightforward and relies on using a defined set of steps to move from identifying whether or not a decision needs to be made to evaluating the outcome of the decision and whether or not the chosen strategy was effective for the identified health-related situation. The skill of decision making is also prominent outside of health, especially in today's world where data-driven decision making is commonly used in fields from education to business. However, even if it is covered in other classes, decision making must be covered in the health education classroom as well. The process of making decisions in other contexts is similar, but students must practice decision making specifically within in the context of health in order to achieve proficiency in making health-enhancing decisions. In addition, decision making in health education supports a **data-driven approach**—students must use some form of evidence when weighing pros and cons and thinking about the consequences of a decision.

Another benefit of including decision making in a health education curriculum is that students spend time thinking about some health-related decisions that they make every day, some that they only make occasionally, and some they may not have faced yet. This helps prepare students not only for decisions they have to make in the present but also ones that

they may face in the future. In health class, students have the opportunity to practice the decision-making process and reflect on what those decisions mean for their health. Similar to analyzing influences on health behaviors, much of what occurs in our daily lives is automatic, and we must make an effort to thoughtfully reflect on the impact of decision making, thereby increasing our awareness of it.

Although specific performance indicators have been identified (as discussed later in the chapter), it is important to complement other school efforts to get students to proactively consider their decisions. This is not a one-sized or prescriptive skill. Many decision-making models exist, and many contain elements that are similar to the National Standards. The key takeaway for students in a health education course is that they become proficient in recognizing when to be thoughtful about health-related decisions, why it is important to do so, and how to work through a health-related decision in a way that leads to a health-enhancing outcome. This last step is crucial—we don't just want students who can make a decision if that decision is detrimental to their health. We must encourage our students to go one step further toward maintaining or enhancing their health through the decisions they make. Figure 7.1 presents the steps of the skill development model for this chapter.

STEP 1: SKILL INTRODUCTION

Decision making is a higher-order skill and is the process by which a person thoughtfully proceeds through a series of steps in order to "identify, implement, and sustain health-enhancing behaviors" (Joint Committee, 2007). The performance indicators for this skill move students beyond identifying a decision to be made and ask them to analyze, predict, and distinguish various aspects of making a decision. Finally, students are asked to evaluate the effectiveness of the decision. To apply the steps contained within the skill of decision making, students must already know some basic principles of health education, including how to analyze influences on themselves and others, how to find valid and reliable information, products, and services how to communicate with others during the decision-making process, and how

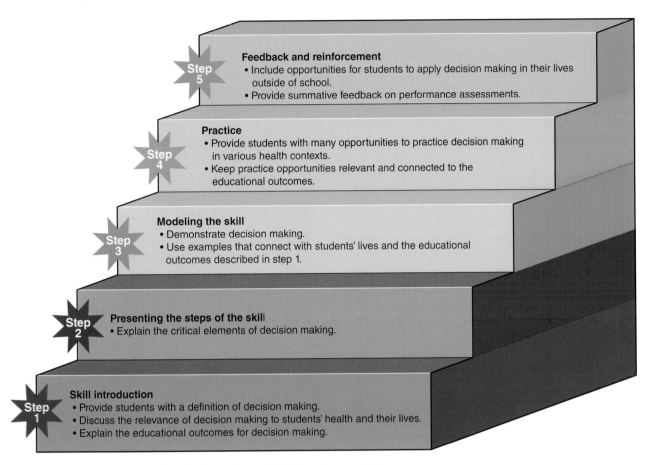

Step 5
Feedback and reinforcement
• Include opportunities for students to apply decision making in their lives outside of school.
• Provide summative feedback on performance assessments.

Step 4
Practice
• Provide students with many opportunities to practice decision making in various health contexts.
• Keep practice opportunities relevant and connected to the educational outcomes.

Step 3
Modeling the skill
• Demonstrate decision making.
• Use examples that connect with students' lives and the educational outcomes described in step 1.

Step 2
Presenting the steps of the skill
• Explain the critical elements of decision making.

Step 1
Skill introduction
• Provide students with a definition of decision making.
• Discuss the relevance of decision making to students' health and their lives.
• Explain the educational outcomes for decision making.

FIGURE 7.1 Steps for developing the skill of decision making.

to convey their intentions to others and stand by their decisions. After learning this skill, students will be able to use a decision-making process to support other skills. For example, decision making supports advocacy because students must make decisions about causes worth advocating for.

Decision making encompasses many dimensions of wellness and occurs regularly in multiple contexts, so the decision-making unit could include many health topics. For example, topics could include the top six health risk behaviors identified by the CDC—unhealthy dietary behaviors, physical inactivity, injuries and violence, sexual behaviors, alcohol and other drug use, and tobacco use. Many decisions need to be made in order to maintain and enhance health within these risk areas. Specifically, students must decide if the decision will increase their risk of a negative outcome or will help them avoid or reduce the specific risk. For example, will a student who needs to get home choose to

accept a ride from a friend who has been drinking, or will she find another way home? Will a student who is in an argument with a friend choose to throw a punch out of frustration, or will he use conflict resolution to work through the problem? Since these are only some of the many topics that could be used as relevant and meaningful context for developing decision making, you should determine the topics most relevant and meaningful to your students.

Educational Outcomes

Similar to the skill of analyzing influences, decision making is personal. Your role as the health educator is to provide a foundation for your students' success. In this case introduce the steps (procedural knowledge) of a decision-making model and give students time to practice working through health-enhancing decisions. In the lower grades, students begin by thinking about situations where they need to make decisions that affect their health (such as wearing knee pads while skating, choosing water over juice, or answering the door without an adult present) and then considering when they could make those decisions on their own and when they would need to ask for help. Up until this point in their lives, it is possible that no one has ever asked them to consider why they make a decision, let alone how that decision could have an impact beyond the immediate moment. Once students move into the later grades, they are asked to identify the decision (such as whether to add protein powder to their diet, whether sunscreen is important, or whether it's worth trying out for a sport team they are interested in) and then take it further by considering potential options for the decision, predicting future effects of the deci-sion on their health, and defending why their choice is a healthy one. The high school level includes a final step where students evaluate the effectiveness of their decision. They must be able to reflect on the decision they made and explain whether it had a positive, negative, or neutral effect on their health.

Although the performance indicators for this skill are relatively straightforward (see table 7.1), following are a few considerations.

Step 1: Choosing Indicators

Unlike skills where students are able to work through some of the performance indicators on their own, this standard requires students to demonstrate all of the performance indicators in a sequential order for the same decision.

TABLE 7.1 Performance Indicators for Standard 5 of the National Health Education Standards

PREK-GRADE 2	GRADES 3-5	GRADES 6-8	GRADES 9-12
5.2.1 Identify situations when a health-related decision is needed. 5.2.2 Differentiate between situations when a health-related decision can be made individually or when assistance is needed	5.5.1 Identify health-related situations that might require a thoughtful decision. 5.5.2 Analyze when assistance is needed in making a health-related decision. 5.5.3 List healthy options to health-related issues or problems. 5.5.4 Predict the potential outcomes of each option when making a health-related decision. 5.5.5 Choose a healthy option when making a decision. 5.5.6 Describe the outcomes of a health-related decision.	5.8.1 Identify circumstances that can help or hinder healthy decision making. 5.8.2 Determine when health-related situations require the application of a thoughtful decision-making process. 5.8.3 Distinguish when individual or collaborative decision making is appropriate. 5.8.4 Distinguish between healthy and unhealthy alternatives to health-related issues or problems. 5.8.5 Predict the potential short-term impact of each alternative on self and others. 5.8.6 Choose healthy alternatives over unhealthy alternatives when making a decision. 5.8.7 Analyze the outcomes of a health-related decision.	5.12.1 Examine barriers that can hinder healthy decision making. 5.12.2 Determine the value of applying a thoughtful decision-making process in health-related situations. 5.12.3 Justify when individual or collaborative decision making is appropriate. 5.12.4 Generate alternatives to health-related issues or problems. 5.12.5 Predict the potential short-term and long-term impact of each alternative on self and others. 5.12.6 Defend the healthy choice when making decisions. 5.12.7 Evaluate the effectiveness of health-related decisions.

Because of this, you should present the performance indicators as a group and then discuss them individually to explain what each indicator anticipates that students should be able to do at the end of the unit. If decision making has been taught in a previous grade within the grade span, reinforce what was discussed previously and encourage students to go deeper in their exploration of health-enhancing decisions or to tackle a harder decision they may face. For example, if a student previously decided to wear a helmet while skiing, now the student could compare brands of helmets to find one that would best meet her needs, including an analysis of factors such as size, price, and protection factor.

As noted previously, if you are using a specific decision-making model throughout the school or district, the skill cues in this chapter (discussed in step 2) may be replaced with the steps of the schoolwide model. Within the health classroom, the schoolwide model is then used to discuss health-related decisions and students use that model to make decisions. It is more important for students to have a consistent decision-making process that they can transfer to multiple areas of their life than it is to use a specific approach. The following is an example of choosing performance indicators for a unit.

You are teaching decision making in your fourth-grade classroom. The performance indicators need to be included in the unit as a group, so you choose 5.5.1 through 5.5.6. As you consider this unit, you realize that this is an area of need because the students haven't had formal health education in their previous years of schooling. Therefore, you decide to make this unit longer than other units and include decision making in a variety of health-related areas, specifically nutrition, tobacco, drugs and alcohol, and puberty.

Step 2: Coverage of Indicators

Because the skill of decision making is a sum of the parts (i.e., each performance indicator is a necessary component of the skill), all of the performance indicators must be included in an overall assessment to determine students' level of proficiency. Given this, students must learn about each performance indicator and have sufficient time to understand and complete the task required.

You recognize that not only do all of the performance indicators need to be included, but also each indicator needs to be covered in its entirety. You also realize that you will have to cover each indicator within each topic area in the unit. This confirms for you that decision making will be a long unit, and you plan other units accordingly.

Step 3: Student-Appropriate Terms

Many of the terms used within the decision-making steps will be familiar to students. However, as you review each performance indicator, check for understanding and provide examples as appropriate.

You use the performance indicators as written in the National Standards for the educational outcomes for the fourth-grade unit. You post the educational objectives in the room for students to reference during the unit.

Step 4: Educational Outcomes

The educational outcomes for decision making are likely going to be the performance indicators with little to no modifications necessary. You may add other outcomes, but the primary outcomes are directly related to the appropriate demonstration of a decision-making model as included in the performance indicators.

The following scenarios demonstrate how step 1 of the skill development model may look in the classroom for decision making. The two examples show how educators at all levels can implement participatory methods to address step 1 in one lesson. Although presented here as a single lesson, actual implementation time for step 1 may vary based on the length of your class period, student learning needs, or types of activities used.

Step 1 in the Classroom: Skill Introduction

Scenario A: Grades 3 to 5

The students in the fifth-grade classroom have had little formal health education to this point and no previous discussion of decision making as it relates to health behaviors. You create a chart listing the performance indicators and hang it at the front of the room. As students are settling in, you ask them to think about something they did today that helps to keep their bodies healthy. After students write down their ideas, they participate in a group brainstorm

KEY POINTS

- This skill is about demonstrating the ability to make health-enhancing decisions. Even though students may be able to work through the model, they have not fully demonstrated the skill unless the outcome is health enhancing.

- The decision-making skill is the sum of its parts, and no part of the skill can operate in isolation. Students must understand and demonstrate each part within the context of the whole skill.

- Decision making is critical for many aspects of health and should be practiced within multiple health-related topics and domains.

to write many of the ideas on the board. Using the brainstormed list as a starting point, you then talk about how the actions on the list are choices they make each and every time they do them. Students come to realize that they have control over their health and that the decisions they make every day can have a profound impact on whether or not their body stays healthy. You then transition into explaining the goals and educational outcomes of the unit.

Scenario B: Grades 9 to 12

In your class of 11th-grade students, decision making is at the top of their minds. You know that students are thinking about the upcoming summer vacation and getting excited for all the free time. At the start of class, you show a short video clip where students are discussing an upcoming end-of-the-year party where alcohol will be available. One character, Luke, is trying to persuade the other, Hunter, to attend the party and drink alcohol. After watching the video, students transition into small groups and each group is assigned a character from the video (either Luke or Hunter). The groups discuss what decisions were made in the video and what decisions would be the healthiest in this scenario. After some discussion, each group reports to the class and you make a list on the board of all the possible decisions that Luke and Hunter could make. You then explain that each scenario is complex and each character has his own point of view, values, and opinions. You continue to explain how decision making is a complex process that can result in many possible outcomes. However, by using the process identified in the performance indicators, students will leave the unit feeling more confident and able to apply the steps to the decisions they encounter.

STEP 2: PRESENTING THE STEPS OF THE SKILL

The skill cues presented in step 2 mirror the performance indicators of the skill but break them down into useable parts. Each skill cue is necessary and should be included in successful demonstration of the skill. Although students could theoretically make a decision without using all of the steps, it is important that students learn and practice all steps so that they can make thoughtful, thorough decisions and evaluate the outcomes of those decisions. Sample skill cues for decision making are presented in table 7.2.

As with step 1, there are many ways to introduce step 2 that are participatory. Following are some examples for implementing step 2 in the classroom.

Step 2 in the Classroom: Presenting the Steps of the Skill

PreK to Grade 2

Before the start of the unit, you prepare a list of scenarios that are relevant for students and that end with the character having to make a decision. You print the scenarios on handouts so the students can read along with you. During the lesson, you read each scenario and ask students what is the decision in the scenario? Write the decision underneath the scenario. Then ask the students, Who needs to help the character? You should also write these answers on the paper. Continue with a few scenarios until you feel that the students understand the skill cues.

TABLE 7.2 Skill Cues for Decision Making

PREK-GRADE 2	
Focus: Determining whether students can make the decision themselves or whether they need help	*What* is the decision? *Who* needs to help? (Note: These are similar to skill cues in previous skills, which should result in positive transfer because the students can see how the same steps are consistent through multiple skills.)
GRADES 3-5	
Focus: Introducing the steps of thoughtful decision making	DECIDE **D**etermine the decision—what is it? Does it require thought? Do I need help? **E**xamine options. **C**onsider consequences. **I**dentify values and possible influences that may affect the decision. **D**ecide on the healthiest option and act on the decision. **E**valuate the outcome.
GRADES 6-8	
Focus: Applying steps of decision making and increasing levels of critical thinking	DECIDE **D**etermine the decision—what is it? Does it require thought? Do I need help? **E**xamine options (healthy and unhealthy alternatives). **C**onsider consequences. **I**dentify values and influences that may affect the decision. **D**ecide on the healthiest option and act on the decision. **E**valuate and reflect on the outcome.
GRADES 9-12	
Focus: Using critical-thinking skills during the decision-making process	DECIDE **D**etermine the decision—what is it? Does it require thought? Do I need help? **E**xamine options (explain healthy and unhealthy alternatives). **C**onsider consequences. **I**dentify values and influences that may affect the decision. **D**ecide (act on the healthiest option) and justify why this is the healthiest option. **E**valuate and reflect on the outcome.

Grades 3 to 5

In preparation for the unit, you find out what shows or characters students are interested in and search for clips or situations from books where the character has a decision to make. (This is also a potential opportunity for interdisciplinary connections with English language arts or social studies.) You and the students read or watch the scenario (or even act it out) and then walk through the skill cues from the DECIDE model. As you cover skill cues, write them on an anchor chart that will remain in the room. If necessary, run through another scenario with students or have them work in pairs on a new scenario using the skill cues.

Grades 6 to 8

You make note cards that each state a health-related scenario, such as, "I am always hungry after school, but when I eat a snack I get cramps at my sports practice," "My friend is being picked on by other kids, but I don't want to say anything because they might pick on me too," or "I am not sure what to do—I told my grandma I would go home and visit with her after school, but I really want to hang out with my friends." As students enter the class, they receive a note card and pair up with another student who has the same notecard. They begin discussing what decision the character on the card needs to make and how that decision could positively or negatively affect their health by using the skill cues from the DECIDE model (these should be on a worksheet that the students will use during the activity). Each group explains their thoughts on the scenario using the skill cues as a framework.

Grades 9 to 12

On the first day of the unit, you give the students a story in which a character faces a dilemma and makes a choice. The students try to identify the skills cues that are presented in the story. They need to use their prior knowledge and critical-thinking skills to determine the skill cues in the story. The class reviews the story, focusing on reinforcing the skill cues of the DECIDE model.

STEP 3: MODELING THE SKILL

Modeling decision making is a straightforward process. The best way to model this skill is to choose a decision that is relevant for students and then walk through the steps as a class. Unlike other skills that are more nuanced and require approaching the skill from a variety of angles (e.g., analyzing influences has students consider the influences of family, peers, media, technology, and other factors), the decision-making steps are fixed. No matter how simple or complex the decision, the procedure is the same.

Note that students will likely bring up examples of both unhealthy and healthy choices. By recognizing both sides of the decision, students become better able to apply the learning to their world, which is full of healthy and unhealthy decisions. Furthermore, most decisions students must make are not black and white—they are not automatically healthy or right. Provide the space for students to question options, and encourage critical thinking that is supported by accurate information in order to lead students toward health-enhancing choices. Do not teach decision making in such a way that students feel obligated to give you the healthy answer. When they give examples that are relevant to the choices they would make in real life, they are more likely to embrace a decision-making model. Having an open dialogue in the safe space of your classroom about why a student might choose an unhealthy option and brainstorming ways to help students feel more comfortable with a health-enhancing choice is at the heart of a skills-based approach because it is authentic and meaningful. Following are examples of modeling activities.

PreK to Grade 2

■ Students read a story about a person (who is similar to your students) who is facing a dilemma. Ask students what the character should do to solve the dilemma.

■ Students describe a time when they were able to choose their own snack. How did they decide what to choose? Be sure to reference the skill cues during this discussion.

■ Students observe a picture of a child about to ride a bike (or perform another healthy behavior) and discuss why that would be a healthy behavior.

■ Students are given examples (e.g., taking medication, going outside to play, making themselves something to eat, going to bed on time), and they discuss whether the decision in the example is something they can handle on their own or whether they need someone else's help.

KEY POINTS

■ If your district uses a specific decision-making model, you should use that in place of the skill cues in step 2. The skill cues presented here are based on the National Standards but will likely align with other decision-making models.

■ Although students could make a decision without all of the skill cues, have them work through the process in order to better understand the "why" behind making decisions.

■ When presenting the skill cues, help students see the cues in context and connect the cues to real-life situations.

Fotolia - Joanna Zielinska

When students develop the ability to make health-enhancing decisions, they are better able to keep themselves safe and healthy for a lifetime.

Grades 3 to 5

- Students read a cartoon where the character faces a health dilemma and works through a decision-making approach to solve the problem in a health-enhancing way.

- Students receive a decision-making worksheet that lists a decision at the top (such as "Should I put on sunscreen before I go outside today?" or "I want to play my video game, but I have a lot of homework to do. What should I do first?"). As a large group, students work through the sheet to result in a health-enhancing outcome.

- Students sit in small groups and discuss a scenario that is posted in the classroom. They work through the decision-making model in the groups, and then the whole class works through the example together. Allow opportunities for students to ask questions, share answers, and so on.

Grades 6 to 8

- Students read two stories. Each story offers a different perspective on the same dilemma (e.g., feeling ill and not knowing what to do because they don't want to miss an upcoming extracurricular activity, seeing another student getting bullied and questioning what they should do to help). Even though the characters face the same dilemma, they come to different health-enhancing solutions. Then students discuss which steps the characters took in order to reach their solution.

- Students watch a video clip of two students (or relevant characters) discussing whether or not to smoke. Stop the video before the students make a final decision. In small groups, students review the decision-making steps and then use those steps to finalize the decision of the video characters.

- As a class, students look at a food label and then work through the steps of decision making to decide if the item is worth eating. Then pairs of students compare two food labels and work through a decision-making process to determine which item would be a better choice to eat.

- Write a scenario (that ends with a decision to be made) on the board. Give each student a slip of paper with one step of the decision-making model on it. Students form groups by completing the decision-making model (i.e., all groups will have D, E, C, I, D, and E). As a group, they determine the healthiest option for the scenario. Then discuss the scenario as a class to ensure students are correctly implementing the steps.

KEY POINTS

■ Students like to make decisions. By providing a framework for students to think about decisions they make you allow them to take ownership of their health.

■ Step 3 is about more than solving problems. It demonstrates that the easy choice is not always the best choice and that the right choice is not always easy.

■ This step should reinforce the relevance and applicability of the skill cues. It is important to explore multiple examples and allow students time to process healthy and unhealthy options before they ultimately choose a health-enhancing decision. If this is not done, students may leave the class feeling as if the discussions were not authentic to their world.

Grades 9 to 12

■ Students discuss local news stories that describe teen behavior. In groups, students discuss the behavior in the story and then work through the decision-making steps and decide if the behavior was healthy. If not, what would be a better choice?

■ Students brainstorm things in the community they feel are unhealthy (e.g., idling cars in front of school, lack of sidewalks and crosswalks, lack of parks, cigarette butts all over the ground). Students then discuss the steps of decision making and what it would take to solve the identified problems.

■ Using a book currently being read in an English language arts class (especially one that has a health focus), students discuss a character's dilemma or a decision that was (or will need to be) made in the story. If the character does not have any health-related decisions, create one and use the character as the focus of the discussion.

■ Students view pictures of people contemplating a decision. Working in small groups, students create a story for the picture. They then use the story to walk through the decision-making steps in order to solve the characters' situation. Review the decision-making process as a class (have groups share and discuss).

STEP 4: PRACTICE

Step 4 provides the opportunity for practice. Whereas step 3 has students work through the steps of decision making, usually as a class or a group, step 4 provides opportunities to practice individually and in small groups, making the skill real to the students' world. As previously mentioned, you should provide flexibility in any assignment and require that students explore both the easy choice and the more difficult ones. Allow students to question themselves and their decisions. To ensure that students fully grasp the entire skill, be sure that assignments require students to work through all of the steps. When sufficient time is not available to fully work through a decision (from determining the decision to evaluation), ask students to hypothesize what might happen. If time allows, have students complete the final step of reflection or evaluation one to two weeks after the rest of the assignment is due. This allows the student to implement their decision and reflect on the results.

Additionally, consider setting aside time for students to reflect on their personal **values**. If students have not done this previously, it will be necessary to consider how personal values and beliefs may affect decisions because identifying and exploring values is a key step of the decision-making process. Not all students (or even many adults) have taken the time to self-reflect and clearly identify what they value and how it influences their choices, so be sure to spend time on this before practicing the skill steps.

To give students feedback and to reinforce the importance of being thoughtful in making decisions, use peer feedback, teacher-directed feedback, or self-assessment as appropriate. For example, in a ninth-grade health class, students have just completed a poster that outlines their decision and how they arrived at that health-enhancing decision. In partners, students share their decision and receive feedback from their partner about potential outcomes of

■ Scenarios should be relevant for students. When possible, allow students to choose decisions that are important to them.

■ Consistently reinforce skill cues by working through all of the cues each time the decision-making process is discussed.

■ Practice opportunities should be varied and connect with events in students' lives and with other classes.

the decision. When set up appropriately by the teacher, this form of feedback could provide valuable insight as students think through their decision and the thought process that brought them to their decision. Regardless of the method, it is critical to build feedback into practice opportunities. Here are some considerations when planning your decision-making practice opportunities:

■ As described earlier, it is important to work through the entire decision-making process when practicing the skill. If necessary, spend more time on certain parts of the process, but do not cover the parts without the context of the whole. A general framework for practicing decision making is to (1) provide students with a scenario, (2) have the students work through the decision-making skill cues for the scenario, (3) reflect on the possible outcomes of the decision, and (4) evaluate the decision-making process.

■ You may need to make some modifications and vary the practice opportunities. For example, a possible modification is developing scenarios based on data from surveys (e.g., in-class survey, youth risk behavior survey).

■ Students can develop scenarios based on situations they are facing.

■ Students could choose their own scenarios with prepared cards. For example, there could be five characters with five settings and five problems. Students pick one card from each category (characters, settings, and problems).

■ Scenarios are taken from current news stories, social media, YouTube, or other real-life situations.

■ Scenarios are taken from situations in other classes such as English or social studies.

■ The students work through each step of the decision-making process based on this scenario.

■ Scenarios are completed individually or in small groups with each group or student responsible for completing one skill cue and then passing the scenario to another student to complete the next step based on the previous students' ideas.

■ Students complete worksheets that include the skill cues with open-ended statements that require students to work through the steps without prompting.

■ Students act out the decision-making process.

■ Students create stories, comic strips, or other creative deliverables that demonstrate the skill cues in various scenarios.

Once students have practiced decision making using the framework described earlier, they may be ready to explore the skill from a perspective that emphasizes evaluating decisions and defending healthy choices (which can provide opportunities for critical thinking as well). For example, students could receive a scenario where a decision was made and they have to evaluate whether or not the decision was the healthiest option. If it was, then students should defend the decision and their evaluation of the scenario. If the healthiest choice was not made, then students should complete a decision-making process that would lead to a healthier decision and then justify why this was a healthier option. This practice opportunity provides a slightly different context for examining the decision-making process while reviewing and reinforcing skill cues, shifting the focus from *making* the decision to *defending* or *justifying* decisions. This can be important in real-life situations, especially when the healthy decision isn't the easy or popular one.

STEP 5: FEEDBACK AND REINFORCEMENT

Step 5 for decision making is the time in the unit when you evaluate students for proficiency and reinforce the steps of the skill to ensure that all students are both proficient and confident in their ability to make health-enhancing decisions. This is also the time when students make adjustments to previous choices, fine-tuning them in real-life situations.

As mentioned throughout the chapter, this skill has students take deliberate steps to work through a process that leads to making a decision to maintain or improve their health and then reflecting on that decision to see if it had the desired outcome. It is this last part of the skill that many students find difficult. Most times, we make a decision and then move on to the next item on our to-do list without taking time to reflect on how things went and whether or not we should do things differently the next time a similar decision arises.

For example, Jonah has recently gotten his driver's license. He knows that the laws in his state are strict about cell phone use while driving. Jonah is always connected to his friends via text and social media—it's how they communicate. Although Jonah knows he shouldn't text while he is driving, he hasn't yet come up with a strategy for where to put his phone to ensure he isn't tempted to use it while he's on the road. Jonah decides to use this dilemma for his decision-making assignment and works through a decision-making process to decide how to handle all the texts coming in while he is driving. As a result, Jonah decides he is going to leave his phone in his bag on the seat next to him in the car. After he uses this approach for a few days, he realizes that even though the phone is in his bag, he can still hear all of the texts coming in and finds himself reaching for the phone. When asked to evaluate how his decision worked out, Jonah realizes that he needs a new plan. As a revision, he decides to put his phone on silent and place it in the backseat so that he no longer hears the texts coming in and can't reach it. This plan works much better and Jonah doesn't have to worry about getting into an accident because of texting.

Your role as the health educator is to provide the structure to promote reflection and evaluation. Because reflection and refinement are not natural steps for adolescents to take, guidance is crucial as your students try to navigate through making decisions, recognizing when things are not working, and adjusting those decisions.

SUMMARY

The skill of decision making is a structured, straightforward process that requires thoughtful action. This skill builds on previous ones and requires students to be able to locate valid and reliable information, products, and services; communicate with others effectively; and analyze the influences around them in order to make health-enhancing decisions. As a precursor, the ability to make decisions helps with

KEY POINTS

- Reflection is an integral part of the decision-making process. Without reflection and evaluation, we run the risk of maintaining behaviors that are not working, or worse, harming our health.
- Reflection is hard for students. It requires them to look critically at their actions and then constructively assess what is not working and why.
- Understand that reflection could cause some anxiety for students as they struggle to find what works for them. The more structured the format for students to use while they reflect, the more likely it is that reflection, evaluation, and even a new decision may occur.

TEACHING DECISION MAKING

Heidi Stan
Riverside Junior High, Fishers, Indiana

What is your best strategy for teaching decision making?

Decision making is covered in many of our content areas, so we approach it differently depending on what unit we are in. I never use the same teaching strategy in the different units. First and foremost we talk about how to make a good decision. We always follow the HELP (healthful, ethical, legal, parent approval) criteria. Here are strategies I use:

- pair and share
- vote and revote
- poll everywhere
- tic tac toe choice boards
- student written and conducted surveys (ways to avoid risk)
- information cubes
- skits (puppet show)
- commercials and iMovies
- journals
- analyzing graphics
- persuasive writing

What is one pitfall to avoid when teaching decision making?

Never assume students know the steps to follow to make a decision. Some students follow in their parents' footsteps and assume they already know the best decision. Ultimately we must help each child individualize and prepare for making their own good decisions (even if it goes against friends or peer pressure).

What piece of advice do you have for other health educators in the field?

You must constantly be willing to find new ways to teach and reach your students. I believe that teachers will witness the greatest amount of learning when they use a hands-on health approach. Students must be able to apply their learning in a hands-on experience in class so that when real-life opportunity comes they are able to apply it.

---

setting goals, self-managing behaviors, and choosing which causes are important enough to advocate for.

Decision making, like most other skills, requires you to be a coach throughout the process. This role is best served by introducing the skill and setting the context for how a sound decision-making process can affect many aspects of life. Following this, create a founda-tion for students to practice the skill steps and then apply them to a decision that is relevant to them. In the final part of the process, you must include time for reflection and evaluation of decisions and the impact they had in real life. Coaching students helps them to internalize the decision-making process and sets them up for success as they navigate the numerous decisions in front of them.

Review Questions

1. Why is it important to use data to inform decisions?

2. What are some strategies that encourage students to be thoughtful in their decision making and to reflect on the outcomes of their decisions?

3. Why is it important that a health educator serve as a coach for the skill of decision making?

To find supplementary materials for this chapter, such as worksheets and extended learning activities, visit the web resource at
www.HumanKinetics.com/TheEssentialsOfTeachingHealthEducation

Matthew Antonino/fotolia.com

CHAPTER 8

Goal Setting

Learning Objectives

After reading this chapter, you will be able to do the following:

- Implement all steps of the skill development model for goal setting.
- Describe appropriate student outcomes for goal setting at each developmental level.
- Create high-quality classroom activities for developing the skill of goal setting.

Key Terms

goal setting

long-term goal

needs assessment

short-term goal

SMART goal

Goal setting is critical for successful behavior change across a variety of health dimensions. Being able to set goals allows students to dream, to aspire, and to plan for the future. When students are able to set goals, they are able to identify needs, make a plan, implement the plan, and reflect on progress and success. They are able to plan both short- and long-term goals that work toward a desired outcome. *Short term* and *long term* are relative to the person and the goal being set. However, a **short-term goal** is one that will be achieved within a relatively small amount of time (day, weeks), whereas a **long-term goal** requires more time (months, years) and often takes more effort to accomplish. For example, a high school freshman might have a short-term goal of getting an A on an exam and a long-term goal of getting an A in the course. This same student could have a short-term goal of getting an A in a course with a long-term goal of earning a GPA of 3.5 or above. There is no specific time limit that distinguishes long-term and short-term goals, but a short-term goal is something you want to accomplish in the near future and a long-term goal is further in the future.

When students have the ability to set health-enhancing goals, they become empowered and motivated to make changes that have a positive impact on their health. For example, a teen who has grown up in a chaotic environment where few people in his life have gone to college learns about his ability to control the outcomes of his future because he has learned how to set and achieve goals. He now can see a future beyond his current circumstances. Whether this includes college or future job training, the important thing is that the student recognizes that his health and well-being (including his future potential) are not limited by those who currently surround him. In the health education classroom, it is important to facilitate experiences where students experience success in setting goals. This does not mean that all students will achieve the desired or anticipated outcomes for the goal they set, but rather that they gain confidence in their abilities to perform the components of the skill and they feel confident setting goals outside the classroom.

Goal setting is considered a higher-order skill because it requires students to synthesize information in order to systematically set goals that enhance their health. However, it is similar to accessing valid and reliable information, products, and services in that it is more of a standalone skill that you can teach at any point. You wouldn't necessarily need to teach other skills first; in fact, it might be effective to teach goal setting at the beginning of a course so that students can work toward their goals during their entire time with you. This would allow for an in-depth exploration of the skill and would not be confusing for students because other skills aren't critical to the successful application of goal setting.

In addition, reinforcing the importance of goal setting in later units such as decision making (i.e., after students have already learned about goal setting) recognizes that health-related goals should be a consideration when making important decisions. For example, Lillian, a high school junior, is offered the opportunity to participate in a pill party. Part of her decision-making process is to weigh pros and cons and to reflect on personal values. Lillian recognizes that taking unknown pills could be dangerous, but she also feels that if a doctor prescribed them then they are probably not that dangerous. However, Lillian has a goal of getting an academic scholarship for college and recognizes that taking unknown pills might cause adverse side effects, get her hooked on using, or even affect her desire to study. She must decide how to handle the situation—does she participate in the pill party, attend the party but choose not to take the drugs, or stay away from the party altogether? Lillian needs to understand that her choice about how to handle the pill party could have a direct effect on whether or not she is able to achieve her goal.

In another example, goal setting may provide a context for advocacy. A critical part of advocacy is passion and conviction. Students may choose to advocate for a topic that relates to a personal goal, or their goal may provide further conviction for the cause they choose to advocate for. For example, Carlo has a goal to clean up a local park because he wants to improve the health of those around him. He believes it is important to keep the earth clean and have safe, accessible spaces for recreation. Therefore, he decides to promote his cause during the advocacy unit.

Similar to the skill of decision making, a health education course probably isn't the first time students have heard about the importance of setting goals. However, it may be the first time that the goals are focused on health-enhancing outcomes. It is valuable to set goals in many areas of life, but you must capitalize on the opportunity to guide students to consider how goals can specifically contribute to their health.

Also, it is not merely enough to have students set goals. Your role as health educator includes guiding students as they set goals and providing opportunities for students to work toward their goals. Taking time to review students' goals will allow for constructive feedback about the selected goal which can increase the likelihood that the goal is realistic and that the student might experience a health-enhancing outcome. After this, you must provide students with a chance to work towards and hopefully to achieve their goals. Note that it is important to focus on the process of applying the skill cues

and sticking to a goal as opposed to focusing on successfully accomplishing the goal. You want students to be able to set goals, work toward them, evaluate their outcomes, adjust as necessary, and feel confident in setting new goals. Figure 8.1 presents the steps of the skill development model for goal setting.

STEP 1: SKILL INTRODUCTION

Goal setting is the process of setting and working toward a goal. It includes the steps necessary for addressing both short- and long-term goals. The performance indicators of the National Health Education Standards are clear in their intentions. Beginning with the younger grades, students are asked to identify a goal and take some action toward accomplishing it. By the time students are in high school, they must not only recognize what areas of their life they should set goals for, but they also

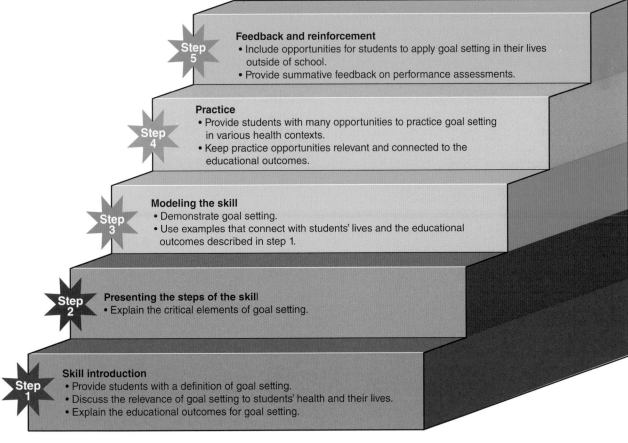

Step 5
Feedback and reinforcement
• Include opportunities for students to apply goal setting in their lives outside of school.
• Provide summative feedback on performance assessments.

Step 4
Practice
• Provide students with many opportunities to practice goal setting in various health contexts.
• Keep practice opportunities relevant and connected to the educational outcomes.

Step 3
Modeling the skill
• Demonstrate goal setting.
• Use examples that connect with students' lives and the educational outcomes described in step 1.

Step 2
Presenting the steps of the skill
• Explain the critical elements of goal setting.

Step 1
Skill introduction
• Provide students with a definition of goal setting.
• Discuss the relevance of goal setting to students' health and their lives.
• Explain the educational outcomes for goal setting.

FIGURE 8.1 Steps for developing the skill of goal setting.

should implement a distinct process of working through a goal that includes thoughtful reflection on how to sustain the goal over the long term. Goal setting has five distinct aspects:

1. Assessing needs
2. Setting a goal
3. Making a plan to achieve the goal
4. Working toward the goal
5. Evaluating and reflecting on the experience

Assessing Needs

A **needs assessment** is a process through which people evaluate aspects of their health and use the results to determine current areas of strength and areas in need of improvement. Typically, goals are based on areas of need, but setting goals to maintain or enhance current health practices can also be beneficial and lead to long-term changes in health behavior.

For example, Brynn participates in a class assignment that asks her to rate her behaviors in areas related to personal health. After participating in this needs assessment and reviewing the results, she learns that she is doing well in the emotional dimension (she has the ability to understand her feelings, has pretty solid self-esteem, and even recognizes that she has areas of health that could be improved), in part due to her consistent journaling. However, she realizes that one area she could improve upon is in the physical dimension—specifically, how much soda and energy drinks she consumes. In many cases, a health educator might encourage Brynn to set a nutrition-related goal, but perhaps she could set a goal to record when she drinks soda or energy drinks and describe what she is feeling and why she is choosing that beverage. This goal can help Brynn capitalize on a behavior that she is already engaging in (journaling) but helps increase her self-awareness around the choices to see if they are related to her emotions or something else such as she only consumes these drinks when she is stressed or upset. Although consuming fewer soda and energy drinks is important, the nutrition area for improvement might not be as important as helping Brynn understand why she is making those choices (more in the emotional dimension). What Brynn may not realize is that the main reason she turns to energy drinks is

because she feels overwhelmed by the pressures in her life and the added boost seems to be an easy way to keep her going.

The most important considerations of a needs assessment are that students examine multiple dimensions of wellness (not just the physical dimension) and that they use the results of the assessment to guide goal selection. Students should choose a goal that is relevant and meaningful to them. If they don't, they may learn the process of goal setting, but the practical application is missing. This may result in a missed opportunity for goal setting to serve a meaningful and relevant purpose in a student's life.

Setting a Goal

Before setting goals, students should be introduced to the *SMART* acronym. This acronym will be too sophisticated for younger students, but you can help them write clear, realistic goals that are modified versions of SMART goals. **SMART goals** are **s**pecific, **m**easurable, **a**ttainable, **r**ealistic, and **t**imely or time based. However, we suggest replacing *attainable* with *adjustable* for two reasons. The first is that *attainable* and *realistic* can be hard to differentiate and it may be difficult for students to understand the distinction. If something is attainable, then isn't it realistic? The second reason is that many goals need to be adjusted even if they are realistic when they are originally set. Giving students permission to adjust their goals based on assessment of their progress can lead to experiences of success and control over the situation rather than failure if they don't meet the original goal (see sidebar).

Making a Plan to Achieve the Goal

After setting a SMART goal, the next step is to work toward the goal. When helping students with this aspect of goal setting, ensure that they have identified specific strategies that will help them work toward their goal. You should also make sure that they have identified at least one person in their lives who can provide support as they work toward their goal.

The specific strategies are less important than their purpose. The strategies should serve as building blocks that break the larger goal

Comparing a SMART Goal With a Not-So-SMART Goal

Which goal is SMARTest?

	I WILL CUT DOWN ON THE NUMBER OF ENERGY DRINKS I CONSUME.	I WILL DRINK A TOTAL OF 3 ENERGY DRINKS OVER THE COURSE OF 7 DAYS FOR THE NEXT 6 WEEKS.
SPECIFIC?	No—How many energy drinks? How often?	Yes—Only 3 energy drinks per week are allowed.
MEASURABLE?	No—What does *cut down* mean? Less than what? How many?	Yes—You can measure if more than 3 energy drinks are consumed.
ADJUSTABLE?	Yes	Yes
REALISTIC?	Yes (but keep in mind that determining the extent to which a goal is realistic is ultimately up to the individual student)	Yes (but keep in mind that determining the extent to which a goal is realistic is ultimately up to the individual student)
TIME-BASED?	No—For how long? When will this start? Over what period of time?	Yes—7 days over the next 6 weeks

into manageable parts. The strategies should be realistic and may take the form of short-term goals or include actions such as sticky-note reminders or phone reminders. Students should be thoughtful about making plans for reaching their goal and choose strategies that are relevant for them and the goal. The aim is for students to identify practical strategies to help them achieve their selected goal.

Working Toward the Goal

As mentioned, the skill of goal setting includes more than just identifying a goal to accomplish. The skill requires that students actually work toward the goal. Sufficient class time should be set aside for students to implement their ideas and track their progress. No predetermined amount of time is specified for working toward meeting a goal, but behavior change takes time. The more time you can give students, the more effective the experience will be. Class time is the perfect opportunity to support students as they track their progress and consider what may be helping them to accomplish the goal and what may be hindering them. This can increase motivation (when students see their success or have a chance to work through problems, they feel more confident and competent), increase self-awareness, and help students understand

the goal-setting process. Remember, when people feel a high level of self-efficacy about something (i.e., they have confidence in their ability to complete the action), they are more likely to try it in the first place and continue to do it.

Evaluating and Reflecting on the Experience

Finally, students need to evaluate and reflect on their experience. This step is both meaningful and necessary to the process of setting and achieving a goal. Evaluation and reflection provide time to not only see what has been working (or not) but also to think about the original goal and what it means for our life over the longer term. Sometimes we get caught up in whether or not the goal was accomplished. Although this is one important aspect, it is not the only outcome or indicator of a successful goal-setting process. Students should not focus solely on whether or not they achieved their goal but also on the experience. Sometimes we need to fail to achieve our goal and realize that it was the wrong goal to begin with or that the goal strategies did not sufficiently address all of the necessary variables.

During this step, students should think about the following questions:

- Was my plan appropriate?
- What went well?
- What could have been improved?
- Did I make progress toward my goal?
- Did I adjust my goal? Why? Did it help?
- Can I continue with this goal? Do I need to set up any additional strategies or supports to keep working on this goal?

It would be helpful for students to journal about their experiences (this could be a good connection to technology by using Twitter, a blog, a journaling app, or another technology medium). This provides both an immediate mode of feedback and a record of successes and challenges associated with the process. A journal can also provide the opportunity to document when students needed assistance and whether the source of support they chose provided the information, resources, or guidance in a helpful way.

Students should also complete a summative evaluation, which looks at the goal-setting experience overall, including any documentation of the process, and encourages reflection on the entire process. The reflection serves as a way to both critically evaluate the process and to make a plan for moving forward.

Educational Outcomes

Educational outcomes for goal setting are directly tied to the steps of goal setting. Teaching students the procedural knowledge of goal setting is directly related to the performance indicators identified in the National Standards (see table 8.1). As students get older and advance developmentally, they are better able to work through all of the goal-setting steps. In the earliest grades, students are asked to identify or set a personal health-related goal, but they are not asked to modify the goal when it is not going as planned or to describe a long-term strategy for making the behavior change last.

When designing educational outcomes for goal setting, a few steps must be completed:

1. Examine the performance indicators and decide which ones you will cover in the unit.
2. Determine the extent to which you will cover the objectives.
3. Recognize if you need to adjust the language of the performance indicators in order to make the outcomes relevant for your students.

The following section highlights some considerations during this process.

Step 1: Choosing Indicators

Indicators for goal setting are more straightforward than for some of the other skills. However, in many cases you need to include more than one indicator in a unit. For example, it wouldn't be as meaningful to include indicator 6.8.2 (develop a goal) without also including at least 6.8.3 (apply strategies) and possibly 6.8.4

TABLE 8.1 Performance Indicators for Standard 6 of the National Health Education Standards

PREK-GRADE 2	GRADES 3-5	GRADES 6-8	GRADES 9-12
6.2.1 Identify a short-term personal health goal and take action toward achieving the goal. 6.2.2 Identify who can help when assistance is needed to achieve a personal health goal.	6.5.1 Set a personal health goal and track progress toward its achievement. 6.5.2 Identify resources to assist in achieving a personal health goal.	6.8.1 Assess personal health practices. 6.8.2 Develop a goal to adopt, maintain, or improve a personal health practice. 6.8.3 Apply strategies and skills needed to attain a personal health goal. 6.8.4 Describe how personal health goals can vary with changing abilities, priorities, and responsibilities.	6.12.1 Assess personal health practices and overall health status. 6.12.2 Develop a plan to attain a personal health goal that addresses strengths, needs, and risks. 6.12.3 Implement strategies and monitor progress in achieving a personal health goal. 6.12.4 Formulate an effective long-term personal health plan.

(how goals can change). To truly be proficient in the goal-setting process, students must be able to demonstrate all of the performance indicators.

While planning a second-grade goal-setting unit, you notice that the performance indicators are strongly connected. You decide to have students identify a short-term goal (performance indicator 6.2.1) and then identify when they might need help to reach their goal (6.2.2). Students covered goal setting in first grade, but not much emphasis was placed on the strategies and people who can help to achieve goals. You also recognize that this would be an opportunity to connect with previous learning from the unit on accessing valid and reliable information, products, and services by discussing community helpers as people who can help with certain goals. This becomes a good time to challenge students by encouraging them to identify a goal in a health dimension other than physical health (such as social or emotional dimensions). This allows students to build upon their previous learning while expanding their understanding of their health.

Step 2: Coverage of Indicators

This step is also more straightforward for goal setting than for other skills. Examining the performance indicators for all grade levels reveals that the entire indicator needs to be covered during a goal-setting unit.

During a fifth-grade goal-setting unit, you address both performance indicators—you ask students to set a health goal and track its progress (performance indicator 6.5.1) and then identify the resources necessary for meeting the goal (6.5.2). You realize that each performance indicator must be discussed completely, and when the opportunity presents itself in class, you direct students to apply previous learning about accessing information and analyzing influences. Students see that they must consider what sources of information are valid and worth using, but they also must consider the influences that may affect the plan they are developing. This crossover between skills shows students that they use their previous learning at other times in their lives. You reinforce the performance indicators and ask students to share with the class some examples that will reinforce each indicator. This exercise sets the stage for the course-long project in which students identify a goal, track their progress, and document the resources they will need.

Step 3: Student-Appropriate Terms

All of the indicators use simple terms that students need to be familiar with. It might be necessary to provide definitions of certain terms, but overall the performance indicators are clear and should be used without major modifications. To reinforce the indicators, use posters and visuals to provide a quick reference as students work through the steps of the skill. The visuals can be as simple as the written indicators along with pictures to help students remember or to support English language learners in the classroom.

Step 4: Educational Outcomes

Completing the previous steps will result in the educational outcomes for the skill unit. These will frame the unit and should be provided for students.

The following scenario demonstrates how step 1 of the skill development model for goal setting may look in the classroom.

Step 1 in the Classroom: Skill Introduction

Scenario A: PreK to Grade 2

The grade 2 unit will include 6.2.1 (identify a personal health goal) and 6.2.2 (identify who can help). The second graders have been studying poetry, so you decide to start the goal-setting unit with a poem related to setting and achieving goals. This helps students to start thinking about goals they have for themselves. You lead a group discussion in which students describe some health behaviors that they know are healthy but think they could do a better job at. This leads to identifying some specific goals they have and why it is important to set goals. Student examples include setting goals to play more outside, wear a bike helmet, brush teeth every morning and night, and get homework done. These ideas are written on an anchor chart and kept in the room for the duration of the unit. After this, you explain that students will be setting their own goals and that they will work to achieve those goals. You refer to the educational outcomes for the unit, which are posted in the room.

Scenario B: Grades 6 to 8

Your eighth-grade unit covers all performance indicators in the National Health Education Standards. Students will need to assess personal health practices

KEY POINTS

- Goal setting is a process that can help students achieve short- and long-term goals.

- Goal setting is relevant in many areas of students' lives. Throughout the unit, it will be important to remind students that the process can be applied to many types of goals.

- All five aspects of goal setting should be included in some capacity at every grade level (assessing needs, setting a goal, making a plan to achieve the goal, working toward the goal, and evaluating and reflecting on the experience). Although the aspects remain constant, the sophistication evolves at higher grade levels.

(6.8.1), set a goal to maintain or improve their health (6.8.2), apply strategies and skills to achieve the goal (6.8.3), and describe how the goal can change as the student realizes what is or isn't working (6.8.4). You start the unit by having students complete a vision board to emphasize the value of having long-term goals and dreams. This gives students a chance to see themselves being successful in the future, even if their vision feels hard to reach right now. You know that students will enjoy this opportunity to be creative and think about their future plans. You use this assignment as the context for discussing how goals and dreams are connected (goals can help you work toward a dream), and then you transition into the educational outcomes for the unit. Students will use the vision boards when determining the goals they will work on over the course.

STEP 2: PRESENTING THE STEPS OF THE SKILL

Once you have introduced the skill of goal setting, the next step is to present the steps of the skill, or the skill cues. These are the parts of the skill that are necessary for successful demonstration of the skill and for meeting the educational outcomes presented in step 1. Sample skill cues for goal setting are presented in table 8.2.

The focus of step 2 is to present the steps of goal setting so that students know exactly what they need to do in order to perform the skill. Emphasize the skill cues using health-related examples in a variety of contexts that are relatable and relevant for students. The following scenario provides some examples of ways to address step 2 for goal setting in the classroom.

Step 2 in the Classroom: Presenting the Steps of the Skill

PreK to Grade 2

In class, ask students guiding questions about healthy behaviors (e.g., How often should we wash our hands during the day? What are some foods that can help our body grow? What are some ways that we can protect our body from getting hurt when we are playing?). Once you have written the responses on the board, pick one to focus on and use it to guide the discussion about setting a goal to improve the identified health behavior. In this instance, you choose to use a response related to the question, What are some ways we can protect our body from getting hurt while we are playing? One student suggests, "Wait my turn before going on the monkey bars," and this provides an entry into discussing the importance of playground safety. Explain that lots of kids get hurt on the playground (include how many accident reports have happened on the playground) and that setting a goal to stay safe on the playground could be one way to make recess safer for everyone. As a group, come up with one goal that all students can agree to try on the playground, such as, "I will wait patiently in line for my turn on playground equipment" (set the goal). Ask the students to tell you why this could keep them safe from injury on the playground (explain the importance). Then have the group decide who is a good person to talk to if they are having a hard time waiting their turn (tell someone and ask for help). Next, determine how they will stay patient when they are eager to get on a certain piece of equipment (make a plan). Because students are in class, not on the playground, review the next step of acting on the plan by asking students to try to meet this goal the next time they are on the playground. Let the students know that the next time you are together in class, you will ask them how it went. Be sure to reinforce

TABLE 8.2 Skill Cues for Goal Setting

PREK-GRADE 2	
Focus: Setting and working toward a goal with help	PreK-K **GOALS** **G**et a plan. **O**ne step at a time. **A**ct on the goal. **L**earn from the goal. **S**tart again. Grades 1-2* **SET GOALS** **S**et a goal based on the results of a needs assessment. **E**xplain why it is important. **T**ell someone you trust and ask for help. **G**et a plan. **O**ne step at a time. **A**ct on the goal. **L**earn from the goal. **S**tart again. *If needed based on the students' understanding of goal setting, grade 1 can use the *GOALS* acronym for reinforcement.
GRADES 3-5	
Focus: Setting a quality goal, tracking progress, and getting help (Note: The skill cues are the same, but there should be greater emphasis on setting a quality goal and planning steps to accomplish the goal.)	**SET GOALS** **S**et a goal based on the results of a needs assessment.* **E**xplain why it is important. **T**ell someone you trust and ask for help. **G**et a plan. **O**ne step at a time. **A**ct on the goal. **L**earn from the goal. **S**tart again. **Skill Cues Used During Goal Planning** *Steps*—What steps need to be taken to reach goal? *Track*—How are you going to track progress? *Help*—Does this goal require help? *Who*—Who can help? *At this age, a needs assessment will not be data driven but will result from personal reflection.
GRADES 6-8 AND 9-12	
Focus: Introducing SMART goals and increasing the extent of the needs assessment	*Assess* the positive areas and areas for improvement of your personal health. *Identify* the areas of health that need improvement or that you want to maintain or enhance. *Create* a SMART goal that will address the improvement or maintenance of one health need. *Apply* strategies and skills to assist with accomplishing the goal. *Record*, *reflect* on, and *evaluate* goal progress.

skill cues during the discussion so that students can clearly see the connection between their actions and the associated skill cues.

Grades 3 to 5

Provide students with a story to read that has a main character who gets mad easily and yells at her friends. Have students discuss with a partner whether or not the main character is acting in a positive way to express her feelings. As each group reports to the class (hopefully the response is that the character is not effectively dealing with her anger by yelling at her friends), ask students to list ways that the character could better handle her anger when she is frustrated. Use the responses provided, and as a class, set a goal for the character to take a deep breath, count to 10, and form an assertive (not aggressive) statement before she responds to a situation that frustrates her (set a goal). Then discuss why this is a good approach (explain importance). (This is also a good example of how goal setting connects with interpersonal communication). Next, have the class list types of people who might be good supports in reaching this goal (tell someone and ask for help) and make a plan for how this might play out in real life (make a plan). Have students practice calming themselves down and write an I-statement that they could use when faced with this situation (act on the plan). Students might create a statement such as, "I feel angry when Brady yells at me because it makes me feel bad about myself. When Brady's actions make me feel this way, I will count to 10 and then get help if I need to." Ask students how it felt to practice calming themselves and if they feel this will work the next time they are upset. Finally, explain that as the unit progresses, they will set and work toward a goal for the final assessment, and they will be asked to say whether the goal worked out as planned or whether they needed to make any changes to the goal. As you go over the plan for the unit with the students, make sure to review the skill cues and show students how the skill cues connect with the unit goals.

Grades 6 to 8

As students enter the class, they review risk behavior data that illustrate the number of teens who have reported bullying and then write a short response as to why they think bullying is an issue for middle school students. Once students have had time to respond to the prompt, explain that this unit is about setting a goal. To start, they are going to discuss the role that bystanders can play in preventing bullying. After explaining that a target of bullying is never at fault for the aggressor's actions, discuss how the students who watch an aggressor target someone with hurtful actions contribute to allowing the behavior to continue. Ask the class to commit to being vocal bystanders by setting a goal to do one thing to stand up to bullying (connection to advocacy). Next, conduct a form of needs assessment by having students list positive behaviors they could engage in that may help prevent bullying and have them list behaviors that might contribute to bullying. Next, identify one positive behavior that students in the class feel could reduce bullying behavior in their school. As a class, create a SMART goal related to the behavior and determine strategies for achieving the goal. Be sure to check in on progress throughout the semester. During the discussion be sure to reinforce the skill cues.

Grades 9 to 12

Begin the class with a brainstorm about what students want do after they graduate from high school. This could be college, work, military, or any combination; the intent is to get students to identify the possibility of success after high school. In small groups, students compare state and national data related to teen alcohol use, especially binge drinking. Discuss what this means to them and how binge drinking could have negative effects on the hopes and dreams they just mentioned. Provide statistics demonstrating the relationship between binge drinking and negative academic outcomes and other risky behaviors (e.g., unprotected sex, violence, drug use). Reminding

KEY POINTS

■ Skill cues should be comprehensive and address all aspects of the skill that need to be covered.

■ Skill cues should apply across multiple health contexts and situations. Goal setting in particular is easily applied in any health dimension.

■ Engaging students in the process of developing or reviewing the skill cues can make this step more meaningful and relevant.

Goal setting is a skill that can help students gain control over their lives and help them to be successful and healthy.

students that alcohol use is illegal under the age of 21, ask them to consider a goal of avoiding situations where binge drinking is likely to occur. Point out that in this demonstration, you are working through a single example, but during their assignment they will personally assess the goal they wish to make. The area for improvement in this instance is binge drinking. As a group, create a SMART goal that helps students to avoid situations where binge drinking is likely to occur and then list strategies that the group is willing to take in order to achieve the identified goal. Finally, have the group make a plan that could be used to evaluate or reflect on the goal with a built-in opportunity to refine the goal as needed. As a review, ask the students to identity how they used skill cues throughout the class discussion.

STEP 3: MODELING THE SKILL

Step 3 is when goal setting is modeled for students in ways that are relevant and meaningful. This step should focus on effective application and examples that highlight the educational outcomes presented in step 1. As with all other steps, the modeling must be done using methods and examples that are engaging for students. Following are examples of modeling activities for goal setting.

PreK to Grade 2

- Ahead of class, create a poster with pictures of health-related items or activities (e.g., riding a bike, two friends smiling, an alarm clock). Students examine the poster and tell you what kinds of goals someone might make that relate to the pictures. Then follow up with a question about whether students could achieve that goal on their own or whether they would need help from someone else (reinforcing each skill cue during the practice).

- Students listen to a story about a character who wants to be a better friend. Then the class discusses ways to be a good friend and a goal related to something they could do that would make them a better friend. Students ask each other for feedback about their goals.

- Students discuss a Venn diagram you have drawn on the whiteboard. The diagram has two competing issues in each circle, such as doing homework and playing outside. As a group, students make a list of goals that could help to make both things possible (these go in the middle of the Venn diagram). Extend the example to include what the entire goal-setting process might look like, from making a plan to evaluating it (using the skill cues).

- Students review a list (or pictures) of community helpers who could provide assistance in meeting a health goal. As a group, discuss what the helpers do and the types of goals they might be helpful for. Discuss how the students could access the community helper as a part of the development of their plan (connection to accessing information, products, and services).

Grades 3 to 5

- Students complete a worksheet that has prompts for each skill cue. As a class, walk through the worksheet for a predetermined goal.

- Students list resources that could be helpful in determining a goal to improve their health. Then they pick a resource and write a goal statement and plan that include the chosen resource. Review as a class.

- Students create a calendar that helps chart their progress toward an identified goal and list the steps and resources necessary for achieving their goal.

- Students create a brief statement to share with the class about the goal they are selecting and how they are going to track their progress. They identify one or two resources they will use to support them.

Grades 6 to 8

- Students read a newspaper article about teens engaging in risky behavior and create a list of ideas to help prevent the behavior. Students then work through a goal-setting worksheet with a goal specifically related to the article.

- Students interview a trusted adult about a personal health goal of theirs and ask a set of questions specifically related to the skill cues. They also ask the interviewee to provide strategies that could help the student meet the goal.

- Students list three goals related to a topic that is listed on the board. For example, the topic of increased physical activity could include goals such as walk the dog every day for 30 minutes, try out for an athletic team, or organize a game with friends in the neighborhood once a week. Then the students choose one of the goals and work through a goal-setting process.

- Students research and present a biography of a person who is successful in her field. They identify what has made that person successful and consider what goals she may have set along the way. Students then set a personal health goal that could help them reach their own dreams.

Grades 9 to 12

- Students work through a goal-setting process using a case study that identifies the character, details about the character's life, and results of a needs assessment. Then review as a class, focusing on the skill cues.

- Students perform a role-play where the characters identify a problem and set a goal to resolve it. Students complete the story via small-group conversations and then review as a class.

- Students explain the *SMART* acronym and how a SMART goal can contribute to the larger skill of goal setting. Review as a class.

STEP 4: PRACTICE

During step 4, students must practice goal setting in varied contexts, ideally for as much time as needed in order to develop proficiency. This section provides considerations and examples for practicing and reinforcing the goal-setting process. You will notice that all examples include not just setting a goal but also working toward the goal and reflecting on and evaluating the process. As with modeling, a critical component of this step is providing practice opportunities that are relevant to students.

KEY POINTS

- Modeling is an important part of the skill development process because it shows students how the skill should look when it is performed correctly. You can perform the modeling, but you can also model the skill using current events, technology, literature, and so on.
- Getting to know your students will enable you to create meaningful experiences that help them see the goal-setting process as one that can benefit their health and help make their dreams a reality.

This will likely include involving students in the process of determining the goal to work on. When students are invested in their goal and are motivated to work hard to achieve it, they are more likely to see success.

Plan practice experiences that address each component of the goal-setting process: perform a needs assessment, set a goal, make a plan, work toward the plan, and evaluate and reflect on the goal and the process. This section provides general ideas for practicing the five components; you can modify them to make the practice developmentally appropriate and relevant for your students.

Assessing Needs

When we think of assessing needs, we often think of a strict process, maybe data driven, that identifies needs of a person, program, or other entity. In health education, we take a more holistic view of needs assessment. The goal is to provide students with time to self-reflect and identify, through formal (e.g., checklists, questionnaires, data) or informal (e.g., journaling, projects, reflection) methods, positive health behaviors and areas for improvement. Areas for improvement could be either risky behaviors that students are engaging in or areas where they need to participate in more healthy behaviors. For example, upon reflection students might realize that they do not engage in any behaviors related to their spiritual health, so they choose to focus on this area for their goal.

A basic format for conducting a needs assessment is to create a project or activity that asks students to highlight behaviors across multiple contexts. Examples include the following:

- Students create a wheel of wellness and list the behaviors that they engage in within each dimension of wellness. They then reflect on an area in which they want to set a goal.
- Provide students with a list of behaviors (healthy and risky) within each dimension of wellness. Students check off which behaviors they currently engage in and which health-enhancing behaviors they want to engage in moving forward. The results are used to identify a goal for the goal-setting activity.
- Students use resources within a specific dimension of wellness (e.g., physical dimension) to evaluate their health status. If they examine the physical dimension, this might include using www.choosemyplate.gov to evaluate their nutritional status or tracking their physical activity and using the Physical Activity Guidelines for Americans (HHS, 2008) to evaluate their current levels of physical activity. You could ask students to look at one dimension or you could provide them with multiple resources in a variety of health domains. Alternatively, you could ask older students to find the resources on their own (connection with accessing valid and reliable information, products, and services).

Setting a Goal and Making a Plan

After students have determined which area of health they want to work on, they need to practice writing a goal statement and making a plan. The practice activity should include writing a SMART goal, justifying how it is a SMART goal, and creating a clear, concise plan to work toward the goal. The best way to do this is to give students a worksheet that guides them through this process. An example is provided in the Sample Health Goal Worksheet sidebar and on the web resource, where it can be modified as needed.

Sample Health Goal Worksheet

Health Behavior to Address:

Why I am choosing to focus on this behavior:

My knowledge about this behavior and how it affects health:

My attitude towards this behavior at this time:

My SMART health goal:

Why my goal is SMART:

It is **s**pecific:

It is **m**easurable:

It is **a**djustable:

It is **r**ealistic:

It is **t**ime based:

My plan for achieving my SMART goal:

One person who will help me is:

KEY POINTS

■ Focus on the process and help students develop confidence in it, not just the end result of achieving goals.

■ Assist students in choosing a goal that is personal and meaningful for the student.

■ Provide feedback as students work through the process including suggestions for improvement.

The focus of this step is to help students write SMART goals and develop plans for achieving their goals. Students should receive feedback on their SMART goals. This step can be challenging for students—writing SMART goals is not an easy task. Be sure that students do not get too far along in the process before they receive feedback on their goal statements. The feedback can be teacher directed, but older students can give peer feedback as well, which may help their own learning and skill development.

Working Toward Achieving a Goal

This aspect of goal setting should be practiced outside the classroom with support and check-ins with the teacher and class along the way. After students have set a goal, give an assignment that requires them to implement their plan and track their progress. This can be done through journaling, blogging, or social media (if appropriate) as well as through in-class check-ins or tracking of progress. Emphasis should be placed on the process, not the outcome. You should monitor progress, assist students with their struggles, and support them on their journey. Encourage students to modify plans and goals as needed for this critical piece of goal setting. Assistance and encouragement will support the development of self-efficacy and instill confidence in their ability to set and work toward goals—not just in their ability to successfully achieve goals. As discussed earlier, the more time students have to work toward a goal, the more meaningful the experience will be and the more perspective and understanding students will have about the process.

Evaluating and Reflecting

The last step is to have students evaluate and reflect on this experience. This is the point where they evaluate their achievement of the goal. Were they successful? Did they achieve the goal? Did they achieve parts of the goal? Did they learn from the process? Should they modify their goal moving forward? Students should not be graded on their achievement of the goal but rather on the depth of their reflections and their evaluation of the experience.

STEP 5: FEEDBACK AND REINFORCEMENT

In the final step, take the time to review the educational objectives established in step 1 and provide feedback that measures students' proficiency in the skill. This step is important for all skills, but goal setting in particular asks students to consider what they need to change or maintain to be healthy and then to employ strategies to actually do this. This component is not only part of the skill development model (to review and reflect on how the process went) but is also explicitly built into the skill of goal setting in the later grades. Even the most diligent and well-intentioned student may set a goal that is unrealistic or requires effort that is unmanageable for the long term. Additionally, in earlier grades, if the person a student chooses to ask for help and guidance in achieving her goal is someone who may hinder her progress (for example, a sibling who smokes is not the best support for a goal of avoiding cigarettes),

TEACHING GOAL SETTING

Kellie Hurst

Winters Mill High School, Carroll County Public Schools, Maryland

What is your best strategy for teaching goal setting?

Students complete numerous personal assessments that address strengths, needs, and risks (self-reflection) specific to core concepts for each dimension of wellness. These assessments are *not* meant to diagnose anyone but rather to create awareness. We then promote challenges that help students make a proactive plan of action, hopefully before various situations occur during their high school experience. Often students forget about guidelines for sleep, good nutrition, water intake, and so on. Health educators must make those connections every day for their students and not assume they know better. Ask if changes are occurring—you might be surprised what students have already put into action! For example, two of my students complained of insomnia and leg cramping at night; when I taught them about the importance of hydration and potassium, they made the change and the ailments disappeared! They were very proud of themselves and became advocates for my class!

What is one pitfall to avoid when teaching goal setting?

Being well is not just about eating right and exercising. Wellness is about the entire person: mind, body, and spirit.

Everyone knows you need to eat right and exercise (physical wellness), but we tend to forget about all the other essential components that are basic human needs. We also need

- mental wellness so we can focus on learning;
- emotional wellness so we keep our emotions in check and protect our hearts;
- social wellness, striving toward building healthy relationships and caring about our reputations; and
- spiritual wellness, or a sense of purpose in our lives.

Self-actualization and wellness take planning and work. They require constant personal assessment and focus in our lives through short- and long-term goal setting.

What advice do you have for other health educators in the field?

Without a strong understanding of the health education standards, the health program becomes unit and content driven; it lacks connection. But teaching the concepts of the dimensions of wellness and Maslow's hierarchy of needs permit us a starting point. The dimensions give us categories for personal assessments so students can see which dimension they need to develop further. This is a starting point for goal setting. Maslow's hierarchy of needs highlights the importance of goal setting. For example, without self-esteem, how can you expect to reach your fullest potential? This connects beautifully; however, I think it's often missed.

---

the goal is not as likely to be achieved. By taking the time to review students' goals and their strategies for the remaining steps of the skill, you can provide meaningful feedback that helps students select the most beneficial supports and strategies.

The second component, also explicit in the skill cues and performance indicators of this skill, is the refinement and adjustment of goals. It is rare that an original goal is the final version that is accomplished. Even subtly, people often give themselves more flexibility (e.g., "It's been a tough week. I'll start exercising next week.") or refine their individual intent (e.g., "Maybe I was being overzealous about my goal to always get to bed before 10:00 p.m. If I do it most nights, that counts, right?"). When time is taken to reevaluate and refine the original goal, the power of slip-ups to derail all progress is gone and the reinforcement of the adjustable part of a SMART goal happens. Students learn that it is OK to refine a goal as long as it is because they have realized that a realistic goal is a more achievable stepping stone than the original goal. Small steps toward a large goal are far better than large steps that are never achieved.

SUMMARY

Goal setting is a dynamic process that can provide a road map for students to be successful. When employed in a health education class, students have the opportunity to realize their hopes and dreams within multiple dimensions of health and how they contribute to a healthy, happy life. They learn how to develop a plan to systematically achieve those dreams, one small goal at a time.

As students participate in the goal-setting unit, they learn more than just the importance of setting a goal. They also learn how to determine if the goal is appropriate, whether help or support is necessary from others, how to make the goal SMART, and how to reflect on the goal in order to make adjustments along the way. Together, these steps form a foundation that students can use across multiple contexts and dimensions. It doesn't matter if the student is setting a goal to eat better or to wear protective clothing while mountain biking—the procedural steps are the same. Through all of this, you are the coach, providing support and guidance as students work through the process. Providing a solid foundation for students to set and achieve goals, coupled with support and feedback as they work through the process, is the best way to approach this skill.

Review Questions

1. What are the five aspects of goal setting?

2. What is a SMART goal, and why is it important to the goal-setting process?

3. How are reflection and evaluation relevant to goal setting, and how does this step encourage long-term behavior change?

To find supplementary materials for this chapter, such as worksheets and extended learning activities, visit the web resource at
www.HumanKinetics.com/TheEssentialsOfTeachingHealthEducation

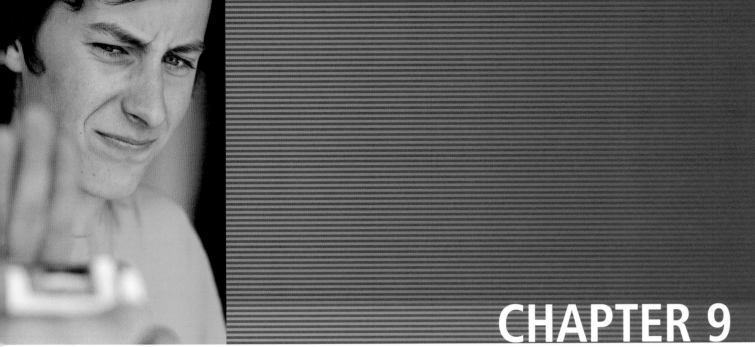

CHAPTER 9

Self-Management

Learning Objectives

After reading this chapter, you will be able to do the following:

- Implement all steps of the skill development model for self-management.
- Describe appropriate student outcomes for self-management at each developmental level.
- Create high-quality classroom activities for developing the skill of self-management.

Key Terms

health-enhancing behavior

interactive health literacy

protective factor

risk factor

risky behavior

self-management

Self-management is the ability to practice health-enhancing behaviors and to avoid risky behaviors. In many ways, it applies all of the other skills of the National Health Education Standards. This skill involves students taking responsibility for their health and demonstrating the behaviors and practices necessary to maintain or improve the health of themselves and others. Practicing healthy behaviors and avoiding or reducing risky behaviors can increase students' quality of life, with positive outcomes related to avoiding disease, being productive, and being happy as well as being healthy. Self-management is critical in all dimensions of wellness for being a healthy person. If students are able to manage their own behavior in each dimension, they are more likely to lead a healthy, well-rounded life. Figure 9.1 represents examples of healthy behaviors in each dimension of wellness.

As you can see in the figure, there are many behaviors that we don't often think about as being related to health (recycling, for example). However, it is important for students to learn that health includes more than just eating right or not drinking too much alcohol. Another example is air quality—when air quality is low, a person with asthma may have trouble breathing. Working on solutions to improve air quality will have an impact on the health of people with breathing issues. There are many ways to be healthy, and behaviors in each dimension contribute to a person's overall health and wellness. Students should take time to examine both **health-enhancing behaviors** (behaviors that make a positive contribution to health) and **risky behaviors** (behaviors that can have negative consequences for health) within each dimension to develop a well-rounded understanding

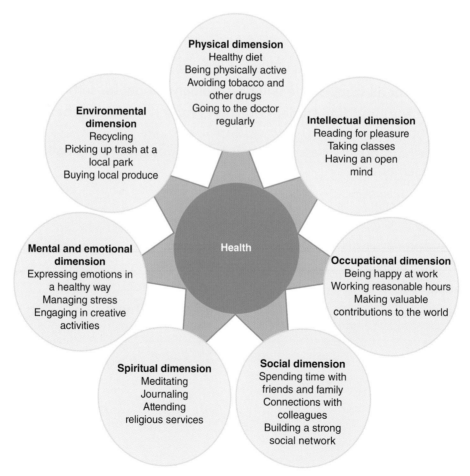

FIGURE 9.1 Examples of healthy behaviors in each dimension of wellness.

of the behaviors that can affect their health and the health of others around them.

Table 9.1 briefly describes how each dimension of wellness can influence health. In the classroom, you should emphasize health-enhancing behaviors, but students also need to recognize unhealthy behaviors to better understand the impact of behavior choices on their overall health as they work to manage their health in a positive way.

In addition to practicing health-enhancing behaviors and avoiding risky ones, two key aspects of self-management are responsibility and awareness. Students must be responsible for their own health and feel in control of their behaviors and, as a result, their health and well-being. This directly connects with self-efficacy (discussed in chapter 2)—people have to believe in their ability to practice or avoid certain behaviors in order to actually do so. In other words, students need to accept responsibility for their behaviors and their health, but

they also need to have the confidence in their abilities to engage in or avoid those behaviors.

Awareness relates to helping students analyze, reflect, and better understand their health status and the effects of their health behaviors. It helps students understand their context, or situation, and take responsibility for how their choices directly affect their overall health status. Students need to understand their context in order to effectively manage their own health and in some cases, the health of others. They must be aware of what factors in their lives may contribute to or detract from their health and be aware of what has (or has not) affected their current health behaviors.

Awareness goes beyond analyzing influences on their health. It also includes recognizing **risk factors** and **protective factors**, things in a student's life that can have a direct impact on health outcomes but may be out of the student's control. For example, having a supportive family and participating in community service

TABLE 9.1 Dimensions of Wellness and Their Impact on Health

DIMENSION OF WELLNESS	POTENTIAL IMPACT ON HEALTH
Physical	Maintaining physical health can help prevent injury and illness in the short and long term.
Social	Maintaining social health helps students use the positive relationships in their life to connect with others and feel supported. *Social health* refers to having positive interpersonal relationships with family, friends, and others; good communication skills; and a support network.
Emotional and mental	Maintaining emotional and mental health can help students positively manage their emotions, which can help them avoid the negative effects of stress, avoid violence, support conflict resolution, and support social health.
Intellectual	Maintaining intellectual health contributes to college and career readiness by helping students develop skills necessary to be successful in school and be lifelong learners. Higher levels of education correspond with positive health outcomes, so this dimension directly relates to health outcomes.
Spiritual	Maintaining spiritual health helps students develop a sense of purpose and connect to something larger than themselves (not necessarily religion). This connects with the holistic level of health literacy, where students are examining issues on a large scale and may be committed to making positive change for others. Having direction and purpose is a protective factor for many health behaviors.
Environmental	Maintaining environmental health helps ensure that students live in an environment (home, school, larger communities) that provides the basic infrastructure for health (clean water, clean air, and minimal pollutants). In the absence of this infrastructure, health is difficult to achieve.
Occupational	Maintaining occupational health helps students be successful in their careers. Being able to find work–life balance and find happiness in their work will have a positive impact on other dimensions of wellness, from physical health to emotional and mental health.

are protective factors related to positive health outcomes. Although students cannot control how much support they receive from family, they can control whether or not they engage in service activities. You want to encourage students to take responsibility for their health but also increase their awareness of the factors that may be outside their control. You want to deepen their understanding of what factors positively or negatively contribute to their likelihood of participating in health-enhancing or risky behaviors. As students gain an awareness of what they can and cannot control, they increase their ability to be responsible for their actions and take control of their behaviors and their health.

Ultimately, students' increased responsibility for their health translates to a higher level of health literacy. Specifically, self-management helps students attain **interactive health literacy** (described in chapter 1), which focuses on "the development of personal skills in a supportive environment" (Nutbeam, 2000, p. 265). As students hone their skills and work toward interactive health literacy, they become better able to use the knowledge and skills they have learned. They are more self-assured and confident in their ability to act on what they have learned during class. This is more likely to occur if the class itself is safe and welcoming for students. Though you cannot control students' external environment, you can provide a classroom environment where students feel valued, encouraged, and safe to step beyond their comfort zone as they try new skills.

Figure 9.2 presents the steps of the skill development model for self-management.

STEP 1: SKILL INTRODUCTION

As described, self-management is the ability to practice health-enhancing behaviors and to avoid or reduce risky behaviors. The focus is not just teaching students what healthy and unhealthy behaviors are but also helping them develop the skills and confidence to practice health-enhancing behaviors and make them a regular part of their lives. Self-management is at the core of what we hope students do as a result of health education—engage in healthy behaviors and avoid or reduce risky ones. When

introducing the skill of self-management, there are three aspects to address:

1. Health behaviors
2. Personal responsibility
3. Self-awareness

Health Behaviors

After you have introduced the term *self-management* and its definition, you will need to explore a variety of health behavior topics with students. Health behaviors should be discussed through examples of both healthy and risky behaviors within all dimensions of wellness. For example, because students make choices about health behaviors all the time, do not limit examples to one topic, such as stress reduction. Rather, show students how being under stress, getting enough sleep, staying hydrated, having good time management skills, and having a network of friends could all affect their desire to be active and exercise. Keep in mind that younger students may not be able to work with many topics and dimensions of wellness all at once, but over time you should expose them to a variety of health behaviors throughout multiple dimensions and show how the behaviors interrelate. Students should be able to identify examples of health behaviors (both health enhancing and risky) in their own lives and in the lives of others. They need to learn what health behaviors are as a foundation for working to practice or avoid them.

When discussing health behaviors, it is best to avoid dichotomizing behaviors as healthy and unhealthy or good and bad. Certainly students need to know which behaviors are health enhancing and which pose risks to their health, but it is equally important to understand that behaviors lie on a spectrum. There is rarely an absolute outcome from behaviors; rather, some behavior choices are more likely to lead to a negative health outcome while others are more likely to result in a positive health outcome.

For example, it is not completely accurate to say that drinking a soda will cause obesity. If a student chooses to occasionally have a soda, that isn't necessarily an unhealthy behavior because it is not likely to lead directly to a negative health outcome. For students who are used to drinking multiple sodas a day, reducing their

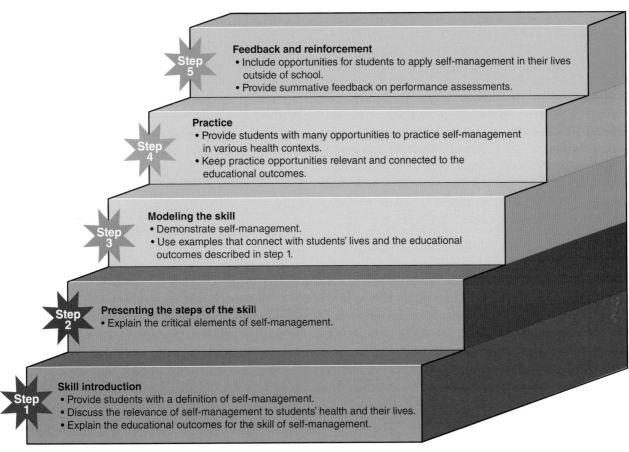

FIGURE 9.2 Steps for developing the skill of self-management.

intake to one per day and then one soda twice per week is health-enhancing behavior because they are limiting their intake and reducing their original risk for poor health outcomes. However, if a student regularly drinks soda, the behavior can lead to poorer health outcomes. It is difficult to find someone who will assert that drinking soda is a healthy choice, but one could argue that drinking soda isn't as unhealthy or harmful as using illicit drugs. The larger concept is the importance of helping students understand that there is a range of behaviors, some of which have more direct, immediate, or significant impacts (positive or negative) on health, and students should consider whether or not the health risks outweigh the potential benefits of the behavior.

Personal Responsibility

Students cannot manage their behaviors without accepting personal responsibility for

their actions and their health. During the introduction to self-management, students should spend some time reflecting on their role in their own health. This role will change over time. When students are younger, they have less control over certain factors in their lives, but there is always something that students can control no matter how young they are. It is important to emphasize this point when discussing self-management. You do not want to stop when students are able to list health-enhancing and risky behaviors; you want them to accept that they can control their behaviors and take charge of their health.

Self-Awareness

In addition to feeling confident and in control, being aware of your context is critical to self-management. In this case, we use the word *context* to encompass the situation that people are currently in, which includes where they are, where they have been, and what they want to do. We all have a variety of contexts, and there is not a one-size-fits-all approach to self-management. As a health educator, your job is to help students understand what has affected their lives, what is currently affecting their lives, and what might affect their future. This relates to identifying barriers and facilitators in SCT (social cognitive theory). Bandura's theory suggests that examining barriers (things in our lives preventing us from being healthy) and facilitators (things in our lives supporting our health) are key contributors to changing behaviors. (Refer to chapter 2 for more about SCT.) Students who understand their context can be more successful when they attempt to practice or avoid specific behaviors.

This aspect of self-management is similar to assessing needs (see chapter 8), but it is not the same. Assessing needs is one piece of understanding a student's context, but is not the only piece. A student's *context* is more than just needs; it is the interaction of multiple factors that influence health, including the built environment in the community, genetics, family, friends, values, and beliefs. Conducting a needs assessment can provide students with information about their context, but in order to measurably increase their awareness, you need to help students see the big picture and recognize the many factors that contribute both positively and negatively to their health.

Educational Outcomes

The performance indicators in the National Health Education Standards relate mainly to demonstrating healthy behaviors and avoiding risky behaviors (see table 9.2). Practicing healthy behaviors and avoiding risky behaviors is the ultimate goal of this unit. Personal responsibility and self-awareness are necessary aspects of self-management that must be addressed for students to be able to meet educational outcomes.

The following section highlights some considerations for establishing educational outcomes.

Step 1: Choosing Indicators

The performance indicators for self-management are straightforward. It would not be appropriate to separate the performance indicators unless you were going to use one of the indicators within another skill unit. For example, within a goal-setting unit, you might want to add a performance indicator from self-management related to practicing health--enhancing or avoiding risky behaviors. As discussed, you could include this indicator in a goal-setting unit either after a self-management unit (this is the best fit) or before it. You would build on the foundation established in the goal-setting unit when you completed the self-management unit.

TABLE 9.2 Performance Indicators for Standard 7 of the National Health Education Standards

PREK-GRADE 2	GRADES 3-5	GRADES 6-8	GRADES 9-12
7.2.1 Demonstrate healthy practices and behaviors to maintain or improve personal health. 7.2.2 Demonstrate behaviors that avoid or reduce health risks.	7.5.1 Identify responsible personal health behaviors. 7.5.2 Demonstrate a variety of healthy practices and behaviors to maintain or improve personal health.	7.8.1 Explain the importance of assuming responsibility for personal health behaviors. 7.8.2 Demonstrate healthy practices and behaviors that will maintain or improve the health of self and others. 7.8.3 Demonstrate behaviors to avoid or reduce health risks to self and others.	7.12.1 Analyze the role of individual responsibility for enhancing health. 7.12.2 Demonstrate a variety of healthy practices and behaviors that will maintain or improve the health of self and others. 7.12.3 Demonstrate a variety of behaviors to avoid or reduce health risks to self and others.

You are teaching a 10th-grade booster session (shortened semester) of health education. You decide that you will start the session with self-management to reinforce the importance of personal responsibility and to provide an opportunity for students to more deeply explore health behaviors and their impact on their health and quality of life. You decide to include all three performance indicators in the first unit of the booster session. By the end, students will be able to analyze the role of personal responsibility in their health (7.12.1), demonstrate a variety of health-enhancing practices and behaviors for self and others (7.12.2), and demonstrate risk-reducing or avoidance behaviors (7.12.3).

Step 2: Coverage of Indicators

The performance indicators for self-management cannot be partially covered. You must address them completely within a unit.

For your seventh-grade health class, you decide to cover all three performance indicators, which relate to personal responsibility, practicing health-enhancing behaviors, and avoiding risky behaviors (7.8.1-7.8.3). You recognize that you must cover all aspects of the indicators during the unit. However, you can also see how following the self-management unit with a goal-setting unit would be beneficial because these indicators will set the stage for students to choose a goal to pursue over the remainder of the health course.

Step 3: Student-Appropriate Terms

This step is when you ensure that the terms that will be used in the educational outcomes are appropriate for your students. In this case, the performance indicators for self-management will likely be appropriate for students but might need some scaffolding. For example, for first grade, you might explain that "*Demonstrate* is another word for *perform*" or "*Demonstrate* is another way to say 'do something.'"

Step 4: Educational Outcomes

Now that you have completed the previous three steps, you have your educational outcomes for the skill.

The following scenario demonstrates how step 1 of the skill development model may look in the classroom for self-management.

Step 1 in the Classroom: Skill Introduction

Scenario A: PreK to Grade 2

You create a visual for your kindergarten students that has an outline of a body. You ask, "What are things that we can do to keep our bodies healthy?" You write the students' ideas on the visual, prompting students with questions such as "What can we do to keep our bones healthy?" and "What can we do to keep our minds healthy?" to help them address multiple aspects of health. Once this is completed, you introduce the self-management unit by telling students that they will be learning about ways to be healthy and that they will have a chance to practice these behaviors during the unit. You show students the educational objectives, which are also posted as a visual. You then ask students to draw a picture of something they do in order to stay healthy.

Scenario B: Grades 9 to 12

You plan to start your ninth-grade unit with a connection to the students' history class. You work to make interdisciplinary connections whenever possible, and the self-management unit provides an opportunity because the students are studying the bubonic plague during the Middle Ages. Students examine historical documents to determine the types of behaviors and conditions that led to the spread of the disease. They then compare those conditions with conditions today and analyze how the spread of disease today is similar to and different from the Middle Ages. This leads to a

---

KEY POINTS

- Self-management is the ability to practice health-enhancing behaviors and avoid risky behaviors.
- During a self-management unit, health behaviors should be discussed along with personal responsibility and self-awareness.
- Avoid labeling behaviors as healthy or unhealthy; instead focus on discussing the relative impact of behaviors.

Self-management provides an opportunity for students to learn more about themselves and the impact of their behaviors on themselves and others.

discussion of personal responsibility and context to set the stage for the unit. You then introduce the skill, its definition, and the educational objectives for the unit.

STEP 2: PRESENTING THE STEPS OF THE SKILL

The second step in the skill development model is to present the critical elements of the skill. Table 9.3 provides examples of skill cues that you can use to reinforce the critical elements of the skill.

The emphasis during step 2 is reinforcing the skill cues so that students are familiar with them. Step 3 provides examples for modeling. The activities listed next are examples of strategies for helping students retain the skill cues.

Step 2 in the Classroom: Presenting the Steps of the Skill

PreK to Grade 2

Begin the unit by having students complete an acrostic poem (a poem that uses the letters of a topic, such as a person's name or object) with their name and

that starts with the "I AM" phrase. They should complete the acrostic poem with positive words to describe themselves. Following is an example for the name SARAH.

I AM

  Smart

  Active

  Runner

  Affectionate

  Happy

I AM HEALTHY!

Discuss how it is important to stay healthy and then introduce the skill cues. The other side of the worksheet should list the skill cues with a place for students to record healthy behavior that they engage in or that they want to engage in.

  Identify health behaviors that keep you healthy.

  Act on health behaviors.

  Make a list of what you do and how you feel.

  I AM healthy, because I . . .

You then move on to modeling how students should work through the skill cues (step 3).

TABLE 9.3 Skill Cues for Self-Management

PREK-GRADE 2	
Focus: Practicing age-appropriate health-enhancing behaviors	**I AM** **I**dentify health behaviors that keep you healthy. **A**ct on health behaviors. **M**ake a list of what you do and how you feel. "I AM healthy" could be a motto for the unit to reinforce both the skill cues and the goal for the unit. The cues are simple but provide information for discussions during health class and support from the teacher and others in their lives. The focus is on the positive, and a "behavior that keeps you healthy" can be avoiding a risky behavior, but you want to keep it simple.
GRADES 3-5	
Focus: Increasing the concept of personal responsibility and the amount of healthy behaviors students are engaging in	**I AM ME** **I**dentify health behaviors that keep you healthy. **A**ct on health behaviors. **M**onitor the impact of the health behaviors. **M**ake a list of what *you* can do to keep yourself healthy. **E**xplain the importance of taking responsibility for your health. "I AM ME and I am healthy" could be a slogan for the unit. *I AM ME* reinforces the skill cues and *I am healthy* reinforces the goal of the unit.
GRADES 6-8 AND 9-12	
Focus: Reinforcing the importance of personal responsibility and variety of behaviors	**I AM HEALTHY** **I**dentify current health behaviors. **A**nalyze your health context. **M**ake a plan for behavior change or reinforcement. **H**elp—get help if you need it. **E**xplain your role in maintaining and enhancing your health. **A**ccess information, products, and services to support health behaviors. **L**ist barriers and facilitators for the behavior change. **T**rack progress on the behavior change or reinforcement. **H**ow did your behavior change work? What would you change? **Y**ou are in control. **I APPEAR** **I**dentify health behaviors, wants, and needs within your context. **A**ccess information, products, and services necessary to support health-enhancing behaviors or behavior changes. **P**ractice health-enhancing behaviors. **P**ractice avoiding risky health behaviors. **E**xplain your role in your health. **A**ssess the outcomes of the behavior changes or of current health practices. **R**eflect on current health practices or changes made. I AM HEALTHY reinforces the desired outcome for students. Although no single behavior makes us healthy or unhealthy, all of our health-related behaviors together do determine our health. I APPEAR may be easier for students to remember and is a possible modification.

Grades 3 to 5

You create a poem that uses the theme "I AM ME and I AM HEALTHY." The poem should provide examples of health behaviors and should emphasize the main character engaging in health behaviors. The class should read the poem aloud as a group or students should take turns reading lines from the poem. You can then use this poem to fill in an anchor chart with the skill cues. This will help students contextualize the skill cues in a real-life scenario.

Grades 6 to 8

Divide students into small groups. Each group has a set of skill cues located around the room (at the other end of the room or throughout the room as appropriate for the space) and each student has a worksheet with blank spaces for the skill cues. In a relay format, students walk to pick up one skill cue card from their pile and bring it back to their group. Everyone records the skill cue and the process repeats until all groups have completed the worksheet. Review and address any questions.

Grades 9 to 12

Review the skill cues, which hopefully are familiar to students. After the review, students should partner up and create their own mnemonic or visual to help remember or reinforce the skill cues. Each set of partners should present to the class (or select partners should share depending on time). If appropriate, student work could be placed in the classroom to serve as supports for students.

STEP 3: MODELING THE SKILL

Step 3 focuses on providing relevant examples of the skill and applying the skill cues effectively. The assumption is that students know the skill cues and are ready to move on to observing the skill being applied.

PreK to Grade 2

- Have a healthy snack day where students discuss what makes a snack healthy (something that gives our body energy and helps our body be the best it can be) and then think about some examples of healthy snacks followed by a taste test of a variety of healthy snacks. Students should record what they liked, what they didn't like, and why. You can prepare a letter for students to bring home asking their families to try one of the new snacks from the taste testing. Encourage students to recommend examples of healthy snacks that are culturally appropriate.

- Students read (or listen to) a book, poem, or other piece of literature that has a character who appropriately expresses feelings of anger or sadness. Students then choose two strategies to try in their own lives. Students should practice in class, and a letter should be sent home to families to inform them of the strategies the students chose and to encourage adults to support the students in practicing these outside the classroom. Students should record how they felt when using these strategies.

- Students assist with the school recycling program. Perhaps students collect recycling from classrooms or support recycling in another manner. After participating, the class should make a list of how it felt to help recycle, why it is important, and how recycling affects their health. A homework assignment could have students ask their families about their recycling practices and how they could improve them.

- Working with the physical education teacher, set up an event that exposes stu-

KEY POINTS

- Emphasize the skill cues during this step. Students should be familiar with and understand the skill cues before moving to step 3.
- Actively engage students in the learning process during this step.
- Provide opportunities for students to interpret the skill cues, and create aids to help them remember the skill cues.

dents to physical activities that they could participate in outside of school. Students record which activities they enjoyed and why. They then make a plan to engage in these activities outside of class.

Grades 3 to 5

■ Small groups of students are assigned a different dimension of wellness. Students are provided with a visual that includes all of the components (e.g., a puzzle, pieces of a pie). Students record examples of health behaviors that people their age can engage in within each dimension. The class comes together to share ideas and address any misconceptions. Then guide students through the skill cues using examples that the students created.

■ Students read a comic strip or other animation (or other technology) that provides an example of a student working through the skill cues.

■ Students play a game in which they are given a scenario and they have to identify what the health behavior is and then work through the skill cues. The whole group should come together to review the scenarios to ensure the skill is modeled effectively.

■ Set up a health fair with a variety of community resources that can help students engage in health-enhancing behaviors. Students must complete a worksheet, scavenger hunt, or other activity to help reinforce the skill cues. (This could work for middle and high school as well.)

Grades 6 to 8

■ Students read a fictional diary entry for a middle school student working on a behavior change. The diary entry should include all skill cues. Individually or in partners, students review the entry and identify the skill cues. Review as a class.

■ Students act out or observe a role-play of two students talking to each other about a behavior change. Be sure the role-play includes all the skill cues. Have students act out the role-play while the rest of the class watches for the skill cues being performed. Debrief as a class.

■ With the assistance of English language arts or history teachers, select examples from texts that highlight some or all of the skill cues. Students work individually or in partners to analyze the text for the skill cues. The whole class reviews the texts and skill cues.

Grades 9 to 12

■ Students are presented with three current topics, such as depression screening, texting and driving, and universal health care coverage. In small groups, students discuss how the skill of self-management relates to the topic. Students should use the skill cues as a framework for their analysis and discussion.

■ Students review the results of the most recent youth risk survey and identify one topic they are interested in discussing. Use that topic to discuss strategies (by working through the skill cues) to help turn that statistic around. Focus on the skill cues and have students explain how each skill cue could be used to address the health behavior.

■ Students view a picture of people engaging in a healthy practice. Create a narrative about what the picture describes by walking students through the skill cues.

■ Refer to Maslow's hierarchy of needs (see chapter 3). Students brainstorm health-enhancing and risk-reducing or avoidance behaviors for one or more levels of the hierarchy. Individually or in pairs, students work through the skill cues for an assigned behavior for that specific level.

STEP 4: PRACTICE

After students have had a chance to learn about the skill of self-management and see it in action, they must employ the skill cues in authentic scenarios related to their world. As with previous skills, the more authentic the scenario, the more likely students are to embrace and employ the concepts presented in class. Because self-management requires students to apply previously learned information and skills, it is important to have a grasp of the students' ability level.

KEY POINTS

■ Modeling provides students with an opportunity to understand the skill in action as it relates to the specific topics presented.

■ The purpose of this step is to provide students with the tools to practice the skill on their own.

■ Modeling is successful when students feel both empowered to try the skill for a health behavior in their life and confident in their ability to maintain a current health practice or make a change to a healthier behavior.

Although the skill cues become more complex with age and grade, each student's ability to analyze or describe may vary. Given this, practice opportunities should be structured to allow for personal growth, not necessarily to arrive at a predetermined destination. For example, even within an overarching topic of stress management, not all students will select the same strategies to reduce their stress or improve their time management. This is acceptable as long as the strategies are appropriate and effective for the student.

The following paragraphs provide a general outline for designing practice opportunities for self-management. The ideas may need to be modified or scaffolded to meet the needs of your students.

Individual Responsibility

At all levels, self-management requires students to think about what it means to make healthy choices. Although this skill does not address how to come to the decision of what is healthy (i.e., the skill of decision making), it does ask students to take responsibility for the choices they are making. As students progress into middle and high school, they must not only talk about what the responsible choice is, but also explain why that is the better choice and then analyze how it is people's responsibility to take ownership of their health and the health-related choices they make. Opportunities to practice individual responsibility include the following:

■ Journal, blog, or do another reflective writing exercise that students use to describe their perceived levels of responsibility for various behaviors.

■ Analyze texts (could be fiction or nonfiction) and discuss the role of individual responsibility in the scenarios.

■ Write a persuasive essay or letter encouraging someone in their lives to take responsibility for their actions.

■ Create a video that explains why and how individual responsibility contributes to health.

Healthy Practices and Behaviors

Self-management requires students to demonstrate health practices that can improve or maintain their health. This moves beyond identifying what is healthy to actually employing strategies to be healthier. The goal for the demonstration is not that students have perfect health practices but that they work toward the healthiest option possible by employing strategies that reduce current risk or enhance health.

Note that the healthiest option is subjective. As discussed in previous chapters, you must take into consideration student backgrounds and cultures when considering your ideal for health. Although you may have a specific idea of how health looks, this view may vary across cultures, communities, families, and so on. You do not want to promote practices that are detrimental to health, but you need to ensure that personal beliefs and biases do not interfere with your students' work toward their own health outcomes. For example, you may have a personal belief that people should only consume organic produce. Although your argument may have merit, it may not be feasible or hold the same importance to students in your classroom. In this instance, it is more important that students recognize that consuming more fruits and

KEY POINTS

■ Classroom practice is the time for students to put their skill cues into action in a way that is relevant to their world.

■ Students should be able to demonstrate both behaviors that are health enhancing and also those that avoid or reduce risk. Both play an important role in overall health.

vegetables carries more weight than whether or not the produce is organic.

Conversely, you may encounter personal health practices that are harmful or perhaps even illegal. In this instance, it is best to discuss behaviors that could better support their health and well-being and, if necessary, report the behavior to the appropriate personnel in your school. For example, during discussions, a student states that he feels comfortable in his ability to manage stress. However, once you speak to this student, you find out that he leaves work until the last minute, stays up all night drinking energy drinks in order to get his work done, and then doesn't stress out again until the next deadline. This may be an excellent teachable moment in which you lead the class in a discussion about healthy ways to manage stress and time, and the negative effects of energy drinks. You might also decide that something a student shares is not appropriate for a class discussion, such as when someone draws a picture of physical abuse after being instructed to draw something that makes them sad. It would not be appropriate to speak about this with the class, but you must address this issue with the student in private and connect the student with the appropriate resources.

An effective way to have students practice demonstrating healthy behaviors is to assign a project on personal behavior change in which students have to decide on a behavior to change or a new behavior to try. They make a plan and try it over the course of a semester. As mentioned, this could tie in well with a goal-setting project. Make sure students record their experience, strategies, and outcomes. You could also expand the assignment to include accessing valid and reliable information by having students explain the health risks and benefits associated with the behavior, and you could

include decision making by having students indicate decisions they have to make relating to the change. This assignment could be modified to meet many objectives and include many skills.

Self-Awareness

Self-awareness is difficult to practice. It is something that needs to be developed, mainly by the students themselves. You can help students increase their self-awareness through in-class activities and assignments that provide opportunities for students to learn more about themselves and explore factors in their lives that are affecting them. Self-awareness comes with the potential for positive outcomes, but it also can have negative outcomes and raise questions about why students are in certain situations or why family members or friends put them at risk. Be prepared and thoughtful when engaging students in these kinds of activities.

STEP 5: FEEDBACK AND REINFORCEMENT

At this point in the unit, students have learned the skill cues, applied the cues to a real-world scenario through modeling, and practiced using the cues in a situation that is applicable to their world. Now they are going to demonstrate the cues as a part of a key assessment.

As discussed in previous steps, deciding to improve students' health depends on what is appropriate for them. For some, the healthiest choice may be harm reduction, whereas for others, completely avoiding a situation is the best option. For example, moving from smoking cigarettes to using a nicotine patch may help a student quit smoking, but for a student who has

TEACHING SELF-MANAGEMENT

Andy Milne

New Trier High School, New Trier Township District 203, Winnetka, Illinois

What is your best strategy for teaching self-management?

The theme of avoiding risky behaviors has to underpin everything that you do. Students should never feel compelled to ask "Why are we learning this?" They should always be aware of why the topic is being discussed and what the implications are to those who don't make the healthy choice.

I present the students with youth risk behavior data (we are lucky to be able to use our own) and highlight the scope of the problem, whether that be binge drinking, sex at an early age, or depression and thoughts of suicide. This promotes a discussion regarding why certain individuals behave the way they do and why some students choose not to engage in risky behaviors. This then leads to discussion about decision-making skills, refusal strategies, and identifying healthy alternatives. The ultimate aim is then to teach students how to identify where there is a problem and how to seek help or advocate for those in need of help.

I finish each unit with a summary of resources within the school building, the local community, and the greater community. I also provide links to videos, NPR radio shows, TED Talks, and extended reading for those students who wish to delve deeper into a topic. I use assessments that link to National Health Education Standards, allowing students to demonstrate their knowledge.

What advice do you have for other health educators in the field?

I encourage health educators to make their teaching as personal as possible. My students are different from all other students. My community has health concerns that might not be prevalent in a neighboring community. I encourage students to discuss these differences and urge them to advocate for others.

---

never smoked, avoiding cigarettes altogether is the best way to go. When students select their behavior of choice and demonstrate the practices that will be health enhancing and also avoid or reduce their overall risk, keep an open mind about how the students are employing the skill as it relates to their own lives. You want students to take responsibility for their health in a way that brings about positive health outcomes. Finally, peer feedback on the application of the skill along with teacher-directed formative and summative feedback are useful and appropriate.

SUMMARY

Self-management requires students to take their previous learning of the other skills of the National Health Education Standards and put them into practice in a way that demonstrates their ability to choose health-enhancing behaviors and to avoid or reduce health risks. In order to do this, however, students must recognize their personal responsibility in keeping themselves healthy and then be motivated to take the action steps necessary to make it happen. For most students, this is far more complicated than it appears.

Keeping in mind adolescent brain development, remember that students will need support and guidance in order to successfully employ the steps of self-management. Once they can do so, however, students will be better prepared and have a stronger sense of how to play an active role in their own health. This is why we teach health education—to help students see their potential and to embrace their role in keeping themselves healthy now and in the future.

Review Questions

1. What are the key components of self-management?

2. How do risk and protective factors affect health outcomes?

3. How do the concepts of motivation and Maslow's hierarchy of needs relate to the skill of self-management?

To find supplementary materials for this chapter, such as worksheets and extended learning activities, visit the web resource at
www.HumanKinetics.com/TheEssentialsOfTeachingHealthEducation

© Eugenio Marongiu/iStock.com

CHAPTER 10

Advocacy

Learning Objectives

After reading this chapter, you will be able to do the following:

- Implement all steps of the skill development model for advocacy.
- Describe appropriate student outcomes for advocacy at each developmental level.
- Create high-quality classroom activities for developing the skill of advocacy.

Key Terms

advocacy

advocate

process check

Being able to advocate for something is as much about having the competence and conviction to persuade someone to believe in your cause as it is about being knowledgeable about the cause itself. Some would even argue that a person's passion and ability to make a compelling, well-reasoned argument are more important than the facts of the argument. However, we want students to be able to support their passion and conviction with facts and evidence to enhance their ability to advocate, whether it is for themselves, someone else, or a cause.

When we teach students to **advocate** for personal, family, and community health issues, we teach them to recognize the value of taking a stand for something that is important to them. Students develop the ability to take control of their future health and, in turn, help others to take control of their health as well. This is the basis of the skill of advocacy within the National Health Education Standards.

Teaching the components of advocacy is straightforward, but understanding and applying them is complex. This is a skill that requires students to think critically and apply previously learned skills and information (e.g., accessing valid and reliable information, deciding what is important to advocate for, analyzing peer influences and social norms, using communication techniques that meet the needs of an intended audience) in order to develop a well-reasoned argument that persuades others to make a health-enhancing decision, to support a cause, or to make a change. Unlike self-management, which asks students to practice healthy behaviors in order to protect and enhance their own health, advocacy has students go further by taking a stand for themselves and by exploring how they can influence the health of others. When positioned on the continuum of health literacy discussed in chapter 1, advocacy is directly related to students reaching the level of critical health literacy, and it can support students in reaching holistic health literacy. Students who are competent at this level are able to understand the perspectives of others in their community, in their country, and potentially even in other countries that may be suffering social inequality or are at risk for poor health outcomes.

Another component of this skill is that in order to advocate effectively, students must consider points of view of various audiences and use that information to shape their argument. Students must recognize that one single message will not result in widespread behavior change because each audience looks at an issue through a different lens. Instead, multiple messages about the same outcome may need to be created for different audiences to buy into the message and change their behavior. For example, when discussing concussion prevention and recovery, student-athletes may need to be persuaded that reporting concussion symptoms to coaches and parents is not a sign of weakness - it is the healthiest decision. It is more important that athletes understand that concussion effects can be cumulative and even a minor concussion could lead to bigger problems the next time. Of less importance to the athletes is what happens in the brain after a concussion. Advocating for athletes to recognize symptoms in themselves and others could truly save a brain. Coaches, on the other hand, would likely want information about the postconcussion brain effects to help them understand the health risks associated with ignoring concussions and their ethical duty to ensure the safety of their athletes. This is an example of how two audiences can have the same position on an issue but need a different frame for the advocacy effort or different evidence to convince them.

When implemented effectively, advocacy is a powerful tool for change. Students learning about this skill have the opportunity to be self-directed in their quest to solve problems and to help those around them maintain or improve their health. When shared outside the health classroom, student advocacy campaigns can also have an impact beyond the immediate school environment. The campaigns provide a stepping-stone for students to become active and engaged citizens in all areas of society.

Figure 10.1 presents the steps of the skill development model for advocacy.

STEP 1: SKILL INTRODUCTION

Advocacy is a skill that teaches students how to build support for a cause and encourage others to adopt or maintain a health-enhancing behavior. The procedural knowledge for this skill evolves from the early elementary level to

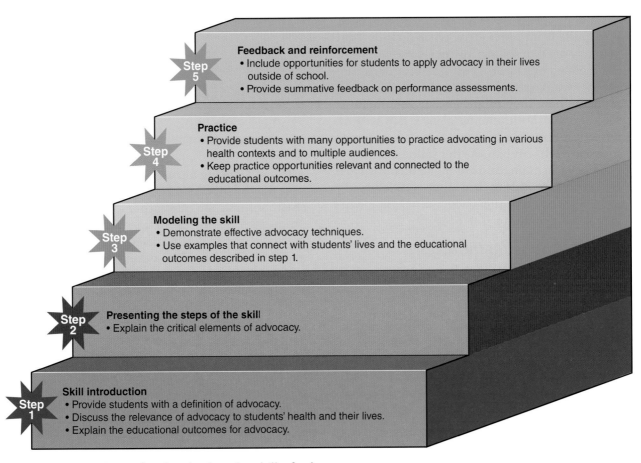

FIGURE 10.1 Steps for developing the skill of advocacy.

the high school level. At the elementary level, students verbalize requests and give their opinion about specific health practices. The importance of this should not be underestimated. Many students have not been provided the guidance and encouragement to effectively and politely verbalize their health needs. Up until this point, many people in their lives have told them what is in their best interest. Given this, many have also not learned how to be a voice that encourages others to make healthy choices. Teaching the youngest students these two skills empowers them. Even from a young age, students can be key players in keeping themselves and others safe and healthy.

At the secondary level, the performance indicators expand beyond stating a health-enhancing message and encouraging others to also include working cooperatively with others as an advocate and recognizing how the audience shapes the development and delivery of the message. Especially at the secondary level, students reflect on social norms and school or community culture and how these affect youth choices. Once students take that information and work with others to improve the health of themselves, their family, and the community, they begin to understand how complex advocacy really is. To many, it appears as if this skill is just about telling others what you think, but actually it requires a thoughtful, measured approach in order to achieve the desired outcome.

Educational Outcomes

Educational outcomes for advocacy focus on students developing the ability to build a compelling argument and then share that argument with others. In class, be sure to explain the performance indicators (see table 10.1) in student-friendly language. In comparison to other skills, advocacy contains few performance indicators at each level. Don't let the absence of performance indicators be misleading.

Although there are few parts to this skill, each part pulls from previously learned skills, and you may need to spend time in class reminding students about the other skills that inform the ability to advocate. For example, when asking students how they might encourage others to make a health-enhancing choice, it would be wise to remind them about assertive communication skills and analyzing influences.

The performance indicators for advocacy are relatively straightforward. However, following are a few considerations when developing educational outcomes for the unit.

Step 1: Choosing Indicators

The performance indicators for advocacy allow for greater depth and sophistication as students progress in age. However, they also need to be covered as a group in order to be most effective. Given this, you will likely include all of the performance indicators in a grade span in order to measure proficiency. The following scenario provides an example of the performance indicators in practice.

You are teaching advocacy in your eighth-grade health class. You know that students have not yet had an advocacy unit in middle school because the sixth-grade curriculum explored other skills in depth and did not have time to cover advocacy. Therefore, you are going to spend more time on the advocacy unit to provide students the opportunity to apply previous skills to an advocacy project. You understand that they have to cover all four indicators (8.8.1-8.8.4) to develop the skill.

Step 2: Coverage of Indicators

Similar to the skills of decision making and goal setting, the performance indicators for advocacy work best as parts of the whole. Although stating a position on a topic is important, if students do not go on to further support their opinion, engage others with a similar philosophy about the topic, and present their message in a way that meets the needs of the audience, they have little likelihood of changing anyone's opinion, let alone behavior. Although each performance indicator can have discrete time and tasks, any assessment of this skill should include all of the performance indicators as a measure of proficiency.

You have decided to include an advocacy unit at the end of the semester in your ninth-grade health class. You will cover all indicators for the grade span because the health education course in the 11th grade does not focus on advocacy. Even though the four indicators are fairly complex, you recognize that students have many of the skills needed to address the indicators. So, you choose to cover all indicators completely and to assess students' performance and application of previously learned skills during the unit.

TABLE 10.1 Performance Indicators for Standard 8 of the National Health Education Standards

PREK-GRADE 2	GRADES 3-5	GRADES 6-8	GRADES 9-12
8.2.1 Make requests to promote personal health. 8.2.2 Encourage peers to make positive health choices.	8.5.1 Express opinions and give accurate information about health issues. 8.5.2 Encourage others to make positive health choices.	8.8.1 State a health-enhancing position on a topic and support it with accurate information. 8.8.2 Demonstrate how to influence and support others to make positive health choices. 8.8.3 Work cooperatively to advocate for healthy individuals, families, and schools. 8.8.4 Identify ways in which health messages and communication techniques can be altered for different audiences.	8.12.1 Utilize accurate peer and societal norms to formulate a health-enhancing message. 8.12.2 Demonstrate how to influence and support others to make positive health choices. 8.12.3 Work cooperatively as an advocate for improving personal, family, and community health. 8.12.4 Adapt health messages and communication techniques to a specific target audience.

Step 3: Student-Appropriate Terms

Many of the terms used within advocacy are straightforward and familiar to students. However, as you review each performance indicator, check for understanding and give examples as appropriate.

To be sure that students understand the terms for each indicator, you stop after presenting an indicator and ask a student to paraphrase what it means. Additionally, you post the skill and performance indicators along with any other skill cues that are used to help students achieve proficiency in this skill.

Step 4: Educational Outcomes

Now that you have completed the previous three steps, you have your educational outcomes for the skill.

The following scenario demonstrates how step 1 of the skill development model may look in the classroom for advocacy. The two examples presented here show how educators at the elementary and secondary levels can implement participatory methods to address step 1 in one lesson. Although presented here as a single lesson, actual implementation time for step 1 may vary based on the length of your class period, student learning needs, or types of activities used.

Step 1 in the Classroom: Skill Introduction

Scenario A: Grades 3 to 5

Within the fifth-grade classroom, students have been divided into groups of three. Each group is given a scenario that discusses a common health issue all fifth graders will encounter—personal hygiene. The scenario discusses how all bodies go through changes, but sometimes we don't realize that these body changes are more than just cosmetic—some of these changes require us to alter our personal care habits in order to keep ourselves feeling, looking, and smelling our best.

You explain to students that in the upcoming unit they will be learning more about the changes that puberty causes in the body and strategies for keeping up with necessary personal hygiene practices. You further explain to students that, by the end of the unit, they will be able to effectively express their opinion about a necessary hygiene practice (performance indicator 8.5.1) and encourage other students to use that hygiene practice as well (performance indicator 8.5.2).

Scenario B: Grades 9 to 12

Students in your ninth-grade health education class know all too well the importance of being successful in and out of school. They feel the pressure to meet parents' and coaches' expectations, keep up with their friends, volunteer to help the community, and work at their jobs. Sometimes the pressure to succeed becomes overwhelming, but when asked about how they handle these overwhelming feelings, many students have difficulty giving examples of positive ways to handle the stress in a health-enhancing or effective manner.

After students settle into the class, they read the story of a character who is overwhelmed with all the things she needs to do and feels there is no way to be what everyone expects of her. This character feels hopeless and decides that the best way to handle the stress is to kill herself—she just wants the pain to go away. After students finish the reading, you do a **process check** with the class, asking the students if they can relate to the character's feelings and what pressures exist in this school that can contribute to those feelings.

Given the previous answers, you ask about possible messages that could be important for high school students to hear about managing their stress and understanding that suicide is never the answer (performance indicator 8.12.1). Then you explain that during this unit, each student will be part of a production team that is responsible for crafting and

KEY POINTS

■ The skill of advocacy empowers students to be vocal about causes important to them and gives them the structure for doing this effectively.

■ Being an advocate requires understanding both the cause being advocated for and how the message will affect social norms and behaviors.

■ Advocacy is a complex skill that may require more time to develop than anticipated.

presenting a message aimed at helping distressed students find the necessary resources and support. Each production will highlight all of the skill cues and be targeted to an audience of high school students, parents, or administrators and their role in helping students (8.12.2-8.12.4).

STEP 2: PRESENTING THE STEPS OF THE SKILL

Similar to other skills in this book, the skill cues for advocacy present the skill in language that is accessible and relevant for students. The cues recognize that persuasion is not about being the loudest voice but rather about being a well-reasoned, effective voice. Sometimes it is the quiet yet persistent voice that prevails.

Sample skill cues for advocacy are presented in table 10.2.

As with step 1, there are many ways to introduce step 2 that are participatory in nature. The following scenarios provide some examples for implementing step 2 in the classroom.

Step 2 in the Classroom: Presenting the Steps of the Skill

PreK to Grade 2

You ask students to list things that they want or need. You record their ideas on the board and then ask students how they think they could get these things and who they could ask for help (covers the I, C, and A skill cues from I CARE). You then lead a discussion about effective ways to get what you want, making sure to focus on getting positive and healthy things. For example, don't choose the fact that students want

TABLE 10.2 Skill Cues for Advocacy

PREK-GRADE 2	
Focus: Promoting personal health and beginning to extend the skill to others	I CARE Identify personal health needs, wants, and desires. Can someone help you? Ask for guidance to promote personal health. Recognize positive health choices. Encourage peers to make positive health choices.
GRADES 3-5	
Focus: Developing informed opinions about health issues and encouraging others	I CARE Identify health issues that are relevant and meaningful. Consider your opinion about the health issue after conducting research about it. What is your position? What is the health-enhancing position? Access information in order to support your position with facts and evidence. Relay your health-enhancing message to your audience. Examine the outcomes. Was your advocacy effective?
GRADES 6-8	
Focus: Continuing to tailor messages and continuing to extend advocacy efforts to larger audiences and issues	I CARE Identify and research a relevant and meaningful health issue. Create a health-enhancing position or message about the issue that is supported by facts and evidence and is geared toward the audience. Act passionately and with conviction. Relay your health-enhancing message to your audience. Evaluate the effectiveness of the advocacy effort.
GRADES 9-12	
Focus: Continuing to apply the skill of advocacy for extended audiences	The same skill cues can be used in grades 9-12. You can add specific references to social norms if you feel it is necessary because this is the main change from grades 6-8. The suggested modification would be to change the C skill cue to "Create a health-enhancing position or message that is based on accurate peer and societal norms, that is supported by facts and evidence, and that is geared toward the audience."

- Clearly reinforce skill cues for students at all levels.
- Provide multiple opportunities for students to understand and retain the skill cues (e.g., using multiple modalities during the presentation, using real-life examples, having students record the cues).
- Allow students to modify cues to help them remember and connect with the cues.

candy; choose the fact that a student wants to go to the playground. (However, you might consider leading a discussion about why candy is not necessarily a health-enhancing item.) Next, ask students to identify positive health behaviors or choices they could make. End with a discussion of how students can use the same techniques to get what they want to help other make healthy choices. Conclude by telling students that this unit will help them develop the skills they need to promote their own health and the health of others using the I CARE acronym.

Grades 3 to 5

Find examples (or use examples from previous units) of advocacy efforts led by students their age, such as Kid President, a boy who has appeared in online videos and believes in the power of kids to make a difference in the world. Show the students the advocacy efforts (e.g., posters, PSAs, news stories) and how the skill cues are represented. (Note: This is also an example of modeling, but combining modeling with the skill cues can be a helpful connection for students as long as you adequately cover the cues and provide other examples of modeling.)

Grades 6 to 8

Place students in small groups. Ask them to discuss what they would need to do in order to advocate for something. This may be a review if advocacy has been covered in other courses or it could be a group brainstorm to access prior knowledge. Once groups have completed this, ask them to share and record ideas on the board. End with a debriefing where you cover the actual skill cues for the skill. Have students record the skill cues using the acronym.

Grades 9 to 12

Show students examples of large-scale advocacy efforts. Ask them what they think are the skill cues for the skill based on the examples provided. Debrief as a large group and then cover the skill cues for the unit. Use the advocacy examples to give students real-life examples of all the skill cues (ones that they didn't cover or ones that needed clarification).

STEP 3: MODELING THE SKILL

Students are surrounded by people trying to get them to buy into a position or cause. Sometimes advocacy takes the form of a friend trying to convince them to finish a video game and delay homework for just a few more minutes. Sometimes the advocacy is less subtle and on a large scale, such as students crafting and delivering a plan to the administration to stop parents and busses from idling their engines during drop-off and pickup so students don't have to inhale the exhaust fumes. When modeling advocacy, it is important to provide multiple examples that show students the many ways that advocacy can influence others.

Modeling the skill of advocacy for students is most successful when the examples are relevant and students can see themselves being an advocate in the given scenario. Because this skill requires students to think about persuading others in a way they may not have previously considered or for something unpopular, some may be uncomfortable and resistant to becoming an advocate. Given this, modeling should provide students with a variety of ways to advocate and language that students can use to promote their health-enhancing message even in the face of adversity. Following are examples of modeling activities.

PreK to Grade 2

- In partners, students observe a picture of children engaged in a healthy activity (e.g., eating a healthy snack, performing physical activity, helping a friend) and then discuss how they could persuade a friend to engage in that activity. Ask partners to share their ideas. You should correct any errors or misconceptions. End the activity with an example of effective modeling (either from you or the students).

■ Students observe puppets discussing how another student in the class is always mean and stating they want to spread the message that being a bully isn't acceptable. Students can suggest strategies for the puppets to advocate for their position and you can act them out for the students.

■ Students view three pictures of children engaging in unhealthy or potentially dangerous activities (e.g., smoking, holding a sharp knife, riding a bike without a helmet). For each, have students think of ways to help the children in the picture make a healthier choice. Record the key points on the board and then model with a final example using the skill cues covered in the discussion.

■ Reference a recent math lesson on telling time and how going to bed and getting enough sleep can influence how the students feel at school. Students should think about what time they go to bed and what they should tell a friend about getting enough sleep each night. Have students share examples and provide feedback so that they clearly understand how to apply the skill.

Grades 3 to 5

■ Write three unhealthy behaviors on the board and assign a small group to each topic. Have the students choose a behavior they would like to use for the modeling. Work together to create an advocacy campaign to prevent students from engaging in the behavior. Be sure to follow the skill cues and call attention to each cue as it is being discussed and used in the class example.

■ Students discuss a character from a book they have recently read who has to make a choice that could affect his health. As a class, come up with a message to tell that character about how to choose a healthier behavior.

■ Students watch an animated clip of two characters in a car who are talking about why they should wear their seatbelts as they go to pick up another child. They have to remind the child to put on the seatbelt and give positive reasons for wearing it.

■ Students brainstorm reasons why it is important to only take medicine in the proper amounts and at the proper times. Together they come up with three small phrases that they could tell other students about why medicine can be dangerous if not taken properly.

Grades 6 to 8

■ Ask for two volunteers to be the characters in a scripted role-play where one character tries to convince the other character that participating in the upcoming walk-to-school day will be fun and get their brain geared up for school. Provide feedback to ensure that students understand how the skill cues were applied in the scenario.

■ Students read or create the story of a student who is in a dilemma about whether or not she should respond to a person whom she has never met and who wants to play an online game with her. Use the facts of the story to create a message as a class that keeps the student safe from unknown people online.

■ After reviewing the skill cues, students form small groups and read a scenario where the main character is being bullied through text messages. Each group creates a message that advocates for antibullying measures and ways to make the school culture less accepting of this behavior.

■ Students choose one dimension of wellness and create a health-enhancing message that promotes the assigned dimension. Make sure there is time for students to share their work and receive feedback.

Grades 9 to 12

■ Students read a newspaper article or watch a news clip about recent legislation related to health (e.g., teen-relationship violence, nutrition standards, texting while driving). In pairs, students develop a health-enhancing message to support the new legislation and identify what other steps they would need to take in order to spread their message to others. Ask students to share their work and review how their examples connect with the skill cues. Facilitate a discussion to cover any cues not addressed.

Courtesy of The Putney School.

When students have the ability to advocate they are empowered to stand up for causes and issues they believe in which can lead to personal growth and community action.

■ Introduce data about youth alcohol use and binge drinking and have the students identify key messages that they need to know in order to prevent this risky behavior. Choosing one of the brainstormed messages, students come up with a way to advocate for their message to three audiences (e.g., other teens, parents, administrators, community members). Provide time for groups to share and for class discussion about the skill application.

■ Students discuss sportsmanship and the role it plays in a successful team. Students create a message that promotes good sportsmanship and then share their message with another classmate. Make sure the message encourages others to be on the team of good sportsmanship. Provide students with a checklist of the skill cues that they can use to evaluate their peers' work.

■ Students read a blog entry written by another teen that advocates for a cause important to them. Ask students to look at the skill cues and determine whether or not the blog entry meets the skill cues, and if not, what would be a better approach to make the advocacy effort more successful.

STEP 4: PRACTICE

Practicing the effective application of skill cues for advocacy is critical. As mentioned previously, although advocacy is a fairly straightforward skill to understand, it is complex to execute. This is mainly because students may not have been taught how to frame a message in a way that gets others to listen—without alienating them. Although students have been advocating for what they want and need since birth, this unit is intended to help them frame a message and move beyond simple messaging to that which is nuanced and tailored to an audience, with the ultimate goal of helping others to be healthy and make positive change.

Because advocacy asks students to think beyond themselves and assess how the needs

KEY POINTS

- Modeling the skill of advocacy should demonstrate multiple approaches to successful advocacy.
- When possible, allow students to come up with the specific topic or healthy behavior to support the introduced topic. This encourages buy-in and a greater willingness to practice the skill cues.
- Modeling sets students up to perform the skill independently, but for advocacy, students may need to see the skill modeled multiple times and have further conversations to come to agreement on the best strategies to use in an advocacy campaign.
- Make sure you always discuss how examples model the skill cues. This should occur whether you provide the modeling example or the students provide the examples. It is critical that students explicitly see how the cues are applied during the modeling phase.

of others will affect their proposed message, you must be conscious of the developmental and social abilities of your students. Not all students will be able to critically assess the needs of others or to rationalize why an argument will be more effective with one group than another. When this is the case, allow students to partner up so as to alleviate the stress of trying to figure out these things on their own. Another suggestion is to allow students to think about how they might be persuaded to engage in the healthy behavior. Then ask the students to imagine that others feel the same way and use that information to practice the skill cues.

Another consideration related to advocacy is for students who are not comfortable speaking publicly. Although the skill of advocacy is the perfect opportunity to have students develop their public-speaking skills, giving a presentation in front of the class is not the only way to advocate. Posters, videotapes, slide presentations, and written dialogues are all ways students could demonstrate the skill without speaking in front of the class.

A third consideration for students is to ensure that any information they use to support their cause is accurate, reliable, and relevant. This skill assumes that students are retrieving valid and reliable information, and it also assumes that the information is relevant and appropriate for the target audience. This can be difficult to determine, so having a class discussion about the types of information various audiences will find useful can go a long way to preparing students to develop a presentation or advocacy campaign.

Given the considerations mentioned here, feedback becomes of the utmost importance. Feedback should be an ongoing process with checks built in along the way. Do not wait until students come in with their final presentation to let them know that their data aren't appropriate or that their audience wouldn't be influential in changing the behavior they are discussing.

The following paragraphs provide a general outline for designing practice opportunities for advocacy. You may need to modify or scaffold the ideas to meet the needs of your students.

Identify Health Issues

The first piece of practicing advocacy is to identify health issues that are of personal interest or that are important for the school, community, nation, and world. Depending on the students' age, this can be more teacher-directed (students choosing from a list you have generated) or independent work (issues identified through research). No matter how the issues are identified, it is important that you provide opportunities for students to connect with issues that have meaning for them.

Access Valid and Reliable Information

After issues have been identified, students need to be able to learn more about the issue in order to create an informed opinion which is a foundation for effective advocacy. This is an excellent opportunity for students to apply the skill of accessing valid and reliable information in a real-life context. The goal is for students to learn more about the issue and to gather evidence that they can use to create and support their position on the issue.

Know Your Audience

Now that students have a clearer understanding of the issue and have developed a position, they need to decide how to address the issue and who the audience is for their advocacy message. Once they have determined the target audience, students need to consider what their audience values and what information or tactics will influence them. This is an opportunity to apply the skill of analyzing influences. Students can think about the factors, messages, visuals, facts, and so on that will influence their chosen audience. They should consider everything from the medium used to transmit their message, to what their message actually is, to colors, pictures, tone, and music used. Whether advocating to a friend or designing a major public health campaign, it is essential to identify the relevant audiences and think about how to best influence and connect with each audience.

Create and Deliver the Message

Students must have an opportunity in class to create their advocacy project (*project* referring here to the broad forms advocacy can take) and actually deliver it. Due to the varied forms advocacy can take, you can narrow this part of the skill development by giving students limited options for the format (e.g., students must create a PSA). However, limiting the options may not allow students to truly connect with their project because a specific format might not be relevant to them or to their audience.

When possible, offer at least two options for the project. It is also important that students deliver their project—ideally to the intended audience but at a minimum to the class—and receive feedback on their work and their delivery. Be sure to instruct the class in appropriate ways to provide and receive feedback. This will make the feedback more constructive and less personal or hurtful for the receiver.

Key aspects of advocacy are passion and conviction. This isn't always easy for students to demonstrate, so it is critical that students receive feedback on the delivery or presentation as well as the project itself. The whole project does not need to be completed in class (students can work on the project outside of class), but there should be opportunity for formative assessment.

STEP 5: FEEDBACK AND REINFORCEMENT

Once you reach step 5 in the advocacy unit, students will most likely be familiar with your classroom strategies to ensure that students are consistently working toward achievement of the identified objectives. As mentioned in step 4, formative assessment for advocacy has the potential to set students up for success or failure due to the higher level of thinking and application required for this skill. Also, if students have class time to develop their advocacy proposal, you could ask the class to work at the same pace, allowing you to reinforce the skill cues and have students share strategies for getting their point across to the intended audience.

The last element of step 5 is to be conscious of whether the topic students are advocating for is health enhancing. Students encounter a vast

TEACHING ADVOCACY

Nichole Calkins, EdD
Mt. Rainier High School, Des Moines, Washington

What is your best strategy for teaching advocacy?

In my teaching experience, providing engaging experiences for students is the most successful tool for teaching advocacy skills. I do this by connecting with community partners who could come into the classroom and show how various organizations operate and the role that individuals can play in creating social change. Students then advocate for a particular organization's cause in a number of ways, such as fundraising for a clinic that treats people with addiction, working in food banks, or volunteering at homeless shelters or a crisis hotline. I believe that our students want to make a difference and want to make positive changes, but they need those behaviors modeled. Students are more equipped to create an influential message because they participated in an experience that influenced them and they were emotionally invested. Connecting students with individuals or organizations that are advocates helps them to develop those same skills.

What is one pitfall to avoid when teaching advocacy?

A pitfall in teaching advocacy skills is not using the power of influence. We can develop lessons in which we ask students to create health-enhancing messages and provide them with the resources to do a social media campaign by making posters or videos. However, if the students do not see the importance of their role and the message in making a difference, then the activity will be just another poster-making assignment. We need to hook our students with the belief that what they are doing will make an impact in some way and show them examples of how it can be done. Avoid assigning the creation of advocacy messages without connecting them to the power of influence.

What piece of advice do you have for other health educators in the field?

In health education there is so much content that it can be very easy to simply assign reading and writing assignments. I think many students expect health to be boring because of sit-and-get lectures. My advice is to create an environment where students are expected to be involved through discussion, role-plays, debates, and interaction. Avoid book work at all costs! Become a master at grouping students so that they can participate in small-group discussions that generate genuine reflection and questioning. I created procedures to help all students in the classroom contribute to the discussion and used those procedures on a daily basis. I brought in current newspaper and magazine articles to capture interest and facilitate relevant discussion. Students knew that they would have to demonstrate knowledge and skills on a regular basis so that they remain engaged.

array of information and opinions on a regular basis, and it is your job to guide students and help them to appropriately advocate for their health and the health of others. This may mean helping students prepare for potential resistance to their argument, even if their position is a different philosophy than yours. Though it may not be easy to support a point of view that is different than your own, as long as the view is factual and based in a reasoned argument, we encourage you to help the student find his voice. If students become proficient in the skill of advocacy, they will recognize that, although it's not easy to do, taking an unpopular stance may be essential to helping others be healthy.

SUMMARY

At its core, advocacy is about taking a topic that is important to you and spreading that message in a way that compels listeners to a healthy action. The beauty of this skill is that there is no one-size-fits-all strategy. Instead, this skill

KEY POINTS

■ Reinforcement and supportive reflection are vital to student success in this skill because they provide an opportunity for students to fine-tune their message along the way.

■ Advocacy for a cause may require sharing an unpopular message. It is your job to help students find their voice and to assist them as they build a foundation for their message.

■ All messages must be health enhancing. Your role is to ensure that students can advocate for their own health and the health of others.

teaches that taking a clear, health-enhancing stand on an issue, providing specific steps to support that message, working cooperatively with others, and having a sound understanding of your audience are the key ingredients. Thus, students in a health education class could present a range of examples advocating for their cause and all of them could demonstrate proficiency. As an educator, your task is to ensure that students understand the developmental progression of the skill yet have the freedom to advocate in a way that feels authentic to them. When you provide this flexibility, you show that you value the unique strengths each student brings to class. Further, allowing creativity in a project or skill demonstration increases the likelihood that students will remember and employ this skill in the future.

Review Questions

1. How does understanding the skill cues and performance indicators for advocacy lead to a better classroom experience for students?

2. What are some strategies that encourage students to apply effective advocacy tactics in a manner that is most appealing to them?

3. Why is it important to provide feedback as students practice advocacy?

To find supplementary materials for this chapter, such as worksheets and extended learning activities, visit the web resource at
www.HumanKinetics.com/TheEssentialsOfTeachingHealthEducation

PART III

Developing Curricula and Assessments

The third part of this text focuses on designing a curriculum that is relevant and meaningful for students and then assessing whether or not students have learned the skills and information in the curriculum. Additionally, you will be able to collect and use data to inform your curriculum decisions. The data will assist you in both meeting the needs of your students and determining which health-related topics and skills to include in your curriculum.

Designing a curriculum that focuses on skill development is a critical step in the implementation of a skills-based approach. The stronger your written curriculum is, the more effective your program will be. As you read through this part, think of curriculum development as an opportunity to create the road map for the skills-based journey. The more detailed, accurate, clear, and purposeful your map is, the smoother the journey will be.

Once you have created your written curriculum and you know where you are going, you will design assessments that let you know when you have arrived. Assessments should be meaningful, relevant, and authentic and should directly measure goals and objectives outlined in the curriculum. If your assessments don't accurately measure your goals and objectives, you won't know when you have arrived at your destination and you may get close or miss the mark altogether.

In this part you will learn about strategies you can implement to create a curriculum and assessments for a skills-based program. You will be able to implement an eight-step approach to curriculum development leading to a written curriculum that emphasizes skills and supports skill development and knowledge acquisition. Finally, you will be able to develop assessments that evaluate the goals and outcomes of your curriculum and that measure both student knowledge and skill level.

© monkeybusinessimages/iStock.com

CHAPTER 11

Using Data to Inform Curriculum Planning

Learning Objectives

After reading this chapter, you will be able to do the following:

- Identify sources of data to aid in the curriculum planning process.
- Use data to determine areas of need in the population.
- Identify topics and functional information that address the needs identified through data.

Key Terms

reliability

socioecological model

statistical significance

validity

To give students a foundation for maintaining or improving their health, each skill must be taught within the context of functional information. It must also be packaged as part of an overall curriculum that moves students through a thoughtful, thorough course of instruction based on predetermined student outcomes. In this chapter, we discuss how choosing topics (which form the umbrella for determining functional information) for inclusion in a health education curriculum is based on multiple factors—not the least of which are whether the topics and information are up to date, relevant, appropriate, and meaningful to the students' world. As we discuss this concept further, you will learn how to identify data, perform a needs assessment in your school and community, and use the data to make appropriate decisions about the inclusion of topics.

COMPILING FUNCTIONAL INFORMATION

You must consider many factors when determining which topics to include. Because information changes at a rapid pace, understanding health data becomes paramount to ensuring that students are learning the most current, accurate, meaningful, necessary, and functional information as it relates to the skills of the National Health Education Standards.

Functional information, as introduced in chapter 2, is information that is usable, applicable, and relevant. It is not arbitrary, traditional, or extensive. Functional information is the *context* in which skills are taught and becomes the basis for students to develop functional knowledge. In this book, the term *information* refers to the facts within a health-related topic area such as alcohol, sexuality, tobacco, or nutrition. The term *knowledge* refers to the compilation of information that has been learned and forms the foundation for future thoughts and actions. The term *content* is not synonymous with *information* because the skills themselves are also considered content that students must learn.

To determine which functional information will provide the context for skill development during class, consider the following criteria. First, the information must be important enough for students to learn in order to do or accomplish something. Ask yourself, "What will happen if my students are not presented with this information? Will they be able to apply this skill in a real-life situation?" For example, when teaching a tobacco unit, the teacher might spend time going over all the chemicals in a cigarette, but in a situation where a friend is offering a cigarette, it is more important for the student to be able to perform an effective refusal. Yes, students need to understand why smoking is a poor choice in order to decide to refuse, but it is possible that the only information they need is that their mom will take away social privileges if she finds out or that smoking could reduce their ability to sing on key. Focusing on the chemicals in a cigarette does not provide students with information that is meaningful or useable. Don't waste valuable time teaching all the chemicals in a cigarette when students may already have the information they need in order to refuse a cigarette. In this example, you could answer "Yes, my students would be able to refuse a cigarette without being able to list the chemicals in a cigarette," and therefore you do not need to include this piece of content in the curriculum. Chemicals in cigarettes may not be vital to learn, but in answering the previous question you may decide that there are other facts that students do need to know (e.g., effects of tobacco on the body, cost of cigarettes) that could support them as they make an effective refusal.

Second, the information must help students to maintain or enhance their health or the health of those around them. Ask yourself, "When my students learn this information, how will they use it to benefit their health or the health of those around them?" This question gets at the heart of why we are teaching students through a skills-based approach. If we are unable to articulate what students will be able to do as a result of learning the information, then the information most likely does not further students' ability to perform a skill. For example, teaching students the anatomy of the lungs will not deter students from smoking. Rather, teaching how the lungs are the primary way the body gets oxygen to survive, the importance of oxygen to brain function and performance, or even how smoking affects body parts and systems (e.g., hair, nails, teeth) could provide a context for students to understand that smoking is harmful and could affect the way they look or feel—both of which will hold more weight for students than the intricacies of the lungs. This is real-time, meaningful information. Students are far more tuned into their immediate world than into the long term or the intricate details, regardless of the topic. This is not to say that teaching the anatomy of the lungs does not have a place; however, in the skills-based health education classroom, you should spend time teaching only the most useful information to help students develop skills. Developing skills to proficiency takes time, so you want to plan more time for developing the skill than for sharing information.

The strategy of using skills as the foundation for the curriculum and functional information as the context for skill development is compelling for a few reasons. The first is based on research about how people learn. Transfer, as discussed in chapter 2, is the ability to use knowledge and skills in new settings and is enhanced when information or skills are taught within multiple contexts (Bransford, Brown, Cocking, Donovan, & Pellegrino, 2000). The goal of health education is for students to effectively use their skill set in a variety of circumstances. To accomplish this, you should teach skills with functional information from multiple topic areas. For example, while teaching students the steps of decision making and asking them to practice making health-enhancing decisions, you may wish to discuss information from various areas in their lives where they have to make decisions. This could include how to decide on boundaries in a relationship, how to decide whether or not to use e-cigarettes, and how to decide whether or not to drink alcohol. Teaching students functional information from multiple topics within one skill, such as teaching about having healthy relationships, staying safe online, and getting enough sleep in the decision-making unit, makes the skill more relevant and increases the likelihood that students are able to transfer the skill of decision making to other contexts in their lives.

The second reason is based on the fact that information is easily accessible and always changing. Just as you must consider the type and amount of functional information during the curriculum development process, it is even more important to consider how inclusion of the chosen information is based on data and student need. Students in today's health education classroom have similar health needs to the students who came before them, but they are not the same students who sat in those seats five years ago or even last year. From the advent of social media to reinvented designer drugs to texting while driving, students are shaped by what is happening around them and pay little attention to those who came before them and how their choices affected health outcomes. Thus, using the most relevant information for your students and using data to help you determine the most current understandings about a topic is the best approach for an effective and engaging curriculum. Teaching information that may quickly become outdated or inaccurate is less meaningful for students than helping them develop skills that they will use for a lifetime.

A third reason is supported by the SCT (social cognitive theory) discussed in chapter 2, which suggests that knowledge is the *precondition* for change—it does not directly lead to behavior change (Bandura, 2004). This concept supports using functional information as a foundation to help students develop, discuss, and explore other determinants needed to change behaviors, including goals and self-efficacy. If our aim is to develop students who have the capacity and competence to make healthy decisions, we need to instill in them the ability to change behaviors or use their knowledge of key principles of behavior change to help maintain their health.

GATHERING AND UNDERSTANDING DATA

Determining the specific topics and information most applicable to students in your class, school, or district requires thoughtful planning. Many health educators take the six risk behaviors identified by the CDC as a starting point for determining what information to include in a curriculum. The six priority areas identified by the CDC (2015) as contributing to the leading causes of death and disability among young people and adults are unhealthy dietary behaviors, inadequate physical activity, unintentional injury and violence, tobacco use, alcohol and other drug use, and sexual risk-taking behaviors. These areas may be a good starting point, but in this chapter we ask you to go beyond them and examine how you can use data to select topics and information, where to find useful data, and how those data can translate into meaningful functional information within the curriculum.

As the educator, it is your job to filter through the wealth of available information and determine what is most important for your students to learn. For example, you may attend a fantastic professional development event where you learn a lot of new information about opioids, but this does not mean you should then give all of that information directly to students. Though this seems simple enough, once you start to consider what students *should* or *could* learn, it is easy to end up with an information-heavy course. You will quickly realize that what you would like students to learn is far greater than what you have time to teach, and it may not be the information most relevant or necessary for your students.

One solution to this problem is to understand the behaviors youth are engaging in and what information your students want and need. This will allow you to plan personalized, engaging instruction based on those needs. For instance, if there is a high rate of distracted driving in your community, the curriculum should include examples and functional information to educate

students on the dangers of this behavior and strategies to prevent it. When you take the time to review the relevant data, you spend less time teaching information that is not relevant to your students. Additionally, using functional information that directly relates to your students' behaviors and needs will encourage authentic conversation about relevant risky behaviors. It will also allow opportunities for students to plan strategies for minimizing or eliminating risk while encouraging the protective factors critical to student success.

To settle on the most appropriate functional information, you must look at data across many levels of influence and determine their relevance and applicability. This could include reviewing data at the classroom, school, or district level; community level; state level; and even national level (see figure 11.1). Each level will provide valuable insight and comparison that can further assist in streamlining the functional information in your health education course.

The **socioecological model** examines the influence of various sectors of society on public health problems. Employing an ecological approach to identifying risk behavior data can yield more comprehensive results (WHO, n.d.). When developing a health education curriculum, taking a socioecological approach can help you to better understand the realities of students in your classroom and community. Next we explore each level of the model as it

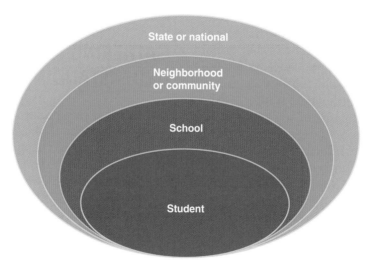

FIGURE 11.1 Socioecological model.

pertains to collecting data to inform curriculum development. Pros and cons for each level are discussed because not all data collected will be necessary or useful at a particular moment.

Student-Level Data

Student-level data are just as described—responses from students highlighting issues of importance or relevance to them. These data may be broader than health behaviors and could include issues of concern, what students would like to learn, questions they have about the topic, interests, ways they learn, connections to their school or adults in their lives, and so on. Additional student-level information can be gained from individualized education plans, anecdotal conversations, attendance records, observation, and student assessments within your health education course.

Pros of Student-Level Data

- Students feel invested in their responses.
- Allows for specificity in topics and functional information identified as areas of concern or need.
- Educators are able to collect specific information.
- People are more motivated when programming is related to their self-interest.
- Gauging student interest provides an opportunity to increase relevance, motivation, and transfer of course content.

Cons of Student-Level Data

- Students may feel anxious about reporting information that could be identifiable.
- The pool of students is limited—depending on how data are collected, the sample is not necessarily representative of the school or district.
- Student wants may not align with other identified needs.

Sources of student-level data include surveys, focus groups, interviews, classroom polls, student assessments, preassessments, activities in which students need to express their thoughts and opinions about topics, and review of records.

School-Level Data

Depending on the systems in place, schoolwide data can provide another level of information, especially if collected and aggregated in a systematic manner. This type of data collection can provide data that are more representative of the student body within the school (as opposed to at the individual class level). Whereas student-level data give a personal look into students' lives and preferences, school-level data help to identify issues that are persistent across the student body. Data at this level could include attendance, assessment, and student indicator data. One of the more common ways to collect school-level health data is through schoolwide surveys such as the Youth Risk Behavior Surveillance System (YRBSS) administered by the CDC or a locally developed risk behavior survey. This type of survey is typically employed in middle or high school, where most students are able to read and answer the questions anonymously with little adult involvement. An additional benefit is that survey data are often analyzed and presented to demonstrate trends and significance.

Some may have concerns about collecting school-level data because surveys such as the YRBSS rely on self-reported student information (CDC, 2015). They may question the validity of the results and whether or not students are truthful in their responses. Although this is important to consider, the data are collected and trends reported across multiple years with different groups of students. If student responses varied dramatically from year to year, or if students were not truthful, trends and patterns could not be traced and there would be great discrepancy in the results. Additionally, well-developed survey protocols (as seen with the YRBSS and similar large-scale surveys) have controls in place to discount individual responses when inconsistent answers are given throughout the course of the survey (CDC, 2015). For example, if a student reports never drinking alcohol on one question and then responds that she has driven five times in the last month after drinking alcohol, both of those responses would be removed from the data pool. Thus, there is little concern about data accuracy because trend lines remain fairly consistent from year to year. For more information about YRBSS, visit www.cdc.gov/healthyyouth/data/yrbs/index.htm.

If you are planning on administering a schoolwide survey, three considerations include parental notification, administrator approval, and methods for sharing results. It is important to alert parents and guardians of the survey administration in order to promote transparency and support. Similarly, gaining administrator approval (and even school board approval) ensures cooperation and staff and student buy-in of the process and results. Additionally, any information worth collecting should be worth sharing. Not only can the results inform curriculum development, but they can also influence schoolwide policies, programs, and community norms and can be used to build support for programs and services. If you are not administering a formal survey, consider encouraging students to research, create, and administer a survey to the student body. They could even use the results to plan an advocacy campaign about a topic that concerns them.

Pros of School-Level Data

- Data trends captured on a regular basis can be used to guide curricula at that level but also at lower levels to help prevent students from initiating risky behaviors.

- The anonymous nature of the data collection encourages students to share their behaviors without fear of retaliation.

- The data collection is not subjective; rather, all students are counted as individuals, not necessarily profiled into a predetermined group (as they would in your individual classes).

Cons of School-Level Data

- Not all students may understand the question being asked, leading to inaccurate responses.

- Information is not collected from students who are absent. Actual rates of a particular behavior may be higher if students who are at the highest risk are not participating in the survey.

- It can be costly to administer or to tabulate data.

Sources of school-level data include surveys (such as YRBSS), attendance records, student assessment data, body mass index (BMI) data, socioeconomic information (e.g., free or reduced-price lunch percentage), and Fitnessgram results.

Neighborhood- and Community-Level Data

Data at the neighborhood or community level may mirror that at the school level, but it may also differ. Each community has a distinct personality and characteristics that differentiate it from other communities. And within the larger community, smaller neighborhoods may exist that have personalities of their own. It is important to take into account the variations among neighborhoods and thus the students who come from those particular neighborhoods when considering what to teach and how to teach it. For example, the community where one of the authors grew up was a suburban city in close proximity to a large urban city. The community has distinct sections and the needs, socioeconomic level, and expectations of the students within those sections vary widely.

Cultural influences at the community level can have a significant impact on the attitudes, beliefs, and values of students who live there. This includes parental and family norms within the community, background of origin, and acceptance of risk-taking behavior among youth. The more you acknowledge and value the diverse backgrounds of your students, the more likely your students are to see the value of your instruction and internalize it.

Pros of Neighborhood- and Community-Level Data

- Educators can gain a better understanding of the norms, expectations, and culture of the community, especially if they do not live in the community themselves.

- Community stakeholders may provide insight into the lives of students that cannot be gained from self-report surveys.

- Data may capture youth not enrolled in school and students in alternative learning settings.

Cons of Neighborhood- and Community-Level Data

- Stakeholders may have preconceived ideas or biases about youth that are not accurately represented by self-report survey data.
- Community-level data may not be representative of students in school.

Sources of neighborhood- and community-level data include teen birth data, police data, socioeconomic status, land-use data, parents and guardians, community agencies, community leaders, and funding for health-related programs at the community level.

State- and National-Level Data

School-level data, which are representative of students within a school building, often feed into a larger sample at the state and eventually the national level. Additionally, much of the research done at these levels may have a greater sample size of students, thus offering an opportunity to compare the behaviors of students in your school with those from another state.

Nationally representative samples of youth data have provided behavioral trends in various locations, an understanding of behaviors that are grounded in adolescent development versus location, and a better understanding of the influence cultural norms have on behavior. Although the data are not ideal as a sole source of information (because they might not be relevant for your students), comparisons between school-level data and state- or national-level data can offer valuable insight into how students in your school compare with students in other parts of the country.

Pros of State- and National-Level Data

- Data can be compared with other locations similar in size and demographics to allow better understanding of youth behavior in your community or school.
- Data are collected in a thorough process that has been reviewed and validated.
- Occasionally, the student population in your school does not have a large enough sample size to provide information in a meaningful way. State- or national-level data may have a larger sample size, thus allowing for a better understanding of a particular population or behavior.

Cons of State- and National-Level Data

- If not compared with local data, information may not accurately reflect the student population in your school.
- Without context, generalizations based on state or national data may not be useful for your school.

Sources of state- and national-level data include vital statistics, youth surveys, crime statistics, aggregated data from state agencies, government records, foundation reports, and research studies (see table 11.1).

KEY POINTS

- Data are all around us. However, finding the most relevant data to meet your needs requires a thoughtful and measured approach.
- Student-level data will be most appropriate when determining a specific approach to take in your classroom or fine-tuning examples. State-level data may be more appropriate if you are trying to determine whether your students' behaviors are consistent with other students' behaviors across the state.
- Whichever type of data you use, the main thing to remember is that data can help you determine which topics and information are most useful and relevant for students in your classroom and district.
- Although other data can be interesting, if they do not help answer the question about choosing functional information, they are likely adding bulk rather than substance to the unit.

TABLE 11.1 Summary of Potential Data Sources

LEVEL	POSSIBLE SOURCES
Student	Surveys Focus groups Interviews Classroom polls Student assessments Preassessments Activities in which students express their thoughts and opinions about topics Review of records
School	Surveys (such as YRBSS) Attendance data Student assessment data BMI data Socioeconomic information (e.g., free or reduced-price lunch percentage) Fitnessgram results
Neighborhood and community	Teen birth data Police data Socioeconomic status Land-use data Parents and guardians Community agencies Community leaders Funding for health-related programs at the community level
State and national	Vital statistics Youth surveys Crime statistics Aggregated data from state agencies Government records Foundation reports Research studies

INTERPRETING DATA TO MAKE DECISIONS ON CURRICULUM

Once you have found quality data, you must use them to inform instructional practice and decisions on curriculum. To collect data and not use it to inform your work is a misuse of time, money, and energy. However, it can be difficult to know how the data in front of you can inform your programming choices. It can be overwhelming to review countless pages of information and numbers that do not seem to have obvious implications or applications. Fortunately, using data does not have to be a daunting task, especially if

done in collaboration with other teachers in your school or district. Working with others in your department and district can expedite the time it takes to review and make sense of all the data, including the most relevant data and their implications for the classroom. Even if you are the lone health educator, you can find a variety of school- and community-level data by talking with people in your school or district. Knowing what you are looking at, however, can be difficult if you are new to reviewing data. This section briefly explains data terminology commonly seen in literature. Understanding these terms will help you to better interpret the information you are reading.

Advice From the Field

DATA TO INFORM PLANNING

Heather Bachman
Prospect Elementary, PE/Health Specialist, West Ada School District, Meridian, Idaho

How have you used data to inform your curriculum?

I have found that formative assessment is most useful at the elementary level when I teach health education. I use exit slips, thumbs up thumbs down, and "Plickers." This data collection helps me to inform curriculum by knowing where we are and where we need to go next. I have used data collection and curriculum mapping to help identify the learning and success of my students. In our school district we do not teach each health concept to every grade level so data collection is crucial for pacing and even scaffolding if needed. Will my fifth grade students remember what they learned in third grade about nutrition since we do not teach nutrition in the fourth grade? I have used data from summative assessments to inform curriculum for this very situation.

What are the benefits of using data to inform curriculum?

Using data to inform your curriculum gives you a chance to readjust where you need to. If large numbers of students do not do well on assessments then we need to use that data to reflect back on the teaching and make necessary adjustments to the curriculum. A benefit of using data to inform curriculum is that it helps in identifying learning needs and success of your students and then making necessary adjustments to your curriculum where needed. Using that data and making minor changes to curriculum can result in improvements in alignment of curriculum, student learning, and achievement.

What piece of advice do you have for other health educators?

My advice to other health educators would be to make sure that you use your curriculum and don't be afraid to make changes where needed. I would also tell them that collaborating with other health educators is key. Sharing ideas and talking about what works and what doesn't when we teach our students is so important to becoming a successful educator.

Statistical Significance

Statistical significance is the likelihood that the results from a research study are due to chance. It is typically reported through a P value. The smaller the P value, the less likely the results are due to chance and the more likely the results are true (Agency for Healthcare Research Quality, 2014). P values can be found in research studies as well as in many data reports. As you look at trends from year to year, there may be slight variations in the numbers, but a statistically significant finding means that there is an actual change in the data (as opposed to a change that seems significant but may just be due to chance). One caveat—if a result appears to be trending in the same direction over a number of years or survey administrations, but it is not significant at a specific interval, you can reasonably assume the results are not a fluke but rather the representation of small, incremental change. In addition, changes in behaviors may still be practically significant—that is, it is still important that there is a decrease in marijuana use even if that change is not statistically significant because a decrease still means fewer students using marijuana.

Let's look at a set of data to help clarify. The 2013 Youth Risk Behavior Survey (CDC, 2015) notes that between 2011 and 2013, the decrease in the number of students across the United States who were in a fight on school property decreased from 12.0 percent to 8.1 percent with a P value of 0.0. A P value of less than 0.05 ($p<0.05$) is statistically significant. You could

Data can be a powerful tool, especially in conjunction with collaboration, to create a meaningful, relevant, and engaging curriculum.

use these data in a presentation to say, "Across the United States there has been a statistically significant decrease in the percentage of fights on school property." However, in Wisconsin the percentage in 2011 was 9.1 percent compared with 6.8 percent in 2013 with a P value of 0.05. Because the P value is not less than 0.05, these findings are not statistically significant (though they're close). In this case, you could not say that this is a statistically significant change, but you might still feel this decrease represents a positive change because there are fewer fights on campus.

Reliability

Another term worth understanding is **reliability**, which is how consistent results are across time and whether they provide a true representation of what has occurred. In addition, reliability includes the likelihood that the results could be reproduced if the same research methods were employed. It is important to understand whether or not the data gathered could be gathered again under similar circumstances, thus strengthening the argument for its use.

Validity

Validity refers to how much you are able to trust the results as an appropriate and accurate measure. Validity often coincides with reliability because, as you review data, you must determine if the data paint an accurate picture and if they were collected in an appropriate fashion. Valid data are answering the questions that are being asked. Additionally, valid data suggest that the information was gathered in a way that allows for others to replicate the study.

Data Sources

The approach to skills-based health education in this text includes reviewing and using data to inform topic selection for your curriculum. It is through the review of multiple data sources that you begin to understand the role that functional information can play within a curriculum. You might not have access to data at all levels, but everyone can gather some data to inform decisions on curriculum (see sidebar). Be thoughtful and thorough about determining what data you have access to. This might also be an opportunity to advocate at the school and

Examples of Using Data to Inform Decisions on Curriculum

Data can be extremely useful in making challenging decisions. Here are two examples of how data can influence decision making.

EXAMPLE 1

The health education staff at a middle school have been given the results of the youth risk behavior survey that was conducted at the high school the previous fall. Additionally, the department head has provided information about student attendance, graduation and dropout rates, the number of discipline reports for bullying and substance use, free and reduced-price lunch percentages, and the number of teen births and STIs among 13- to 19-year-olds. As the staff review the information, they notice a high teen birth rate but low rates of chlamydia. They also notice that an alarming number of students drop out the summer after 10th grade. What might these data indicate about what the staff should teach in their middle school health education classes?

Based on the data, the following topics and skills should be included in the curriculum:

- Healthy sexual relationships
- Delay of sexual contact
- Prevention of STIs
- Impact of pregnancy on health and life
- Goal setting
- Decision making
- Interpersonal communication

EXAMPLE 2

A team at the high school reviews the results of a student health survey completed by their school and schools in the three surrounding towns. The data are given both as a total and broken down by community. The data reveal that their community has a higher prevalence of youth who have ridden in a car with a driver who has been drinking, higher rates of marijuana use, and a greater number of students who have been involved in a relationship where violence has occurred. Additionally, there is a general acceptance by parents and guardians that underage drinking is tolerable as long as it is done at a home and not where kids could get into trouble. Given this information, what skills and information should be included in the curriculum at various grade levels?

Based on the data, the following topics and skills should be included:

- Avoiding alcohol and marijuana use
- Risks associated with driving under the influence
- Norms and values (health-enhancing norms and values)
- Analyzing influences
- Decision making
- Healthy, safe relationships
- Interpersonal communication

KEY POINTS

■ Data can assist you in determining topics to address in the curriculum.

■ Data enable you to sift through the possible information and skills that you *could* teach to identify topics that you *need* to teach.

■ When used appropriately, data can empower you to make confident choices about what to include in a curriculum. In addition, data can provide an opportunity to engage students, parents, and other community members in the curriculum development process. This could lead not only to a more effective curriculum but also to a more engaged community that is invested in health education.

community levels for data collection, whether it is to start collecting data (such as through a youth survey or review of Fitnessgram results) or to expand data collection (for example, students are already completing a risk behavior survey, but it does not include any questions about the amount of physical activity they are participating in).

Do not be intimidated by data! Even if you're working alone, there *are* data that you can access or collect and use to inform your decisions. It might be as simple as giving a preassessment or doing an activity that asks students what they know and want to know at the beginning of the year or unit. Any data will be helpful in creating a meaningful, relevant curriculum that meets the needs of your students.

USING DATA TO BUILD SUPPORT FOR HEALTH EDUCATION

Another key use of data is in building support and demonstrating the need for a well-structured health education program. Although it may be difficult to make direct connections between the lessons taught in a health education class and a specific health outcome, data can help justify *why* students must learn the skills of the National Health Education Standards along with the accompanying topics and information—specifically, how students benefit when they learn these skills and concepts in a well-designed health education course. Using data to develop a strong rationale for the topics being covered is the best way to deter critics and justify the inclusion of the chosen information.

Student- and school-level data should be

used to educate members of the community and school committee about the behaviors youth are engaging in and the effect those behaviors can have on overall achievement. Perhaps it is a yearly presentation to the school committee highlighting trends in student behaviors or a discussion with the parent–teacher association about how their support for healthier snacks in the cafeteria aligns with students learning how to read food labels and make healthier decisions about food. Whatever method is used, sharing data in order to support and advocate for your health education programming is crucial to making meaningful changes and increasing the potential impact of health education.

SUMMARY

Data are extremely useful when determining which topics and information to include in a health education curriculum and whether or not the specific information is functional for students. Data should be collected and analyzed at a variety of levels: student, school, community and neighborhood, and state and national. Even if you do not have access to data at all levels, you should determine what data you do have access to and use them to help determine your students' areas of need. Data are critical to creating an effective curriculum that meets students' needs.

The next part of the process involves identifying topics and functional information to address in your curriculum. There is more to health education than just preventing risky behaviors. Part of being healthy is being well and maintaining or adopting other behaviors across the spectrum of topic areas in order employ a skill set of health-enhancing behaviors.

Review Questions

1. What are the types of data that you can use to help determine the needs of students?

2. Why is it helpful to gather data at a variety of levels?

3. How can data be used in making decisions on curriculum?

4. How can data be used to generate support for the health education program?

To find supplementary materials for this chapter, such as worksheets and extended learning activities, visit the web resource at
www.HumanKinetics.com/TheEssentialsOfTeachingHealthEducation

Photographee.eu/fotolia.com

CHAPTER 12

Eight Steps for Curriculum Development

Learning Objectives

After reading this chapter, you will be able to do the following:

- List and describe each step of the curriculum development process.
- Apply the steps to your health education courses or curriculum.
- Describe how skills and functional information are integrated into the written curriculum.

Key Terms

backward design

benchmark assessment

scope and sequence

In the last chapter, we discussed ways to use data to inform curricular decisions based on the needs of students in your class and community. That serves as the preliminary step in the curriculum development process. The next steps are to plan and create the curriculum. Not every teacher will be involved in district- or school-level curriculum planning, but we feel it is important to outline this process so that, when appropriate, teachers can assume leadership positions during curriculum development or revision. We will also refer to how you can use this same process in your own course-level curriculum. The process is essentially the same; it's just on a smaller scale. In this chapter, we explain each step of the curriculum development process along with strategies for implementing the process at the district, school, and course level.

The curriculum development process in this chapter uses a **backward design**—that is, it begins with student outcomes (Wiggins & McTighe, 2005). The focus is on implementing the general principles of curriculum development rather than on a specific model. We recognize that many curriculum development models are used across the country. If your school or district is aligned with a specific model, use that approach, but we encourage you to see where you might take key points from this chapter and integrate them into whichever model your district uses. This process is based on the backward design approach but is largely informed by our practical experience in curriculum development and in teaching curriculum development in college and university teacher preparation programs. Regardless of the model used, the intention is to focus on student outcomes and to let those outcomes guide your curriculum planning.

This text highlights an eight-step process beginning with the students and the community and ending with specific lesson plans:

1. Get to know the students and the community.
2. Formulate goals.
3. Design benchmark assessments.
4. Determine the health topics, functional information, and skills.
5. Create a scope and sequence.
6. Develop unit plan objectives and outcomes.
7. Develop unit assessments.
8. Create lesson plans.

Even though the steps are presented sequentially, curriculum development is an iterative, ongoing process. The curriculum should be planned, implemented, evaluated, and revised as necessary, and this may not happen in a sequential order. These steps provide a guide for the planning process. Figure 12.1 shows the cyclical, continual nature of the curriculum development process.

STEP 1: GET TO KNOW THE STUDENTS AND THE COMMUNITY

Understanding student and community norms, culture, and expectations is critical for creating effective curricula. If you do not know your students and the community, a well-developed curriculum can easily fall short on implementation because it may not be appropriate for the audience. As discussed earlier in the text, relevance is key to student engagement, transfer, and skill development. Your written curriculum must be relevant in the same way that your instructional strategies are. Imagine teaching a curriculum where you reference resources that aren't available in the community, or you plan units using the Internet but Internet

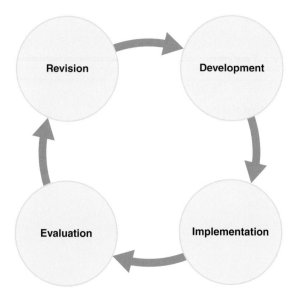

FIGURE 12.1 Curriculum development process.

access (or a computer) isn't available, has a slow connection, or students do not have computers at home. Perhaps you discuss marijuana use when the real issue in the community is prescription pills, or you talk about the importance of being physically active outside but there is a lack of safe outdoor spaces to be active in. Any of these examples can be an opportunity for students to disengage with your curriculum because it doesn't relate to them. One way to ensure this does not happen is to get to know both the students and the community in which you are working.

There are many ways to get to know your students and the community where they live. Some strategies:

- Use data as described in chapter 11.
- Live in or near the community where you work.
- Take a tour of the community and visit the local restaurants and shops.
- Talk to a variety of community members who are representative of all groups within the community.
- Engage in community activities.
- Be active in the school (e.g., lunch duty, after-school clubs, school events).
- Be accessible to your students; provide opportunities for them to talk to you.
- Talk to other teachers and staff.
- Check in with students and ask about their interests and questions.
- Provide opportunities for student voices to contribute to the curriculum development process.
- Conduct surveys in which you ask a variety of informal questions to learn more about the students.

We encourage you to do as many of these things as possible. Any of these strategies will help you learn more about your students and the community where you work. Whichever strategies you choose, you should be able to answer the following questions before moving on to step 2 of the curriculum planning process:

- Who are my students?
- What are their strengths? Areas for improvement? Areas of interest? Languages spoken? Questions and concerns?

- Who are their families? What are their cultures? Where do they come from? Where do they live?
- What health-related resources are available in the community?
- What are the issues in the community? What are the community strengths?
- What are barriers to health in the community? What are facilitators?
- What groups are active in the community? Are these groups supportive and beneficial for students or do they pose a threat to student health?
- What health initiatives are currently in place in the community?

The answers to these questions can be telling, especially once you start to consider that your students may come from a variety of backgrounds with a variety of values, beliefs, and perceptions about community health norms. For example, let's say a local teen center is a resource for students after school, but it is not available to everyone. Perhaps it is located in a part of town that isn't easily accessible, or maybe there are fees to attend the center and students believe the cost is prohibitive because they are unaware of the center's scholarship programs. If this is the case, the resource isn't available in the sense you had originally thought, and you may need to think about other resources that could serve a similar purpose for students. Once you have thoughtfully answered these questions and considered the answers, regardless of whether you are planning at the district/school level or the course level, you are ready to move on to step 2.

STEP 2: FORMULATE GOALS

If goals for the curriculum don't already exist, it's time to create them. If they do exist, you should revisit them before proceeding. When formulating or revising goals for the curriculum, consider the following:

- What do we want our students to be able to do at the end of the health education program? (district or school level)
- What do I want my students to be able to do at the end of my health education course? (individual level)

Keep the goals general and based on the big picture of what you've learned about the community and the students. The goals at this stage should be consistent with the length of the curriculum and should take into consideration the overall district goals for the health education program. For example, you have a district health education curriculum that includes kindergarten through grade 12. You are working with all the health educators in your district to review the entire curriculum. During this step of the curriculum development process, you formulate goals for students to accomplish by the end of grade 12 (i.e., the entire curriculum). You might then break the grades into smaller groups and create goals at each level. Using grade spans helps to ensure that all grade-span educators are aligned in their thinking about the goals and that the goals are aligned with the overall district goals. The same holds true if you are looking at outcomes for a specific course—the goals directly reflect the scope of grades included in the planning process.

Once you've developed overall goals, you identify grade-level goals to delineate the type of instruction that occurs at each grade level. Aim for three to five program goals—fewer than three may not adequately cover the scope of the program but more than five may not be achievable or realistic.

The goals should be written using the stem "By the end of ____ grade, students will be able to. . . ." This allows you to focus on the behaviors, skills, and abilities students should have if your curriculum is successful. Following are some sample goals.

District or School Level

- By the end of 12th grade, students will be able to make informed decisions about personal and community health.

- By the end of 12th grade, students will be able to evaluate and adapt behaviors in order to maintain or enhance their health.

- By the end of seventh grade, students will be able to analyze the influence of peers on health behaviors.

Course or Individual Level

- By the end of this course, students will be able to access resources to enhance their health.

- By the end of this course, students will be able to effectively demonstrate refusal skills.

These big-picture goals are based on a specific audience—your students and community. On the surface, the sample goals seem appropriate for any community. This is intentional because at this stage the goals focus on higher-level outcomes that are common across many health education programs. Even so, be sure there is a clear connection between the goals in this step and the information gathered in step 1.

Also note that these goals do not meet all of the SMART criteria discussed in chapter 8; namely, they are not specific (i.e., the aspects of personal and community health are not specifically identified). This is appropriate given that these are high-level goals and outcomes that will be achieved over multiple courses and years (district and school level) or over multiple units (individual level). Even though these goals are not specific because they cover a broad range, they will likely meet the other SMART criteria. For example, the decision-making goal is measurable. You could evaluate students' ability to make informed decisions or analyze the influence of peers via grade-level assessments, portfolios, or other assessment measures. The goal is adjustable (as all goals are), we assume that it is realistic because the district created the goal based on its needs, and it is time based (i.e., by the end of 12th grade). We encourage you to ensure that these aspects of SMART goals are included at this level. Also keep in mind that the specificity will be included in the identified benchmarks of your district and then even further in courses and units.

STEP 3: DEVELOP BENCHMARK ASSESSMENTS

Once you've identified goals, determine at what point each goal will be measured (benchmark) and how the measurement will occur (assessment). There is no predetermined interval for **benchmark assessments**. They can occur as appropriate but should be aligned with other health education offerings in your school or district.

For example, at the elementary level, goals include all instruction students receive by the end of fifth grade (e.g., By the end of fifth grade, students will be able to . . .) because they represent the end of the elementary health education program. This program has health education in kindergarten and grades 2, 3, and 5. The district decides that grades 2 and 5 should be the benchmarks (points at which progress should be measured). Grade 2 was included because it represents the halfway point of the elementary health education program. This is a good time to check in and evaluate how students are progressing. Another benchmark is included at the end of grade 5 because this is the culmination of the health education program. End-of-program evaluation is important in order to understand student competency and growth as a result of participating in the program specifically as it relates to the goals created for the program in step 2.

Now that you have determined the benchmarks for evaluating student progress, you need to design the benchmark assessments. We discuss assessment in depth in chapter 13, but here are some general considerations when planning benchmark assessments:

■ Create SMART objectives specific to what students should be able to do at the time of the benchmark. For example, your goals discuss a benchmark after fifth grade, but now you need to determine what outcomes your students should be able to demonstrate in second grade that will indicate whether or not students are on track to meet the fifth-grade benchmark. If your fifth-grade goal is "Students will be able to demonstrate effective communication in a variety of health-related situations,"

you might decide that the key outcomes by the end of second grade are that students can appropriately express wants, needs, and feelings; they can listen; and they can ask for help. (Note that these reflect the performance indicators of the National Standards for preK to grade 2 within the skill of interpersonal communication.) You develop the objectives that by the end of grade 2, students will be able to do the following:

- Demonstrate appropriate ways of expressing needs, wants, feelings, and ideas through the effective implementation of the skill cues within a topic of the students' choosing.

- Demonstrate effective listening skills by performing all of the skill cues effectively in a real-life scenario.

- Demonstrate effective communication in situations where help from a trusted adult is needed.

■ These objectives directly contribute to the larger goal and are measurable through a well-designed assessment (see chapter 13).

Results from benchmark assessments should be used to inform students of their progress as well as to evaluate the curriculum and its implementation. Students should be provided with feedback on their work, and the students' performance should be shared with parents and other teachers. One benefit of benchmark assessments is that they allow schools to track student progress toward district goals across grades. This is most successful when the information from benchmark assessments is collected and transmitted to relevant parties

KEY POINTS

- One of the most important parts of curriculum development is getting to know your students and the community. This will allow you to develop an engaging, relevant curriculum that meets the needs of your students.

- District-level goals and outcomes will help inform your decisions on curriculum. If these do not exist, we suggest that your district consider creating goals and outcomes.

- Creating benchmark assessments for district-level goals will assist in tracking student knowledge and skill development throughout the K-12 program. Benchmark assessments will also provide information for teachers and administrators to make adjustments to curriculum if assessments are not showing appropriate growth.

in order to determine student needs and to help inform decisions on curriculum.

STEP 4: DETERMINE HEALTH TOPICS, FUNCTIONAL INFORMATION, AND SKILLS

At this point, you've gotten to know your students and your community, written goals for the curriculum, and created benchmark assessments. The next step is to determine which skills, health topics, and functional information to address in the curriculum so that students develop the skills and knowledge they need in order to complete the assessments and the goals for the curriculum (see the Considerations During the Planning Process sidebar).

One of the overwhelming aspects of curriculum planning is trying to fit in everything you want to cover into the amount of time you have with students. A well-designed curriculum across grade levels can help alleviate concerns about trying to cover everything in a short amount of time. It also helps to ensure that the curriculum is comprehensive and systematically advances students through skills and topics. At this stage, it is important to communicate with other teachers in the school and district to make sure there are no unnecessary repetitions or gaps across the curriculum.

It is useful to keep a running list of the topics and functional information to be considered for inclusion in the curriculum as they come up. When appropriate, take note of specific functional information within those topics (e.g., list *alcohol* as a topic and make a note to address specific information such as alternatives to drinking, impact of alcohol use, and saying no to alcohol). Due to the creative nature of this step, it might also be prudent to record any thoughts, lightbulb ideas, or other information that arises. Being open to ideas and being flexible will lead to a more coherent, comprehensive curriculum and better outcomes for your students. Figure 12.2 highlights the process of generating topics for a curriculum.

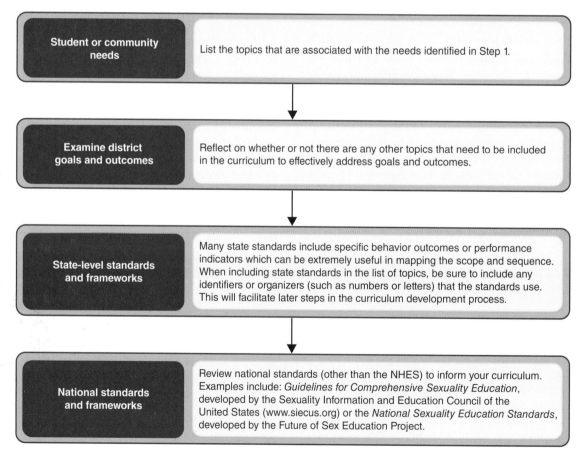

Student or community needs
List the topics that are associated with the needs identified in Step 1.

Examine district goals and outcomes
Reflect on whether or not there are any other topics that need to be included in the curriculum to effectively address goals and outcomes.

State-level standards and frameworks
Many state standards include specific behavior outcomes or performance indicators which can be extremely useful in mapping the scope and sequence. When including state standards in the list of topics, be sure to include any identifiers or organizers (such as numbers or letters) that the standards use. This will facilitate later steps in the curriculum development process.

National standards and frameworks
Review national standards (other than the NHES) to inform your curriculum. Examples include: *Guidelines for Comprehensive Sexuality Education*, developed by the Sexuality Information and Education Council of the United States (www.siecus.org) or the *National Sexuality Education Standards*, developed by the Future of Sex Education Project.

FIGURE 12.2 Process of generating topics for your curriculum.

Considerations During the Planning Process

DISTRICT LEVEL

When examining district-level goals and outcomes, you might find goals and outcomes that include skills or topics that did not show up as needs in the data review. If this is the case, you should discuss the extent to which the goal or outcome should be addressed. You might find that there is a need to cover the skill or that there is an issue in the school even though students didn't report it. Also consider that you may need to reexamine district-level goals and outcomes to revise existing ones or add new ones.

STATE STANDARDS

After reviewing district-level goals, examine your state health education standards. States vary in their levels of accountability and systems of evaluation and assessment; however, these standards are valuable resources when planning and also supporting and justifying topics in the curriculum. A review of state-level standards can help determine if any important topics need to be addressed that are not on your list or if there is specific functional information within a topic that should be included in the curriculum. The state standards can also help your team decide what topics to address and when to address them.

NATIONAL STANDARDS

National standards provide guidance and support for topics and information included in the curriculum. This can be especially important for topics that are highly contested and sensitive, such as sexuality. Being able to reference national documents can assist you in justifying their inclusion. It is also important to know your district and school policies related to topics such as sexuality education when deciding which topics to include.

Making Sense of the Topics

Your list of topics is now comprehensive, inclusive, and well rounded. However, it might just be one long list that hasn't taken shape, because we have not addressed the big issue of how to match these topics with skills. Taking seemingly unconnected topics and creating meaningful, relevant themes or connections can lead to a more integrated curriculum that reflects the dynamic, intersecting nature of health and health behavior. Health is like a web—it is delicate and intricate but clearly has a pattern and function. Your curriculum can reflect this through the creation of themes that help students see the connections, patterns, and functions. Using your list of topics and functional information in this step, a step that is unique to this text, we describe how to make sense of the topics. It is important to synthesize and analyze multiple health topics so that the information can be presented to students in a meaningful, relevant, and connected manner.

Making sense of the topics begins by grouping topics into themes that serve as cornerstones of your units. A benefit of this approach is that the same process can be used by an educator who is developing a course and by a curriculum team planning the district curriculum. To identify possible themes, take some time to reflect on the list of topics you have created with the following questions in mind:

- Will these topics meet the needs of my students?
- Are there topics that can be combined?
- Are there topics that should be addressed in other grade levels or other courses?
- Are there themes among the topics?

After grouping topics into themes, you may have something that looks like figure 12.3.

The example in figure 12.3 is for a high school. If you are doing this process at the district level, you will need to create a similar

District A: High School Topics and Themes

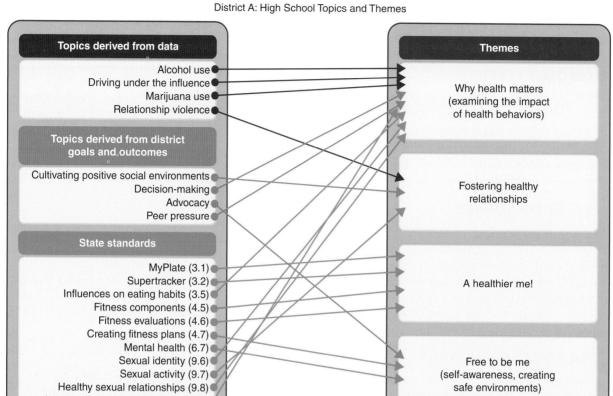

FIGURE 12.3 Creating themes from topics.

chart for all levels where health education is taught. Alternatively, you can create a district-level list where the themes remain the same throughout all levels but the sophistication and coverage of the information will change. All the themes in the figure could also be appropriate for elementary through middle school, though the specific topics might need to change in order to be developmentally appropriate. For example, A Healthier Me could involve hand-washing and fire safety in elementary school and could involve nutrition and physical activity or drug abuse in middle school. The theme is the same but the functional information and topics are different. This approach encourages health educators to show students the inter-connectedness of health and health behaviors. It shows students that health always matters; that we should always try to foster healthy relationships with family, friends, and romantic partners; and that we should always work to understand and be comfortable ourselves at any age. This larger context for health educa-tion reflects the reality of health—we always need to be working on our health because our lives are constantly changing and we need to manage changing needs, demands, desires, and challenges.

Matching Topics and Skills

The next part of step 4 is to match the themes or topics with the most applicable skills. This matching allows you to further focus in on how the topics within a theme allow students to apply the skill. Remember, all topics should pro-vide the context for students to apply the skill cues and thus result in skill development. When making the match between topics and skills, you may find that the original matches do not make sense once they are placed into the scope and sequence. Allow for flexibility at that stage and be open to moving topics around if you see a better fit within the scope and sequence. The

Examples of Matching Themes and Skills sidebar shows two examples of what you might have after matching skills and themes. An example is provided for a health teacher working at the district level and at the individual level.

There are three important things to note about the charts in the sidebar:

1. Each of the seven skills from the National Standards is covered at each grade level (except self-management at the elementary level).

2. The themes incorporate a variety of skills, again reflecting the nature of health (e.g., fostering healthy relationships requires many, if not all, of the skills discussed in this text).

3. Specific topics to be included in the themes are not listed here, but it may be helpful during the planning phases to have all three pieces (themes, topics, and skills) in one chart.

Now that you have matched your themes (and therefore your topics) with your skills, you are ready to move on to the next step of the curriculum development process: creating the scope and sequence.

STEP 5: CREATE A SCOPE AND SEQUENCE

A **scope and sequence** outlines what content is being covered and when it is covered; it is a way to organize your curriculum so that you know what you are teaching (scope) and when you are teaching it (sequence). A scope and sequence is a useful tool because it provides a framework for skill progression and for examining which topics are covered in which grades and with which skills. It also provides an overview of benchmarks and expectations for what students at certain grade levels have learned. The process of creating a scope and sequence

Examples of Matching Themes and Skills

SEVENTH-GRADE HEALTH CURRICULUM (INDIVIDUAL LEVEL)

WHY HEALTH MATTERS (EXAMINING THE IMPACT OF HEALTH BEHAVIORS)	FOSTERING HEALTHY RELATIONSHIPS	A HEALTHIER ME	FREE TO BE ME
• Accessing valid and reliable information, products, and services • Decision making	• Analyzing influences • Interpersonal communication	• Goal setting • Self-management	• Advocacy

DISTRICT CURRICULUM

	WHY HEALTH MATTERS (EXAMINING THE IMPACT OF HEALTH BEHAVIORS)	FOSTERING HEALTHY RELATIONSHIPS	A HEALTHIER ME	FREE TO BE ME
Elementary school	• Accessing valid and reliable information, products, and services	• Interpersonal communication	• Decision making	• Analyzing influences • Goal setting • Advocacy
Middle school	• Analyzing influences • Decision making	• Interpersonal communication • Self-management	• Goal setting • Advocacy	• Accessing information
High school	• Accessing information • Decision making	• Analyzing influences • Interpersonal communication	• Goal setting • Self-management	• Advocacy

at the district level is the same as at the course level. Writing a district-level scope and sequence before writing a grade-span or course scope and sequence will allow for better sequencing and planning at each grade span. When creating the scope and sequence, be sure to include administrators or other health teachers to ensure that everyone is on the same page about the topics and skills to be taught at various grade levels. Curriculum documents should be living documents that are fluid and dynamic. A scope and sequence can also allow individuals to further develop course and unit content.

Scope and sequences come in many formats, and there is no single correct way to create one. The goal for this step is to have an easy-to-read, quick reference for what is being taught in your curriculum and when it is being taught. Before beginning, you will need all three pieces of the curriculum development process: topics, themes, and skills. The theme and skill charts created in the previous step are a place to start. At the end of this step, you will have a comprehensive scope and sequence that can be adjusted as necessary to meet the needs of your district or your school.

First, determine the format. We suggest the format shown in table 12.1.

You will notice that the skills of the National Health Education Standards are placed across the top in this format. Having the skills at the top of the chart highlights the skill emphasis of the curriculum and helps to ensure that any functional information that is included will advance skill development.

The next step is to fill in the chart (see table 12.2). Note that the themes are listed in each box under the skills. This is a visual way of reinforcing that the skills are the focus of the curriculum.

After looking at the first stage of the chart (table 12.2), let's say you decide to move the decision-making unit to the beginning of the course (after accessing valid and reliable information, products, and services) so that there is a flow to the course. The remainder of the skills will be presented in the same order listed. You have already decided that the focus of the year will be relationships, especially romantic relationships (based on the need in the community and the ninth-grade topics determined in the previous curriculum development step). The units will be Why Health Matters, Fostering Healthy Relationships, A Healthier Me, and Free to Be Me, in that order. Alternatively, you could use the skills as the unit titles because the focus within each unit is to develop the skill identified in the scope and sequence using the

TABLE 12.1 Sample Scope and Sequence Format

	ACCESSING VALID AND RELIABLE INFORMATION, PRODUCTS, AND SERVICES	ANALYZING INFLUENCES	INTERPERSONAL COMMUNICATION	DECISION MAKING	GOAL SETTING	SELF-MANAGEMENT	ADVOCACY
6th grade							
7th grade							
8th grade							

TABLE 12.2 Sample Ninth-Grade Curriculum

	ACCESSING VALID AND RELIABLE INFORMATION, PRODUCTS, AND SERVICES	ANALYZING INFLUENCES	INTERPERSONAL COMMUNICATION	DECISION MAKING	GOAL SETTING	SELF-MANAGEMENT	ADVOCACY
9th grade	Why Health Matters	Fostering Healthy Relationships	Fostering Healthy Relationships	Why Health Matters	A Healthier Me	A Healthier Me	Free to be Me

themes and topics as the context. At this point, the curriculum might flow something like this:

The course will start by discussing why health matters, focusing on the consequences of health-enhancing and risky behaviors relating to relationships, drug and alcohol use, and sexual activity. The first unit is about accessing valid and reliable information, products, and services. This unit will provide opportunities to discuss how to find valid and reliable information on the Internet about these topics. Students will work in groups to create presentations on each of the three topics. Their presentations will be the method for covering the functional information necessary for the unit. Next, the course will discuss how decisions can result in positive or negative consequences. The specific focus will be how decisions related to drugs, alcohol, and sexual activity can affect relationships with those around us. Next, the course examines how internal and external influences can affect our relationships, segueing into how to communicate effectively within a relationship. The goal-setting unit is where students will set a goal relating to improving a personal relationship in order to make them healthier. They will set goals and work to achieve them (self-management). Finally, the course will culminate with students completing advocacy projects in which they advocate for healthy relationships to an audience of their choice.

The next step in the scope and sequence is to further fill in the boxes with the specific objectives to be achieved. These may be in the form of the National Health Education Standards performance indicators, state frameworks, other specific objectives that your curriculum should address, or some combination of these (see table 12.3).

Now you have your scope and sequence! The format of the scope and sequence should match the needs of your course, school, or district. If you're completing this at the district level, you will need to create an additional scope and sequence for each grade level of health education to build from the district-level scope and sequence and to provide further detail and clarification. Remember, the district scope and sequence is the compilation of all grades, and all other course decisions should be driven by the district-level goals and outcomes for health education. If it doesn't appear at the district level, it will not appear at the grade level. Also note that you have not yet completed the steps of planning for the educational outcomes for each skill (think back to the skill chapters). Here, you are planning which performance indicators are relevant (from the National Standards) and

TABLE 12.3 Aligning Standards With Skills

	ACCESSING VALID AND RELIABLE INFORMATION, PRODUCTS, AND SERVICES	ANALYZING INFLUENCES	INTERPERSONAL COMMUNICATION	DECISION MAKING	GOAL SETTING	SELF-MANAGEMENT	ADVOCACY
9th grade	**Why Health Matters** National standards: 3.12.1 3.12.2 State standards: 1.3 1.5 2.7 9.3	**Fostering Healthy Relationships** National standards: 2.12.1 2.12.2 2.12.3 2.12.8 2.12.9 State standards: 3.6 3.8 8.1	**Fostering Healthy Relationships** National standards: 4.12.1 4.12.2 4.12.3 State standards: 4.2 4.3 SIECUS standards: Concept 3 Topic 3 Level 4	**Why Health Matters** National standards: 5.12.1 5.12.2 5.12.3 5.12.4 5.12.5 5.12.6 5.12.7 State standards: 7.10 7.13 9.4	**A Healthier Me** National standards: 6.12.1 6.12.2 6.12.3 6.12.4 State standards: 3.4 3.5 3.10	**A Healthier Me** National standards: 7.12.1 7.12.2 7.12.3 State standards: 4.4 4.5	**Free to Be Me** National standards: 8.12.1 8.12.2 8.12.3 8.12.4

Having a thorough, thoughtful scope and sequence can give you direction and help you purposefully plan assessments and lessons to help your students meet course, school, and/or district goals.

which state standards you will cover. You will use the process outlined in the skill chapters when you move toward unit planning in the next step. Once this work is completed, you will have a plan for a curriculum that is sequential and comprehensive and that meets the needs of your students and community.

STEP 6: DEVELOP UNIT PLANS

At this stage, it may be the case that your units have essentially been planned for you. As with the previous example, the units are the themes,

so the health teacher's objectives would be as shown in table 12.4.

However, it may not always be this straightforward. You may find that you have a large number of objectives under one skill or under one theme. It may make more sense to create smaller units to keep the material manageable for students. Different teachers may have different approaches for writing unit plans. Variability is permissible as long as the objectives set forth in the scope and sequence are covered within the agreed-upon units and as long as the units do not place an emphasis on

KEY POINTS

- When determining curriculum topics, look at the following levels: the students and community, district-level goals, and state and national standards.
- Once the list of topics is determined, organize the topics into comprehensive, connected themes.
- The written curriculum should reflect the skill emphasis. Develop skill-based or theme-based units (e.g., so that you have a goal-setting unit rather than a nutrition unit).
- The scope and sequence should demonstrate what content is being taught (skills and themes) and when the content is being taught (grade level).

TABLE 12.4 Sample Unit Objectives

WHY HEALTH MATTERS	
Focus: Decision-making with accessing valid and reliable information, products, and services	
NATIONAL HEALTH EDUCATION STANDARDS	**STATE**
3.12.1	State
3.12.2	1.3
5.12.1	1.5
5.12.2	2.7
5.12.3	7.10
5.12.4	7.13
5.12.5	9.3
5.12.6	9.4
5.12.7	

the health topics rather than keeping the focus on the skills and skill development.

This stage is where you should use the process outlined in part II of this text to modify the performance indicators in order to create educational outcomes for each skill. The outcomes for each skill will form the foundation of your skill-related unit objectives. Keep in mind that an educational outcome is in essence an objective because it is a target for what you want students to be able to do with each skill. However, earlier in the book you developed educational outcomes (or objectives) specifically related to the skill itself and within the context of skill development. In the curriculum planning process, you now combine the work you did when developing skill outcomes with other considerations for the curriculum, such as state standards. Some states may have frameworks or standards that are already aligned with the National Health Education Standards, in which case your job will likely be easier because there is already a clear alignment. In other states, the framework or standards may be more content based, which does add a small challenge but can also be useful for grounding the objective within a topic.

Let's look at an example using the objectives for accessing valid and reliable information, products, and services for the sample unit in table 12.4. We start by implementing steps 1 through 4 presented in part II of the text related to educational outcomes.

■ Step 1: choosing indicators. This has already been done in the curriculum planning process. The unit will include 3.12.1 (Evaluate the validity of health information, products, and services) and 3.12.2 (Use resources from home, school, and community that provide valid health information).

■ Step 2: coverage of indicators. You decide to focus on health information in this unit because it is the first unit of the course and you want the students to be able to apply the skill of accessing valid and reliable information to determine and present the functional information for the topics in the curriculum. You modify 3.12.1 to "Evaluate the validity of health information."

■ Step 3: student-appropriate terms. These are ninth graders who are familiar with the vocabulary and concepts, so no modifications are necessary.

■ Step 4: educational outcomes. Your educational outcomes for accessing valid and reliable information are as follows:

● By the end of the unit, students will be able to evaluate the validity of health information.

● By the end of the unit, students will be able to use resources from home, school, and the community that provide valid health information.

At this point, you have yet to integrate your state frameworks. In this example, we will assume the state standards are content based and that 1.3 and 1.5 are about nutrition, 5.7 is about physical activity, 9.10 and 9.13 are about healthy relationships, and 11.3 and 11.4 are about mental health. At this point, you can add these topics to your educational outcomes:

■ By the end of the unit, students will be able to evaluate the validity of health information about nutrition, physical activity, healthy relationships, or mental health.

■ By the end of the unit, students will be able to use resources from home, school, and the community that provide valid health information about nutrition, physical activity, healthy relationships, or mental health.

Note that we used *or* here because not all students will achieve the objectives for each content area. As you work through the objectives, you are beginning to formulate ideas for the assessment (step 7), which includes groups of students covering each topic area and then presenting to the class. This is also the time to include any secondary unit objectives that relate to the functional information for each topic area. In the end, your objectives might look something like this:

■ By the end of the unit, students will be able to evaluate the validity of health information about nutrition, physical activity, healthy relationships, or mental health.
  • Students will be able to list the effects of healthy behaviors in all topic areas.

  • Students will be able to list the effects of risky behaviors in all topic areas.

  • Students will be able to list strategies for peers to implement to support their health in these topics areas.

■ By the end of the unit, students will be able to use resources from home, school, and the community that provide valid health information about nutrition, physical activity, healthy relationships, or mental health.
  • Students will be able to list valid and reliable resources that provide information about the topic areas.

  • Students will be able to locate resources from home, school, and the community that provide information about the topic areas.

You would repeat a similar process for the other skills, such as decision making. The topics remain the same, but the functional information will likely be different within each skill. This emphasizes to students that the skill of accessing valid and reliable information is necessary and transferrable. The skills they just learned are directly applicable to finding the functional information they need for the decision-making unit.

STEP 7: DEVELOP UNIT ASSESSMENTS

At this stage, you are ready to create assessments for your units that will measure the objectives you created in step 6. The focus is

KEY POINTS

■ Once you have created the scope and sequence, units have essentially been planned! At this point, organize the objectives for each unit in whatever format is appropriate for your school.

■ After the unit and unit objectives have been created, you need to plan unit assessments to appropriately measure the unit objectives.

■ The final step in the curriculum development process is to create lesson plans that include activities to develop the students' knowledge and skills so that they can successfully complete the assessments and achieve unit objectives.

DEVELOPING A MEANINGFUL CURRICULUM

Terri Bowman
College and Career Readiness Academy at Lehman Middle School, Canton City Schools, Canton, Ohio

What is your best strategy for developing a meaningful curriculum?

When it comes to developing a meaningful curriculum, I find that it is most important to know your population well. Know your students, know your parents and caregivers, know your community, and most importantly know which health disparities exist within that community. This can be done in numerous ways depending on the resources allotted in your district. In some school systems, a youth risk behavior survey can be formally given and assessed for pertinent information. If your school system does not have the resources to provide for professional assessment, it is up to you, the health educator, to learn as much as you can about your community. At the beginning of the school year, I require students to fill out a survey that gives me some basic information about their prior learning in health education. I ask them to share information about their personality, family, and past life experiences. I also provide time for students to share which topics in health they already feel very comfortable with as well as the topics that they know very little about. I also make it a point to get to know their counselors, provide multiple opportunities for family interaction, and read up on any available health-related data and statistics pertaining to the community before the school year begins.

What is the biggest challenge to curriculum development and how have you dealt with the challenge?

I have had multiple challenges when it comes to curriculum development. I'm one of three health educators in a district with over 9,000 students. This district is located in one of the only two states in the country without any adopted health education standards. For much of my teaching experience, I have felt isolated, on my own little island, without many district- or state-led resources. Instead of letting these barriers hold me back, I have used my island status to my advantage. I have been able to create a curriculum designed specifically for my population using the National Health Education Standards as a guide. There are days when I feel that the outside world is unaware of the work we are accomplishing in my classroom, but I remind myself that my students are learning the necessary skills to make well-informed health-related decisions that will affect their personal futures as well as the future of their community.

What advice do you have for other health educators in the field?

Embrace your island status. Although it can be isolating and frustrating to work within the field of health education, we are often given much more instructional freedom than other disciplines. My non-health-education colleagues are driven by their premade state and national assessments, but I am able to tailor my instruction for the needs of my student population. In addition, I also recommend that health educators emphasize real-world connections within the classroom. Whereas a math or social studies teacher may be struggling to show application to the outside world, the health educator is at an advantage. I suggest using real-life examples, scenarios, and stories throughout instruction. The nature of our subject can be quite personal. It is particularly important for health educators to set boundaries and guidelines to make their classroom an inviting, warm, and safe space for all students.

on developing summative assessments for your unit that will effectively and appropriately measure the objectives that you wrote earlier. We will cover assessment in depth in chapter 13.

STEP 8: CREATE LESSON PLANS

One of the advantages to a backward design is that, by the time you are planning lessons, the hard work has been done. You can think of backward design as a sort of filter where the big things such as the learning outcomes for the curriculum are filtered down to the point where the lessons have almost planned themselves. You know what you want your students to know and be able to do (your assessments), and you have the learning objectives for the unit. Now is the time to design the learning activities to support students' skill development and knowledge acquisition. Organize the unit objectives into lessons based on the amount of time you have for the unit and what is realistic for your class. Once you have outlined the objectives for your lessons, plan the lessons based on the principles described in chapters 2 and 14.

SUMMARY

Curriculum development is an ongoing process in which a curriculum is drafted, implemented, assessed, revised, and repeated. A backward design begins and ends with the students, working through a process where the outcomes for students are filtered into learning activities, thereby ensuring alignment, cohesion, and purpose. You can begin anywhere that is appropriate for your situation, whether you are working at the district level or the individual level. The important thing to remember about this process is that you need to know your students and community and work through the process based on their needs.

Review Questions

1. List and describe the steps of the curriculum development process.

2. Explain why it is important to get to know the students and the community.

3. How can organizing topics into themes support student learning?

4. What are the benefits of a scope and sequence?

Monkey Business/fotolia.com

CHAPTER 13

Designing Meaningful Assessments

Learning Objectives

After reading this chapter, you will be able to do the following:

- Explain various types of assessment and their uses within a health education classroom.
- Describe how various assessment strategies affect curriculum design.
- Employ a variety of assessment strategies in your own practice.

Key Terms

authentic assessment

exemplars

feedback

formative assessment

grade weighting

performance task

prompt

rubric

summative assessment

Assessment is a key part of curriculum development because it provides the opportunity for students to perform the skill evaluated. When assessment is implemented effectively in a skills-based approach, it provides more than just a demonstration of student knowledge. In fact, demonstrating the knowledge acquired is a small portion of the assessment; instead, assessments are opportunities for students to demonstrate their skill performance. You are able to evaluate their competency, proficiency, or mastery of the skill using a rubric or other assessment tool (see the Levels of Skill Performance sidebar).

Throughout this chapter, we discuss ways you can use assessment to measure progress toward your desired student outcomes. We also explore assessment strategies that you can use to guide instruction (formative) or at the end of a unit or course (summative).

PURPOSE OF ASSESSMENT

The purpose of assessment is to determine how well students are able to perform based on a specific set of criteria. The results of the assessment do more than provide a grade for how well a student completed the assessment. In addition to providing data for grades, the assessment should also be used to inform teacher practice—what you do in the classroom. For example, if you use the results of a formal assessment to guide instruction, you will look at how students performed and identify areas where they successfully demonstrated skills and knowledge and areas they need to work on. You will then make changes to instruction or curriculum to address the areas students need to work on.

When you use assessment results to guide what you teach in class and the strategies you use to achieve the stated outcomes, student outcomes improve. A good rule to remember is if it is worth teaching, it should be worth assessing, and if it is worth assessing, it should be worth taking the time to ensure students learned it. Further, if it is worth assessing, it is worth using the information from the assessment to modify instruction to ensure that objectives are being met. This may mean extending the length of a unit or reteaching skills or content, but this approach will lead to more meaningful outcomes for your students. Because you will be assessing students at multiple times and for multiple reasons, it is important to consider why the assessments are important and what they mean for you as an educator and in terms of student performance and outcomes.

TYPES OF ASSESSMENT

There are two types of assessment: formative and summative. When most people think of assessment, summative assessment is what comes to mind first. Whereas **formative assessment** is an assessment *for* learning, **summative assessment** is an assessment *of* learning. Formative assessment is used to

Levels of Skill Performance

There are three main levels of skill performance: competency, proficiency, and mastery. You may see slightly different terms used in other resources but the concepts are the same. Competence is the lowest level of skill performance and mastery is the highest. This does not mean that competence is a negative outcome but rather that you want to focus on developing competence during your teaching and then assess students' proficiency through summative assessments. In an ideal world, all students would acquire the necessary knowledge and skills at the same pace and would be given ample time to develop a skill to the level of mastery. Unfortunately, this is not reality. Not only do all students learn differently and at their own pace, but it is rare for a health education course to provide the time and real-world experience to master a particular skill, let alone multiple skills. Instead, it is your job to aid students as they work toward proficiency. Table 13.1 provides a definition of each level and sample activities for measuring students' competency, proficiency, or mastery.

support learning; it occurs along the way as students are engaging with the information and skills within a unit. Formative assessment should be used to provide students with the feedback they need to work toward achieving learning objectives. Summative assessment occurs at the end of the unit and is used to measure the extent to which students can demonstrate unit objectives. The remainder of this section explores each assessment type in more detail.

Formative Assessment

We will begin our discussion of assessment types with formative assessment (assessment that is used *for* learning) because you use formative assessment to inform your practice and to help students work toward achieving objectives. Specifically, formative assessment provides an opportunity for you to evaluate and adjust ongoing teaching and learning to improve students' achievement of intended instructional outcomes (Council of Chief State School Officers [CCSSO], 2012) That is, you should use the results of a formative assessment to help determine appropriate instructional strategies to meet student needs and to gauge how well students are progressing toward the intended outcomes. As the name implies, this type of assessment is done while the students are learning new information or skills or reviewing previously learned information or skills in class. You would use formative assessment to gauge whether or not students are keeping up with your pace of instruction, whether or not students are

TABLE 13.1 Examples of Competency, Proficiency, and Mastery

	DEFINITION	CLASSROOM APPLICATION	SAMPLE ACTIVITIES
Competency	The ability to correctly, appropriately and effectively apply the critical parts of the skill in a given context although some error may occur	Application occurs in a controlled environment. Students are walked through examples and given guidance and step-by-step instruction for implementation. Often developed through classwork and assignments. Can be measured during formative assessments.	• Group discussion • Worksheets • Jigsaw activities where students are given the skill steps in random order and must list the steps in the proper order • Think-pair-share • Prewritten role-play that students perform • Skill steps posted on the wall and frequently referred to during class
Proficiency	The ability to do something successfully with little error in varying contexts	Application occurs in a structured environment, such as a classroom, but students must use prior learning to solve the problem. This level requires students to have a firm understanding of the skills and concepts in order to apply them in a situation that simulates a real-world example. Students are able to see how the skill applies in multiple contexts. Measurement occurs during the summative assessment.	• Performance tasks • Self-written role-plays • Written dialogue between two characters • Storyboard • Student-developed PSA
Mastery	The ability to successfully and automatically perform a skill or task at a high level without prompting and to demonstrate the skill or task to another	Application occurs in an independent environment with no prompting or intervention necessary to accurately perform the skill in a real-world setting. Students are able to apply the skill or task in multiple contexts with ease.	Mastery is typically not measured in a health education class; students must independently apply the skill in a real-world setting outside the classroom.

KEY POINTS

■ Assessment should be used to determine how well students have learned what has been taught.

■ A key element of assessment is using the results to refine classroom instruction. If students are consistently performing well, the instruction is a good match. If many students are struggling to produce the expected level of work, there is a disconnect and teaching strategies and format should be reconsidered.

■ Students are provided an opportunity to achieve proficiency as a result of participation in your course. Although it is always a goal for all students, only some will develop proficiency. Even when proficiency does not occur, students should at least leave with a level of competency. All units, lessons, and activities should move students toward proficiency.

■ Skill mastery is a long-term outcome not likely achieved through one course of instruction. However, students should be encouraged to apply the skills in a real-world setting to further develop their ability and to strive for mastery.

progressing toward objectives, and what areas of functional information and skills may need more work. You would then make adjustments to increase students' likelihood of success and proficiency. Some would even argue that formative assessment is the first step of differentiating instruction for students in your class.

One benefit of formative assessment is that it can be a low-stakes assessment. Formative assessment should not be used to finalize students' grades or to make a final determination of learning. Instead, it should inform students about where they are related to successfully achieving the objectives and performing the skill with proficiency. It can also be used to provide students feedback on a specific assessment or even on their final grade so that they know what they need to work on to improve their performance.

This is different from a benchmark assessment, which is a formal assessment of student learning at a given point in time and is used to ascertain if students are progressing toward broader goals. It is similar in purpose to a formative assessment because it is used to support students' learning before they are evaluated on their achievement of the broader goals. However, a benchmark assessment should be designed using principles related to summative assessment. Because it is a tool to evaluate student learning at the end of a given time frame, the format should be aligned with summative assessment principles (discussed in the next section). On the other hand, formative assessments are done in real time during your

instruction and provide immediate feedback. They are not intended to denote whether a student has met a specific benchmark.

Table 13.2 gives some examples of when and how to use formative assessment. It is not divided by grade span; because formative assessment is a type of assessment and not a specific set of responses or criteria, the strategies can be used at various grade levels. You can determine how much or how little information is necessary to determine student progress and growth needs.

Let's look at two examples of what formative assessment could look like in the classroom.

You have just finished modeling decision making for students and your next activity is small-group work. Before you move to small groups, you want to make sure that students know the skill cues, so you decide to do a quick formative assessment. You ask students to work with a partner and write the skill cues on a piece of paper. You then review as a whole class (pairs check their own work) and provide opportunities for students to ask questions. You ask students to leave their answers out during group work so that you can circulate while students are in their groups to see how well they did remembering the skill cues and identify any areas that need to be reinforced at the end of the lesson.

You designed an exit ticket for students to complete before they leave class. The exit ticket includes questions about the topic of the lesson as well as a question about the students' level of engagement and a question about the extent to which students feel that the lesson objectives were achieved. You review the exit tickets as you are planning or reviewing your

TABLE 13.2 Sample Uses for Formative Assessment

WHEN TO USE FORMATIVE ASSESSMENT	EXAMPLES OF FORMATIVE ASSESSMENT
• To review at the beginning of class • To check for understanding in the middle of a lesson • Before an exam or quiz • Before leaving class	• Instant activity as students enter the classroom • Gallery walk to posters around the room, adding one new answer to the questions posed on each poster • Think-pair-share • Graphic organizer • Checkpoints (placing check marks on worksheets to prompt students to check their work) • 5-4-3-2-1 (students hold up one hand and the number of fingers for how confident they feel with the directions just given) • End-of-class prompt • Red, Yellow, Green (students place the appropriate colored chip on their desk to show their understanding)

next lesson. You notice that students were able to answer the questions about the topic correctly but that many students didn't feel the objectives of the lesson were achieved. You decide to make time at the beginning of the next lesson to review the previous lesson, and you add some review activities to provide students the opportunity to revisit the objectives from the lesson before moving forward in the unit.

Summative Assessment

Summative assessment is a measure of students' ability to achieve unit objectives and of their skill proficiency. Summative assessment requires students to use everything they have learned during a specific amount of time, typically at the end of a unit or, in the case of a benchmark assessment, at the end of a longer time (e.g., multiple grades). For example, a summative assessment will measure whether or not a student can use all the steps of the decision-making model in a meaningful and relevant way that leads to a healthier outcome. Typically, summative assessments include a combination of the following strategies:

- Selected response
- Constructed response
- Performance task

Table 13.3 briefly describes summative assessment strategies with examples.

Each assessment type described in table 13.3 can play a role in a skills-based classroom.

At times, the most appropriate way to quickly check knowledge of factual information is with a selected-response test. However, a selected-response assessment should not be the only assessment of learning because it cannot measure skill proficiency. It only measures whether a student is able to list skill components or recognize which skill to use in a particular situation.

AUTHENTIC ASSESSMENT

Whether you are using a formative or summative assessment, it should be authentic. In skills-based health education, you are encouraged to use assessment that goes beyond identifying what information students know to find out what they are able to do with the skills and information they have learned. For example, have students formed a base of knowledge and are they able to use that knowledge to apply a skill in an appropriate context? The ideal way to ascertain whether students are proficient in a skill is to have them complete an assessment where they must demonstrate learning in a meaningful and relevant way. This is best achieved with authentic assessment.

The word *authentic* can be defined in a variety of ways, but at the heart of its definitions is that being authentic is akin to being true, real, and meaningful. The term **authentic assessment**, then, refers to assessments that are meaningful and relevant to a student's

TABLE 13.3 Summative Assessment Strategies

TYPE	EXPLANATION	EXAMPLES
Selected response	Measures knowledge acquisition (specifically, if a student can pick the correct answer out of a group of answers).	• Multiple choice • True or false • Matching
Constructed response	Requires students to apply information or a skill in an improvised way. They must know the information well enough to apply it, but they are not responsible for generating a novel concept or idea. The response is based on a predetermined set of responses.	• Fill in the blank • Short answer
Performance task	Students do an assignment or project that requires them to follow a set of directions in order to demonstrate their learning of a concept or skill.	• Extended response • Self-created role-play, PSA, diorama, comic strip, or brochure • Portfolio

circumstances. Additionally, authentic assessment requires students to demonstrate their learning by applying the skills and information they have learned in order to solve the question posed in the **prompt** (the directions given for an assessment).

Some characteristics that help to determine whether an assessment is authentic include the following (Wiggins & McTighe, 2005):

■ The assessment is realistically contextualized—the prompt considers real-life scenarios and settings.

■ It requires judgment and innovation to perform—students must reflect on what they have learned and determine how to use their learning in a real-life scenario.

■ It asks students to apply the subject and solve the problem in new or novel ways.

■ It replicates key situations that test adults in a real-world setting, such as work, home, or civic life; it demonstrates the complexities of solving a real-world problem.

■ It assesses students' ability to use their knowledge and skills to solve complex problems; it looks at the problem as a whole rather than as isolated parts.

■ It allows opportunities to rehearse, practice, consult others, and get feedback in order to refine the final product. The process is not intended to be done as a test or in one sitting; rather, the process includes time to perform, get feedback, revise, and perform again.

What does this mean in your classroom

and assessments? How do you make sure that your assessments are authentic? In short, your assessments should be structured such that students can demonstrate learning and skill ability in a way that maintains or improves their health in realistic situations. Although there are many ways to demonstrate learning and skill ability, having students do a performance task is a great example of authentic assessment.

Performance Tasks

A **performance task** is an assignment or project that requires students to demonstrate their learning of a concept or skill. Performance tasks can be structured as an assignment that is completed during class, over multiple sessions, or as a take-home assignment. A well-designed performance task provides the parameters of the assignment and the scoring criteria so students know what is expected of them as they work to demonstrate proficiency.

Performance tasks are an effective way of determining student learning and growth; however, an ill-designed performance task will not elicit a response that fully demonstrates learning, measure the desired objective, or provide students an opportunity to demonstrate proficiency. A well-designed assessment includes four key elements (Joint Committee, 2007, p. 97):

1. The setting and role
2. A goal or challenge for the students
3. A product or performance for students to complete
4. An audience

Meaningful assessment engages students and provides an opportunity for educators to understand more fully what their students know and are able to do.

The National Health Education Standards (Joint Committee, 2007, p. 97) have identified other components of a well-designed performance assessment:

- Alignment with one or more performance indicators within a specific skill
- A clear description of the tasks of the assignment
- Information about the topics and skills students will know and be able to do once they complete the task
- Description of the product the student will create to demonstrate understanding of and ability to perform the skill
- Step-by-step directions, including process steps, feedback, and how to complete the task
- Assessment criteria, including rubrics, and tips for a well-designed response or project
- **Exemplars** (samples of previously completed work that show students what high-scoring assignments look like)
- Support from the teacher via instructions and opportunities for students to receive feedback and revise their work

Combining the key elements and components of well-designed assessments helps to ensure that you are providing students with performance tasks that are relevant and useful while also allowing the students to demonstrate their learning in a way that is measureable.

The following example outlines the prompt used for a summative, authentic performance task in a sixth-grade classroom at the end of a unit on accessing valid and reliable information, products, and services. The unit objective to be measured is "Students will be able to analyze the validity of health information and services" (modified from National Health Education Standard 3.8.1).

ACCESS

Accuracy— Is the information given on the site true? How do you know?

Credibility— What makes this source credible? What are the credentials of the person giving this information? How long has the source been providing information?

Current— Is the information less than five years old?

Ease of use and access— Is the source easy to find? Can anyone get this information?

Situations— What types of situations is this information best used for?

Sources— Cite your sources of information.

KEY POINTS

- Summative assessment allows students to demonstrate how well they have learned the concepts and skills taught in class. In a skills-based classroom, authentic assessments are most likely to provide the information necessary to determine whether or not a student has reached skill proficiency.

- Authentic assessment is meaningful for both students and teachers. Students have an opportunity to apply their learning in a real-world scenario and teachers are able to see what application would look like.

- Formative assessment is an assessment *for* learning that can be used at any time during instruction. Formative assessment is not intended to be a formal or scored process but rather a time to check for learning, provide clarification, and follow up for deeper understanding.

- When designing performance tasks, keep in mind the design elements most associated with high-quality prompts. This includes being specific and providing clear instructions, exemplars, and feedback throughout the process. Using a variety of strategies is important to keep the assessments fresh and meaningful.

Assessment Prompt

Isaiah and Jenna are playing in their neighborhood when Jenna tells Isaiah about a girl at school who keeps calling her fat. The girl has been saying that no one wants to tell Jenna that she should lose some weight, but if she doesn't no one is going to want to be her friend because she is too ugly. Jenna tells Isaiah that this girl has even sent her text messages and posted negative things about her on a site where kids from school like to communicate. Jenna is hurt by this and doesn't want to go to school anymore because she is afraid of what other kids are saying behind her back.

Part 1

Imagine you are Isaiah and that you want to help Jenna but don't know how. Identify three valid and reliable sources of information and at least one valid and reliable service you could share with Jenna to deal with this situation. The sources of information and the service(s) should provide support to Jenna, help her develop the language to respond to the negative comments, and provide her with tips to protect herself. Each information source and service should be evaluated using the ACCESS skill cues presented in class to explain why it is a valid and reliable source.

Part 2

Using the sources you identified in part 1, create a brochure for other sixth-grade students. It should provide valid and reliable sources of information and services that could help in a situation like this. For a sample assessment based on this example, see figure 13.1.

This prompt is an example of an authentic assessment, specifically a performance task, because it is relevant and meaningful to students, uses all the components of the skill they have just learned, and provides you with enough information to know whether or not students have an understanding of the skill and topic. The assignment may be given all at once or in parts. Breaking the assignment into two parts allows you to determine if the students have selected appropriate examples and to give constructive feedback before students move on to part 2.

RUBRICS AND GRADING

Summative assessments provide the structure for determining how well students have learned and can apply their learning and **rubrics**, the scoring criteria that outline the performance measures. They provide the parameters for demonstrating success. Although the process of creating criteria seems straightforward, we caution you to consider the criteria you wish to include in your rubric (for both information and skills) and whether you have articulated the criteria to students in a way that is understandable and achievable.

Analytic Versus Holistic Rubrics

Two types of rubrics are commonly used to score student work: analytic and holistic. Both types have value when scoring student work.

An analytic rubric measures each component of the criteria. For example, an analytic rubric for part 1 of the previous prompt related to Isaiah and Jenna could include listing three specific sources and each of the ACCESS skill cues, with a score for each component. In contrast, a holistic rubric is one that measures the product as a whole. For example, using the same prompt, a holistic rubric would score students on whether or not they met all of the criteria for part 1 at an acceptable level. Table 13.4 compares analytic and holistic rubrics.

Some factors to consider when deciding whether to use a holistic or an analytic rubric include:

- **Number of readers scoring the student work**—Analytic rubrics may make it easier to score among multiple readers, but inter-rater reliability (the likelihood that everyone scoring the students will fall within an acceptable range of each other) can be achieved with a holistic rubric given training and consensus about acceptable responses is provided.

- **What is being measured**—If the rubric is specifically for skill application, a holistic rubric may be sufficient. If you wish to score additional criteria that are separate from the specific skill, an analytic rubric is necessary. Students should not be marked down on a holistic rubric for skill application just because they do not earn style points.

- **Translation of rubric scores to grades**—An analytic rubric is more likely to provide enough score points to determine a grade for student work. A holistic rubric, on the other hand, is not intended to produce a grade but rather to score students on their ability to demonstrate skill proficiency. In this instance, additional criteria or measurement points would need to be considered for grade determination.

Figure 13.1 shows a sample rubric for the skill of accessing information.

Rubric Language

As stated earlier, you shouldn't use a rubric in a formative assessment unless you're using it to provide feedback to assist students in improving their work before final submission; rather, use rubrics during summative evaluations. Another caveat is that students can use a rubric as a self-assessment tool to determine if they are meeting the criteria before turning in their assignment.

Rubrics clearly define the level of work a student must demonstrate in order to receive full credit and to demonstrate proficiency of the skill and other required components of the assignment. Rubrics have points or scores to clearly articulate the expectations. You may determine the number of points you wish to use. Most rubrics contain at least 3 points but no more than 6. For example, some rubrics range from 4 to 1, others from 3 to 1, and others from 5 to 1. The upper number states what students will demonstrate in order to show proficiency, while the lower numbers indicate that some (or all) of the required components are missing. Using fewer than 3 points typically provides a large range from one point to the next, while

TABLE 13.4 Analytic Versus Holistic Rubrics

ANALYTIC RUBRIC	HOLISTIC RUBRIC
• Provides specific feedback on areas of achievement and growth.	• Allows students to see whether they are able to perform an entire skill.
• Allows students to focus on specific criteria and points within an assignment.	• The scoring scale looks at the sum of student work versus specific areas of growth or achievement.
• Establishes a minimum threshold (points) for each part in order to be considered proficient.	• Requires students to think about the big picture while they are applying the skill as opposed to each specific part.
• Each component can be weighted and give priority to specific criteria.	• All components are weighted equally.
• Often includes criteria unrelated to a specific skill (e.g., grammar, spelling, length of presentation).	• Criteria should be related to skill development; nonskill criteria may unfairly score students on their ability to apply the specific skill.

FIGURE 13.1 Sample rubric for accessing valid and reliable information and services

Criteria

4 Student work is thorough and applies the skill cues appropriately and effectively.

3 Student work is mostly complete. The response applies the skill cues but may not be done effectively or appropriately.

2 Student work is somewhat complete and does not apply the skill cues appropriately or effectively.

1 Student work is incomplete and applies the skill cues inappropriately or ineffectively.

CRITERIA	4	3	2	1
Accuracy	The student thoroughly (and without errors) explains the accuracy of 3 information sources and at least one service.	The student's explanation of the accuracy of the 3 information sources and at least one service is mostly appropriate and has only minor or few errors.	The student's explanation of the accuracy of the 3 information sources and at least one service consists of errors.	The explanation does not demonstrate an ability to explain the accuracy of the information or services.
Credibility	The student thoroughly and appropriately explains the credibility of 3 information sources and at least one service.	The student's explanation of credibility is mostly complete and appropriate for the 3 information sources and at least one service.	The student's explanation of the information and services' credibility contains errors.	The explanation does not demonstrate an ability to explain the credibility of the information or services.
Current	The information sources and services listed are less than 5 years old.	The information sources and service(s) are 5-7 years old.	The information sources and services listed are 7-10 years old.	The information sources and services listed are more than 10 years old.
Ease of use and access	The three sources and service(s) are easily accessible to 6th-grade students.	The three sources and service(s) are somewhat accessible to 6th-grade students.	At least one of the three sources is inaccessible to 6th grade students and/or the service is not accessible.	The sources and service(s) are not accessible for 6th-grade students.
Situations	Student work excellently identifies the types of situations the information and services are best used for.	Student work adequately identifies the types of situations the information and services are best used for.	Student work satisfactorily identifies the types of situations the information and services are best used for.	Student work inadequately identifies the types of situations the information and services are best used for.
Source citation	Student work includes citations with no inaccuracies.	Student work includes citations that may have minor inaccuracies.	Student work includes the three sources and service(s) with inaccuracies.	Student work does not include citations and/or has major inaccuracies.
Brochure	Brochure design is very appealing to a 6th-grade student.	Brochure design is appealing to a 6th-grade student.	Brochure design is somewhat appealing to a 6th-grade student.	Brochure design is not likely to be appealing to a 6th-grade student.
Turned in on time	The assignment was turned in on time.			The assignment was turned in late.

using more than 6 points may make it difficult to differentiate between responses. Our preference is a 4-point scale. Using an even number in the rubric forces you to clearly delineate what is expected and provides a measure of quality for the submitted student work. When an odd-number point scale is used, it can be easy to default to the middle score (e.g., a 3 on a 5-point scale) because we often want to give students the benefit of the doubt and see their work as average. When the scale only includes 4 points, the score becomes either a 2 or a 3—either below average or above average.

Note that the inclusion of 0 as a rubric score is open for debate. Some would argue that it is needed in order to note that the criteria were not met or that the student did not make any effort. We encourage you to only add a 0 to your scale to indicate that specific criteria were not submitted or demonstrated a complete lack of effort. If work was submitted and a reasonable attempt was made to complete the assignment, a score of 1 is usually appropriate; a 1 can most often be used to denote poorly constructed work while recognizing some effort. As a practical matter, whether students receive a 0 or a 1, their overall score will reflect that they have not achieved proficiency in the skill and further work is needed.

Because rubrics determine skill proficiency, they must use understandable and meaningful language. As with the steps of the skill development model, the students should review the rubric as part of the assignment and understand its criteria. Be sure to include all criteria you will be scoring, and do not score students on any criteria that you have not explicitly stated in the rubric. Because your students do not have the advantage of knowing the thoughts in your head, scoring them on criteria you have not listed in the rubric is an unachievable standard.

Table 13.5 shows some examples of language to use in your rubrics.

Weighting and Scoring

As mentioned previously, a rubric score does not necessarily translate into a letter grade. Assigning a grade is a complex process that requires multiple variables, such as attendance, homework assignments, tests and quizzes, and performance tasks. Though we advise against using the rubric score from one particular assignment to assign a letter grade at the end of a course, it is appropriate to assign each assignment, performance task, and so on with a point value. When the point values are combined, they can help to determine a student's level of performance in the course.

Even in this scenario, not all assignments, activities, or assessments are equally important. Because of this, you may wish to weight your grades. **Grade weighting** is when some variables are worth a larger percentage of the final grade than others. For example, classwork may count for 10 percent of the final grade while the performance assessment accounts for 25 percent. Even if both of these criteria have 50 points associated with them, the performance assessment score will hold more weight than the 50 points for classwork. Many schools have a grade-weighting policy or criteria, so be sure to review any related policies before establishing weights for assignments and assessments.

TABLE 13.5　Examples of Rubric Language

4	3	2	1
• Always	• Mostly	• Usually	• Rarely
• Clear	• Sufficiently clear	• Little clarity	• Unclear
• Exceptional	• Satisfactorily	• Incomplete	• Limited
• Thoroughly	• Adequately	• Partially	• Incompletely
• Excellent	• Thorough	• Somewhat	• Unsatisfactory
• Exceeds	• Meets	• Needs Improvement	• Below
• Comprehensive	• Complete	• Basic	• Negligible
• Demonstrates	• Some demonstration	• Little demonstration	• Poor demonstration

KEY POINTS

■ Rubrics provide the structure to score student work against a predetermined set of criteria. Without a rubric, students are left to guess how their work will be scored.

■ Both holistic and analytic rubrics serve important functions. Their use should be based on what you are measuring.

■ In any assignment, no two criteria are identical and there are always a few aspects of the assignment that are more important for students to master. Grade weighting allows you to decide which criteria or assignments are most important and give students credit accordingly.

CONSTRUCTIVE FEEDBACK

Giving and receiving feedback is vital to skill development because it allows for deeper understanding. **Feedback** is the process of assessing a specific action or piece of work in a way that promotes growth and strengthens learning. The most useful feedback is constructive and directly related to the task at hand. Although some consider criticism to be a form of feedback, it is actually the opposite. Criticism is the act of passing judgment on an action or work product. Feedback can be beneficial to students as they develop their skills, but criticism (as a form of judgment) does not have a place in a classroom. The intent is to provide feedback that helps students perform better and is not merely a negative response to students or their work. In this book, we focus on feedback as the appropriate method of providing students with information and strategies to improve their work.

For example, telling a student who has just turned in an incomplete assignment that he produces poor work is not feedback; it is criticism. An appropriate use of feedback would be to return the paper to the student, ask him to review the directions for clarity, and explain that the current assignment does not fulfill the criteria in the directions. This feedback is constructive and helps the student to revisit the assignment and improve his work.

The biggest reason to use feedback in a skills-based classroom is that without quality feedback, learning and skill proficiency occur at a slower or reduced rate. Students most likely continue working at the same level, which may or may not be appropriate, and they have a harder time increasing their knowledge and ability. The simple reason is that in the absence of feedback that tells or shows them that there

is a more appropriate way of accomplishing something, they have no reason to think that doing something different will result in a better outcome. A second reason is that feedback should encourage and motivate students to do better work and take ownership of it. Showing students that they are on the right track and can make their work even stronger with some constructive changes helps them to see that their initial work has value. If the student first presents work that is outside the directions or is of poor quality, feedback becomes even more important to help that student get on track to producing high-quality work.

For example, a student completes part 1 of the assessment prompt described earlier and presents an example that is neither current nor accurate. The source is from the 1992 version of a brochure from a local community agency that says it is best for kids to immediately confront the person picking on them and to show their strength by hitting the other person. A good use of feedback would be to ask the student to explain to you why her sources meet the criteria. Remind the student of the skill cues (what do we mean by *accurate* or *current*?) and ask if her sources meet the criteria. If the student says the sources look fine to her, identify the sources that do meet the criteria and why the remaining sources are outside the criteria.

Although constructive feedback is vital, some educators give minimal feedback because they feel it takes too much time away from other teaching. Feedback does take time, but it does not need to occur in the absence of teaching—feedback itself is a form of teaching. Regardless, feedback can be given in multiple ways, including from the teacher, from other students, or by self-monitoring. Table 13.6 identifies some ways to provide feedback.

TABLE 13.6 Types of Feedback

TEACHER-DIRECTED FEEDBACK	STUDENT FEEDBACK	SELF-MONITORED FEEDBACK

• Provide a model or an example.
• Write comments on assignments.
• Make verbal comments while students are working.
• Have students check in with you as they work through the steps of a project.
• Refer to anchor assignments or previous work.
• Address three areas for the student:
  • Do more . . .
  • Do less . . .
  • Keep doing . . .
	• Students complete a worksheet that lists the assignment criteria and provide three strengths of the work and up to three areas to improve.
	• Students score a partner's work using the assignment rubric.
	• Students complete a feedback form created for the assignment.
	• Students verbally explain their project and ask their partner for suggestions to improve a particular aspect of the project.
	• Students provide the skill cues or criteria and have a partner check off the criteria met.
		• Students score themselves using the assignment rubric.
		• Students list three areas they would like feedback on and why these areas are causing a problem.
		• Students answer questions on a worksheet aimed at improving work.
		• Students record a video of themselves giving a presentation and write a reflection.
		• Students fill out an assignment checklist to determine if all criteria are met.
		• Students write a reflection about the assignment, identifying areas of strength and for improvement.

Ultimately, feedback is a mechanism to improve student work while empowering students to take ownership of what they produce. Feedback should always be used to move students to the next level, whether from being a novice to being competent or from proficiency to mastery. The process is smoother and more successful with high-quality feedback.

SUMMARY

Assessment is as necessary for student growth as it is for informing teacher practice. Growth occurs when students are required to thoughtfully apply their learning. Formative and summative assessments measure students' competency or proficiency in applying what they have learned. Quality assessments assist students in identifying their strengths as well as the areas they need to work on. If it is our intention to produce students who are health literate and can use the skills of the National Health Education Standards in a real life, then we must take the time to understand the level they currently are at and how we can help them to progress in their understanding and ability.

When we fail to use effective assessment strategies, we fail to provide a learning environment that should be valued. Even though there are challenges to completing high-quality assessment in the health education classroom, students who are assessed and provided with quality feedback are more likely to use their learning. This holds true across content areas and is not unique to health education. We encourage you to develop assessments that fit within your scope of work and requirements. Assessments can range from low stakes and

■ Feedback is both important for student growth and necessary to further the likelihood of achieving proficiency.

■ High-quality feedback can be from the teacher, other students, or even self-reflection. Each can be effective in providing constructive suggestions for improvement.

low impact to high stakes and high impact; most often they fall somewhere in between. In any case, students will leave your class better prepared and you will have a better sense of how your teaching is helping students reach the intended goals and outcomes of your course.

Review Questions

1. Why is assessment important in health education?

2. What is authentic assessment, and how can it be used in a health education classroom?

3. What is the difference between formative and summative assessment? Provide two examples of each.

4. What is the role of feedback, and what strategies should you take to ensure it is effective?

To find supplementary materials for this chapter, such as worksheets and extended learning activities, visit the web resource at
www.HumanKinetics.com/TheEssentialsOfTeachingHealthEducation

PART IV

Strategies for Effective Instruction

Teaching students is a complex process. In previous parts of the book, you learned about the steps of planning a skills-based health education program. This part takes a deeper look at how to implement those plans through effective instructional practices. We begin with a discussion of how to create a positive learning environment. The learning environment is critical to the success of a skills-based approach. It sets the stage for participatory methods, which are a core component of this approach.

After learning how to create a positive learning environment, you will explore strategies and tips for using participatory methods to support skill development. If part III was about creating the map for the journey, then this part includes ways to ensure the trip itself is successful—how to prepare for the journey (by establishing a positive learning environment) and how to have a safe, enjoyable, effective journey. The final chapter focuses on assisting instructors who are teaching health education at the elementary level. Recognizing that the elementary level poses unique challenges, we discuss strategies for implementation in a setting that often has nontraditional health education programs.

By the end of this part, you will be able to establish a positive learning environment to support your skills-based approach. You will be able to implement participatory methods to support knowledge acquisition and skill development in your classroom. You will also be able to apply strategies for a skills-based approach at the elementary level.

Syda Productions/fotolia.com

CHAPTER 14

Creating a Positive Learning Environment

Learning Objectives

After reading this chapter, you will be able to do the following:

- Describe the importance of a positive learning environment.
- List the components of a positive learning environment.
- Apply a variety of strategies to achieve a positive learning environment.

Key Terms

contextual aid

icebreakers

movement activities

movement bursts

positive learning environment

A **positive learning environment** is one of the most critical components of a skills-based health education classroom. A positive learning environment is created when you value participatory teaching and learning and when there is trust and rapport among students and between yourself and students. To establish trust that leads to true participation and engagement in learning, you first need to set the stage by establishing a learning environment in which all students feel valued, safe, and supported.

Let's further define the characteristics found in a positive learning environment:

- Students feel physically and emotionally safe. They see the classroom as a place where they can be themselves and express themselves and their ideas without judgment.

- Students know that they are valued and respected, regardless of other factors such as ability, gender, sexuality, race, ethnicity, or religion.

- Students have ownership and input related to class structure and expectations. This can range from creating spaces specifically for student use to having a class discussion to establish norms and expectations.

- All students are challenged to achieve high expectations, and all students receive the support necessary to meet those expectations.

- Standards of behavior are established and are consistently and equitably enforced for all students.

- Class structure provides multiple and varied opportunities for students to experience success.

- The teacher gets to know all students and uses that knowledge to create meaningful experiences.

- There is a positive rapport (relationship) between the teacher and students and among students in the class.

Creating a positive learning environment begins with the teacher's self-reflection, continues with planning, and then is ongoing and dynamic during the implementation of the curriculum. Maintaining a positive learning environment is a work in progress—you must always consider how to maintain a positive learning environment and must be thoughtful about how the learning environment is perceived by students.

As with curriculum development, a positive learning environment takes planning and thought. It is important to continually monitor and adapt your strategies to meet the changing needs of your students. No two students are the same and no two classes are the same. You need to be aware of the differences in your classes (e.g., personalities, dynamics, interests, strengths, learning styles) and adjust your strategies to meet your students' needs. Also keep in mind that students' needs can change within a semester, term, or year. You should do the best you can to plan ahead of time, but be aware that once you get to know your students, you may need to adjust your strategies to ensure that everyone feels safe, supported, and valued. This chapter will discuss strategies for creating a positive learning environment in the classroom. Some ideas may work better for you than others, but we hope to give you plenty of ideas that you can use to develop and maintain a positive learning environment.

KNOW YOURSELF

Before planning the specifics of your positive learning environment, take time to reflect on who you are and how you arrived at your values, beliefs, behaviors, and attitudes. If you haven't explored how your beliefs and values shape your personality and decisions, it is difficult to guide students as they think about who they are. The Exploring Personal Beliefs and Values sidebar poses a few questions to use as a starting point.

After you have taken some time to explore your personal beliefs and values, the next step is to think about how you will influence the learning environment in your classroom. Take time to consider how you can build on your strengths while also addressing your weaknesses. Remember that weaknesses aren't necessarily negatives; they represent areas for improvement. As long as you recognize your areas for improvement and don't let them negatively affect your students' experience, they can be opportunities for growth. For example, you

Exploring Personal Beliefs and Values

- What are my beliefs about teaching? About health?
- Why do I teach? Why do I teach health?
- What do I value about myself? My teaching? My health?
- What are my strengths? What do I bring to the table?
- What are my blind spots? What are my weaknesses?
- Do I have any biases? Do I treat any group of students differently because of a preconceived opinion?
- Do I have any prejudice about certain students?
- How has my experience shaped who I am today?
- What are the greatest influences on my life? My health?
- Do I feel uncomfortable with certain health topics?
- Where do I place myself on a scale of cultural competency?
- Am I passionate and excited about teaching?

may have a strong belief that poor personal hygiene is a reflection of a person's self-esteem. However, you have a student who does not use deodorant for cultural reasons. You will need to respect your student's beliefs and not let your personal views affect how you teach or interact with that student. It is equally important that you model appropriate interactions with people who have different beliefs, ideas, or values. Your classroom should be a place where students learn, observe, and practice positive interactions with others regardless of differences. When you reinforce healthy and appropriate discourse, you provide students with an opportunity to share beliefs, take into account another person's point of view, and then filter through everything they have learned in order to form their own opinions.

Self-reflection is not an evaluative exercise in which you criticize yourself or try to identify things you are not good at. Rather, this is a time to get to understand yourself better, to understand where you are coming from, and to discover where and how you can build on your strengths to support your students.

HAVE A PLAN

The next step in creating a positive learning environment is to plan for it! You can plan many

aspects of the environment. Following are some areas that you'll want to think about before the school year (or class) begins.

Curriculum

Planning a curriculum that is relevant and engaging is one way to establish a positive learning environment. We have discussed the issue of relevance throughout this text. Specifically, students not only respond more positively to information that feels relevant to their world, but they also have a vested interest in maintaining or improving their health when they are empowered to use the skills in personal situations. Having a relevant curriculum can influence many facets of a health education program, including the learning environment. If students are engaged and can relate to the curriculum, they are more likely to be active participants who are on task and willing to contribute to the class. As an example, let's look at the difference between a learning environment that uses a relevant curriculum and one that does not.

Imagine you are teaching a curriculum in which the scenarios describe characters whose circumstances aren't relatable to your students. Maybe they have names that are not similar to your students' names, they live in a different community (e.g., your students live in a suburb but the characters are trying to navigate city streets), they are in situations that your students are not likely to find themselves in (e.g., the characters are going to a fair but your students live in an urban area and have never been to a fair), or the situations reference resources that are not available to your students (e.g., a teen health clinic, sidewalks for walking to school). For example, perhaps the scenario is about increasing fruit and vegetable intake but your students live in a food desert (a geographic area where healthy foods are not readily available). In this case, the students may have trouble relating to the situation because increasing fruit and vegetable intake isn't as simple as trying new foods, going to the store, or asking parents to buy more fruits and vegetables.

Put yourself in your students' shoes—would you pay attention or feel any connection to a curriculum that you couldn't relate to? Probably not. If you aren't engaged and can't relate to the experiences of the characters, why would you pay attention? What is going to motivate you to be an active participant?

Now, imagine you are teaching a curriculum using scenarios that you know your students are facing because you have been tracking health behavior data and providing students with opportunities to share their experiences. Your activities make specific references to school staff and places in the school and community. You are making the curriculum personalized and immediately relevant in some way to all students. Let's reframe the previous example to fit the context of your students. Now the scenario asks students to consider how they could increase their intake of fruits and vegetables while considering that there are few options for fresh and local produce nearby. The scenario includes references to the local convenience store and to the closest resource that carries fresh fruits and vegetables.

Put yourself back in your students' shoes. Even if you haven't experienced the specific situations being described, you know that others in your class have, and you know the people and the community being referenced in the scenario. You are now more engaged because you can relate in some way to the scenario.

Students connect with things that they find familiar or relatable and tune out things that they can't relate to or have no interest in. Doing your best to make sure that each of your students will be able to relate to your curriculum will lead to more motivation and engagement.

Along the same lines, having a curriculum that is sequential and builds on prior learning can also help keep students interested and engaged. You want to ensure that students are being appropriately challenged and also that you are showing students how their learning in the present relates to their learning in the past (both in their classes as well as in their personal experiences). If students are bored because they are learning the same thing they learned last year, or if they are confused because they don't understand what the current unit has to do with the last one, then they aren't going to be as engaged. Disengaged students are more likely to detract from a positive learning environment or to not make positive contributions.

Teaching Methods

Teaching methods that are interactive and engaging can contribute to a positive learning environment, but their success also depends on a positive learning environment. Interactive and engaging methods will be less successful in environments where students do not feel safe and supported. For some, being in a classroom that uses interactive teaching methods is a new experience. Perhaps previous teachers have not required students to go outside their comfort zone, to get up in front of their peers in what might be an uncomfortable situation, or to be a talker if they are usually quiet or a listener if they are accustomed to being a talker. For example, you may have students who don't feel comfortable speaking in front of the class, but your class involves role-plays, presentations, and other activities that require them to do so. If they don't feel safe and secure in the class, they might be less willing to fully participate in the activities and engage in their own learning. The flip side is that using interactive, engaging methods can help students feel invested in the curriculum and that they are valued members of the class whose ideas matter. We address teaching methods in more detail in chapter 15.

Resources for Students

Along with a relevant curriculum, you need to plan to have resources available for students that include multiple perspectives and represent a broad range of students. The term *resources* includes readings, books and other texts, websites, articles, magazines, and brochures from local community organizations. You should provide a variety of resources that reflect the diversity of your community. Resources should also be varied to provide opportunities for students of all abilities. All students should be able to find resources (either in the classroom or through direction) to meet their needs. It might not always be possible to have all of these resources available in the classroom, but you can connect with community resources or have a list of resources available for students.

Put yourself in your students' shoes again. You are always excited for the read-alouds at the beginning of class. Each time you hope that there will be a book with a character who looks like you, or talks like you, or lives in a place like you do. But it doesn't happen. You stop looking forward to the read-alouds and stop paying attention. Or, as a struggling reader, when it comes to the time in class when everyone finds a text to read and analyze, you can't find a text that you can confidently read. You sit quietly and do your best, but you aren't able to fully apply yourself during this time and you are consistently receiving negative feedback.

These examples emphasize the importance of having resources available that your students can relate to. However, it is also important to broaden students' perspectives and introduce them to viewpoints that are different from their own. There is a balance between providing resources that students can connect with and helping students develop an understanding of issues or topics that they may disagree with or that they may not have been exposed to yet. This is especially valuable when discussing personal goals and expectations. For example, if a young girl has always dreamed of being a ballerina but has never seen a ballerina who looks like her, she may be quick to give up on her dream. Showing her pictures and stories of ballet dancers from other cultures could be the impetus for her to continue with her dream.

Physical Space

A final area to consider when planning the learning environment is how to maximize the physical space to enhance learning. The physical space can play a significant role in setting the stage for the learning environment. Some aspects of the physical environment will be out of your control, but here are some things to consider.

Seating

Grouping desks or using tables will provide opportunities for students to interact with each other. However, students must also be able to see you during a lesson and see content if you're using a presentation program or other visual teaching methods.

Space for Students

Creating a space that is for students—whether it is a reading nook, a relaxation corner, or a physioball in the corner—can increase students' feelings of ownership in the classroom and show them in a concrete way that they have a place in the classroom. You must also make it clear that this is a space that students can use. It would be ineffective to have a space but not allow students time to use the space when needed.

Student Work

Showcasing student work in the classroom can enhance the learning environment at any level. This is typically more common at the elementary level, but providing space for student work at all levels can elicit a sense of pride, ownership, and respect for their work. Even at the middle or high school level, students love to see their work displayed. Displaying the posters, brochures, or visual PSAs that students develop will go a long way toward showing that their work is valued and will educate other students in the process.

Contextual and Other Visual Aids

Include **contextual aids** that can help all students in the class be successful. These can be sentence stems, visual representations of the skill cues, or even posters with vocabulary words and definitions. In addition to the contextual aids, you want to make sure that pictures, posters, and other visuals are diverse.

KEY POINTS

- Self-reflection is an important first step to establishing a positive learning environment. You need to assess your personal beliefs, values, and what you are bringing to the classroom before you can help students do the same.

- There are many ways to prepare for a positive learning environment even before the class starts.

- You should consider your curriculum, physical space, resources, and teaching methods to ensure that they support all students in the classroom.

KNOW YOUR STUDENTS

Getting to know your students is another key aspect of creating a positive learning environment. We discussed strategies for getting to know your students in chapter 12. Strategies implemented during the curriculum development process to get to know your students will also assist you when working to establish a positive learning environment. We will explain some additional strategies here.

Getting to know your students will facilitate relationship building, engagement, interest, and motivation. Knowing your students' likes, dislikes, learning styles, interests, and experiences can help you tailor your examples to connect with students, include students in the learning process, and increase student engagement. Another benefit to asking students to share information about themselves is that it could lead students to be more self-aware. There are many strategies for getting to know your students, but here are a few to get you started.

- **Icebreakers:** Plan **icebreakers** and get-to-know-you games for the beginning of the course. This will not only help you get to know your students but will also help students learn more about each other and feel more comfortable sharing information about themselves. As with all activities, it is important to put parameters on icebreakers. Ground rules for the activity could include not sharing private or confidential information, never using the information shared to tease another person, and only sharing about yourself (it is not OK to disclose something about another person to the group). This works best when your prompts are thoughtful but not intended to elicit responses that

could cause someone to share inappropriate information. This is the beginning of the year and you want these activities to help students feel comfortable. An added benefit is that icebreakers can also help you learn correct pronunciation of names. All of these results will help develop a positive learning environment. If students are reluctant to participate in these kinds of activities, a good strategy is to have them come up with an activity to lead the class. The students will surely get excited about having their game chosen.

- **Surveys:** Create a survey that asks students a variety of questions that will assist you in the classroom. Suggestions include likes, dislikes, hobbies, interests, languages spoken at home, and health-related questions they might have. This could also be an opportunity to engage families if you send the survey home and ask students to complete it with parents or guardians or include specific questions for parents or guardians.

- **Reflection assignments:** Design assignments that ask students to reflect and share their reflections. Assignments can include essays, autobiographies, poems, illustrations, and collages. If this is a visual assignment, students' work could be posted in the classroom.

ESTABLISH CLASSROOM NORMS, CONSEQUENCES, AND REWARD SYSTEMS

Establishing classroom norms and consequences provides structure and consistency. It also helps students develop a sense of responsi-

Establishing a positive learning environment in which students feel safe and supported and empowered to take ownership over their learning is critical to the success of a skills-based approach.

bility for their behavior in the class and creates an environment where it is both acceptable and necessary to hold each other to high standards. Make sure that any classroom policies align with school policies, but when possible, use this as an opportunity to engage students and allow them to be part of the decision-making process. You might work as a group and ask students to share their ideas for norms and consequences. Even young students are able to tell you what is appropriate behavior in the classroom.

You might put students into small groups, have them create a number of norms, and then bring the groups back together. You might use a text or book to introduce the idea of appropriate behavior and then lead a discussion about how to act in the classroom. However you do it, ensure that students have a voice in the process. Following are some considerations when creating classroom norms, consequences, and rewards.

Use Norms, Not Rules

The term *rules* has a negative connotation—we have to follow rules or else there are negative consequences. On the other hand, the term *norms* suggests that this is what we do and how we act. Norms are not intended to dismiss the idea of consequences, but rather to set the foundation for the classroom culture. Using *norms* instead of *rules* also introduces a term that might be used in the health education class in the future. Students will be able to make connections between class norms and societal norms, which may be more meaningful for them.

When creating norms, always use positive language. Instead of saying "Don't talk when others are talking," say "Listen when others are talking" or "One person speaks at a time." Focus on what students *should* be doing rather than what they *shouldn't* be doing. This should be a theme throughout the health education curriculum. You don't want to always focus on what not to do (e.g., "Don't do drugs," "Don't drink alcohol," "Don't drink soda") but rather what to do (e.g., "Drink more water," "Avoid using alcohol," "Make responsible decisions").

Have students sign a list of the class norms or a statement in which they acknowledge and accept the norms. These actions help keep students accountable for their actions and puts responsibility on them to follow the norms. Having students come to consensus for the final set of norms is a great opportunity to introduce a group decision-making process that may be used throughout the course.

Posting the norms can also be useful as reminders for students. In addition to posting

CULTIVATING A POSITIVE LEARNING ENVIRONMENT

Melissa Jackson

Westside Middle School, Westside Community Schools, Omaha, Nebraska

What is one key component of a positive learning environment?

Make sure that all students feel safe and important. Walk around and interact with the students.

How do you keep the environment positive and safe for students?

At the beginning of the year, I shake every student's hand, introduce myself, and say "Welcome to health." My students create ground rules for establishing a safe and respectful learning environment. The ground rules include what a safe and respectful learning environment sounds, looks, and feels like. I make copies of the ground rules, laminate them, and place them at every table so that students can see them daily. We visit the rules multiple times throughout the year. I talk to every one of my students every day and actively participate with my students. I also make three to five positive phone calls home each week.

What advice do you have for other health educators in the field?

Have fun, make the learning pertinent to your students' lives, and engage your students. Connect with other health teachers. They are great to share ideas and lessons with.

---

them in the classroom, you can put them on a class website, in binders, or on a digital platform.

Be Consistent

It is critical to uphold the established norms and consequences with all students. If you do not enforce the consequences, students will be less likely to take the norms seriously and it will be more difficult for you to manage the class. It is also important to focus on recognizing positive behavior—the times when students are demonstrating the norms. For example, you might say "Thank you for listening when others are talking" or "Thank you for raising your hand before speaking." If you focus on the negatives—the times when students are not following the norms—you set a negative tone for the class. Though it is important to address behaviors that are not meeting the norms, the focus should be on positive behaviors.

Develop a Reward System

Consider developing a positive reward system for behavior in addition to enforcing conse-

quences. This system could be classroom or school based depending on policies in your school. However you decide to do this, make sure you have a systematic way of rewarding positive behavior for all students that is meaningful for students and that will be a source of motivation. Rewards, however, should not become the norm for doing the right thing. Students don't need a prize every time they do what they are supposed to. Maybe they have to earn a certain number of tickets before they can pick from a prize box, or maybe there is a combination of individual and class levels and incentives. We encourage you to choose health-enhancing rewards. Be sure that you are not handing out candy or pizza tokens—use this opportunity to show students that rewards can be healthy and enjoyable. Base the rewards on what motivates your students, such as more recess time or a homework-free night.

Plan for All Situations

Be sure to plan for a variety of situations in your classroom. Have a plan for lining up, going to the bathroom, transitioning between activities, forming groups, getting students' attention, and so on. Don't underestimate the importance of these transition times for class management. The more effective your management is, setting behavior expectations at the beginning of the course, the more time you will spend on task and the less opportunity there is for actions that detract from the learning environment.

Incorporate Movement

There are many benefits to using movement in the classroom. In terms of the learning environment, movement can provide simple, quick bursts for students that energize them and help them stay on task. For example, have students stand at their desks and jog in place, march in place, and perform arm circles, jumping jacks, and trunk twists. This will get oxygen to their brains, give them time to process information, wake them up, and help them refocus on learning. Younger students can sing songs and incorporate movements, and you could do yoga with students of any age. Movement is fun and can add enjoyment to the classroom (see Sample Movement Bursts and Movement Activities sidebar).

Encourage Positive Attitudes

Health education is unique in that it relates to each and every student in the class—it's all about them—which is perfect for adolescents. Your class should be a chance for them to engage in a way they may not be able to do in other classes. The focus on participatory learning in skills-based health education in and of itself encourages positive interactions. Make sure that this is clearly articulated to students through the norms.

Communicate Expectations

In addition to establishing class norms, you must clearly define your expectations. Students will be more successful when they know what you expect of them—you can't expect them to do something a certain way if you don't tell them how to do it. You can communicate expectations verbally or in written format—or even better, do both. Review expectations with your students multiple times and through multiple modes. We suggest clarifying expectations for the following.

- **Learning objectives:** Tell students the objectives for the course, the unit, the lesson, and (when appropriate) the activity. Objectives should be orally communicated to students and also written along with an agenda for each lesson.
- **Assignments:** Use rubrics or other strategies to outline the expectations for

---

Sample Movement Bursts and Movement Activities

Movement bursts are short in duration and do not have to connect with course content.

- Thirty seconds of jumping jacks or jogging in place at their desks
- Yoga or stretching
- Laps around the classroom
- Dancing (they can dance however they want for one minute)
- Acting out various movements (e.g., swimming, swinging a bat or tennis racket)

Movement activities integrate content into the experience.

- Students walk to one end of the classroom to collect skill cues for a skill and then complete a worksheet.
- Students perform various movements between stations that are set up around the room.
- Students act out a story as it's being read.
- Students toss a beanbag or other manipulative back and forth while listing the cues for a skill as a class.

assignments, including when assignments are due, what is necessary to complete them, and how they will be evaluated.

■ **Feedback:** Tell students how and when they will receive feedback in class. You should also explain how students can respond to feedback (how to communicate with you if they have an issue or a question). In addition, it may be helpful to establish guidelines for appropriate ways to give and receive feedback. You could connect this to interpersonal communication and provide a real-life example of the importance of effective communication.

■ **Peer-to-peer interactions:** Clarify expectations for peer-to-peer interactions in the classroom. This can include how to listen, how to respond if they want to share an opinion that may conflict with someone else's, how to show respect, and how to work out conflicts. You may include these in the norms as well, but it is important to be explicit about how students should interact in the class. With participatory methods, it is critical that peer-to-peer interactions support the positive learning environment and a safe, judgment-free zone.

FOSTER STUDENT LEADERSHIP AND INVOLVEMENT

Providing students with opportunities for leadership and for sharing their voice can support a positive learning environment. As discussed at the beginning of the chapter, a positive learning environment is one in which students are valued. One way to demonstrate students' value is to provide leadership roles in the classroom and to give students a chance to have an impact on the curriculum and the class. Suggestions for student leadership include the following.

■ **Involve students in the planning process.** This could be done through a reflection paper, an end-of-course evaluation where students provide feedback that you use to modify the curriculum for the next class, or even an in-class discussion about what they enjoyed most about the class and what they wish they had more of. You could also do midcourse check-ins to get students' perspectives about the extent to which objectives are being achieved, whether there are areas that need to be revisited, and whether there are areas that they want to address moving forward. Another option is to have students complete a preassessment of their knowledge related to various topics and areas of interest. However you involve the students, you need to take their feedback into account and make changes based on their ideas. You'll need to use your professional judgment, but if you ask for feedback and do not use it, you will not truly be giving students a voice.

■ **Provide leadership opportunities throughout the course.** There are many ways to integrate leadership roles into the class. Not every student is a leader, but every student should have a chance to be

KEY POINTS

■ Getting to know your students is important for relationship building and can help you personalize your teaching to be relevant and meaningful for them.

■ Establish norms and consequences for the classroom. Engage students in the process so that they have ownership and accountability.

■ Be consistent in your enforcement of consequences. You need to do what you say you will do and hold all students accountable.

■ Focus on the positive behaviors students are demonstrating in your classroom, not just the negatives. Establish a reward system to recognize these behaviors.

■ Clearly communicate your expectations for classroom behavior.

a leader. You may have line leaders, group or team captains, readers, students to distribute papers or other resources, students to write on the board, group assignments outside of class, and so on. Positions should rotate, and you should ensure that every student has a chance to lead in some capacity. Providing leadership in a variety of roles is a way to build group cohesion, strengthen personal skills, and contribute to the success of the group.

■ **Provide opportunities for student voices and choices.** With a participatory approach, there should be many opportunities for student voices to be heard through partner work, small-group and large-group work, student questions, student projects, and in-class activities. Another way of giving students a voice is to let them create scenarios for in-class activities and other assignments. This allows them to create situations that are meaningful for them and gives them some control over the curriculum in a direct way. In addition, you can design activities and assignments that allow students to choose which option they would like to complete. You may design options with varying levels of challenge, options for different styles of learning, or options with a choice of scenarios. This requires more planning but can be valuable for students' learning experiences.

■ **Foster connections outside the classroom.** The goal of health education is to provide students with the knowledge and skills necessary to be healthy outside the classroom. Therefore, when possible, learning should be taken outside the classroom. You might have a project in which students connect with leaders in the community and then students present to the class or to community organizations. You can also have students complete projects that they must present to other students in the school or district (e.g., high school students present to elementary school students).

BE A POSITIVE ROLE MODEL

A final aspect of creating a positive learning environment is being a positive role model—show students how you want them to behave. If you ask them to be positive, you must be positive when teaching. If you ask them to listen when others are speaking, you need to listen when others are speaking. Do not underestimate the influence your actions have on students. You need to model and contribute to the learning environment as you ask students to do the same.

■ Be enthusiastic and positive.

■ Model appropriate behavior.

■ Have fun when you teach.

■ Model healthy behaviors.

■ Be aware of your teacher talk—what you say and the language you use—both in class (while teaching and while speaking to students) and out of class (students can often hear what you're saying when speaking to other teachers about exercising, stress management, your plans for the weekend, and so on).

■ Stay current and engaged in your profession (more on this in chapter 17).

■ Be a lifelong learner.

■ Admit when you do not know something and model appropriate ways to find answers to questions.

SUMMARY

Creating a positive learning environment is critical to a successful skills-based health education classroom. A positive learning environment is one in which all students feel safe, valued, and supported and in which all students can experience success. There are multiple strategies for creating a positive learning environment, but we addressed some of the most critical here. The learning environment is dynamic and must be monitored and evaluated consistently during the course and throughout the year.

Review Questions

1. What are the components of a positive learning environment?

2. How does self-reflection support the development of a positive learning environment?

3. What considerations for a positive learning environment are relevant in the planning process?

4. What strategies can you use in your classes to establish and maintain a positive learning environment?

5. How does being a positive role model contribute to a positive learning environment?

To find supplementary materials for this chapter, such as worksheets and extended learning activities, visit the web resource at
www.HumanKinetics.com/TheEssentialsOfTeachingHealthEducation

Susan Chiang/iStock.com

CHAPTER 15

Implementing a Skills-Based Approach

Learning Objectives

After reading this chapter, you will be able to do the following:

- Describe the role of the teacher in skills-based health education.
- Describe key aspects of implementation for a skills-based approach.
- Apply effective teaching strategies in your classroom.

Key Terms

active learning

do-now activities

essential questions

internalization

personalization

scaffolding

self-reflection

Socratic seminar

Previous chapters of this text have explained why a skills-based approach to health education is valuable. We have also taken a closer look at the considerations and strategies for helping students develop the skills of the National Health Education Standards, and we have provided strategies for planning a curriculum, assessing student learning, and creating a positive learning environment. What we haven't discussed yet is how to put it all together and implement a skills-based approach in the classroom.

To connect the pieces we've discussed thus far, you must be thoughtful about the methods and strategies used during class. If your goal is to prepare students to manage problems they encounter outside the classroom, you must use methods and strategies that get at the heart of what students know and are able to do in order to improve their likelihood of maintaining or improving healthy behaviors. You must focus on effectively implementing skills-based instruction while reinforcing the skills necessary to be contributing members of society. In addition to the ideas presented in this chapter, Appropriate Practices in Health Education (2015) is a resource which can support you in the implementation of a skills-based approach to health education.

How you teach students is just as important as *what* you teach them, if not more so. This chapter focuses on classroom methods to support a skills-based approach. There are five main goals when implementing a skills-based approach:

1. Facilitate learning experiences that engage students with the content.
2. Use a lesson format that supports knowledge and skill acquisition.
3. Provide engaging, relevant experiences for students.
4. Foster participation and active learning.
5. Provide opportunities for self-reflection, internalization, and personalization of content (information and skills).

FACILITATE LEARNING EXPERIENCES

The teacher's role is to be a guide or a facilitator. As a health educator, you plan activities for students that provide opportunities to engage with the functional information and develop skills. In the classroom, you facilitate those experiences through the strategies we will discuss in this chapter. Being a guide or facilitator (also discussed in chapter 2) does not mean taking a passive role in the classroom; in fact, it is quite the opposite. Being a guide or facilitator means that you set the stage for learning, monitor the class during activities and make adjustments as necessary, reflect on each lesson and determine if modifications are needed, differentiate instruction for your students, and model engagement, enthusiasm, and participation. It also means that you occasionally use direct instruction to provide students with the functional information they need. However, direct instruction should only be used when necessary because there are usually more effective ways of helping students learn and retain information.

We can also think of the teacher in a skills-based classroom as a gardener. Just as a gardener prepares the garden bed to ensure the best conditions for the plants to grow, a teacher establishes a positive learning environment that helps students feel safe and supported and ready to grow as they learn the functional information and develop skills. The gardener then determines what plants to put in the garden and where to plant the seeds for maximum growth. The teacher determines the content (functional information and skills) to include and plans out the sequencing for maximum learning and skill development. Next the gardener plants the seeds; similarly, the teacher plants the seeds with an engaging approach that provides students with the knowledge and skills that will help them to lead healthy lifestyles. The gardener then monitors growth and provides support as needed, such as water, fertilizer, or other resources. Likewise, the teacher monitors student progress and adjusts the curriculum and instruction to meet students' needs. The teacher may also add support, scaffolding, or differentiation for students to help them learn. Finally, as the gardener assesses the garden, enjoys its successes, and begins to prepare for the next year, the teacher uses assessments to determine student growth and to plan for the next year.

Importantly, the gardener plays an active role in fostering the growth of the garden, but she cannot make the plants grow. She can plant the seeds in the best conditions and provide resources and support to help the plants, but she can't force the plants to grow or to bloom. Similarly, the teacher cannot make students learn or apply their learning to enhance their health. However, he can take an active role by providing the best experience for his students in order to support their learning and skill development, make the health education class meaningful and relevant, and foster positive attitudes and health behaviors.

FORMAT LESSONS TO SUPPORT SKILL DEVELOPMENT AND KNOWLEDGE ACQUISITION

Before we continue, it is necessary to review the basic structure of a lesson. Every lesson should include a beginning, middle, and end. Routines for the beginning and end of class should be similar so that there is structure and consistency across lessons. When students can predict classroom patterns (such as the entrance and exit routines), classroom management takes less time and more time can be focused on instruction and learning.

As discussed in chapter 12, each lesson should have specific objectives that contribute to the unit objectives and the assessments. Each learning activity in the lesson should relate to those objectives. There is limited time for health education and there is much to accomplish. Lessons must include activities that are purposeful and related to achieving objectives (because the objectives are the outcomes that have been identified as the most important for students). We also suggest that you include some type of formative assessment in each lesson to help monitor student progress (see chapter 13).

A consistent format with clear and measurable objectives can support student learning and engagement. Purposefully planning activities to meet objectives will help maximize your time with students. Your lesson plan format is a simple but important part of implementing a skills-based approach. We will now examine strategies for each part of the lesson plan.

Beginning of Class

The beginning of class provides a transition time for students to focus on the material for the day while attendance and other housekeeping tasks occur. The routines at the beginning of class set the tone for the rest of the lesson. The more consistent your routine is in the beginning of class, the more students learn what to expect and the more likely they will be to come into class, sit down, and focus on the task at hand.

Beginning-of-class routines often include an oral review of the lesson objectives as well as references to a location where the objectives are posted in the room (e.g., whiteboard, poster) and an activity that gets students thinking about the lesson skill or topic. For example, as students enter the room, they are directed to a written assignment on the board. This **do-now activity** (see table 15.1 for examples) acquaints students with the lesson content, focuses their energy on the task at hand, and gives you time to take attendance and collect assignments. You could begin with an individual activity and as students complete the activity, they turn to a partner and share their response. You could also have the do-now activities involve small groups or even the whole group. The format should be determined by the needs of your students and the purpose of the lesson, and it should be varied often to prevent students from getting complaisant during the activity. Any responses generated are then used to frame the lesson for the day and serve as a lead-in to stating the lesson objectives. A do-now activity should be something that students can work on without direct support from you but that gets students thinking about the material for the day.

Another way to focus students on the task at hand is to post an **essential question** on the board or screen to get them thinking about the topics of the day or other related course material. An essential question is an open-ended question that fosters critical thinking about the content. There is no one right answer; the goal is to provide students with an opportunity to apply what they have learned and think critically as they form their own understandings. You could think of it as a guiding question for your lessons and activities.

TABLE 15.1   Sample Activities for the Beginning of Class

Do-now activities	• Students complete a sentence stem. • Students look at a set of skill steps and place them in the appropriate order. • Students journal about a healthy choice they have made in the last 24 hours. • Students read a short story or paragraph and formulate an argument for or against the statement. • Students complete a matching activity between topic words and their definitions. • Students complete a 3-2-1 activity to review material from the last class.
Essential questions	• What does it mean to be healthy? • What do we need to be healthy? • What influences your health? • Are you healthy? • Why is it important to make healthy choices?

Middle of Class

The middle of class is when the main learning activities occur that advance student knowledge and skills. During your planning, make sure to consider the order of activities so there is a clear progression. Also, determine the prerequisite skills, concepts, and vocabulary needed for the activities. If students do not have these, you should take time to teach them. If students do have the prerequisites, a review is still always helpful (and can be used to assess their understanding). Other considerations for this part of the lesson include the following:

■ Ensure that activities are engaging and purposeful rather than just being fun. We want students to enjoy being in class, but every activity during class time should help students meet one of the stated lesson objectives. We have all participated in activities that were fun but did not help us to do anything differently, teach us anything new, or challenge us to step outside our comfort zone. Students can enjoy activities that are engaging and relevant and that directly contribute to their learning and skill development. We encourage you to implement activities that will be enjoyable for students but to limit activities that are just for fun. Fun activities have their place, but their inclusion should be thoughtful and should serve a purpose.

■ Scaffold activities to ensure students have the opportunity to experience suc-

cess. **Scaffolding** is a way of building to more complex information and skills in a methodical and thoughtful way. In addition to ensuring that students have the prerequisites they need, you also need to ensure that activities are scaffolded so that everyone can participate. Remember that not all students learn at the same pace or advance through lessons at the same speed. Scaffolding will be largely based on your students' needs. Strategies could include providing preprinted notes, assigning roles for activities, creating levels or stages for an activity, and arranging groups to combine students of varying skill levels so they can support each other.

■ When discussing information about health-related topics, ensure that you present the functional information in relation to the skill students are learning and make meaningful connections between the information and the skill that are relevant to their world. For example, if you are teaching information related to underage drinking in your interpersonal communication unit, you may present statements that students can use to support their refusal (e.g., "I want to stay in control of my body," "Alcohol affects everyone differently and I don't know what it will do to me," "I had an energy drink earlier and alcohol and energy drinks can be dangerous," "I don't even want to start because I don't want to spend all that money on alcohol") rather than just presenting facts (e.g., how alcohol is made, a demonstration of how it feels to be intoxicated). Or, if you are presenting tobacco information in your advocacy unit, you might present facts that students can specifically use to support their anti-tobacco position. You need to model how to use the functional information and help students to see connections between the information and the skill.

■ Meeting the needs of all students takes planning and consideration. You may want to use a specific framework such as Universal Design for Learning (www.udlcenter.org). While the UDL framework can also apply when planning goals and assessments, it is especially relevant as you design your lessons and learning activities so that your students all have the opportunity to learn in ways that are meaningful and appropriate for their needs. You may need to connect with others to ensure you are aware of any specific needs a student may have. Whether or not you use UDL or other resources, the most important thing is that you are implementing a skills-based health education program that meets the needs of all learners and that provides all students with the opportunity to learn and grow.

End of Class

Just as having a routine in the beginning of class is important, having a structured ending (or closure) is important to wrap up the lesson and to explain homework or assignments due at the next class. For example, include time to debrief and review lesson objectives to formatively assess if they were met, highlight the key points of the lesson, answer any outstanding questions, and preview the next lesson. One strategy that can be useful is exit tickets. Similar to do-now activities at the beginning of class, exit tickets are quick activities for students to complete before they leave the classroom. A do-now activity helps students focus and preview the lesson, whereas an exit ticket reviews the lesson. Exit tickets can be especially useful as formative assessments to help determine how well students are able to meet lesson objectives or articulate key takeaways from the lesson.

Finally, preview the next lesson for students and explain the connections between what they have been learning and their assignment or what is coming next. As with the introduction, it is crucial to be consistent with your procedures and closing activities. You do not have to use the same activity every class, but there should always be closure to send students on their way.

Table 15.2 presents sample activities for the three parts of the lesson.

TABLE 15.2 Sample Activities for the Three Parts of the Lesson

BEGINNING	MIDDLE	END
• Students reflect on a quote related to the content. • Students answer an open-ended question related to the topic of the day. • Students work in small groups to review readings due that day. • Students answer a series of questions related to content that will be covered that day. • Students are given a scenario related to the skill of the unit. Students must attempt to resolve the scenario in a health-enhancing way. • Students journal (can be free writing or prompted).	• Hold a Socratic seminar. • Students perform role-plays. • Do a jigsaw activity where groups of students read parts of a text, discuss the text, and then present to the class. • Students give presentations of an assignment. • Students do skill practice activities. • The group brainstorms about a topic or skill.	• Hold a group debriefing where you ask questions about the lesson. • Students complete exit tickets individually. • Check in with students and have them share what they learned. • Hold small-group discussions about the main messages of the lesson.

KEY POINTS

- In a skills-based classroom, the teacher acts as a facilitator or a guide to assist students with activities that are designed to engage them with the topics and skills.
- The teacher has an active role in the class, from setting the stage for learning through monitoring progress to adjusting lessons and curriculum.
- Lessons should have a consistent structure with a clear beginning, middle, and end. The beginning activities should prepare students for the lesson, and the closing should include a review of key points from the lesson and a preview of the next lesson.

PROVIDE ENGAGING, RELEVANT EXPERIENCES

Ensuring that students have engaging and relevant experiences starts with curriculum planning, but it doesn't end there. Before each unit and then each lesson, you need to review what you are going to teach and the tactics you will use to keep the instruction fresh, relevant, and interactive. For example, make sure you are using up-to-date materials, references, and resources. This means that you must not only stay abreast of current issues within the community, state, and nation but also that you must connect with students so that you can include meaningful examples during learning activities.

Another way to engage students is to allow them to share their input about the topics and materials used in class. The best way to find out what will engage students and what is relevant to them is to ask! Asking students for their input serves a couple of purposes. First, you get a better sense of what information is on your students' minds. This can alert you to any potential misunderstandings or allow you to debunk any myths they believe. Second, asking for student input keeps you present in their world. Because you are no longer at the same stage of development as your students, it can be easy to slip into adult mode and think about issues from an adult lens. Failing to remember the nuances of the adolescent brain can cloud your perception of how students view situations and topics.

Another strategy to provide engaging, relevant activities is to include many opportunities to get to know your students. This will help you develop rapport with the students, and

it may facilitate opportunities for students to share concerns as well as situations they may have been in (or heard of) that you can use in your classroom. Further, it may make students more comfortable with sharing ideas, thoughts, and situations during class, which will support authentic discussions and skill development using situations that are occurring in their lives.

You might also allow students to find their own resources and conduct their own research (which can provide an opportunity to apply skills such as accessing valid and reliable information). You could create an assignment where students have to research an area of interest, or you could assign topics based on curriculum needs, which would provide less opportunity for **personalization** but would still give students an opportunity to pick an area they are interested in. Students conduct the research using the skill cues for accessing valid and reliable information, products, and services. Students then create a deliverable (e.g., presentation, brochure, video) to share with the rest of the class. This kind of activity directly engages students in the planning and disseminating of information through the application of skills. It can also provide insight into areas of interest for your students and perhaps even show you a new technology or other innovation to use in your classroom.

FOSTER PARTICIPATION AND ACTIVE LEARNING

A key aspect of skills-based health education is the use of participatory and interactive methods. The best strategies for your class will depend on factors such as class size, student age, and class dynamics, but the following principles should be considered.

Modeling and Observation

As discussed in the skill chapters, step 3 of the skill development model is to model application of the skill in authentic situations. This is important because students need the opportunity to observe the skill being implemented correctly. However, this does not mean that students are passive during the modeling or observation. You could have a checklist where students need to watch for certain skill cues, you could stop at certain points during the demo and ask questions to check for understanding

---

Advice From the Field

IMPLEMENTING A SKILLS-BASED APPROACH

Andy Horne
New Trier High School, Winnetka, Illinois

What is your best strategy for engaging students?

In recent years, I have relied on interactive-response and game-based learning technologies to give students immediate feedback. These technologies allow me to create interactive quizzes, surveys, and discussion questions using text, images, and multimedia. Students can participate with any mobile device and earn points for their responses. These activities are great for review games, bell-ringers, or exit slips and can allow students to respond anonymously if they wish. I like how these technologies engage students in their learning and also provide them each with a voice. Not only are they great formative assessment tools, but they also can serve as avenues to generate classroom discussion. As a classroom teacher I know time is valuable. These technologies collect behind-the-scenes data about your class or individual students in real time. The spreadsheets can be used to check for understanding and efficiently identify areas of concern without giving up much of your teaching time.

Another key strategy I employ often is storytelling and current events. When students hear true stories, it oftentimes hooks them into becoming more interested in the topic. This can be an effective strategy to create engagement in the classroom.

What is the most critical attribute of an effective teacher?

There are many skills or components that make up being a great teacher. One of the most critical attributes is presence. Passion often drives presence. Students know when a teacher is fully engaged or excited about teaching something. Teachers must have a presence in the classroom in order for students to be engaged. Stay true to who you are because students will know if you are faking it, but presence comes with having confidence and showing students you are not afraid to take risks. You have to have that teacher radar to gauge the temperature of the room and to figure out when to switch gears if things are not working the way you had hoped. Your presence creates the tone of the classroom. Like any great entertainer who has presence on stage, great teachers must find ways to entertain their students. You need to put on a show sometimes. One way I try to do that is by performing live rap songs in my class (check out www.youtube.com/ahorne23 to view some examples). Try to give students something that they will remember for perhaps the rest of their lives.

What advice do you have for other health educators in the field?

My best advice for other health educators in the field is to consistently find ways to grow and try new ideas. It's easy to settle and get comfortable in our ways. When things feel a little uncomfortable, it means you are growing as a teacher. The best teachers I know make it a priority to consistently attend conferences and learn from like-minded teachers through social media like blogs, Twitter, Pinterest, and Voxer. Do not be afraid to fail and try new lessons. The minute you think you know it all, you should probably retire.

(formative assessment), or you could use technology to engage students during this time (see part II for more information about modeling skills). Once students have learned the skill, you might have them create the models that can be used in future classes. This provides an opportunity for students to apply what they have learned, and it makes the modeling and observation more relevant in the future because students will be observing their peers rather than the teacher.

Social Interactions

Another aspect of participatory learning and teaching is social interactions (WHO, 2003). The implication is that the teacher must provide many opportunities for students to interact with each other during class. To do this, ensure each lesson has at least one opportunity for students to work together in partners, small groups, or large groups. This might include think-pair-share activities between partners, activities for students to accomplish in small groups, discussions, presentations, hands-on activities, and other activities in which students are working collaboratively and engaging with each other and with you. Another opportunity for social interactions is **Socratic seminars**, a discussion-based format in which students are asked to think critically and collaboratively about an open-ended question typically based on a text (Filkins, n.d.).

It is especially important to establish norms and expectations for social interactions in class (see chapter 14). Students may not be comfortable or familiar with this level of class participation. You will need to build up to these types of activities and monitor situations to ensure that all students have a chance to contribute and that students are not placed in a situation that is too far beyond their ability level. It is good to challenge students to participate in class, but take note of students who may have difficulty communicating with peers and provide the supports necessary for them to be successful.

Additionally, consider strategies for maintaining on-task behavior, which includes how you will monitor group work, expectations for what happens if some students finish early (have a list of activities for students once they have completed the initial task), and how you will enforce the established norms and expectations. For example, you give students a task where they are working in small groups. You instruct students that once they have finished the first task, there is one other task to complete and then a bonus task if they finish both. You have planned this in advance because you want students to accomplish tasks 1 and 2 within the class, but you also want to make sure students who complete tasks 1 and 2 quickly will have something to do to stay engaged with the material. This is a bonus activity because it isn't necessary for the lesson but will be enjoyable for students and will keep them engaged. A caveat to adding a bonus activity is to be sure that students who do not finish the first two tasks do not feel as though they missed out because they didn't go fast enough.

Tell the students to raise a hand when they have completed each task. Students begin to work and you walk around the class, listening to conversations, reminding students to stay on task, answering questions, and giving support. When groups complete tasks, you review their work, ask them to address any issues, and then provide them with the next task. If you see positive behaviors, you should point them out while also reminding students about norms and expectations (especially if you are seeing negative behaviors).

Participation and Active Learning

Participation is greatly influenced by the learning environment in your class, and **active learning** is a result of the activities you plan. However, there are some other considerations when working to foster participation and active learning:

■ Get buy-in from students. If students aren't on board with what they are learning or why they are learning it, they will be less likely to participate. You may not be able to get every student fully on board, but you should attempt to get some level of buy-in from all students. For some, this may be an acknowledgment that they will keep an open mind or respectfully listen to all points of view on the topic under discussion.

- Create participation systems that reward students for meaningful participation. Design a system that does not just reward the talkers of the class. You might think about having maximum rewards or increased rewards for students who identify as shy or as listeners in class. One way of doing this is to have students set participation goals for themselves after engaging in self-reflection about their comfort with participation. Students who are talkers would set goals that allow them to participate but also prompt them to think about giving others a chance to speak. Perhaps their goal is to participate three times in a class period. Listeners might have a goal of participating only once, but for them, this represents an effort to get out of their comfort zone. Students can be rewarded for reaching their goals. You can also track the goals over time and have students adjust them, allowing them to apply the skill of goal setting. This may not seem fair; however, fair doesn't mean equal but rather that everyone has the supports they need to succeed in the class.

- Design systems in which any student may be called on at any time. For example, all students have a wooden craft stick with their name on it and you pick out sticks during discussions. All students must be prepared to answer. See www.ascd.org for more information on total participation techniques.

- Create norms where students can pass if they don't feel comfortable or where they can reach out to other students for help. If this is a norm, it doesn't put students on the spot; instead it enhances the sense of collaboration and community because students know they can both reach out for help and help each other.

- Call students by name and encourage the use of names during class interactions. Students must feel comfortable with each other, and being able to refer to each other by name is a simple but important part of this.

- Use a variety of activities, including independent, partner, small-group, and large-group or whole-class activities. Think of participation on a continuum ranging from students participating in activities on their own all the way to being part of a large group. Make sure that you cover all parts of the continuum during your lessons and that students understand the parameters for each type of participation.

- Employ questioning techniques often in the classroom. Use open-ended questions that do not have one right answer in order to encourage students to expand their thinking. This also works well as a small-group technique. Pose a question, and in small groups students work to form an answer and justify their answer with information they have learned during the activity time.

- Include problem-solving and critical-thinking activities. Some of the best solutions are found when we think objectively about a problem. As discussed in the introduction to this text, critical-thinking and problem-solving skills are highly sought after in the workforce. They are foundational skills for preparing students for college and careers (www.p21.org). Providing opportunities for students to develop critical-thinking skills sets them up for success in other areas of their life as well.

- Differentiate instruction so that all students have opportunities for success during activities and participation.

- Provide options for assignments that allow students to design (or choose) a method of showing their knowledge and skill. An example could be presenting students with a prompt and asking them to successfully complete it in the way they feel is most appropriate, or it could be a student deciding to create a brochure or write a role play to demonstrate skill proficiency. When you provide options for students to demonstrate what they have learned, you honor their individuality while maintaining control over the outcome expectations.

- Be mindful of learning styles in your classroom. Plan activities that can be differentiated to meet the needs of many students or use a variety of methods so that every student experiences success and confidence during an activity.

You can foster participation and active learning in many ways. As discussed in chapter 14, one of the most important ways is to get to know your students so that you can plan and modify activities that will meet their needs.

PROVIDE OPPORTUNITIES FOR SELF-REFLECTION, INTERNALIZATION, AND PERSONALIZATION

The goal of a skills-based approach is to help students develop the knowledge and skills they need to engage in health-enhancing behaviors and avoid risky behaviors *outside the classroom*. This means they need to increase their self-awareness and understanding of who they are, they need to make connections between what they have learned in class and their own lives, and they need to understand how to apply the knowledge and skills to their world.

Self-reflection means that students have time to reflect on their own situations, skills, beliefs, values, ideas, attitudes, understandings, and so on. These activities should not be graded, and you might never see students' work. You will likely notice that some students can do this well but others struggle. Students need to be supported in their ability to reflect and to know themselves better. The development of reflection skills and the ability to be honest with oneself are critical to leading a healthy lifestyle.

Internalization relates to the extent to which students embed the knowledge and skills into their beliefs, values, attitudes, and actions. It means that students are adopting what they have learned so that it becomes their frame of reference for health and health behaviors.

Personalization is the extent to which students can see themselves in the curriculum. This includes the extent to which they can connect with activities, apply skills, and relate to content.

It is hard to make distinctions between these three aspects of a skills-based approach because you can use self-reflection to address internalization and personalization, and if you don't provide opportunities for reflection, students will be less likely to internalize and personalize the curriculum. Here are some strategies to consider:

■ Incorporate journaling in the class. This could be done during the opening or closing sections of the lesson. For example, have students take five minutes to complete a 3-2-1 activity or to write about what they have learned or still have questions about.

■ Include activities that ask students to apply learning to situations in their lives. For example, ask them to describe a time when they used interpersonal communication outside of school.

■ Make time for check-ins (e.g., "How are you feeling on a scale of 1 to 10 today?", "Does anyone have something to share?") or other quick activities that allow students to share something about themselves. This is a formative assessment that can yield big results and provide insight into students' personalities.

■ Incorporate activities where students have to write to themselves now and in the future or give advice to their past or future self about a situation they have been in.

■ Provide opportunities in homework and assignments for students to engage with an adult they trust. Engaging trusted adults supports the connection between adults and adolescents, and it also gives the adults a glimpse into your health class. This is a great way to share what you are teaching. As a note, although most students will have a parent or guardian they can talk to, not everyone will. Shifting the language to *trusted adult* rather than *parent* and then providing examples (e.g., parent, guardian, grandparent, other relative, counselor) shows those students that you recognize that not everyone comes from the same circumstances.

■ Engage families in the development and implementation of your curriculum. Sharing what you do is paramount to getting support for your programs. If you want parents to vote (by their voice or their ballot) to support what you teach, you must take the time to engage them in meaningful conversations.

■ Host events in the community or at the school and invite members of the community to take part as students show how their learning applies not only in class but in the real world as well.

- Ask students to share stories and questions during class that are relevant to the topic. Periodically review group norms and expectations to remind students about appropriate levels of sharing and how to acknowledge what others have shared.

- Design assignments and assessments that ask students to apply knowledge and skills in their own lives.

- Providing multiple options for assignments and assessments and allowing students to choose topics for a project will allow them to connect more personally with their learning.

PROVIDE OPPORTUNITIES FOR SKILL DEVELOPMENT

A core principle of a skills-based approach is that skill development is paramount to student success. Never forget that building dedicated practice time into the curriculum is both necessary and meaningful. If we expect students to use the skills outside the classroom, we need to develop their proficiency and their self-efficacy around the skills. This takes time and dedicated practice.

Remember from chapter 2 that self-efficacy is one's belief in one's ability to do something. This can be enhanced through practice and feedback within the classroom. Keep in mind that skill practice can take time and that students will progress at their own pace. You may have to dedicate a few days during your unit for meaningful skill practice. When implementing practice opportunities in your classroom, consider the following:

- What types of scenarios are most authentic and relevant for students?

- What type of practice do students need in order to demonstrate proficiency in the assessment? Practice in class should mirror what you will ask of them in the assessment. If the assessment allows students to choose their format, practice should be offered in a variety of ways to allow for variability of student work.

- How much time do you think your students need to practice this skill? Be thoughtful and practical. Practice takes more time than we like to admit, and it takes away

Providing time for and including activities that allow students to self-reflect, personalize, and internalize what they are learning make them more likely to engage and stick with healthy behaviors.

© WILLSIE/iStock.com

time from other instruction. Do not let this dissuade you from providing sufficient time. Remember, practice time can be more valuable than direct instruction when students are provided with a solid foundation and parameters.

- What resources do you need for the practice? For example, does practice need to occur in a computer lab? Do students need access to certain materials? If students do not have the necessary resources, frustration and class disruption are likely.

- How will students receive feedback? Who provides the feedback? Be sure to discuss the parameters for peer feedback and make sure students understand how they should use the feedback to shape their work moving forward.

- How will you monitor the practice? Aside from time parameters, clear expectations for the practice time should be given to students. Perhaps they need to complete a worksheet or find a source. During the practice time, your role is to keep students on track and provide the guidance and support needed for success.

KEY POINTS

- Instruction should be centered on the students and should provide meaningful opportunities to engage with the content.
- Instruction should foster participation and active learning.
- The implementation should include opportunities for self-reflection, personalization, and internalization through multiple methods.
- Practice is a critical component of implementation.

■ How will you know when students are ready to move on? This is something many teachers struggle with and may require you to consider multiple factors. A good rule is to set a time and then check in with the class as the time frame draws to a close. If the majority of the students are not ready, more time may be necessary. If most of the students are ready but there are a few outliers, you must determine whether students could successfully move on to the next step if the current step hasn't been completed. Perhaps they can move on to the next step and complete the unfinished work on their own.

The importance of practice in the classroom cannot be overstated. Developing skills to competency and proficiency takes time, but it is critical to the ability to apply the skills outside the classroom and ultimately to become a master. You also need to monitor and provide feedback, allow time for discussion about the implications of behaviors in real life, and debrief situations so that students have not only practiced the skill but also spent time thinking about the implications in real-life situations.

SUMMARY

The methods we use to teach students are as important as what we teach students. In a skills-based approach, we have the opportunity to help students develop the knowledge and skills necessary to lead healthy and productive lives. To be most effective, a skills-based approach must focus on achieving five main goals: facilitating learning experiences through which students engage with the content; using a lesson format that supports knowledge and skill acquisition; providing engaging, relevant experiences for students; fostering participation and active learning; and providing opportunities for self-reflection, internalization, and personalization of the content (functional information and skills).

When we consider each of these goals as a part of a greater whole, we create a health education program that keeps students at the center. This is, after all, an important goal of teaching—to advance our students through a series of benchmarks toward an intended target. The more methodical we are in our planning, the more likely we are to achieve success in advancing student growth and development.

Review Questions

1. What are the five goals of implementing a skills-based approach?

2. What is the role of the teacher in a skills-based classroom?

3. What is the structure of an effective lesson plan? Give examples of activities within each part of the lesson.

4. How can you foster participation and active learning in your classroom?

To find supplementary materials for this chapter, such as worksheets and extended learning activities, visit the web resource at
www.HumanKinetics.com/TheEssentialsOfTeachingHealthEducation

© Christopher Futcher/iStock.com

CHAPTER 16

Meeting the Unique Needs of Teaching Elementary Health Education

Learning Objectives

After reading this chapter, you will be able to do the following:

- Discuss considerations for teaching health education at the elementary level.
- Discuss and apply strategies for integrating health education skills and concepts into other subjects.
- Use children's literature to support health education at the elementary level.
- Implement effective health education at the elementary level.

Key Terms

Appropriate Practices in School-Based Health Education

Health Education Curriculum Analysis Tool (HECAT)

School Health Index (SHI)

Elementary school provides a unique opportunity to reach students at an age when they are developing the knowledge, skills, and attitudes that will influence their health behaviors in adolescence and beyond. So far, this text has provided information for licensed health educators teaching a dedicated health education course at all levels, including the elementary level. However, there are often educators at the elementary level who may have little to no training in health education. Further, there is often limited or no time dedicated for health education in elementary grades. You may be a classroom teacher who is trying to fit in health lessons when you can or a physical educator who has been asked to include some health education for students. The goal of this chapter is to provide practical strategies for implementing a skills-based approach at the elementary level. We hope that anyone teaching health education at the elementary level will find the information they need in previous chapters to design a curriculum, develop skills in elementary students, and implement effective teaching practices. This chapter provides additional considerations and supports at the elementary level.

MAKING TIME FOR HEALTH EDUCATION

The most effective way to implement health education at the elementary level is to dedicate time for health along with other core subjects. Teachers are pulled in many directions and seem to be constantly barraged with the next new idea or initiative. In addition, teachers need to address many content standards and prepare students for formal and state-wide assessments. However, if your students aren't healthy, no amount of teaching will help them perform at their best. Healthy students are more ready and able to learn (CDC, 2015). Dedicating time to health education in elementary school sets a critical foundation for developing positive health behaviors that will help students throughout their lives. At a minimum, we recommend that you spend 30 to 45 minutes per week on health education and health education alone. However, in this section we offer strategies to incorporate health into other subjects and throughout the school day.

Integrating Health Education Into Other Subjects

In addition to the time you dedicate to health education in your classroom, we encourage you to think about ways to incorporate health topics into other subject areas as well. Doing so can increase students' awareness about health and how their own health and the health of others affect them in many ways. When students engage with health content and skills throughout the school day, it is likely to lead to increased transfer outside the health classroom and into their everyday lives. The more interaction students have with the skills and topics, the more likely this is to happen.

However, we want to be clear that we are advocating for having dedicated time for health education *plus* integrating health topics into other subject areas. If you only integrate health topics into other subjects and don't teach health education on its own, you diminish its value and potentially undermine efforts to include health education as a subject equal to or even more important than other content areas. Table 16.1 suggests ways to integrate health into other subjects.

Strategies for Including Health Topics Throughout the Day

There are many ways to integrate health into other parts of the school day and to make it part of your classroom routine. Discussing health can become a norm and an expectation in your classroom. This section presents several ways to develop positive norms around health.

Morning Meeting or Message

The morning message or morning meeting can be a great time to discuss health. Integrating health into the morning meeting or message can promote discussion about health, show students the many dimensions of wellness, and help students feel comfortable discussing health-related topics. Some ideas for integrating health into this part of your classroom routine are presented in table 16.2.

TABLE 16.1 Strategies for Integrating Health Into Other Subjects

Math	• When writing word problems, include health scenarios. For example, you and your three friends want a snack but there is only one apple. How would you need to divide the apple to make sure that everyone has an equal portion? • Use health-related polls to gather data and then analyze it. • When creating worksheets, use health-related items or objects. For example, if students need to count a number of objects, use healthy foods, physical activities, bike helmets, and so on. If students need to create or interpret graphs, use health data for the graphs, such as the percentage of students who walk to school. • Have students track physical activity, vegetable consumption, or other health-related behaviors (connection to self-management) and then make graphs or charts. • Use food labels to create math worksheets and problems. • Use numbers in real-life contexts, such as discussing how body temperature can indicate illness or how many seconds students should wash their hands. • Have students collect health-related data (or conduct a survey in the school or in families), plot the data on a chart, and interpret it.
English language arts	• Use health-related nonfiction books and articles when teaching students. • Have students access valid and reliable resources for research assignments or projects. Refer to the skill cues previously learned. • Have students keep a journal, blog, or other ongoing writing assignment on a health-related issue. • Have students write letters as a part of an advocacy campaign. • Have students create books about healthy behaviors to share with other students. • Have students read two opinions or texts about a health issue and then have a debate.
Science	• Use the scientific method to make hypotheses about certain health-related data and have students gather and analyze data. • When discussing body systems, include discussions of how certain health behaviors can affect the systems. • When discussing environmental issues, make the connection to the environmental dimension of wellness. • Plant fruit and vegetable seeds. Discuss the benefits of consuming what you planted. • Discuss how certain health behaviors (e.g., gasoline consumption, cigarette smoking) affect the environment. • Make a connection to how the five senses connect to health and healthy behaviors (e.g., smell and taste affect what we eat and what we like).
Social studies	• Examine the diets and food availability of other cultures, present and past. • Discuss differences in health behaviors in various parts of the world, past and present. • Use historical figures to demonstrate the skills of advocacy, decision making, or goal setting. Discuss the role those figures played in solving health crises or concerns. • Use various cultures or times to help students analyze influences. • Connect with the school librarian and have students work on a project to explore health practices, beliefs, and behaviors of cultures in their school or community. • Discuss the role of government in health and health care (e.g., public policy).

Around Your Room

It can be helpful to represent health around your classroom. Examples include the following:

■ Dedicate a bulletin board to health tips, skills, and content.

■ Hang student work from health class around the room.

■ Have a variety of health-related books for students to read.

■ Have an anonymous question box in your room where students can write down questions.

TABLE 16.2   Morning Message and Morning Meeting Ideas

Morning message	• What did you eat for breakfast today?
	• What is your favorite _____? (physical activity, fruit, vegetable)
	• How much sleep did you get last night? Making sure to get enough sleep helps you to be ready to learn in school.
	• Don't risk spreading lice - keep heads apart, only use your own hat, and tell someone if your head is itchy.
	• Did you try to "eat a rainbow" each day?
	• Did you know that singing the alphabet while washing your hands for 20 seconds helps ensure you wash long enough to stop germs from making you sick?
	• Did you know that taking deep breaths and counting to 10 can help you calm down when you are angry? Do you know of other things that you can do to help you calm down?
Morning meeting	• Ask students to share how they are feeling.
	• Ask students to tell you when it is safe to help a friend who is being picked on.
	• Ask students what they know about how their bodies work.
	• Sing a song about health.
	• Read a health-related book.
	• Tell a health-related story using puppets.
	• Discuss any current events in the school or community.

■ Have pictures or posters of students engaging in healthy behaviors.

■ Hang posters of the skill cues around your room.

■ Have manipulatives that are health related (e.g., fruit and veggie beanbags, body-part beanbags).

■ Have a calendar that lists health tips or challenges.

■ If you have costumes or dress up in the classroom, be sure to include health-related occupations, especially ones that students may interact with such as physicians or dentists.

Class Initiatives

Another strategy for integrating health into the general school day is to have health-related class initiatives or challenges. This can also be a great way to engage the school, families, and larger community. Some ideas for health-related initiatives and challenges include the following:

■ Hold a step-a-thon where students (and maybe their families) track their steps for a certain amount of time to reach a goal (e.g., walk across the country, walk to a certain place, walk a certain mileage). This would also be an opportunity to work with the physical educator at your school.

■ Give families a health-related challenge that they must document and complete. The possibilities are endless, but some ideas include cooking a meal together, trying a new healthy food, seeing how long you can avoid watching TV, eating dinner as a family for a certain number of nights, being physically active together, and talking about something that happened at school.

■ Have Thank You Thursdays (www.thank youthursday.org) or class shout-outs where students share something positive about a classmate or teacher. This can connect to self-esteem, communication, and social and emotional health.

■ Have the class complete a health-related challenge. Perhaps students need to create an A-to-Z list of healthy behaviors, come up with five ways to say no to alcohol or other drugs, or set a class goal to reach.

CONSIDERATIONS FOR THE ELEMENTARY LEVEL

In this section, we discuss certain challenges that elementary health educators may face when implementing a skills-based approach to health education. The issues addressed here are

KEY POINTS

■ Integrate health content and skills into other subjects in addition to the specific time you spend on health education.

■ Include health in all aspects of your classroom—your routines, the physical space, and class initiatives.

---

not exhaustive, but they are some of the most common challenges.

■ **Concern: The skills of the National Standards aren't appropriate for elementary students.** As noted throughout part II, the verbs in the National Health Education Standards performance indicators were selected to be developmentally appropriate. Although you aren't going to have second graders come up with the factors influencing them and then analyze them on their own, you can have them demonstrate developmentally appropriate behaviors that will set a foundation for developing the skill as students move up in age and grade. For example, students could look at product packaging with princesses and superheroes and then discuss how the characters are put on the package to try to influence them to buy the product.

■ **Concern: Don't I have to give up content to teach skills?** As we discussed earlier, a restructuring of content needs to take place in order to determine the functional information necessary for your elementary students as they begin building the base of health knowledge. However, given that you are laying a foundation and students may have limited knowledge and experience, you may need to include more content than you will in later years. We suggest that you use your state learning standards as a starting point for determining what information to cover. Additionally, get to know your students and identify areas where they need more content knowledge in order to effectively apply the skills. For example, your students may need to spend some time on basic body parts (e.g., role of the heart, lungs, brain). There is no magic amount of topics to cover. The takeaway is that you start with the skills, use the topic to teach the skills, and

give students opportunities to apply their knowledge and skills.

■ **Concern: Interactive teaching methods are difficult with elementary students.** Students in kindergarten (or prekindergarten) through grade 5 have short attention spans, are fidgety, like to talk, and require frequent check-ins to ensure they are on task (see chapter 3 for more on the developmental stages of students). This can pose challenges when trying to implement strategies such as role-playing or group discussions because it may be difficult for students to stay on task without getting distracted. You'll need to consider your students and get to know what will work for them, but activities should be simple and straightforward. You'll also need to consider the amount of scaffolding necessary for your students to successfully complete the activity, and you'll need to have a plan B! For example, your fourth-grade class might be able to handle large-group discussions, but maybe your third-grade class still has trouble with this strategy so you have them work in partners and then present their answers or record them on a whiteboard. Another example is that instead of doing a traditional role-play to practice interpersonal communication in grade 1, you read a story and have students simultaneously say certain lines, which helps them practice effective communication, or you give them statements to read to a partner.

■ **Concern: We don't have an elementary health education curriculum.** As discussed in chapter 12, it is important to have a written curriculum that is aligned with national, state, and local standards; is skills based; is sequential from kindergarten to grade 12; and has health-related topics that are informed by local data. We suggest that you coordinate with other health educators in your district to determine the skills and content most relevant to students in your school along with the skills and information that will provide a foundation for students as they move into later grades. Look into available tools such as the *Health Education Curriculum Analysis Tool,* the *School Health Index,* and SHAPE America's *Appropriate Practices in School-Based Health Education* to help evaluate your school health policies and practices and determine what to teach in your curriculum as well as how to plan your scope and sequence.

Including meaningful health education at the elementary level can feel like a big challenge but with planning and commitment, you can create an effective health education program for your elementary students.

- The **Health Education Curriculum Analysis Tool (HECAT)** is designed to evaluate an existing curriculum to determine its feasibility in your classroom, school, or district. However, you can also use the *HECAT* to help shape your curriculum as you develop it. This resource provides guidance about what information should be addressed within a variety of health topics, how many skill practice opportunities you need, and other information. The *HECAT* can be found at www.cdc.gov/healthyyouth/HECAT/.

- The **School Health Index (SHI)** helps schools conduct a self-assessment to evaluate the extent to which they are addressing the components of the Whole School, Whole Community, Whole Child model (see chapter 18). Much of this tool would not necessarily be relevant when you are trying to plan your curriculum (though it provides other valuable information), but there is a whole section on health education that could support your work. The *SHI* can be found at www.cdc.gov/healthyyouth/shi/.

- *Appropriate Practices in School-Based Health Education* provides guidance for key stakeholders in school-based health education. The document articulates best practices and includes a section specifically on curriculum. You can use this tool to identify key items to include in the curriculum as well as overarching principles to consider during development. The document can be found at www.shapeamerica.org/publications/products/upload/AppropriatePractices SchoolBasedHealthEducation.pdf.

KEY POINTS

- It is important to carve out time in the elementary schedule exclusively for health education.
- Aim for a minimum of 30 to 45 minutes per week for focused health education.
- Health education at the elementary level has unique needs that must be addressed through a variety of methods, but that should not prevent schools from including health education at this level.

■ **Concern: I have limited time with the students.** You may be in a situation where you are not the classroom teacher but you are a physical educator who is trying to integrate health lessons, or you are a health teacher who travels to multiple schools, or for other reasons you have limited contact with the students beyond the time that is dedicated to health education. In these instances, it can be difficult to implement a sequential curriculum because students may not remember material from week to week. You'll want to make sure that the takeaways are clear at the end of each session, so have students repeat the takeaway multiple times during a lesson. Plan review time into your lessons so that at each session students expect to review previous learning. Be prepared to scaffold activities if students don't remember content or skills. And repeat, repeat, repeat—repetition helps form long-term memories, especially in younger children. Repeat key concepts and skills often to help them stick.

■ **Concern: I don't have training in health education.** This is one of the most significant challenges that teachers may face. However, the good news is that a wealth of support and information is available from resources such as the CDC, SHAPE America, and state organizations (e.g., state affiliate physical education and health education organizations). You can also seek out and advocate for professional development opportunities that can help you develop the knowledge and skills to be a more effective health educator (see chapter 17).

USING CHILDREN'S LITERATURE TO SUPPORT HEALTH EDUCATION

As an elementary health educator, you have a wonderful opportunity to support both literacy and health education using children's literature. There are many excellent texts that you can use to cover course topics and help students develop health-related skills. You can use these texts as a part of your health education class or as a supplement or extension to the class.

Planning

As with all activities in your curriculum, you want to be purposeful in planning to use literature. Figure 16.1 is a template to help with your planning. As you are selecting texts, be sure to consider the following:

■ Themes
■ Characters
■ Diversity
■ Skills in the text (or that could be connected to the text)
■ Fiction and nonfiction texts
■ Vocabulary
■ Literacy goals and objectives
■ Health topics in the text

Make sure to use the texts in a purposeful way to support the goals of your curriculum. These may not be all the considerations that you need to address, but they will help you in your planning.

In addition to thinking about the elements in figure 16.1, you should plan how to use the texts. For example, think about the following questions:

■ Will you use the text primarily for discussion? You may take this approach if you are using the text to introduce a topic or skill, to hook students on a topic, or to reiterate a theme or message from the class. You may also take this approach if you have students read about a particular health topic or skill and then have them use the characters as the actors in your discussions.

■ Will you use the text to support a certain step of the skill? You may find that a text can be helpful in step 1 of the skill development model when you are introducing the skill and in step 3 when you are modeling the skill.

■ Will you use the text to support a practice opportunity (step 4 of the skill development model)? You may want to use a text to set the stage for a practice opportunity. Perhaps you use a nonfiction text to provide students with the information to use in a decision-making scenario or you want the students to change the outcome of the

FIGURE 16.1 Template for Planning Lessons Using Children's Literature

Title:	Author:
Grade levels:	

Summary:

Connections to health-related skills (list and briefly explain):

Health topics in the text:

Vocabulary from the book (include words and age-appropriate definitions):

Discussion questions (list key discussion questions you could use before or after reading):	Key takeaways or focus points (list the ideas, skills, and concepts that you want students to take away from the book):

Follow-up activity (describe, in enough detail for someone to implement the activity, a skills-based activity that reinforces key ideas, skills, and concepts from the text, making sure to highlight which skill is being introduced, modeled, or practiced):

Using literature can be an excellent way to reinforce other school goals (literacy) while also creating more time for health education.

story through better interpersonal communication.

- Will you use the text to help establish classroom norms or expectations? You may want to use certain texts at the beginning of the year to help establish a positive learning environment, review expectations in the classroom, and so on.

You are now ready to use fiction and nonfiction literature in your classroom to support your health education curriculum!

Assessments and Assignments

In addition to developing activities to support literacy and health education, you can design assignments and assessments that integrate literacy. Examples include the following:

- Journaling and writing assignments and assessments that have a prompt related to a health topic or skill
- Reading a book and writing a book report that includes specific questions related to health outcomes of the characters
- Researching a health-related topic and creating a poster or presentation
- Writing a role-play or comic strip of two characters solving a health problem

Also, be sure to assess your health lessons and units in a similar fashion to other subjects. Though every unit may not have a project, health should be considered a part of the grade and students should understand its importance.

ENGAGING FAMILIES AND THE COMMUNITY

In addition to spending time each week on health education, we encourage you to think of ways to bring health education to your school, to parents, and to the community. For example, you could have students create projects that advocate for a healthy behavior. After the project is complete, have a showcase in the school library where families can come to see the work. This also reinforces the health message to the students' families. Or maybe you have a health fair where community partners come in and families attend. Finally, you might start an after-school club or program that reinforces health knowledge and skills and that includes families. The more health is present throughout the school, the more effective your health education will be because students see it beyond the classroom and there is increased awareness in their families.

Consider designing strategies for directly engaging parents and families in health education. Design homework assignments in which students must speak with parents about a topic or work with them to complete an activity. No matter what the homework entails, providing opportunities for families and students to engage in the material can make it more meaningful for students and might even increase families' awareness about health and wellness. You might also send home letters or use another method such as social media to update families on topics being covered, activities to try at home, and health tips. You could have family nights or events where families engage in health-related activities. Some schools have even invited parents to a classroom showcase that includes a cooking demo of a healthy recipe and sends the family home with a bag of groceries. Regardless of the method, increasing family engagement with the school and with your health education class will increase the value of the short amount of time you have during the school day.

Finally, we encourage you to think of ways to engage the larger community in your health curriculum. You could bring in community helpers and other community members approved by the district to work with students on a certain topic (e.g., have a doctor or school nurse come in when discussing communicable disease or a dentist come in when discussing oral health, both of which could be connected to the skill of self-management). You could organize walk-to-school days or other initiatives that engage multiple stakeholders. You could have students from the middle or high school come to your class to deliver health lessons, discuss health topics, or simply help out with a project or assignment. You could take field trips to local resources in the community (e.g., restaurants, stores) or bring in local businesspeople to discuss staying healthy and ways they can assist students.

SUMMARY

Everyone teaching health education faces unique challenges. However, the elementary level also presents opportunities to immerse students in health and to lay a foundation for positive attitudes, norms, and expectations around health. We encourage you to dedicate time specifically to health education each week. More health education is always better, but we recommend at least 30 to 45 minutes per week. You can supplement this time by bringing health outside the classroom and into the school, families, and community. You can also support your work by integrating health into all aspects of your classroom. In sum, health education should be an integral part of a well-rounded elementary curriculum, and there are multiple ways to help health education at this level make an impact on students and the school, families, and community.

Review Questions

1. What are some strategies for integrating health into the elementary classroom?

2. Describe two ways you could integrate health into each of the core subject areas.

3. How can you use children's literature in the elementary classroom to reinforce health topics and skills?

4. How can you engage the school, family, and community to support health education at the elementary level?

To find supplementary materials for this chapter, such as worksheets and extended learning activities, visit the web resource at
www.HumanKinetics.com/TheEssentialsOfTeachingHealthEducation

PART V

Beyond the Classroom

Although a skills-based health education program can provide students with the skills and information to lead healthier lives, classroom-based instruction alone cannot ensure students are healthy and ready to learn. Parts I through IV provide the tools, strategies, and tips for developing and implementing a skills-based approach. In part V, we look at how you can advance your professional practice, how you can advocate for health education, and how you can extend health education beyond your classroom.

As health educators, we play a vital role both for students and for the profession. It is our collective responsibility to ensure that the field of health education stays current, relevant, and meaningful. Additionally, we must be the voice of the profession. We all must be ready to share our successes and work to ensure that health education is a core component of every student's educational experience. We hope these chapters inspire you to continue your own journey and to think about how you can make an impact beyond your classroom.

By the end of this part, you will be able to create a plan for your professional development, evaluate professional development opportunities, and advocate for yourself and your profession. You will also be able to implement strategies to extend the reach of health education beyond the classroom by supporting a Whole School, Whole Community, Whole Child approach and by integrating health education into other subject areas.

kasto/fotolia.com

CHAPTER 17

Professional Development and Advocacy

Learning Objectives

After reading this chapter, you will be able to do the following:

- Identify types of professional development to improve health educator practice.
- Create a plan for ongoing professional learning.
- Describe strategies you can take to advocate for and educate about skills-based health education.

Key Terms

advocacy

authentic environment

job-embedded learning

personalized professional development plan

professional development

professional learning opportunities

In health education, two things are constant: People will always have an opinion about what should be taught and how it should be taught, and the topic of health is ever evolving. Although these constants can cause challenges for health educators, it is important to accept them. One way to do this is by being proactive in your professional practice. Here are two ways to do this:

1. Stay up to date on trends and emerging evidence. This includes staying current on best practices, keeping up with the latest health trends and data, being aware of education and school initiatives locally and nationally (perhaps even internationally), understanding how other academic goals and standards affect the health classroom, and identifying areas for personal and professional growth. You should participate in professional learning opportunities that advance your practice as an educator and teach you to better meet the needs of students.

2. Maintain a presence in the field of health education and work to educate others about its value in schools. You must be an advocate for the profession while ultimately being an advocate for your students. You must be an active participant in the conversation to make health education not only relevant in education circles but a necessary component of overall student success.

These tasks may seem daunting, but this chapter will provide several suggestions and strategies. We discuss what role professional learning plays in staying current, what constitutes high-quality professional development, and how to engage in professional learning opportunities that are meaningful and useful. Then we take a closer look at how to educate and advocate to others about the profession and strategies for increasing support for health education programs in schools.

STAYING CURRENT AND RELEVANT

The fields of health and education are constantly changing, and it is important to stay as up to date as possible. You can do this in many ways—for example, you can participate in professional groups on social media with other health and education professionals, read blogs related to emerging topics of interest, watch the news, subscribe to journals in the field (and take time to read them), or attend community events. You might decide to dedicate some time to this task every night, once a week, or even once a month, reading and reflecting on what you learn. Another benefit to this approach is that it will help you keep your curriculum relevant, which, as we discussed in chapter 12, is a critical aspect of effective curricula.

ENGAGING IN PROFESSIONAL DEVELOPMENT OPPORTUNITIES

Health educators enter the field in a variety of ways. Some complete an undergraduate or graduate preservice program focusing on the pedagogy of health education. Others begin their teaching career in another field such as physical education or science and then teach health education due to scheduling, budget cuts, or the desire for a new challenge. Some enter the field with little experience in schools but a background in a health-related topic or community health education. Regardless of the point of entry into classroom-based health education, staying current on best practices and advancing as a professional are paramount. As we've discussed throughout this book, information changes at a rapid pace, teaching methods and pedagogy are refined over time, and new methods for assessment and measuring student learning are continually being discussed. The best way to stay current while also growing as a professional is to proactively learn about new teaching methods and then implement your learning in the classroom. It is through meaningful professional learning opportunities that we improve our practice and our ability to influence student outcomes.

Just as you walk students through a skill progression model and allow time for practice, feedback, and application in a real-world scenario, you should do the same as you learn new teaching strategies and approaches. Whether you're learning an easy concept or an in-depth approach to classroom management, the more time you spend mastering the new concept, the more likely it will result in a change in your classroom practice and ultimately in student outcomes. Research shows that educators need approximately 49 hours of professional development in order to see a 21 percent change in student outcomes (Yoon, Duncan, Lee, Scarloss, & Shapley, 2007). Mastering a new skill takes time. It may take ongoing and multiple touchpoints, practice, feedback, and refinement before you feel comfortable using a new piece of information in the classroom, and it will likely be even longer before you start seeing the positive results from your students.

Professional development has a greater likelihood of resulting in change when single learning opportunities are part of a larger plan. Many educators are familiar with single-session professional learning opportunities such as teacher in-service days or day-long conferences. However, this approach alone is unlikely to result in changes to educator practice or student outcomes. In addition, the idea of participating in a professional development day may elicit a variety of thoughts and emotions. For some, learning a new teaching technique or becoming familiar with a new curriculum is an exciting challenge. For others, professional development is something they are forced to do; it feels like a poor use of time away from students. Regardless of your feelings about professional development you have experienced in the past, well-designed professional development should challenge you and invigorate you to be a better educator. If it doesn't, then it is time to find a new opportunity. Let's take some time to discuss what high-quality professional development entails and then look at some types of professional development that will improve your teaching practice and student outcomes.

Professional development is an overarching term that encompasses the formal and informal learning experiences that help us to grow as professionals. **Professional learning opportunities** are the discrete opportunities or experiences that, when bundled together, provide a foundation for professional growth and development. High-quality professional development is composed of learning opportunities that adhere to some generally recognized criteria:

■ *Contains goals, objectives, and learning activities that lead participants toward predetermined outcomes.* Stating goals and objectives frames the learning opportunity, and doing activities that work toward the identified outcomes helps to ensure that the outcomes are met.

■ *Engages participants through collaboration with adult learning strategies.* We are social beings, and collaboration is key to learning from one another. Adult learners must feel invested in their learning, understand why it is important to learn, see the relevance and applicability of learning to their classroom, and be engaged in the learning process. Adults come to the table with previous knowledge and experience that should be honored and incorporated into the learning experience (Knowles, 1990).

■ *Engages participants prior to the learning opportunity and encourages prepreparation and assessments of learning.* When participants have been told about the expectations and intended outcomes before attending a professional learning event, they are more likely to have expectations that are aligned with the intended outcomes. In addition, giving participants a preassessment aids the instructor in learning the background and level of the people in attendance. At the end of a session, a postassessment indicates how well the participants moved from their initial level of knowledge and skill toward the intended outcomes of the learning opportunity.

■ *Aligns with local, state, or federal learning standards.* To grow as a professional, you should consider the standards you are held to and use professional development opportunities to become a better educator in an effort to meet those standards and improve student outcomes.

■ *Provides an appropriate amount of time and resources to accomplish the outcomes.* Professional growth is a process. Meaningful, high-quality professional development opportunities are often ongoing, and at minimum they provide ample time for participants to meet all of the other criteria in this list. Although not all professional development is going to occur in multiday sessions, there is general agreement that onetime trainings that only last for a short amount of time without any follow-up or connection to teacher practice have little to no impact on educator practice. For example, attending a short informational session or sitting through a lecture might provide interesting information but will not result in changes to teacher practice or student outcomes. Professional development should allow participants time to learn the new information and skills, practice their learning, and receive feedback. In addition, the learning should occur in an environment that affords the necessary supports and resources to apply the learning. For example, computers are available if the professional development is about using a new computer program, sample student work is used during an event intended to calibrate educator scores on an assessment measure, or a copy of the latest needs data is presented and reviewed if the professional development is intended to identify topics and functional information for new lessons or units in the curriculum.

■ *Is relevant and meaningful for participants.* As we've discussed, units and lessons for students must be relevant and meaningful. The same is true for professional development—if it is not meaningful or relevant to your classroom, teacher practice, or student outcomes, it is unlikely to have an impact. Professional development should be directly applicable to the participant's classroom and desired student outcomes. However, sometimes you may be asked to attend professional development on topics you do not view as applicable to your teaching. In these instances, we challenge you to find ways to integrate your learning from that opportunity into your classroom. Perhaps you can bring sample classroom lessons with you to the training, review the new material, and use it to update or enhance current lessons. You might even consult with non-health-education colleagues about how to implement the new learning in a health education classroom. We also encourage you to advocate for health-related professional development opportunities and to work with fellow health educators and administration to ensure that you are able to participate in sessions that promote better practice and in turn support the desired academic outcomes.

■ *Includes follow-up opportunities at predetermined intervals.* Follow-up is key. Learning should be reinforced, whether formally (e.g., reconvening with fellow participants in person or in an online forum) or informally (e.g., e-mails reminding you of the actions you committed to taking). This not only brings the topic back to the front of your thinking, it also allows an opportunity to clarify confusion, solidify learning, and remind you of key elements.

■ *Is evaluated for effectiveness.* How we do we know that what we are doing is successful? We evaluate our outcomes to see if they are in line with our expectations and claims. The same is true with professional development. High-quality offerings have an evaluation component that asks participants to rate both their confidence and their competence as a result of attending the session. In some cases, the session provider will also do a follow-up evaluation to assess the teacher's implementation of strategies and concepts along with changes in student outcomes.

In general, professional development that leads to changes in teacher practice and has the opportunity to affect student outcomes is well designed and purposeful. The event or series of learning experiences requires you to examine current practice and learn a new skill or approach to implement upon return to the classroom. When teacher practice has been positively influenced, there is also likely to be a positive change in student outcomes over time. Let's examine some learning opportunities that could be part of your professional development and are likely to result in improved teacher practice and student outcomes.

Job-Embedded Learning

Job-embedded learning consists of learning opportunities that occur in an **authentic**

environment, that is, an environment closely related to our actual experiences and circumstances. *Job-embedded professional development* has been defined as "teacher learning that is grounded in day-to-day teaching practice and is designed to enhance teachers' content-specific instructional practices with the intent of improving student learning" (Croft, Coggshall, Dolan, Powers, & Killion, 2010; Darling-Hammond & McLaughlin, 1995; Hirsh, 2009). Professional development that is job embedded meets teachers where they are and continually demonstrates application back to the classroom. When done appropriately, this approach is a gold standard for professional development. Not only is job-embedded learning practical, it is often embraced by high-performing schools that understand that helping teachers be successful is often the best way to help them change their practice and improve student outcomes. Job-embedded professional learning opportunities can take many forms, but a few tenets are explained here (see table 17.1 for examples).

Job-embedded learning

■ takes place in or near the classroom or job location and is directly applicable in your classroom;

■ occurs in collaboration with other educators from your school or district who are familiar with you, your students, and the health education course requirements;

TABLE 17.1 Examples of Job-Embedded Professional Learning Opportunities

TYPE OF ACTIVITY	EXAMPLE IN ACTION
Peer observation *Educators observe peer colleagues as they go about their work. This could be teaching, talking with a student, managing a difficult situation, and so on. Following the observation, debriefing occurs to discuss what went well and what areas might be improved.*	The elementary health teachers all gather at one of the elementary schools to watch Mr. Jackson teach a new lesson on advocacy related to pedestrian safety. This is a new topic for the teachers and they are not all sure that the lesson content has been developed in the best way. The teachers watch Mr. Jackson teach the lesson and then gather in the conference room with him to discuss what worked well in the lesson and what they should consider altering before making this lesson part of their curriculum.
Coaching *An educator works with someone who is trained to identify areas of growth and to offer strategies to improve educator practice. A coach may also work with a team of teachers on a common issue of concern.*	An instructional coach visits the team of health teachers and shows a video of a health class learning the skill of analyzing influences. After watching the video, the group discusses the strategies that worked well and those that didn't work so well. The instructional coach then has each teacher write down three ways they would like to improve their teaching. The group discusses the responses, groups them, and prioritizes them for future meetings. With the instructional coach, the group works through strategies to improve the identified areas.
Study circle *A group of educators with a common interest or assignment meets multiple times to discuss a problem or improve practice by relying on the collective wisdom of those in attendance.*	A group of middle school health teachers gathers to review the performance assessment given to their students for the goal-setting unit. With examples of student work on hand, the group discusses what proficiency looks like for this performance assessment and then reviews student work to ensure the teachers are scoring the students in a similar way.
Learning walks *A group of educators assembles to solve a problem or answer a question. The group then observes a variety of classrooms and lessons in order to collect baseline information related to the identified concern or question. The information gathered is then used to inform future solutions or educational approaches.*	A group of health, physical education, art, and music teachers has been tasked with integrating more math concepts. A nearby school has done some interesting work integrating math into lessons, and the teachers are interested in seeing how it is going. The group decides to visit a nearby school and observe lessons in each subject area to see how math is integrated into the lessons. After the visit, the teachers gather to come up with strategies to use within their own lessons.

■ focuses on lessons, strategies, or concepts that you are teaching to your students currently, recently, or in the immediate future (it is not theoretical or long-range planning); and

■ may rely on examples from your actual teaching such as student work, observation, or video of your teaching.

Course or Series of Workshops

As mentioned, a single event or day-long session is not likely to dramatically change teacher practice or improve student outcomes by itself. Workshops or training events can improve practice and outcomes if they are part of a longer series or course. The amount of time spent in professional development makes a difference. When looking for a course or workshop series, check to see if it has the following aspects:

■ The sessions are sequential and have a defined progression of learning. Multiple shorter sessions over a few weeks or months can provide the time necessary to influence teacher practice and student outcomes. Look at the agenda for the training sessions to see if there is a logical sequence of learning and that the sessions build upon one another.

■ Includes an assessment of learning. This will help you know if you have learned the new information or skill in a way that allows you to use it in your classroom.

■ Relates to standards you are required to teach. If the professional development opportunity is intended to improve your teaching, you must consider how it fits in with local, state, and national standards you are required to follow.

■ Is research based or theory driven. Does the opportunity have a research or theory behind it to support what it is demonstrating? Although something untested may be interesting to learn about, it may not provide sound evidence that could improve your practice or student outcomes.

■ Course instructors or facilitators are knowledgeable and hold relevant credentials. Many people provide trainings, but unfortunately not all of them hold the credentials, training, or experience necessary to advance your practice. Be sure to review the instructor's credentials before registering for a course.

Self-Directed Learning

Learning can take place in many ways and venues. Similar to participation in learning opportunities that are job embedded and part of a longer course, self-directed learning can build your foundation of knowledge and solidify learning. There are many ways to engage in self-directed learning, including the following:

■ Reading professional journal articles and responding to the associated quizzes

■ Taking an online course

■ Participating in a study circle with professionals outside your school or district

■ Submitting a proposal to present at a conference

■ Creating a research project and publishing the results or sharing them within your district

■ Submitting to a professional journal or writing an informational piece for your local paper

■ Researching a new teaching strategy and then implementing the strategy in your classroom or rewriting your curriculum or lessons to incorporate the strategy

DEVELOPING A PERSONALIZED PROFESSIONAL DEVELOPMENT PLAN

Take a moment to think of the last time you were asked to learn something new. Maybe it was taking a class that you didn't know you needed or attending a conference to help fulfill requirements for your teaching license. Perhaps you were the one to decide that you wanted to learn a new skill to improve your teaching. Regardless of the answer to "Why did you participate in that learning opportunity?", the more important question to answer is, "What did you do as a result of attending?" For many, the answer to the second question

ADVOCACY AND PROFESSIONAL DEVELOPMENT

Judy LoBianco
South Orange-Maplewood Schools, Maplewood, New Jersey

How can health educators best advocate for themselves and the profession?

It is extremely important to be an advocate in our profession and to be immersed in the health field. Over the years I have raised money in the schools for causes that not only I am passionate about but the students are passionate about too—Pennies for Patients, Hoops for Heart, Jump Rope for Heart, ALS, AIDS Walk, breast cancer, and others. Not only did we raise money but the students became advocates for each cause by interacting with various speakers and patients with these illnesses. It is important to bridge the gap between the school and the community. When you do this, the community becomes educated about health and wellness and becomes interested in making their own lives more positive physically, emotionally, and socially.

I have organized health fairs during the past 10 years. Every year the fairs get bigger and the crowds become larger. The fairs educate students, parents, teachers, and the community about the most up-to-date health and wellness education. They also provide people with free health screenings and materials for them to use in their everyday lives. This is a way to send the message to others that health education is one of the most important fields of study. During the week of the fair you can also have a Health and Wellness Week. Each day focuses on an important topic (e.g., bullying, saying no to alcohol and drugs, nutrition, fitness). Speakers can come in and educate the students, you can organize a parent night, you can hold a blood drive, and so on. When you organize different weeks during the year and have whole-school or whole-community involvement, everyone starts to become excited for health.

Another way to be an advocate for our field is to be successful in your own classroom. Make health education fun and let the kids know you mean business. They will want to come to your class and they will know that this is the most important class of their day.

How do you stay current as the field of health education changes?

I am a news junkie so I watch the world news and local news every night. I watch 60 Minutes, various documentaries, YouTube videos, podcasts, and so on to stay up to date. It is important to attend local, state, and national conventions. I stay involved with various nonprofit organizations. It is important to continue conversations with professionals in your field. I have my go-to websites that are always updated with new info. I love F.L.A.S.H. and Advocates for Youth. I love Teenshealth.org. I also live and die for Tom Jackson's *Activities That Teach* books. These books teach the skills that all students need to be successful in life: communication, problem solving, decision making, interpersonal relationships, values formation, and healthy lifestyle choices. The students become part of the lesson, not just bystanders. The activities from the book allow students to think for themselves and draw conclusions from their own thought processes, not from mine.

What advice do you have for other health educators in the field?

Be the very best you can be each day. Continue to be a learner. Adapt to changes in education as well as in the health field. Be a role model for your students. Have great character every day because it is contagious. I love my students and I respect them. Even on my worst days I give 100 percent. It is my goal as an educator to teach not only information but lifelong skills so that my students can absorb the information and assume responsibility for their decisions regarding their personal lifestyle choices. Inspire them to go out there and make a difference, and let them know they can do it.

KEY POINTS

- Professional development is intended to improve educator practice and student outcomes. For this to happen, it must be ongoing as well as relevant and meaningful to participants.

- Multiple professional learning opportunities exist, so be sure to look for opportunities that meet the standards of quality described earlier. This will help to ensure that the experience is a good use of time, energy, and money.

- Professional learning is best done with others who have similar goals and outcome expectations, such as coworkers, other health educators, or other grade-level educators. When you participate in learning experiences with other professionals who have similar goals, you are better able to focus on learning in relevant and meaningful ways.

---

is often something along the lines of "It was a great training; I just wish I had the time to try what I learned" or "I wish I would have known what we were expected to do ahead of time; that wasn't what I was expecting."

Both of these responses are important to explore. The first response ("It was great, but I haven't done much . . .") highlights that we are often energized after a good training but fail to take the action (or don't know the steps to be taken) in order to implement the new learning in our practice. The second answer ("I wish I would have known . . .") is more of a practical issue. Why did you attend the training in the first place, and how did you anticipate it would fit in with your learning goals? Or better yet, did you think about your learning goals before attending the professional development? In this section, let's explore some strategies to tackle both of these questions.

A **personalized professional development plan** is your opportunity to identify what learning goals are important to you while reflecting on what will help you to achieve your plan. When you take time to consider the types of professional learning you want to participate in, you are more likely to end up in learning opportunities that will advance your practice. There are always professional learning sessions required by the school or district that all educators must attend, but a personalized plan goes beyond these requirements. In fact, having a personalized plan is one way of showing the administration that you care enough about advancing your practice that you have taken the time to identify areas where you would like to improve. When all health education staff have personalized plans, prepare a summary of the goals and learning outcomes. Then you can use this summary to ask the administration to support specialized professional development for the health education staff.

Personalized plans may also be used for to evaluate education and to support staff growth. Additionally, many states require educators to participate in professional learning opportunities in order to maintain a teaching license. Because of this, many states also have requirements for educators to create an individualized professional development plan that relates to their professional goals, ways to help students meet academic outcomes, and ways to improve school and district performance.

Each state has its own criteria for individualized professional development plans. However, the Criteria for a Personalized Professional Development Plan sidebar lists five key categories to consider as you think about your learning goals.

USING WHAT YOU LEARN

Just as it is important to thoughtfully select professional learning opportunities, it is important to use the skills, information, and strategies learned during these events. Use it or lose it! We have all attended events where good intentions for classroom or workplace change are derailed by the crisis of the moment. Good intentions often get sidelined for legitimate reasons, but this prohibits us from taking advantage of our learning and ultimately has an impact on our ability to change our classroom practice. The following strategies can assist you in taking full advantage of your learning.

Criteria for a Personalized Professional Development Plan

1. **Identify learning goals.** Similar to asking your students to set a goal during a goal-setting unit, identify two to four learning goals per year that you would like to achieve. Some goals may be more in depth and require previous learning or multiple years to complete (e.g., working with an instructional coach to align all lessons to be more culturally inclusive), while other goals are more simplistic and can be achieved by attending one or two training sessions (e.g., learning about new risk behavior data and updating lessons as appropriate).

2. **Identify resources necessary to achieve your goals.** All goals require resources to achieve them. Resources include the following:

   ■ Time
   ■ Money
   ■ Expertise (coaching, mentoring, other educators)
   ■ Technology
   ■ Training
   ■ Substitute coverage
   ■ Any specific resources necessary to accomplish each goal

3. **Identify supports and barriers.** Similar to resources, certain factors support the likelihood of achieving a goal and others inhibit it. Be thoughtful and reasonable when identifying what may help or hinder progress on your goals. This includes the supports necessary from the administration.

4. **Set time parameters.** Identify how long each goal should take.

5. **Define success.** What does successful completion of your professional development goals look like? Is partial completion acceptable for long-term goals? Are you factoring in student performance? Does success hinge on others being able to assist you in achieving your goals?

■ **Create an action plan.** If you haven't already done so during the learning event, take some time to establish three to five concrete steps for using the information that you learned. With each action, similar to the personalized professional development plan, consider what may help or hinder you in achieving each objective. Be realistic about your actions, but challenge yourself to try something new. Lastly, place a time frame on your actions in order to hold yourself accountable.

■ **Check on action plan progress.** After returning from a professional learning opportunity, make a note in your calendar to review your action plan and to complete any outstanding items. If the action plan is far from being completed, reevaluate if the stated actions were appropriate or if they need to be revised.

■ **Tell a friend.** When we vocalize our goals, they become more real. Enlist the support of a colleague and hold each other accountable to your learning and implementation goals.

■ **Educate other staff.** Upon returning from a well-designed learning opportunity, plan a time to meet and share the information. Use this time to discuss how the new learning could have a positive impact on classroom practice and student outcomes. If possible, consider sharing the learning at an all-staff meeting. This will demonstrate your commitment while also providing cross-curricular connections.

■ **Follow up with contacts.** We all make contacts at events. Make a pointed effort to follow up with at least two other participants and the presenter or facilitator following the event. This will also help you stay energized about your learning and discuss strategies for implementation with another person who has the same knowledge base.

■ **Participate in follow-ups.** Many professional learning opportunities that run over a length of time have follow-up mechanisms, such as an online community, an in-person session to discuss how implementation is working in the classroom, or connections to other resources. Using the provided forums gives you the support you need and answers questions for smoother implementation.

Participation in well-designed professional development helps you to be a better educator, benefitting not only your practice but also your students. Similarly, participation in high-quality professional development advances the profession. When we have health educators who are strong in the classroom, we build our credibility overall. Another way to advance the profession is through advocacy. Let's take a deeper look at what it means to be an advocate for the profession.

ADVOCATING FOR HEALTH EDUCATION

All successful initiatives have one thing in common—a consistent message that people use to improve the visibility of the initiative, inform about the benefits of the initiative, and demonstrate the support behind the initiative. If we want health education, and specifically skills-based health education, to become an indispensable part of children's schooling, we must be the voice to make that happen. In fact, not only must we be a strong voice for this, we must encourage others to raise their voice, too.

Advocacy is an overarching term that covers any action or process intended to support a cause, program, or proposal. Forms of advocacy range from providing basic information to giving testimony before a local, state, or national committee with the intention of shaping policy outcomes. For many people, the idea of participating in advocacy efforts typically falls somewhere on the continuum between "That's not my responsibility" and "I have an obligation and desire to be a strong voice for my profession." Where you land on this continuum may vary; there are many reasons why some people are active in promoting the profession while others are less engaged. We encourage you to advocate for skills-based health education as a component of the core academic education that all students receive. When you choose to be a strong voice for skills-based health education, you will find that change *can* happen and support for your program *can* grow stronger.

Advocacy is about more than saving the jobs of teachers. It's about informing others (administration, community members, parents, legislators, the public) of the value of skills-based health education for students. Our goal in this section is to provide you with a better understanding of how to advocate so that you can feel confident in becoming an active voice for health education. We provide simple, concrete strategies that you can implement in order to advocate and build support for the health of children and the health and well-being of the profession.

Before engaging in advocacy efforts, you must learn your district's policy about advocating for your program. It is common for employees of a school district to be prohibited from using their official position to advocate for something that could bring them financial gain. However, as a private citizen, in your free time you are able to advocate for causes as long as you do not use your official position, school district, or other public resources.

Even with this distinction, it can be difficult to know if you are within your scope to advocate for skills-based health education and the field of health education as a whole. Following are some strategies to assist with this concern.

■ **Read your employment policy to understand what is permissible.** If in doubt (or if unable to officially advocate), build awareness and educate others about your program. Increasing awareness and educating others about skills-based health education does not ask a person to commit to a decision or to take a specific action. These actions are about providing factual information that allows the recipient to make an informed decision. Raising awareness and educating others is an important step that all health educators can participate in.

■ **Know your facts.** It is difficult to build your credibility as an advocate if you are not using accurate information. Never provide information that you know is false or that you haven't researched. If you are in doubt about a specific piece of data or question, check the facts and get back to the person. It is better to follow up with the correct answer than to risk losing credibility with misinformation.

■ **Become the "health person"—every school needs one.** The more you talk about skills-based health education and the role that health education plays in youth development and positive outcomes for students, the more you become the expert when there are questions in your school about health education. This includes searching out your school or district's wellness committee, parent–teacher organization, and student government.

You can advocate for your skills-based health education program in many ways, ranging from lower- to higher-profile courses of action. Remember, advocating for your program or for the greater cause of health education in schools occurs one conversation at a time. Following are some examples of how you might advocate. Remember to learn your district's policy first to ensure you are complying with it.

Educating and Building Awareness

As teachers, we educate our students, but as professionals, we must educate others about the role that skills-based health education can play in the health and well-being of children. We do this by providing appropriate information and correcting misinformation in order to help someone make an informed choice. The outcome is providing an opportunity to learn something new or encouraging discussion about health-related topics and behaviors. Educating may take place as a part of your formal responsibilities and may be an appropriate use of school or district resources. Awareness initiatives or campaigns provide a foundation for and can be considered a precursor to change. Examples of education and awareness activities include the following:

■ Dedicate a bulletin board in your school to health-related information, such as promoting a health observance for the month. You can also use a bulletin board to showcase student work, explain the steps of the skill development model, or show connections between the National Health Education Standards and 21st-century skills.

■ Create a newsletter or website for parents that highlights health-related topics applicable to their children, information about new trends, and activities to engage the family in healthier activities. Consider partnering with the physical education and/or nursing staff to broaden the scope and reach of the newsletter or website.

■ Include health messaging as part of the morning announcements.

■ Have students enter a poster contest that advocates for a healthy behavior. Promote the contest to the parent–teacher association as a way to build support.

■ Sponsor a health fair or event that brings in local community agencies and practitioners that promote the health and well-being of students and families. Finding ways to cosponsor an event with a community agency builds support for both programs.

■ Become a member of the district wellness committee. Use your voice at the table to inform other members about how students are taught and what support is needed in order to address students' needs.

■ Provide a yearly presentation to your local school committee about current youth risk data that highlights improved health outcomes and growing concerns for district youth. The presentation may also include talking points related to what skills and information are included in the curriculum and how they are conveyed during class.

Soliciting Support

Soliciting support for your program goes a step beyond educating about what a skills-based health education program is and why it is important for student growth. When you solicit support, you are using materials to educate a person or group for a specific purpose. This is the step where you ask stakeholders and decision makers for support to maintain or improve your program. When you are able to clearly ask for what you need and support your request with compelling information, stakeholders are more likely to listen to what you have to say and give the support you are asking for.

Here are some examples of soliciting support:

■ Talk with your principal about updating your current health education curriculum. Explain what aspects of the curriculum are working well along with new data to support updating areas that are no longer useful or relevant. This conversation may include examples of student assessment data, current research on best practices in the health education classroom, and examples of how the proposed changes will make the curriculum stronger and more relevant for students.

■ During a presentation to school staff about the new wellness policy, address areas of concern and ask the staff to support the changes by talking positively about the policy to students and being role models within the school and their classrooms.

■ While attending a community forum in your town, voice your concern over proposed cuts to health education and provide data to support how health education can address the risk factors of youth in your town.

■ During a meeting with members of a local youth-serving organization, ask them to review what you are currently teaching in health education and to support your efforts through their after-school program.

Lobbying

Lobbying is an effort to influence a public or governmental organization such as your school board, city or town council, state legislature, or even national legislature. Lobbying requires you to understand the issue, formulate a specific request for change, and understand the needs of the stakeholders or decision makers you will be speaking with. Lobbying differs from soliciting support in that it focuses on local, state, and national policy makers. Examples of lobbying include the following:

■ Write a letter to your state commissioner of education and ask to include health education as part of the graduation requirements in your state.

■ Participate in SHAPE America's SPEAK Out! Day. In preparation, SHAPE America trains people to be advocates with the skills to lobby federal legislators to improve access and quality of health and physical education programs.

■ Visit your town council to speak about how supporting the school budget helps to provide students with the opportunities to learn how to lead healthier lives.

SUMMARY

As health educators, we must protect the integrity of the profession. There are two key ways

KEY POINTS

- Without a voice, the field of health education is sure to fall out of the purview of decision makers. It is both our right and our responsibility to be strong advocates for health programs in schools.

- Advocacy is vital to protecting the health, well-being, and academic outcomes of students. We must be a voice that makes the connections for others who are unfamiliar with the impact that a skills-based health education program can have on students.

- Advocacy can take many forms. It is imperative to choose some way to support the field of health education and then follow through on efforts to advocate.

to do this: high-quality professional development and advocacy. Professional development advances the ability to improve classroom instruction with the intent of improving student outcomes. When we do this, we demonstrate our dedication to the overall outcomes of youth—they are, after all, at the core of why we do the work we do. Choose professional learning opportunities based on your personal goals to improve your practice. This helps you to both engage in learning opportunities that challenge you to learn new skills and strategies for your classrooms and also to be proactive as you discuss your growth as an educator with your administrators.

The second is to be an advocate for the profession and the well-being of children. Advocacy is necessary to ensure that stakeholders and decision makers understand what skills-based health education is and why it needs to be a regular part of school. In addition, we cannot expect others to advocate for health education if we are not willing to do the same. We must all play an active role in advocating for the profession. We hope you will consider how you can be an advocate for our field.

Review Questions

1. What are the key elements of high-quality professional development?

2. What are ways that you can use what you learn from professional development?

3. What are some ways to advocate for skills-based health education? List three examples.

To find supplementary materials for this chapter, such as worksheets and extended learning activities, visit the web resource at
www.HumanKinetics.com/TheEssentialsOfTeachingHealthEducation

Making Cross-Curricular Connections

Learning Objectives

After reading this chapter, you will be able to do the following:

- Identify components of the Whole School, Whole Community, Whole Child (WSCC) approach and how it affects student outcomes.
- Engage stakeholders in a plan of action to support student health and academic outcomes.
- Describe strategies for integrating health education material across curricular subjects.
- Discuss ways to increase the impact of school-based health education through integration with multiple areas of the school.

Key Terms

health coordinator

local education agencies (LEAs)

local wellness policy

Whole School, Whole Community, Whole Child (WSCC)

Student health comes up in conversation for many reasons. A group of health educators may be discussing what is taught in the curriculum, a group of school nurses may be thinking about the physical health of students, school-adjustment counselors and social workers may be discussing how students are being bullied, administrators may be thinking about the recent flu outbreak that has kept an unusually high number of students out of school, and parents may be concerned that their children are not getting enough sleep because of the early school start times or about the challenge of getting their child to eat breakfast before school. All of these issues are important and have an impact on both health and academic outcomes. Additionally, none is unique to a single group. Whether it is bullying in the cafeteria, being absent from school, managing life threatening allergies, or students unable to concentrate because they are tired, the impact is felt across many groups.

To tackle these wide-ranging issues, we must gather together as a team and look across disciplines. When we work across departments and specialties, we have a greater chance of creating an environment in which students can be successful—both in terms of health and academics. We have dedicated this chapter to exploring collaboration and coordination inside and outside of schools in order to improve health and academic outcomes for students. Specifically, this chapter explores the WSCC approach and how the integration of a coordinated approach can prove beneficial. We also explore how health-related topics and skills can intersect with other areas in the curriculum with the goal of making health a regular part of conversations in schools. The overarching goal of this chapter is to provide ideas and strategies for bringing health education beyond the classroom in order to increase its impact on not only student health but academic success as well.

A COORDINATED APPROACH TO STUDENT SUCCESS

Most will agree that healthy children are important to a healthy society. Many will also agree that student health and academic success are linked. If students aren't healthy and aren't

in school or aren't able to fully concentrate while in school, they are not likely to achieve academically at the highest level. This means we need to take into consideration the needs of the whole child when planning education systems.

Unfortunately, many students have health-related problems that affect their learning. Although not all health issues among youth are tracked in a systematic way, there are some that have been shown to have a negative effect on student achievement. Some examples include vision problems, asthma, attention-deficit/hyperactivity disorder (ADHD), teenage pregnancy, lack of physical activity, and not eating breakfast (Basch, 2010). These health problems would hinder any child, but we have also learned that they are more likely to disproportionately affect urban minority youth from low-income families (Basch, 2010). Young people face many health-related issues, but we know that these problems in particular can negatively affect teaching and learning. Therefore, a critical role of the school is to create an environment that addresses student health in a meaningful and effective manner. This means going beyond the health education classroom into other areas of the school building and grounds to consider how your school can become a place where students can grow and thrive.

Even though evidence supports the need to address health issues and their effect on academic achievement, differences of opinion occur when we start discussing *how* to make this happen in schools. Specifically, people tend to disagree when discussing the structures, supports, and education that students need in order to be healthy and academically successful and when discussing whose role it is to ensure that these structures, supports, and educational approaches are in place. It would be unrealistic to place the entire burden of health and educational outcomes on schools, but in order for students to be successful and well adjusted, school systems must take a thoughtful look at the needs of students from multiple dimensions. Healthy students are better learners, and schools play a vital role in student outcomes and success.

Student success can occur on many levels, and our role as educators is to ensure that we provide students with the greatest chance for success. Having a coordinated approach to student success, regardless of life circumstances outside of school, levels the playing field, allows students to focus on their academics, and helps create a healthier and more successful society.

An approach that coordinates the efforts of many within the school and community is the **Whole School, Whole Community, Whole Child (WSCC)** model (see figure 18.1). This approach, formalized in 2014, brings together the original coordinated school health approach, the Coordinated School Health model, and the Whole Child Initiative of ASCD (formerly the Association for Supervision and Curriculum Development). The development of the WSCC approach integrates and coordinates the "goals of the education and health sector" and "as the next evolution of CSH, the approach speaks to leaders and practitioners of both sectors on the local level" (Lewallen, Hunt, Potts-Datema, Zaza, & Giles, 2015, p. 735). It is an updated approach designed to provide a framework to advance the "educational attainment and healthy development for students" (Lewallen, Hunt, Potts-Datema, Zaza, & Giles, 2015, p. 737).

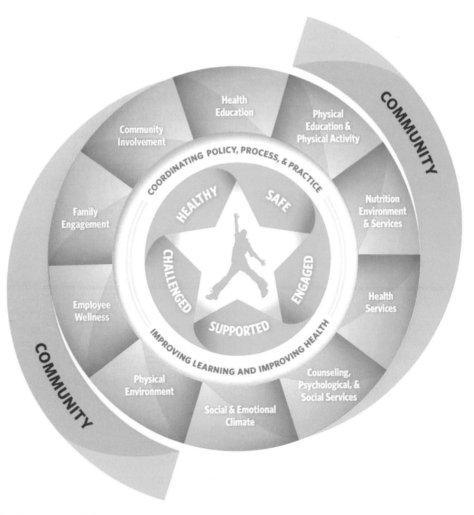

FIGURE 18.1 WSCC model.

The WSCC model has 10 components:

1. Health education
2. Physical education and physical activity
3. Health services
4. Nutrition environment and services
5. Counseling, psychological, and social services
6. Physical environment
7. Social and emotional climate
8. Health promotion for staff
9. Family engagement
10. Community involvement

The intention is that children are at the center of everything we do in schools. The role of adults is to ensure that students are healthy, safe, engaged, supported, and challenged at school (ASCD, 2014). This occurs when each component works together, and it becomes a necessary factor in making sure that policies and practices improve the learning and health of students. We discuss each component in this section, but if you want more information as well as a tool for self-evaluation, you should explore the School Health Index (SHI; http://nccd.cdc.gov/DASH_SHI/default/Login.aspx), the Health Education Curriculum Analysis Tool (HECAT; www.cdc.gov/HealthyYouth/HECAT/index.htm), and the Comprehensive School Physical Activity Program (CSPAP; www.cdc.gov/healthyschools/physicalactivity/cspap.htm) from the CDC. All will be helpful as you begin to examine how your school can better meet its students' health needs.

Health Education

The foundation of the first WSCC component, health education, is a comprehensive and developmentally appropriate skills-based health education program that is taught as a regular part of the school curriculum and guided by a formalized scope and sequence. As discussed throughout the book, and specifically in chapter 2, a well-designed and implemented preK-12 health education program is most likely to bring about changes in students' knowledge and skills. When health education is sporadic or ineffectual, it limits the likelihood of change in student behavior and may increase negative student outcomes related to risky behaviors.

Physical Education and Physical Activity

The WSCC component of physical education and physical activity was expanded from the previous coordinated school health approach. Similar to the health education component, this component recognizes the importance of a well-designed physical education program that follows the National Standards for K-12 Physical Education, provides adequate resources (including time, space, and equipment), and is taught by a certified physical education teacher. Physical education should have a goal of getting all students engaged and moving for the majority of the class regardless of ability level. When we offer students a physical education program that helps them to develop the skills to be physically active throughout their lives, we help to shape their physical health.

The original coordinated school health approach only included physical education. However, physical activity before, during, and after school is increasingly seen as vital to student success. In a 2013 report, the Institute of Medicine (IOM) made recommendations for increasing physical activity in order to improve health and academic outcomes. Specifically, the report highlighted ways for students to meet the Physical Activity Guidelines for Americans, which recommend that kids get at least 60 minutes of physical activity per day (IOM, 2013).

Health Services

Health services encompass all professional health-related services that students may need or that are provided within the school environment. This includes school nurses, school-based clinic staff, school physicians, dental professionals, vision professionals, or any other health professionals who screen, evaluate, treat, or monitor physical conditions. If students are not physically well, their ability to focus on academic work is greatly diminished. Think of the last time you had a toothache or a stomachache. Were you able to concentrate on what you were doing? Now, imagine you have this toothache all the time but have never been to a dentist or that you cannot see the board clearly and have never had your eyes tested and you do not realize that the words on the board should be clear and not blurry. Or, imagine that you have a life-threatening allergy or chronic condition that you need to manage while you are at school. For a large number of students, these situations are a reality. Without supportive health services, school could be dangerous, if not inaccessible, for some students.

Many people are familiar with school nurses and their role in providing onsite support and care to students. Fewer are familiar with the role of a school physician or a school-based health center. Some schools have partnered with community and nonprofit organizations to ensure that students receive the health care, dental care, and vision care they need. Having strong policies and supports that address the health needs of students is the intention of this component.

Nutrition Environment and Services

This WSCC component encompasses the food made available during the school day and on school property. For school meals, this includes the cafeteria, whose lunches and breakfasts are governed under the Healthy, Hunger-Free Kids Act rules pertaining to the National School Lunch Program and the School Breakfast Program in schools that receive reimbursement for meals served (www.fns.usda.gov). This may also include when and where breakfast is served to students—in the cafeteria, in the classroom, or through grab-and-go kiosks. A second area of this component includes foods that are sold to students à la carte during lunch time, in school stores, at concession stands, in booster sales, and so on. The third area of this component is the foods that are offered to students during the school day, such as classroom parties, pizza parties for good behavior, bake sales, or even candy dishes on the teacher's desk.

All of these examples represent ways that students are given food throughout the day. The food available (either offered or sold) is a reflection of the social norms in the school. When healthy meals are sold, highly nutritious foods are sold in à la carte lines, and minimally nutritious foods are limited, students see that the school is committed to maintaining a healthier nutrition environment. We encourage schools look at their nutrition environment, including where and when food is offered and sold,

to determine if the items are high quality. If foods with low nutritional value are offered or sold, then consider the parameters surrounding those sales. If schools identify areas for improvement, they should engage in a dialogue with multiple stakeholders in order to find ways to improve the offerings or environment.

Counseling, Psychological, and Social Services

Counseling, psychological, and social services encompass all of the services available to support the mental health of students. These services can include testing students for special needs, providing counseling and support to students who are struggling, and partnering with community agencies to provide wraparound services to students in need. Many students have complex mental health needs. Students may witness violence in the home, struggle with depression or anxiety, be dependent on alcohol or another substance, face bullying, or be abused by a partner or someone they know. Professionals such as psychologists, social workers, and counselors are critical to address students' mental health needs and help them feel safe in the learning environment.

Physical Environment

The physical environment in WSCC considers the physical space—the buildings and grounds of the school. Many areas of the physical environment can affect the health and safety of students, such as the exhaust released as busses idle in the parking lot, how pests are managed and controlled, whether or not the building is in compliance with the Americans with Disabilities Act, or even whether or not playground equipment has been checked regularly to ensure safety. Unfortunately, the physical environment is often overlooked when school health measures are considered. In failing to include the physical environment in our conversations, we may miss cues that could keep students safe. For example, in the planning of a new school, the architects should take into consideration the size and functionality of the school kitchen—how can cafeteria staff prepare healthy food with inadequate space or equipment? Or, it may be a custodian who understands where students hide when skipping classes or knows how to ventilate an area after a science experiment goes bad. The physical layout of the school becomes essential should an emergency arise.

The physical environment is where students and teachers spend their time. When the space is conducive to learning and development, great things can happen.

Social and Emotional Climate

The social and emotional climate encourages schools to create an environment that is welcoming and nurturing for students. When students feel connected to their school, they are more likely to experience academic success and better health outcomes (CDC, 2009). This component is unique in that it is not necessarily staff directed. Although it is important for teachers and administrators to put the appropriate supports and curriculum in place to encourage a welcoming, safe, and accepting atmosphere, it is also important for students to help create this climate. Students who feel invested in their environment and feel a responsibility to their peers are more likely to work to create a safe space where everyone can thrive.

When assessing the strength of the social and emotional climate, there are many areas to consider:

■ Policies that promote inclusiveness

■ Student involvement in extracurricular activities and clubs

■ Attendance and tardiness rates

■ Open conversations and displays promoting diversity

■ Class sizes that allow for engagement and personalized attention

Ultimately, a school with a positive social and emotional climate is one that both talks about tough issues and then follows up those conversations with actions that demonstrate support for all students in an inclusive way.

Health Promotion for Staff

This WSCC component recognizes that when school staff (i.e., everyone from the principal to the cafeteria staff and bus drivers) are good models of health for students, it sets the tone for the entire school. This component encourages schools to support opportunities for staff to be healthy.

For some schools, this includes allowing staff to use time within their schedule to walk around the building or work out in the fitness center. For others, it may be providing an employee assistance program that is free and encourages employees to reach out for help. Additionally, it may include establishing policies and protocols to support staff wellness, connecting staff to health screenings and resources, supporting staff efforts to get healthier (e.g., walking clubs, weight management challenges, bringing a farmer's market to campus), and having vending machines that offer healthier items. Perhaps it is even making opportunities for skills-based health education available for staff and their families.

Family Engagement

Family engagement considers the role that families play in the development of their children. Parents and guardians have a profound influence on the health and health care decisions that youth make. In many cases this can be positive, but in some unfortunate scenarios students are left to navigate the world with little family support.

For both health education and school programs as a whole, engaging parents and families is a way to build support, gain trust, and increase the protective factors of youth (CDC, 2012). As students become independent (in middle and high school), they need to feel a connection to parents and caregivers. In order to improve family engagement, the CDC (2012) recommends three steps:

1. Connect with parents.
2. Engage parents through a variety of opportunities.
3. Sustain the relationship by addressing challenges of getting parents involved.

Community Involvement

Community involvement requires schools to look to the community for support and leverage. No one teacher or parent can be responsible for the health, education, and well-being of a child, and getting the community involved builds support across domains. As the saying goes, it takes a village to raise a child and the same is true to support the health and academic outcomes of students in schools. At any given time, only a small percentage of community members have children who attend school. However, all community members are responsible for funding school programs and will be the direct recipients of services that today's students will provide. We believe that all communities have dedicated individuals who want to see the school succeed. There is also a core group of people who have the skills and expertise to make this happen but may not be currently involved with school initiatives.

For school personnel, opening the school doors to community members requires an investment of time and effort. To make community involvement valuable, organize opportunities for meaningful engagement with the community, such as creating a community forum to solicit feedback or calling local businesses to sponsor student clubs, events, or internships. Establish fair-use policies that define what an open-door policy looks like—we want to invite the community into our schools but must be conscious of safety protocols.

Ultimately, every community has a vast array of stakeholders and valuable assets. Tapping into those stakeholders in meaningful ways can have multiple benefits for students and the community as a whole. This could include soliciting student feedback on policies that promote a positive environment, assessing student perceptions of the school climate and ways to improve it, or creating a taskforce of students and staff to take a thoughtful look at student engagement and how to improve it.

Table 18.1 provides examples for each component of the WSCC approach.

SHAPING LOCAL WELLNESS POLICIES

We've discussed how the WSCC model provides the framework for integrating health and education in schools. For this integration to be successful, there must be a core group of people at the school and district level who are responsible for making it happen. Those are the people who take the lead in creating the policies, procedures, and protocols that result in implementation at the local level. When the U.S. Congress reauthorized the Special Supplemental Nutrition Program for Women, Infants, and Children (WIC) in 2004, it required all **local education agencies (LEAs)**, or school districts, receiving federal dollars for child nutrition programs, including school lunch and breakfast, to create a wellness policy by 2006. In 2010, the Healthy, Hunger-Free Kids Act strengthened the requirements for LEAs by adding more criteria. At present, LEAs are required to have a **local wellness policy** that does the following (U.S. Department of Agriculture [USDA], 2010):

■ Includes goals for nutrition promotion and education, physical activity, and other school-based activities that promote student wellness.

■ Includes nutrition guidelines for all foods available in each school district in order to promote student health and reduce childhood obesity.

■ Permits parents, students, representatives of the school food authority, physical

KEY POINTS

■ The WSCC model highlights 10 components that work together to increase the likelihood of engaging students and promoting their success.

■ Student success increases when we are thoughtful about engaging partnerships and resources in the school and community, and everyone benefits. No one can succeed alone.

■ Each component of the model offers examples of involvement and success, but there is no single strategy that will work for all schools. Each school must identify the needs of its students and community and craft solutions to meet them.

TABLE 18.1 Examples of the WSCC Approach

Health education	• Ensure health education is part of the curriculum for all students across grades. • Base your health education program on student needs. • Write a developmentally appropriate scope and sequence that supports a positive youth development model. • Dedicate time for health education taught by qualified educators.
Physical education and physical activity	• Provide quality physical education to all students at all levels. • Provide opportunities for physical activity before, during, and after school as part of a comprehensive school physical activity program. • Write policies to support the role that physical activity plays in academic achievement.
Nutrition environment and services	• Ensure that school meals offered meet USDA requirements and are acceptable to students. • Integrate school nutrition professionals into the wellness committee. • Create a school food environment that supports healthy food choices.
Counseling, psychological, and social services	• Integrate mental health professionals into the school community and make their services available to students. • Ensure access to mental health services that minimally disrupts a student's day, including minimal removals from special or elective subjects. • Promote community mental health resources to students. • Make connections with mental health resources within health and physical education curricula.
Physical environment	• Employ policies that promote the health of all students by supporting strategies such as improving indoor air quality or pest management. • Ensure that the physical space is accessible to all students. • Inspect all playground, physical education, and physical activity equipment to ensure safety. Replace worn-out equipment when necessary.
Social and emotional climate	• Value the culture of all students in the school. Recognize that each student brings a unique perspective to the classroom. • Create a safe-space for learning that does not tolerate hurtful or hateful language. • Ensure that class sizes are consistent across subject areas and for the classroom structure.
Health promotion for staff	• Allow staff to pursue physical activity within their schedule during the school day. • Host voluntary competitions that promote wellness. • Offer educational sessions for staff and their families.
Family engagement	• Connect parent activities with student performances. Create an accessible way for parents to get engaged. • Hold morning coffee with administrators—parents may find it easier to come in the morning than in the evening. • Solicit parent feedback and create opportunities for dialogue.
Community involvement	• Reach out to community organizations and businesses to gain support for school health initiatives. • Hold a career fair for students that emphasizes how current and future choices will affect career choices (bring in local employers). • Actively engage with community members by asking them to serve on the wellness committee.

© Chris Schmidt/iStock.com

Collaborating with multiple stakeholders within a school who are committed to improving health and academic success will lead to improved student outcomes.

education teachers, school health professionals, the school board, school administrators, and the general public to participate in the development, implementation, and review and update of the local wellness policy.

■ Informs and updates the public (including parents, students, and others in the community) about the content and implementation of local wellness policies.

■ Is measured periodically to evaluate the extent to which schools are in compliance with the local wellness policy, the extent to which the local wellness policy compares with model policies, and the progress made in attaining the goals of the local wellness policy. This assessment is made available to the public.

Table 18.2 provides suggestions for ways that schools can address the criteria for the wellness policy.

School Wellness Committees

As discussed, the Healthy, Hunger-Free Kids Act of 2010 requires LEAs to establish a committee for the purpose of developing and implementing the local wellness policy (www.fns.usda.gov). Having a school wellness committee as a component of the local wellness policy provides a forum for stakeholders to discuss health issues and to create policy that will apply to all schools in the district. Although health educators are not specifically listed in the regulation, it is important to be involved in your school wellness committee. Being involved in both the wellness committee and the development of local policies provides an important avenue to influence the health and well-being of students. If you are not already involved, seek out the head of the committee and inquire about getting involved. The Healthy, Hunger-Free Kids Act stipulates that parents, students, representatives of the school

TABLE 18.2 Sample Language and Strategies for Meeting the Requirements of Local Wellness Policies

Goal for nutrition promotion and education	• Students will receive nutrition education as a part of their skills-based, sequential, comprehensive health education course. • Nutrition education will be integrated with other core academic subjects as appropriate. • Nutrition education and promotion activities will meet the diverse needs of students in the school community. • The cafeteria will be a pleasing and welcoming environment for all students. • Positive food messages will be included throughout the school and in notices to parents. • Teachers will not use food as a reward or a punishment.
Goals for physical activity	• Students will receive physical education as a required component of their schooling and all courses will be standards based, sequential, and developmentally appropriate. • Students will be provided with recess before lunch. • Physical activity will not be taken away from students as a punishment. • Teachers are encouraged to integrate physical activity interventions at least three times per day at the elementary level and at least once per class period at the secondary level. • The physical education curriculum will encourage lifetime physical fitness and provide students with multiple opportunities to engage in physical activity. • Schools will provide multiple opportunities for physical activity before, during, and after school.
Other school-based wellness initiatives	• School-sponsored fund-raisers will involve nonfood options or promote an increase in physical activity. • Food-free classroom celebrations are encouraged. Classroom celebrations including food will occur no more than one time per month. • School policies will allow for students to self-carry emergency medication (such as inhalers and epinephrine). • Indoor air quality will remain at a level safe for all students and staff. • The comprehensive skills-based health education curriculum will include topics deemed most relevant based on local youth risk data.
Nutrition guidelines for all foods sold in school	• The school nutrition program will remain in compliance with all requirements for the National School Lunch and School Breakfast programs. • All foods sold will comply with state and federal competitive food regulations. • School menus will provide nutrition information for all meals served. • Food labels will be made available to parents and staff as requested. • Schools will be encouraged to adopt a Breakfast in the Classroom model to ensure all students start the day ready to learn. • Students will be given, at minimum, 20 minutes to eat their meal after being seated.
Development of local wellness policy	• Key stakeholders and community members will be engaged in the development of the local wellness policy. At a minimum, members will include parents, students, representatives of the school food authority, physical education teachers, school health professionals, the school board, school administrators, and the general public. • Policy development will include other key stakeholders, such as health educators, school counselors, local community organizations, and so on. • Leadership of the wellness committee will be by the district health coordinator or comparable. • The wellness committee will meet a minimum of four times per year and will establish goals for the committee. • Annual goals and objectives will be written to advance the implementation of this policy.
Inform the public about progress	• The wellness policy will be published on the school district website with all other school policies. • Meetings of the wellness committee will be open to the public. • The wellness committee will compile and publish an annual report documenting the implementation efforts, and measurement related to identified outcomes will occur.
Monitoring and evaluating the wellness policy	• The wellness committee will publish an annual report documenting the implementation efforts, and measurement related to identified outcomes will occur for each school within the district. • The wellness committee will conduct a semiannual review of the wellness policy to update requirements and to ensure compliance with state and federal mandates. • The wellness committee will integrate feedback from stakeholders (including students, parents, and staff) regarding policy implementation.

- The Healthy, Hunger-Free Kids Act of 2010 reaffirms the importance of creating a policy that outlines criteria for the nutrition and physical activity environment in schools.

- Playing an active role on your school or district wellness committee is an opportunity to engage in the policy and protocols related to the health and well-being of students.

- Health coordinators are key to creating a coordinated structure of support for the health and well-being of students.

food authority, teachers of physical education, school health professionals, the school board, and school administrators should participate in the policy development, so we encourage schools to include all of these individuals on the school wellness committee as well.

Along with the federal regulations, it is important to find out whether other regulations exist at the state level about who should be included on a local committee. A well-designed committee will also consider components outside of nutrition and physical activity (i.e., the components of the WSCC model). You may find that having such a well-rounded committee allows for greater depth of discussion and the ability to address student issues in a thoughtful and systematic way.

School Health Coordinator

Similar to having a comprehensive school wellness committee, having a point person to manage the health and wellness initiatives in the school district is more likely to lead to policies that promote the health and well-being of students. The role of a **health coordinator** will vary from district to district, but we suggest having a person who is the district leader for all curricula, programs, and policies related to the health and well-being of students. This position should involve coordinating health education and physical education curricula along with establishing connections among all areas of the coordinated approach. In some districts, the health coordinator may be a lead health educator who has additional administrative responsibilities, in other districts it may be a school nurse who dedicates some time to leading the district wellness committee, and other districts it may be a person who is an administrator and acts as a department head, providing both administrative oversight of curriculum and coordination of other services and supports for students.

MAKING INTERDISCIPLINARY CONNECTIONS FOR SCHOOL IMPROVEMENT

School improvement is a process within a district to address student outcomes and improve them in a systematic way, and it is governed by state and federal requirements. The National Association of Secondary School Principals (NASSP) suggests that collaborative leadership, personalizing your school environment, and curriculum, instruction, and assessment are key to improving student performance (www.nassp.org/school-improvement). The NASSP recommendations are only one example of ways to address school improvement, however. Districts have the opportunity to identify the specific outcomes to improve upon based on student academic performance. In order to do this, student-level data and outcomes must drive improvement plans. For example, selected outcomes might include improving graduation or dropout rates, absentee rates, student growth from year to year, performance of special education or English language learners, student discipline rates, family and community engagement, emergency response plans, staff absenteeism (through the implementation of wellness initiatives), or student performance on state assessments. Though each district varies in the outcomes selected for improvement and the strategies they will use, they all have areas they target to improve on a yearly basis.

One way to support school improvement efforts is by understanding the areas your school and district have identified as most in need of improvement and then educating the administration on how the skills-based health education curriculum can help to meet the identified goals. For example, if improving the academic outcomes of special education students has been identified as an area of growth, you could inform the administration of how the skills-based approach provides opportunities for all students to be engaged via differentiated instruction and assessments. You also might point out how your work to address the risk factors of special education students increases the likelihood that they stay connected to school.

A second way to support school improvement is to work with the administration and school board to add health-related objectives to school improvement goals. For example, you could educate the school board on the role that risk and protective factors play in academic achievement and the local youth risk behavior data that indicate increased rates of relationship violence. The school board might then include goals related to improving the social and emotional health of students and designate health education as the primary place where students learn about healthy relationships, friendships, interpersonal relationships, and management of emotions.

Another way to connect with school improvement efforts is by thoughtfully integrating health education with the traditional core subjects of math, English language arts, science, and social studies. One conversation that doesn't often happen is how these core subjects may be a strategy for extending the reach of health education and perhaps even part of a larger strategy to improve the health outcomes of students. As previously discussed in chapter 16, we encourage you to consider how you can integrate other subject areas with health education. This can show students how health crosses multiple dimensions, strengthen the potential for transfer of core skills and knowledge beyond the health class, and support student outcomes in other subject areas.

It may be helpful to meet with teachers in other disciplines to better understand what students are learning and to integrate opportunities for practice into your classroom activities. For example, interpretation of statistics may be a learning goal for students in high school. Using data on youth risk behavior, you can support student understanding and application of the statistical concepts they learned in math class while you discuss health data points and what they mean to students' health and well-being. In addition, the math teacher can use health-related data to explore the concepts of statistics and probability. Another example is meeting with the reading specialist to determine the best strategies to support the emerging readers in your elementary health education class. You can then incorporate those strategies into your health class to support literacy goals, and the reading specialist can use more texts that support health themes. Thinking about how to include more of the core subjects in your health education class and how other subjects can support health education will lead to improved student outcomes.

This does not mean you must be a math or language arts expert; rather, you must be a willing collaborator who seeks out connections

KEY POINTS

▪ Integrating other subjects into health education allows health educators to support other academic areas while teaching students health-related topics and skills.

▪ No two schools are alike. The best way to integrate other subject areas into health education is to meet with the subject-matter experts in your school to determine how best to integrate other standards into your course.

▪ Integration of other subjects into your health education course may be already occurring. Understanding the requirements of other subjects helps to support your efforts and demonstrates collaboration.

with other staff members. If you make these connections and find ways to integrate other core subject standards into health education and vice versa, you maintain a presence in the conversation about increasing students' health literacy and how that can influence academic performance. Specifically, as discussed in chapter 1, when you show students how health-related concepts and skills transfer across contexts, you set up a foundation for application in the real world. You also help to maintain the integrity of health messaging in the school. Conversely, when other subject-matter experts are asked to add in health topics without coordinating with the health educator, the skill development component may be lost. Instead, we encourage a collaborative relationship between health educators and others in the school. This provides students with an appropriate skills-based health education course that supports the teaching of other disciplines. As an expert on skills-based health education, we encourage you to take an active part in conversations about how to improve student outcomes by using what is taught in the health education classroom. Table 18.3 presents some ideas to inspire you in integrating other subjects in your program.

SUMMARY

The saying that it takes a village to raise a child is true. However, just having the village does not ensure success; the village must work together to meet the needs of all children. In a school, the same is true—we must work to meet the needs of all students. This can only happen if we recognize that students have unique needs and unique perspectives as members of the school community.

The WSCC model provides the framework for meeting the needs of all students, with 10 components surrounding the student in the center and the components surrounded by the community influence. At its heart, this model starts the conversation of collaboration and coordination at the school and district

TABLE 18.3 Strategies for Integrating Other Subjects Into Health Education

SUBJECT	INTEGRATION METHODS
Math	• Students compile statistics from health-related surveys. • Students create charts and graphs based on data about youth risk behavior. • Students calculate the cost of regular tobacco use. • Use MyPlate (www.choosemyplate.gov) to discuss fractions.
Science	• Students use the scientific method to answer health-related questions. • Students connect with experts (or local groups) about the environmental health of the state or community. • Students create a presentation about cause and effect related to health issues (e.g., drug use and addiction, sleep and academic performance). • Discuss how the structure of the human body relates to its health-related functions.
English and language arts	• Students use relevant literature to explore health-related skills (e.g., *Romeo and Juliet* can be used to discuss decision making, analyzing influences, and interpersonal communication). • Students practice writing skills by keeping a health journal. • Students complete a research paper on a topic of personal interest (accessing information). • Students predict the health outcomes of characters in a book they're reading in English and how another health choice could alter the characters' life circumstances.
Social studies	• Students explore health issues in certain time periods and focus on how times have changed and why certain issues don't exist now (and perhaps why we face new ones). • Students explore health practices in other cultures. • Students explore different views on health across time periods and cultures. • Students analyze food choices around the globe and how they affect health outcomes.

levels. When schools formalize the conversation through a wellness committee or local wellness policy, they create an opportunity for growth. This conversation requires a thoughtful approach and goes beyond purely looking at academic outcomes. We must address the needs of students to set them up for academic success and achieve high academic outcomes.

Review Questions

1. What are the components of the WSCC approach?

2. How does the school wellness committee contribute to the WSCC approach?

3. What strategies can your school implement to meet the needs of students across multiple domains?

4. How can you integrate other subjects into health education?

To find supplementary materials for this chapter, such as worksheets and extended learning activities, visit the web resource at
www.HumanKinetics.com/TheEssentialsOfTeachingHealthEducation

Glossary

active learning—Process in which students engage with the content; when students are *doing* things with content and *thinking* about content.

advocacy—Any action or process intended to support a position, cause, program, or proposal.

advocate—Educating and persuading others to believe in a specific position, claim, message, or cause. To advocate is to speak favorably on a topic for others to hear.

anchor chart—Visual tool on which the teacher writes lesson reinforcements or strategies for students to refer to during and after the lesson.

Appropriate Practices in School-Based Health Education—A guidance document from SHAPE America that is a detailed blueprint for designing and delivering effective skills-based health education within the PK-12 setting.

authentic assessment—Assessment measure that is meaningful and relevant to a student's real-world circumstances and surroundings; requires students to demonstrate learning by applying the skills and knowledge in a way that appropriately responds to the question posed in the prompt.

authentic environment—An environment that is closely related to our actual experience and circumstance and that increases our ability to apply learning to our lives directly following a learning experience.

authentic situation—A situation that accurately represents the experiences of an audience.

backward design—Curriculum development beginning with student outcomes and working through the process of establishing goals and outcomes, creating benchmark assessments, choosing skills and topics, creating a scope and sequence, developing units (including assessments), and designing lesson plans (adapted from Wiggins & McTighe, 2005).

benchmark assessment—A specific point in a program when student progress is measured.

competency—The ability to do something successfully.

conflict resolution—The methods and process of resolving a disagreement or conflict in a healthy way.

contextual aids—Visual aids that help all students in the class be successful.

culture—The beliefs, customs, ways of thinking, and behaviors shared among a group of people.

data-driven approach—The process of gathering and analyzing data for the purpose of making a decision based on facts, data, and information, not opinion.

decision making—The process by which a person thoughtfully proceeds through a series of steps in order to "identify, implement, and sustain health-enhancing behaviors" (Joint Committee, 2007).

do-now activity—An activity that is completed at the beginning of class that can help students focus on content to be covered in the lesson, review material previously taught, or provide time for self-reflection.

e-health literacy—The capacity to apply health literacy competencies in an online environment (Paek & Hove, 2012).

essential question—Open-ended question that fosters critical thinking about the content.

exemplars—Samples of previously completed work that show students what a high-scoring assignment looks like.

external influence—Anything that affects our feelings, actions, and beliefs and is introduced from an outside source.

extrinsic motivation—Motivation that is driven by factors outside oneself such as fame, money, and consequence.

feedback—Providing an honest and nonjudgmental assessment of a specific action or work in a way that promotes growth and strengthens learning.

formative assessment—An assessment *for* learning that allows you to evaluate and adjust ongoing teaching to improve students' achievements of intended instructional outcomes (CCSSO, 2012).

functional information—Information that is useable, applicable, and relevant. It is not arbitrary, traditional, or extensive. Functional information is the context in which the skills will be taught and the base for students' developing functional knowledge.

functional knowledge—The outcome of internalizing and applying functional information so that the student can retrieve and apply the learning when necessary.

goal setting—The process of setting, creating, and working toward a goal. This includes the steps necessary for both short- and long-term goals.

grade weighting—When an assignment or graded work accounts for a higher percentage of the total grade. Each assignment counts toward a percentage of the overall grade.

health coordinator—An identified point of contact who works to align health-related initiatives within a school or district.

Health Education Curriculum Analysis Tool (HECAT)—A tool that can help school districts, schools, and others conduct a clear, complete, and consistent analysis of health education curricula based on the *National Health Education Standards* and CDC's *Characteristics of an Effective Health Education Curriculum.*

health-enhancing behavior—A behavior that an individual engages in that will benefit their health and well-being.

health literacy—Links to overall literacy levels and focuses on people's knowledge, motivation, and competencies to access, understand, appraise, and apply health information in order to make judgments and decisions in everyday life concerning health care, disease prevention, and health promotion to maintain or improve quality of life during the life course (Sorenson et al., 2012).

icebreakers—Activities to help people get to know each other, feel more comfortable, and warm up in a group setting.

influence—Anything that has an effect on an outcome. In this context, we explore things that can influence a person's feelings, actions, thoughts, and beliefs.

information—Facts, details, or data about a subject.

interactive health literacy—"The development of personal skills in a supportive environment. This approach to education is directed toward improving personal capacity to act independently on knowledge, specifically to improve motivation and self-confidence to act on advice received" (Nutbeam, 2000, p. 265).

internal influence—Characteristics that are an innate part of who we are that can affect our behaviors, such as values, beliefs, motivation, attitudes, and needs.

internalization—Students' ability to embed knowledge and skills into their beliefs, values, attitudes, and actions. It means that students are adopting what they have learned so that it becomes their frame of reference for health and health behaviors.

interpersonal communication—The exchange of information between two or more people. A message is developed and sent by the sender and transmitted to, received, and interpreted by the receiver.

intrinsic motivation—A person's internal drive or motivation to engage in behaviors that are interesting and provide an opportunity to feel competent and self-determined (Deci & Ryan, 2000).

job-embedded learning—Learning opportunities that occur in an authentic environment, such as in the classroom, with other educators in your school, or with other health educators outside your school.

knowledge—The synthesis of previously learned information and experience that forms the foundation of action.

listening—An interpretive action in which the listener (receiver) attempts to understand and make meaning of a message.

literacy—The ability to read and write.

local education agencies (LEAs)—The legal entities responsible for education at the school district level.

local wellness policy—As part of the Healthy, Hunger-Free Kids Act of 2010, school districts must create policies that address the health and well-being of students (www.fns.usda.gov/tn/local-school-wellness-policy-requirements).

long-term goal—A goal that will be accomplished further in the future. A long-term goal often requires additional planning and check-in points to ensure it stays on track.

Maslow's hierarchy of needs—Based on the theory of human motivation, Maslow's hierarchy outlines basic human needs and the importance of meeting those needs before being able to concentrate on more complex needs. The hierarchy includes biological and physiological, safety, belongingness and love, self-esteem, and self-actualization needs.

motivation—The desire and drive to do something. Motivation can be derived from either internal (self) or external (others) factors.

movement activities—Activities that integrate content into the experience.

movement bursts—Short pauses in instruction that get students up and moving. These bursts of activity provide opportunities for students to increase their energy, process information, and refocus.

need—Something that is innate and not learned or placed upon us by others.

needs assessment—Process to measure performance against a specific criteria. Students may evaluate aspects of their health and use the results to determine current areas of strength and areas in need of improvement.

negotiation—When two or more parties come to an agreement about an issue.

outcome expectations—The expectations people have about the outcomes of their health-related actions (Bandura, 2004).

participatory methods—Instruction that uses the methods through which people naturally learn, including observation, modeling, and interaction. An important component of participatory teaching, especially relating to skills-based health education, is that students have time to practice the skills they have learned (WHO, 2003).

performance task—An assignment or project that requires students to follow a set of directions in order to demonstrate their learning.

personalization—The extent to which students can see themselves in the curriculum. This includes the extent to which they can connect with activities, apply skills, and relate to content.

personalized professional development plan—Plan developed by an educator to identify the learning opportunities that will help the educator to achieve professional goals. The plan may also be used by administrators to measure educator growth.

positive learning environment—Learning environment in which all students feel valued and safe, and which supports learning and personal growth.

procedural knowledge—Learned information that is applied during the performance of a task or in a given situation.

process check—Classroom strategy that assesses whether or not students understand and are following along with current instructions and activities.

product—Something that can be provided to meet a want or need.

professional development—The learning experiences (both formal and informal) that help us to grow as professionals.

professional learning opportunities—Discrete learning opportunities or experiences that, when bundled together, allow professional growth and development to occur.

prompt—Directions given for an assessment that explain the criteria a student must complete and will be scored on.

protective factors—Characteristics or behaviors that support healthy development and can decrease the likelihood of a person engaging in risky behaviors.

refusal—The act of saying no.

reliability—When results are consistent across time and truly represent what has occurred, including the likelihood that results would be reproduced if the same research methods were employed.

risk factor—Anything that increases the likelihood of engaging in a behavior that is detrimental to one's health.

risky behavior—Behavior that can have negative consequences on one's health.

rubric—A standard of performance that provides the criteria for assessing students' work.

scaffolding—Designing learning activities that build upon students' ability to complete progressively more complex tasks as they acquire new information and skills in a methodical way.

School Health Index (SHI)—The *School Health Index (SHI): Self-Assessment & Planning Guide* is an online self-assessment and planning tool that schools can use to improve their health and safety policies and programs.

scope and sequence—Outline of the content being covered and when it will be taught.

self-actualization—Obtaining personal fulfillment through our actions and meeting our greatest potential.

self-determination theory—Relates to individuals' needs, specifically competence, or the desire to effectively handle our environment (Deci & Vansteenkiste, 2004; White, 1959); relatedness, or the need to be connected to others (Baumeister & Leary, 1995; Deci & Vansteenkiste, 2004); and autonomy, or acting in accordance with one's beliefs and values, whether out of a personal choice or a duty to others (Chirkov et al., 2003; Deci & Vansteenkiste, 2004).

self-efficacy—The "foundation of human motivation and action. Unless people believe they can produce desired effects by their actions, they have little incentive to act or to persevere in the face of difficulties" (Bandura, 2004, p. 144).

self-esteem—One's general feelings about one's self-worth or value.

self-expression—Transmission of one's thoughts, feelings, needs, wants, or ideas through verbal or nonverbal communication.

self-management—The practice of engaging in health-enhancing behaviors and avoiding risky behaviors.

self-reflection—Reflection that focuses on one's situations, skills, beliefs, values, ideas, attitudes, understandings, and so on.

service—Action taken to help someone.

short-term goal—Something you want to accomplish in the near future.

skills-based health education—A planned, sequential, comprehensive, and relevant curriculum that is implemented through participatory methods to help students develop skills, attitudes, and functional knowledge needed to lead health-enhancing lives.

skill proficiency—Level of skill performance in which the person can apply a skill by implementing the critical parts appropriately in a given context.

SMART goal—A goal that is specific, measurable, adjustable, realistic, and time based.

social cognitive theory (SCT)—Addresses the multidimensional aspect of skills-based health education and provides a strong theoretical basis for its use in the classroom. SCT proposes that health behavior is determined by knowledge, perceived self-efficacy (that one has control over one's health habits), outcome expectations, health goals, and perceived facilitators and impediments to action (Bandura, 2004).

socioecological model—Framework that highlights the multiple factors and levels that can influence behavior.

Socratic seminar—Discussion-based format in which students are asked to think critically and collaboratively about an open-ended question typically based on a text (www.readwritethink.org/professional-development/strategy-guides/socratic-seminars-30600.html).

statistical significance—The likelihood that the results from a research study are due to chance, typically reported through a P value. The smaller the P value, the less likely the results are due to chance.

summative assessment—An assessment *of* learning that is designed to measure outcomes at the end of a predetermined amount of time or content coverage.

transfer—Occurs when learning (knowledge, skills) in one context assists in learning or application of the learning in a new context (Bransford, Brown, & Cocking, 2000).

validity—How much one is able to trust results as an appropriate and accurate measure.

values—Principles, standards, and characteristics that represent what is most important to a person.

Whole School, Whole Community, Whole Child (WSCC)—Combines and builds on elements of the traditional coordinated school health approach and the whole child initiative. The CDC and ASCD developed this model in collaboration with key leaders from the fields of health, public health, education, and school health to strengthen a unified and collaborative approach to learning and health (ASCD, 2014).

References

Chapter 1

Armitage, C.J., & Conner, M. (2000). Social cognition models and health behavior: A structured review. *Psychology and Health, 15*, 173-189.

Association for Supervision and Curriculum Development (ASCD). (2011). *Making the case for educating the whole child.* Alexandria, VA: Author.

Bandura, A. (2004). Health promotion by social cognitive means. *Health Education & Behavior, 31*, 143-164.

Basch, C.E. (2011). Healthier students are better learners: A missing link in school reforms to close the achievement gap. *Journal of School Health, 81*(10), 593-598.

Beachum, F.D., McCray, C.R., Yawn, C.D., & Obiakor, F.E. (2013). Support and importance of character education: Pre-service teacher perceptions. *Education, 133*(4), 470-480.

Bradley, B.J. & Greene, A.C. (2013). Do health and education agencies in the United States share a responsibility for academic achievement and health? A review of 25 years of evidence about the relationship of adolescents' academic achievement and health behavior. *Journal of Adolescent Health, 52*(6), 523-532.

Centers for Disease Control and Prevention (CDC). (2015). Health and academics. Retrieved June 17, 2015, from www.cdc.gov/HealthyYouth/health_and_academics.

Centers for Disease Control and Prevention (CDC). (2012). Health and academics data and statistics. Retrieved June 17, 2015, from www.cdc.gov/healthyyouth/health_and_academics/data.htm.

Cha, E., Kim, K.H., Lerner, H.M., Dawkins, C.R., Bello, M.K., Umpierrez, G., & Dunbar, S.B. (2014). Health literacy, self-efficacy, food label use, and diet in young adults. *American Journal of Health Behavior, 38*(3), 331-339.

Diley, J. (2009). Research review: School-based health interventions and academic achievement. Retrieved June 17, 2015, from http://here.doh.wa.gov/materials/research-review-school-based-health-interventions-and-academic-achievement/12_HealthAcademic_E09L.pdf.

Fisher C., Hunt, P., Kann, L., Kolbe, L., Patterson, B., & Wechsler, H. (2003). Building a healthier future through school health programs. In *Promising practices in chronic disease prevention and control: A public health framework for action.* Atlanta: CDC. Retrieved June 17, 2015, from www.cdc.gov/HealthyYouth/publications/pdf/PP-Ch9.pdf.

Hale, D.R., Fitzgerald-Yau, N., & Vine, R.M. (2014). A systematic review of effective interventions for reducing multiple health risk behaviors in adolescence. *American Journal of Public Health, 104*(5), e19-e41.

Health Resources and Services Administration (HRSA). (n.d.). Adolescent and young adult health program. Retrieved June 17, 2015, from http://mchb.hrsa.gov/programs/adolescents/.

Ickovics, J.R., Carroll-Scott, A., Peters, S.M., Schwartz, M., Gilstad-Hayden, K., & McCaslin, C. (2014). Health and academic achievement: Cumulative effects of health assets on standardized test scores among urban youth. *Journal of School Health, 84*(1), 40-48.

Institute of Medicine (IOM). (2004). Health literacy: A prescription to end confusion. Retrieved June 17, 2015, from www.iom.edu/Reports/2004/Health-Literacy-A-Prescription-to-End-Confusion.aspx.

Joint Committee on National Health Education Standards. (2007). *National Health Education Standards: Achieving excellence* (2nd ed.). Athens, GA: The American Cancer Society.

Kolbe, L.J. (2002). Education reform and the goals of modern school health programs. *State Education Standard, 3*(4), 4-11.

Lewallan, T.C. (2004). Healthy learning environments. *ASCD: Info Brief, 38.* Retrieved June 17, 2015, from www.ascd.org/publications/newsletters/policy-priorities/aug04/num38/toc.aspx.

Lewis, S.V., Robinson, E.H., & Hays, B.G. (2011). Implementing an authentic character education curriculum. *Childhood Education, 87*(4), 227-231.

Manganello, J.A. (2008). Health literacy and adolescents: A framework and agenda for future research. *Health Education Research, 23*(5), 840-847.

Michael SL, Merlo CL, Basch CE, Wentzel KR, & Wechsler H. (2015). Critical connections: health and academics. J Sch Health. *85*, 740-758.

Murray-Johnson, L., Witte, K., Boulay, M., Figueroa, M.E., Storey, D., & Tweedie, I. (2005-2006). Using health education theories to explain behavior change: A cross-country analysis. *International Quarterly of Community Health Education, 25*(1-2), 185-207.

National Governors Association Center for Best Practices, Council of Chief State School Officers. (2010). Common Core State Standards. Retrieved June 17, 2015, from www.corestandards.org/about-the-standards/branding-guidelines/.

National Network of Libraries of Medicine. (2013). Health literacy. Retrieved June 17, 2015, from http://nnlm.gov/outreach/consumer/hlthlit.html.

NGSS Lead States. 2013. *Next Generation Science Standards: For states, by states.* Washington, DC: The National Academies Press.

Norman, C.D., & Skinner, H.A. (2006). eHEALS: The eHealth literacy scale. *Journal of Medical Internet Research, 8*(4). Retrieved June 17, 2015, from www.jmir.org/2006/4/e27/.

Nutbeam, D. (2008). The evolving concept of health literacy. *Social Science & Medicine, 67*(12), 2072-2078.

Nutbeam, D. (2000). Health literacy as a public health goal: A challenge for contemporary health education and communication strategies into the 21st century. *Health Promotion International, 15*(3), 259-267.

Paek, H.J., & Hove, T. (2012). Social cognitive factors and perceived social influences that improve adolescent eHealth literacy. *Health Communication, 27*, 727-737.

Rask, M., Uusiautti, S., & Maatta, K. (2013-2014). The fourth level of health literacy. *International Quarterly of Community Health Education, 34*(1), 51-71.

Rosemond, T.N., Blake, C.E., Jenkins, K.A., Buff, S.M., & Moore, J.B. (2015). Dietary improvements among African American youth: Results of an interactive nutrition promotion program. *American Journal of Health Education, 46*, 40-47.

Sorenson, K., Van den Broucke, S., Fullam, J., Doyle, G., Pelikan, J., Slonska, Z., & Brand, H. (2012). Health literacy and public health: A systematic review and integration of definitions and models. *BMC Public Health, 12*(80), 1-13.

St. Leger, L. (2001). Schools, health literacy and public health: Possibilities and challenges. *Health Promotion International, 16*(2), 197-205.

U.S. Department of Health and Human Services (HHS). (n.d.). Quick guide to health literacy. Retrieved June 17, 2015, from http://health.gov/communication/literacy/quickguide/factsliteracy.htm.

Wartella, E., Rideout, V., Zupancic, H., Beaudoin-Ryan, L., & Lauricella, A. (2015). Teens, Health, and Technology: A national survey. Retrieved June 17, 2015, from http://cmhd.northwestern.edu/wp-content/uploads/2015/05/1886_1_SOC_ConfReport_TeensHealthTech_051115.pdf.

World Health Organization (WHO). (2003). Skills for health. *Information Series on School Health, Document 9*. Retrieved June 17, 2015, from www.who.int/school_youth_health/media/en/sch_skills4health_03.pdf.

Chapter 2

Allensworth, D.D. (1994). The research base for innovative practices in school health education at the secondary level. *Journal of School Health, 64*(5), 180-188.

Arborelius, E., & Bremberg, S. (1991). How do teenagers respond to a consistently student-centered program of health education at school? *International Journal of Adolescent Medicine and Health, 5*(2), 95-112.

Bandura, A. (2004). Health promotion by social cognitive means. *Health Education & Behavior, 31*, 143-164.

Bongardt, D., Reitz, E., Sandfort, T., & Dekovic, M. (2014). A meta-analysis of the relations between three types of peer norms and adolescent sexual behavior. *Personality and Social Psychology Review*. Retrieved June 17, 2015, from www.researchgate.net/profile/E_Reitz/publication/263365399_A_meta-analysis_of_the_relations_between_three_types_of_peer_norms_and_adolescent_sexual_behavior/links/5523df650cf2c815e0735c9f.pdf.

Borders, M.J. (2009). Project Hero: A goal-setting and healthy decision-making program. *Journal of School Health, 79*(5), 239-243.

Botvin, G.J., Baker, E., Dusenbury, L., Botvin, E.M., & Diaz, T. (1995). Long-term follow-up results of a randomized drug abuse prevention trial in a white middle-class population. *Journal of the American Medical Association, 273*(14), 1106-1112.

Brown, S.L., Teufel, J.A. & Birch, D.A. (2007). Early adolescents' perceptions of health and health literacy. *Journal of School Health, 77*(1), 7-15.

Centers for Disease Control and Prevention (CDC). (2015). Characteristics of an effective health education curriculum. Retrieved June 17, 2015, from www.cdc.gov/healthyyouth/sher/characteristics/index.htm.

Greenberg, M.T., Weissberg, R.P., O'Brien, M.U., Zins, J.E., Fredericks, L., Resnik, H., & Elias, M.J. (2003). Enhancing school-based prevention and youth development through coordinated social, emotional, and academic learning. *American Psychologist, 58*(6/7), 466-474.

Joint Committee on National Health Education Standards. (2007). *National Health Education Standards: Achieving excellence* (2nd ed.). Athens, GA: The American Cancer Society.

Kirby, D., Short, L., Collins, J., Rugg, D., Kolbe, L., Howard, M., Miller, B., Sonenstein, F., & Zabin, L.S. (1994). School-based programs to reduce sexual risk behaviors: A review of effectiveness. *Public Health Reports, 109*(3), 339-360.

Michael SL, Merlo CL, Basch CE, Wentzel KR, & Wechsler H. (2015). Critical connections: health and academics. J Sch Health. *85*, 740-758.

Monahan, K.C., Rhew, I.C., Hawkins, D., & Brown, E.C. (2014). Adolescent pathways to co-occurring problem behavior: The effects of peer delinquency and peer substance use. *Journal of Research on Adolescents, 24*(4), 630-645.

Nation, M., Crusto, C., Wandersman, A., Kumpfer, K.L., Seybolt, D., Morrisey-Kane, E., & Davino, K., (2003). What works in prevention: Principles of effective prevention programs. *American Psychologist, 58*(6/7), 449-456.

National Registry of Evidence-based Programs and Practices. (2014). Retrieved June 17, 2015, from www.nrepp.samhsa.gov/Search.aspx.

Tappe, M.K., Wilbur, K.M., Telljohann, S.K., & Jensen, M.J. (2009). Articulation of the National

Health Education Standards to support learning and healthy behaviors among students. *American Journal of Health Education, 40*(4), 245-253.

World Health Organization (WHO). (2003). Skills for health. *Information Series on School Health, Document 9.* Retrieved July 5, 2007, from www.who.int/school_youth_health/media/en/sch_skills4health_03.pdf.

Chapter 3

Baumeister, R.F,& Leary, M. R. (1995). The need to belong: Desire for interpersonal attachments as a fundamental human motivation. *Psychological Bulletin, 117,* 497–529.

Buckley, L., Chapman, R., & Sheehan, M. (2010). Protective behaviour in adolescent friendships: the influence of attitudes towards the consequences, friendship norms and perceived control. *Journal of Youth Studies, 13*(6), 661-679. doi:10.1080/13676261003801762

Chirkov, V., Ryan, R.M., Kim, Y., & Kaplan, U. (2003). Differentiating autonomy from individualism and independence: A self-determination perspective on internalization of cultural orientations, gender, and well-being. *Journal of Personality and Social Psychology, 84,* 97-110.

Deci, E., & Vansteenkiste, M. (2004). Self-determination theory and basic need satisfaction: Understanding human development in positive psychology. *Ricerche Di Psicologia, 27*(1), 23-40.

Hawkins, J.D., Catalano, R.F., & Miller, J.Y. (1992). Risk and protective factors for alcohol and other drug problems in adolescence and early adulthood: Implications for substance abuse prevention. *Psychological Bulletin, 112*(1), 64-105. doi:10.1037/0033-2909.112.1.64

Joint Committee on National Health Education Standards. (2007). *National Health Education Standards: Achieving excellence* (2nd ed.). Athens, GA: The American Cancer Society.

Li K., Iannotti, R.J., Haynie, D.L., Perlus, J.G., & Simons-Morton, B.G. (2014). Motivation and planning as a method of the relation between social support and physical activity among US adolescents: A nationally representative study. *International Journal of Behavioral Nutrition and Physical Activity, 11,* 42.

Maslow, A.H. (1943). A theory of human motivation. *Psychological Review, 50* (4), 430-437.

Monahan, K.C., Rhew, I.C., Hawkins, D., & Brown, E.C. (2014). Adolescent pathways to co-occurring problem behavior: The effects of peer delinquency and peer substance use. *Journal of Research on Adolescents, 24*(4), 630-645.

Ryan, R.M., & Deci, E.L. (2000). Self-determination theory and the facilitation of intrinsic motivation, social development, and well-being. *American Psychologist, 55,* 68-78.

Search Institute. (2006). 40 developmental assets for adolescents. Retrieved May 12, 2015, from www.search-institute.org/content/40-developmental-assets-adolescents-ages-12-18.

Sznitman, S.R., Kolobov, T., Bogt, T.T., Kuntsche, E., Walsh, S.D., Boniel-Nissim, M., & Harel-Fisch, Y. (2013). Exploring substance use normalization among adolescents: A multilevel study in 35 countries. *Social Science & Medicine, 97,* 143-151.

Tomek, J., & Williams, M.J. (n.d.). Retrieved June 17, 2015, from http://extension.missouri.edu/fnep/lg782.pdf.

van de Bongardt, D., Reitz, E., Sandfort, T., & Dekovic, M. (2014). A meta-analysis of the relations between three types of peer norms and adolescent sexual behavior. *Personality and Social Psychology Review.* Retrieved June 17, 2015, from www.researchgate.net/profile/E_Reitz/publication/263365399_A_meta-analysis_of_the_relations_between_three_types_of_peer_norms_and_adolescent_sexual_behavior/links/5523df650cf2c815e0735c9f.pdf.

White, R.W. (1959). Motivation reconsidered: The concept of competence. *Psychological Review, 66,* 297-333.

Chapter 4

None

Chapter 5

Joint Committee on National Health Education Standards. (2007). *National Health Education Standards: Achieving excellence* (2nd ed.). Athens, GA: The American Cancer Society.

Wartella, E., Rideout, V., Zupancic, H., Beaudoin-Ryan, L., & Lauricella, A. (2015). Teens, Health and Technology: A national survey. Retrieved June 17, 2015, from http://cmhd.northwestern.edu/wp-content/uploads/2015/05/1886_1_SOC_ConfReport_TeensHealthTech_051115.pdf.

Chapter 6

Bransford, J.D., Brown, A.D., Cocking, R.R., Donovan, M.S., & Pellegrino, J.W. (Eds.). (2000). *How people learn: Brain, mind, experience, and school.* Washington, DC: National Academy Press.

Chapter 7

Joint Committee on National Health Education Standards. (2007). *National Health Education Standards: Achieving excellence* (2nd ed.). Athens, GA: The American Cancer Society.

Chapter 8

U.S. Department of Health and Human Services (HHS). (2008). *2008 physical activity guidelines for Americans.* Retrieved June 17, 2015, from www.health.gov/paguidelines/pdf/paguide.pdf.

Chapter 9

Nutbeam, D. (2000). Health literacy as a public health goal: A challenge for contemporary health education and communication strategies into the 21st century. *Health Promotion International, 15*(3), 259-267.

Chapter 10

None

Chapter 11

Agency for Healthcare Research Quality. (2014). Appendix H: Information on statistical significance. Retrieved June 17, 2015, from www.ahrq.gov/professionals/quality-patient-safety/quality-resources/tools/asthmaqual/asthmacare/appendix-h.html.

Bandura, A. (2004). Health promotion by social cognitive means. *Health Education & Behavior, 31*, 143-164.

Bransford, J.D., Brown, A.D., Cocking, R.R., Donovan, M.S., & Pellegrino, J.W. (Eds.). (2000). *How people learn: Brain, mind, experience, and school.* Washington, DC: National Academy Press.

Centers for Disease Control and Prevention (CDC). (2015). Youth Risk Behavior Surveillance Survey (YRBSS). Retrieved June 17, 2015, from www.cdc.gov/healthyyouth/data/yrbs/index.htm.

World Health Organization (WHO). (n.d.). The ecological framework. Retrieved June 17, 2015, from www.who.int/violenceprevention/approach/ecology/en/.

Chapter 12

Wiggins, G.P., & McTighe, J. (2005). *Understanding by design.* Alexandria, VA: Association for Supervision and Curriculum Development.

Chapter 13

Council of Chief State School Officers (CCSSO). (2012). Distinguishing formative assessment from other educational assessment labels. Retrieved April 29, 2015, from www.ccsso.org/Resources/Publications/Distinguishing_Formative_Assessment_from_Other_Educational_Assessment_Labels.html.

Joint Committee on National Health Education Standards. (2007). *National Health Education Standards: Achieving excellence* (2nd ed.). Athens, GA: The American Cancer Society.

Wiggins, G.P., & McTighe, J. (2005). *Understanding by design.* Alexandria, VA: Association for Supervision and Curriculum Development.

Chapter 14

None

Chapter 15

Filkins, S. (n.d.). Socratic Seminars strategy guide. Retrieved June 17, 2015, from www.readwritethink.org/professional-development/strategy-guides/socratic-seminars-30600.html.

World Health Organization (WHO). (2003). Skills for health. *Information Series on School Health, Document 9.* Retrieved July 5, 2007, from www.who.int/school_youth_health/media/en/sch_skills4health_03.pdf.

Chapter 16

Centers for Disease Control and Prevention (CDC). (2015). Health and academics. Retrieved June 17, 2015, from www.cdc.gov/HealthyYouth/health_and_academics.

Chapter 17

Croft, A., Coggshall, J.G., Dolan, M., Powers, E., & Killion, J. (2010). Job-embedded professional development: What it is, who is responsible, and how to get it done well. *Issue Brief April 2010.* Washington, DC: National Comprehensive Center for Teacher Quality.

Darling-Hammond, L., & McLaughlin, M.W. (1995). Policies that support professional development in an era of reform. *Phi Delta Kappan, 76* (8), 597-604.

Hirsh, S. (2009). A new definition. *Journal of Staff Development, 30*(4), 10-16.

Knowles, M.S. (1990) The Adult Learner: a neglected species (4th edition) Houston: Gulf Publishing.

Yoon, K.S., Duncan, T., Lee, S.W.-Y., Scarloss, B., & Shapley, K. (2007). Reviewing the evidence on how teacher professional development affects student achievement (Issues & Answers Report, REL 2007–No. 033). Washington, DC: U.S. Department of Education, Institute of Education Sciences, National Center for Education Evaluation and Regional Assistance, Regional Educational Laboratory Southwest. Retrieved from http://ies.ed.gov/ncee/edlabs.

Chapter 18

Association for Supervision and Curriculum Development (ACSD). (2014). *Whole School, Whole Community, Whole Child: A collaborative approach to learning and health.* Alexandria, VA: Author. Retrieved March 14, 2015, from www.ascd.org/ASCD/pdf/siteASCD/publications/wholechild/wscc-a-collaborative-approach.pdf.

Basch, C.E. (2010). *Healthier students are better learners: A missing link in school reforms to close the achievement gap.* Columbia University. Retrieved May 23, 2015, from www.equitycampaign.org/i/a/document/12557_EquityMattersVol6_Web03082010.pdf.

Birch, D.A., & Videto, D.M. (Eds.). (2015). *Promoting health and academic success: The Whole School, Whole Community, Whole Child Approach.* Human Kinetics: Champaign, IL.

Centers for Disease Control and Prevention (CDC). (2012). *Parent engagement: Strategies for involving parents in school health.* Atlanta: HHS.

Centers for Disease Control and Prevention (CDC). (2009). School connectedness: Strategies for increasing protective factors among youth. Atlanta: HHS. Retrieved June 18, 2015, from www.cdc.gov/healthyyouth/protective/pdf/connectedness.pdf.

Institute of Medicine (IOM). (2013). Educating the student body: Taking physical activity and physical education to school. Retrieved June 19, 2015, from www.iom.edu/Reports/2013/Educating-the-Student-Body-Taking-Physical-Activity-and-Physical-Education-to-School/Report-Brief052313.aspx.

Lewallen, T.C., Hunt, H., Potts-Datema, W., Zaza, S., & Giles, W. (2015) The Whole School, Whole Community, Whole Child Model: a new approach for improving educational attainment and healthy development for students. *J Sch Health.* *85,* 729-739

United States Department of Agriculture (USDA). (2010). Local school wellness policy requirements. Retrieved April 15, 2015, from www.fns.usda.gov/tn/local-school-wellness-policy-requirements.

Index

Page references followed by an italicized *f* or *t* indicate information contained in figures and tables, respectively.

About the Authors

Sarah Benes, EdD, CHES, is a senior lecturer and program director in physical education and health education at Boston University. Sarah teaches a variety of undergraduate- and graduate-level courses in health and physical education, does service projects in local communities,

and conducts research on health education and physical activity in schools. She has numerous publications in refereed journals and chapters examining health education; she has also made more than a dozen presentations on skill-based health education and related topics at state and regional conferences. Sarah serves on a variety of health education committees, including as a member of the health education steering committee for SHAPE America—the Society of Health and Physical Educators—and as the vice president of health education for the Massachusetts Association for Health, Physical Education, Recreation and Dance. Benes consults with school districts on health and wellness issues with a focus on skills-based curriculum development and implementation and is a member of the National Athletic Trainers' Association and SHAPE America. She is a certified and licensed athletic trainer and health education specialist. Sarah received a bachelor's degree in athletic training from the University of Connecticut, a master's degree in education, and a doctorate in curriculum and teaching from Boston University and is currently working on an MPH. She lives in Natick with her husband, two daughters, and yellow Labrador. She enjoys spending time with her family on nature walks and enjoying the sights and sounds of the Northeast.

Holly Alperin, EdM, MCHES, has worked to improve the health and academic outcomes of young people by leveraging partnerships in order to strengthen school-level policies and practices both in the health education classroom and throughout the

school. She provides training and technical assistance to preK-12 educators, administrators, and staff; teaches preservice and graduate students working toward degrees in health education; and develops and implements trainings to advance the capacity of state and national stakeholders to improve the outcomes of children. Holly is a sought-after presenter, having been invited to numerous local, state, and national events. She is an advocate for ensuring that health educators receive high-quality professional development and takes this responsibility to heart through her personal development and participation in professional organizations including SHAPE America. Holly received her bachelor's degree in health education and health promotion from Central Michigan University and her master of education in policy, planning, and administration from Boston University. Holly currently lives in New Hampshire with her husband and two daughters. Together they enjoy the best of New England—ocean, mountains, cities, and countless adventures.